BREST-LITOVSK

THE FORGOTTEN PEACE

MARCH 1918

BY

JOHN W. WHEELER-BENNETT

The Norton Library

W · W · NORTON & COMPANY · INC ·

NEW YORK

TO

BRUCE HOPPER

I DEDICATE THIS BOOK

IN FRIENDSHIP

First published 1938

First published in the Norton Library 1971
by arrangement with St. Martin's Press, Inc.

Books That Live
The Norton imprint on a book means that in the publisher's
estimation it is a book not for a single season but for the years.
W. W. Norton & Company, Inc.

SBN 393 00576 3

PRINTED IN THE UNITED STATES OF AMERICA

1 2 3 4 5 6 7 8 9 0

CONTENTS

LIST OF ILLUSTRATIONS

Following page 172

MAP

NOTE

Exchange Values.—The pre-war values of the rouble and the mark in relation to sterling were 2s. 1½d. and 1s. respectively, although just prior to the war the rouble had dropped to 2s. 0½d. The relation of the rouble to the mark for the same period was approximately 1 rouble to 2 German marks.

Calendar.—Throughout the book the New Style Calendar has been used, the Russian Revolutions taking place, therefore, in March and November, and not in February and October.

PREFACE TO 1966 REPRINT

SINCE this book is being reissued by the process of photo-lithography it is impossible for me to make any alterations to the text as it stands. I do, however, welcome the opportunity presented by this foreword to draw attention to the continuing shadow which the Peace of Brest-Litovsk cast in the middle years of the Second World War—and beyond.

It is a matter of historical fact that the over-all pattern of German-Russian relations over the past two hundred years has been one of alternating bitter estrangements and warm rapprochements. This was true of the policies of Frederick the Great but it became more clearly defined with the re-emergence of Prussia in the 'sixties as a dynamic force in Europe. There then appeared within her counsels two warring schools: one thought of Russia as the natural ally of Prussia in the coming struggle with France and Austria; the other thought in terms of a Greater Germany which included Austria and her traditional hostility to Russia. Between the two the upper echelons of the Foreign Office and the General Staff were divided; sometimes one was in the ascendant, sometimes the other. It was the triumph of the Greater Germany School during the First World War which found its ultimate expression in the predatory Treaty of Brest-Litovsk, by which it was intended to eliminate Russia as a political factor in European affairs.

Hitler fell heir to both of these conflicting policies and did not scruple to exploit both of them. The Nazi–Soviet Pact of August 1939 was a demonstration of the first, and the policy pursued subsequent to the invasion of Russia in June 1941 a reversion to the second. The objectives of the German General Staff in 1918 and of the Führer nearly a quarter of a century later were virtually identical. Like Hindenburg, Hitler needed the Baltic Provinces for the manœuvring of his left wing in the next war. Like Hoffman, he visualised the annexation of the rich black soil of the Ukraine. Like Ludendorff, he aimed at a political partition of Russia which would leave her dismembered and helpless, driven back behind the Urals and eliminated from Europe. Indeed, in this latter respect the parallel is actually documented. On June 9, 1918, Ludendorff had put his views on record in a memorandum to the Imperial Chancellor, and the similarity of his political designs with those of Hitler may be gathered from a comparison of this document with the account of the Führer's conference at the Reich Chancellory on March 17, 1941—before the invasion of Russia had even begun.[1]

Whatever wisdom of hindsight we may have since achieved, this was not considered "a good thing" either in 1918 or in 1941.

The parallel of Russia at Brest-Litovsk as compared with the Second World War is, of course, far less complete—indeed almost non-existent. In 1918 Russia had sustained the greatest military débâcle of her history and the Bolshevik revolution was fighting for survival. She was compelled to accept the victor's terms at Brest-Litovsk, yet survived to assist in the destruction of the Imperial German régime. In the Second World War, having sustained initial disaster, Russia returned to Europe as the strongest single military power on the continent and rapidly became a continuing and growing menace to world peace.

Thus, the importance of Brest-Litovsk as a political factor persists to this day. The parallel between the German policies in the First and Second World Wars is very clear. What they coveted they seized—and lost. And Lenin's prophecy that all that the Bolsheviks had surrendered by the "Tilsit Peace" of Brest-Litovsk would ultimately be redeemed by the Soviet Government—and more, has been fulfilled.

JOHN WHEELER-BENNETT

Garsington Manor, Oxford,
June 1966

---

[1] See Ludendorff, *The General Staff and its Problems* (London, 1920), pp. 571-5, and Document L.221, presented in evidence before the International Military Tribunal at Nuremberg.

INTRODUCTION

Twenty years ago, on March 3, 1918, the first treaty of peace between belligerent parties in the World War was signed by the Central Powers and Russia at Brest-Litovsk. Few at that time appreciated its full significance, and, in the later years, when events crowded hard upon each other, the Peace of Brest-Litovsk was forgotten.

Yet, this Peace of Brest-Litovsk is one of the important milestones in modern history, for with its signature begins a chain of events which leads directly to the happenings of to-day; a chain which numbers among its links some of the greatest incidents in war and peace. The Treaty of Brest-Litovsk not only signified the apparently complete victory of German arms in the East, and the greatest diplomatic and military humiliation which Russia had ever sustained in a long history of defeat, but, with the exception of the Treaty of Versailles, it had consequences and repercussions more vitally important than any other peace settlement since the Congress of Vienna.

It was the course of the negotiations at Brest-Litovsk which prompted President Wilson to promulgate his famous Fourteen Points, in an attempt to keep the Russians from concluding a separate peace. The rapacity of the victor's terms imposed upon Russia disclosed to the rest of the world the domination which the Supreme Command had attained in Germany, and the impossibility of arriving at a " peace of understanding " with a Germany in the hands of such rulers. The realization of this fact produced that final unity of purpose between the United States of America and the Western Powers, that implacable "will to victory", which all previous negotiations had failed to achieve, and which assured the ultimate defeat of Germany.

The Peace of Brest-Litovsk preserved Bolshevism. Its conclusion provided Lenin with the essential " breathing-space " for consolidating the Russian Revolution against the attempts to overthrow it from within. At the same time, the treaty marks the beginning of that infiltration of active Communism into Germany which materially contributed to her collapse some nine months later. For, with the opening of the negotiations, there emerged that new and potent factor in world diplomacy, Bolshevik propaganda ; propaganda carried on by the party which formed the Government of the Soviet State, but of whose activities that Government professed official ignorance. " The Party does not sign the treaty," said Lenin, " and for the Party the Government is not responsible." It was upon this policy of " parallel diplomacy ", first used at Brest, that the activities of the Third International were based after its organization in 1919.

Such were the more immediate results of Brest-Litovsk, but its influence is still discernible in the political life and ideological trends of both Russia and Germany to-day. The psychology of Brest-Litovsk is still strong in both countries, though with strangely different manifestations, and is responsible both for the genesis of the Nazi ambitions for hegemony over Eastern and South-Eastern Europe, and, in some degree possibly, for the actions of those leading members of the Old Bolshevik Party which have recently ended in their own destruction.

Though it is almost impossible to extract any clear and undisputed facts from the mystery which surrounds the Moscow treason trials of 1936 and 1937, it does seem possible to detect in the mental processes and in the activities of the accused, particularly Radek, Sokolnikov, and Pyatakov, a tendency to return to the tactics of what may be called " primitive Leninism " and to the psychology of the Brest-Litovsk period. The Old Bolsheviks, believing that the principles of Lenin and the ideals of the November

Revolution had been betrayed by Stalin, and convinced that the U.S.S.R. could not resist an attack by both Germany and Japan, appear to have reverted to the pre-revolutionary strategy of sabotage and subversion in order to overthrow the Stalinist régime, and to the Leninist policy of defeatism and national immolation in order to placate for the moment the aggressive policies of the two Imperialist-Fascist Powers. The crimes of which they were accused, and to which they pleaded guilty, were none other than those very principles of destruction and disintegration on which Lenin based his fight against the Liberal Government of Prince Lvov and the Socialist régime of Kerensky, while the policy of defeatism was exactly that followed by him in regard to Brest-Litovsk.

This latter doctrine had been established by Lenin again and again. " It is impossible to attain this end [the Revolution] without wishing for the defeat of one's own government and without working for such a defeat ", he wrote in *Against the Current*; and, again, he warned American workers that " he is no Socialist who will not sacrifice his fatherland for the triumph of the Social Revolution ". Nor was he content merely to preach the doctrine. Against the bitter opposition of the Left Communists, particularly Bukharin and Radek, within his own party, he pursued just this same policy in regard to Brest-Litovsk.

What then would be more natural than for the Old Bolsheviks to fall back on these original principles ? Both Radek and Bukharin had publicly declared that in following the doctrine of defeatism Lenin had been right and they wrong. Is it not possible that the psychology of Brest-Litovsk reasserted itself and that, in negotiating with Germany and Japan for the cession of the Ukraine and the Maritime Province, they were reverting to the principle of the " breathing-space " in order to safeguard themselves from external aggression, while setting about the destruction of the Stalin régime which they regarded as having betrayed the Revolution? Moreover, had not Lenin himself accepted the facilities offered by Imperialist Germany on his return to Russia ? Was he not always prepared to spoil the Egyptians if by so doing he could strengthen or advance the Revolution ?

How these strange new allies were ultimately to be disposed of is not clear, but presumably it was hoped to regain all territory lost at some later date, either by the extension of the world revolution or by some revolutionary war. The wisdom of such a course is, of course, clearly questionable. If it is possible to find an explanation of the Moscow mystery in terms of guilt of the accused, this appears to be the only possible clue to a solution. But so complex is the problem that it has even been suggested that Stalin revived the defeatist doctrine of Brest-Litovsk in order to fasten the responsibility for it upon his political rivals and opponents, and to father on these people, very crudely, his own Leninist policy of 1918.

This consideration, however, is of but academic interest, compared with the very practical application of the principles of Brest-Litovsk now obtaining in Germany, since the advent to power of the National Socialist régime. The Weimar Republic, with the support of the majority opinion on the German General Staff, represented by General von Seeckt, sought to reach a *rapprochement* with the Soviet Union, and largely succeeded in doing so by the Treaty of Rapallo and the Military Agreement of April 3, 1922, and the German-Russian Non-Aggression Treaty of 1926. There remained, however, a minority who followed in the Hoffmann tradition, regarding Bolshevism as the root of all evil, and dreaming of the ultimate realization of those far-reaching plans for German expansion in Eastern Europe which so sadly eluded them after Brest-Litovsk.

Added to this is the very definite view which Adolf Hitler himself holds regarding the treaty, and which the National Socialist Party has sedulously fostered into a legend and an attainable ideal. For the ideology which actuated the dictation of the treaty has not been replaced by any other set of ideas, and has become the conviction of a large part of the German people. The present German generation—the generation of Nazi Germany—regards the principles of Brest-Litovsk and the motives lying behind it as an actual political programme.[1] None has been more eloquent in this view than the Führer himself, in his comparison of the treaty with the Peace of Versailles. " I placed the two Treaties side by side, compared them point by point, showed the positively boundless humanity of the one in contrast to the inhuman cruelty of the other ", he wrote in *Mein Kampf.* " In those days I spoke on this subject before audiences of 2000 at which I was often exposed to the gaze of 3600 hostile eyes. And three hours later I had before me a surging mass filled with righteous indignation and boundless wrath." [2] With this as a pointer it is not surprising to find Hitler stating somewhat later in his work : " We [the National Socialists] stop the perpetual migration towards the south and west of Europe and fix our gaze on the land in the East . . . when we talk of new lands in Europe, we are bound to think first of Russia and her border States ".[3] And again: " We must not forget that the international Jew, who continues to dominate Russia, does not regard Germany as an ally, but as a State destined to undergo a similar fate. The menace which Russia suffered under is one which perpetually hangs over Germany ; Germany is the next great objective of Bolshevism." [4]

Here then is combined in one political philosophy the doctrine of pre-war Pan-Germanism, the all-pervading

[1] Cf. " Germany's Present Eastern Policy and the Lessons of Brest-Litovsk ", by " Pragmaticus ", *Slavonic and Eastern European Review,* xv. No. 44.

[2] Adolf Hitler, *Mein Kampf* (Munich, 1938), i. 523-525.

[3] *Ibid.* ii. 742.   [4] *Ibid.* pp. 750-751.

hatred of the Jew, and the ideological opposition to Bolshevism, and the only means by which this philosophy may
be given practical application is through a reversion to the
German mentality of Brest-Litovsk. It is not unimportant
that political writers of 1917 talked as freely of German
equality (*Gleichberechtigung*) as do the Nazi pundits to-day,
but they were more frank in their interpretation of it. " The
issue between us and England constitutes not so much
isolated problems as the conflict between England's world
domination hitherto and our endeavour to obtain *Gleichberechtigung* in the world. That is why the war is being
waged ", wrote Professor Hettner in his book, *Der deutsche
Frieden und die deutsche Zukunft*; and years later Hitler
epitomised this statement in a single sentence : " Germany
will be a World Power or nothing at all ". He admits that
England will not tolerate Germany as a World Power, but
says that this is not for the moment an urgent question, for
Germany is first concerned with uniting the German race
and fighting for territory in Europe.[1]

Reverting to the Ludendorff thesis that " German
prestige demands that we should hold a strong protecting
hand, not only over German citizens but over *all* Germans ",
Hitler aims first at the realization of a *Deutschtum* stretching from Jutland to the Brenner and from Strasburg to
Riga, and later at securing for Germany enough territory
to accommodate 200,000,000 Germans. This expansion,
according to the views expressed in *Mein Kampf*, the undisputed Bible of the Third Reich, is to take place in the
east and south-east of Europe, in those territories to
which German colonization during the Middle Ages was
directed—" We begin again where we left off six centuries
ago "—and to the Ukraine and Southern Russia as a
whole.

Read in this light the attitude assumed by Nazi Germany towards Austria and Czechoslovakia, towards the

[1] Hitler, *Mein Kampf*, ii. 699.

Baltic States and Poland, and towards Hungary and Rumania takes on a new significance. The expansion of Germany thus conceived envisages the readjustment of existing conditions in Central and Eastern Europe corresponding to the political system which the Pan-German Party and the Supreme Command planned during the war, the skeleton structure of which was completed under the Treaties of Brest-Litovsk and Bucharest; that is to say, the political hegemony of Germany over all remotely Germanic States and a meditated acquisition of Russian territory. The methods employed differ in each case. Austria was first terrorised and then annexed to the German Reich. Czechoslovakia is subjected to threats and propaganda calculated to stimulate " spontaneous revolt ". Poland and the Baltic States, as in the days of Brest-Litovsk, are offered compromises and the expectation of security—though it may be recalled that in *Mein Kampf* the Poles are not only dismissed as " inferior ", but Polish children are classed on the same low level as Jews, negroes, and Asiatics. Towards Hungary, Yugoslavia, and Rumania a policy of blandishment and flattery is adopted in the hope of winning away the first from Italian, and the two latter from French influence.

With the *Drang nach Süd-Osten* well under way,[1] the first steps have already been taken to direct the political thought of Germany towards the possible advantages of expansion into Russia. German " colonization " in Russia was proposed by Dr. Schacht at a conference in Rome in November 1932, even before the advent of Hitler to power, and the subject was revived in Herr Hugenberg's famous memorandum to the World Economic Conference in June 1933. The Führer himself made plain reference to it during his speeches against Communism at the Nürnberg *Parteifest*

[1] For good accounts of this movement see *Hitler's Drive to the East*, by E. Elwyn Jones (1937), *Germany Pushes South-east*, by Dr. Gerhard Schacher (1937), and *The German Octopus*, by Henry C. Wolfe (1938).

of 1936. " If the Urals with their incalculable wealth of raw materials, the rich forests of Siberia, and the unending cornfields of the Ukraine lay within Germany,[1] under National Socialist leadership the country would swim in plenty. We would produce, and every single German would have enough to live on ", he told representatives of the *Arbeitsfront* on September 12. No purer example of Brest-Litovsk psychology could be required than this virtual incitement to plunder. The speech might well have been inspired by the Press Department of the Great General Staff in the early weeks of 1918.

The nearing of the completion of German rearmament brings to a close the first stage of the Nazi development towards *Gleichberechtigung*. The second, which overlaps the first, has already begun, and Germany is well on the way to the establishment of her desired hegemony. With each step forward the burden of the psychology of Brest-Litovsk weighs more heavily upon Germany's mentality and makes more inevitable the ultimate effort to fulfil her destiny. Europe has been treated to one display of the effects of this psychosis, and, should Germany succeed in re-establishing the situation which existed for a brief moment after Brest-Litovsk, the results would be even more threatening than they were then. For an industrialized Russia exploited by the organizing genius of Germany conjures up a vision which no Western European can contemplate with equanimity. But in 1918 the will-o'-the-wisp of ambition lured Germany into a slough of dilemma from which extrication proved impossible, and the rest of Europe remembers, what Herr Hitler may have forgotten, that disaster followed in the train of transient glory.

[1] As reported in the British press of September 14-15, this sentence was variously translated as follows: " If he could command " (*The Times*), " If we had at our disposal " (*Daily Telegraph*), " If we had " (*Manchester Guardian*). In the official version of the speech, published in the German press on September 14, the sentence was modified and given the above form.

In the pages which follow, it has been my object, first, to tell the story of the peace negotiations of Brest-Litovsk and of Soviet-German relations up to their rupture in November 1918 ; secondly, I have aimed at explaining the motives behind the diplomatic moves made by either side ; and thirdly, I have endeavoured to establish the very prominent place which the Forgotten Peace holds in world history.

I have used the official documents published by the Governments concerned, together with the contemporary press of Germany, Austria-Hungary, and Russia, and of certain Allied countries, and, in addition, the diaries, memoirs, and biographies of the principal actors in the drama. But I have also tried to supplement the written word by personal conversation with all those participants in the story of Brest-Litovsk who were still alive. With the exception of Joffe, on the side of the Soviets, and Dr. von Rosenberg on that of the Central Powers (both of whom died before I had an opportunity of meeting them), I have been able to discuss the treaty with almost all the leading figures both at the Conference and in the various capitals; with members of the Russian Provisional Governments, and of the *Rada* and Skoropadsky Ukrainian régimes ; with officers of the former German and Austrian High Commands, and also with a number of those who played less prominent rôles, but who have since risen to positions of importance in the services of their countries.

My researches involved numerous visits to Germany, Austria, the U.S.S.R., and further afield, and have left me with many pleasant recollections : conversations with Baron von Kühlmann, a memorable walk with Karl Radek in the woods outside Moscow, and one unforgettable afternoon with Trotsky in Mexico City ; to all those who gave me the benefit of their recollections I am deeply grateful. I have thought it wise to refrain from mentioning by name those to whom my thanks are due for assistance given me in Germany and Russia, where, despite much advertised divergences in ideological outlook, similar difficulties are encountered by the individual citizen. But my gratitude is none the less sincere.

I wish to express my very sincere thanks to those of my friends who, either by criticism and advice, or by assisting me in obtaining material, have contributed to the making of the book. First amongst these are Professor Bruce Hopper, of Harvard University, and Professor L. B. Namier, of Manchester University, to whose great knowledge, trenchant criticism, and friendly encouragement, both I and my work owe so much. In addition, I am deeply indebted to Mr. Bruce Lockhart for allowing me to use his diaries of the period ; to Mr. Nicholas M. Oushakoff, of the Harvard Law School Library, for his invaluable assistance in translation work ; and to Miss Elizabeth Monroe, Baroness Budberg, Sir Frederick Whyte, Mr. De Witte Clinton Poole of Princeton University, Mr. Alexander Gumberg, Mr. Max Eastman, Dr. Kurt Rosenfelt, Professor William Adams Brown, Jnr., of Brown University, Rhode Island, Mrs. P. E. Baker, and to my secretary, Miss Margaret Dunk, all of whom have given me welcome aid at some time during the writing of the book, and to whom I am deeply grateful.

I wish also to acknowledge the generosity of the United States Department of State for allowing me to make use of their library and to reprint, in Appendices II, IV, V, VII and IX, documents from certain of their publications, to thank Messrs. James Bunyan and H. H. Fisher, and the Stanford University Press, California, for permission to reprint the texts in Appendices I and III, and to acknowledge the great kindness and assistance which I have received from the Widener Library of Harvard University and the Information Department and Library of the Royal Institute of International Affairs.

JOHN W. WHEELER-BENNETT

April 1938

I

EXITS AND ENTRANCES

I

EXITS AND ENTRANCES

1

AT Imperial General Headquarters at Moghilev an officer of the Russian Army was writing to his wife. The room was bare, its only decoration a jewelled ikon and some photographs of children. The writer had that morning come back from a brief visit to Petrograd, and wrote in affectionate terms to his family of his safe return to duty. The letter was filled with tender and intimate details. He had had a little cough, but it was better now. He was terribly distressed at the news that two of the children had contracted measles, there was much of it at Moghilev, too ; among the boys of the 1st and 2nd Cadet Corps it was increasing steadily. He was particularly anxious about his little son who was not robust, and was concerned for the inconvenience to his wife. " In any case, it is very tiresome and disturbing for you, my poor darling " ; and he added that it would be much better if all the children fell ill at the same time. " I greatly miss my half-hourly game of patience every evening. I shall take up dominoes again in my spare time"; and he concluded: "Good-night. May God bless your dreams." [1]

He signed the letter " Your little hubby ", and turned to make the day's entry in his diary ; details of his journey from Petrograd, and of his routine work at headquarters. " In all my spare time I am reading a French book on Julius Caesar's conquest of Gaul." [2]

[1] *The Letters of the Tsar to the Tsaritsa* (London, 1929), p. 313.

[2] *Journal intime de Nicholas II, juillet 1914–juillet 1919* (Paris, 1934), p. 93.

A man of tranquil spirit, it may be thought; his life untrammelled by aught else than the everyday difficulties of his duties and the dark shadow of war which rested over the Russian nation; an undistinguished though conscientious officer—and it would have been true: but the man was Nicholas II, Tsar of All the Russias, the date was March 8, 1917, and his Empire was crumbling around him while he wrote of dominoes and patience.

No greater disaster could have overtaken the Empire which he ruled, the dynasty which he represented, and, indeed, himself, than that Nicholas II should have occupied the throne at a time of crisis. No man was less fitted to face the responsibilities and bear the burdens of an autocrat in time of war. No man was less suited to guide the destinies of a hundred and fifty million people who were gradually but irresistibly emerging from the aftermath of serfdom. He was not what historians of a certain school would have called "a bad man", but, which was infinitely worse, he was weak, with all the inevitable obstinacy of weakness. Power in his hands was "not power but its pale shadow", for he was the slave of influence and pressure, yet unreceptive of advice and counsel. Deeply religious, he had the bigotry of a zealot, and his unswerving faith brought him not spiritual comfort, but a detached and stubborn passivity, a fatalism which sapped his better judgement and surrounded him with an impenetrable barrier. Moreover, he was married to an adoring but dominating consort, one who was even more susceptible to things mystic, yet convinced of her qualification and her duty to supply her husband with that militant masculinity in which his strange nature was lacking. Repeatedly in her letters to him the Tsaritsa referred to herself as "wearing the trousers", imploring him not to be persuaded by the counsels of moderation and half-measures. "Only fools and cowards could have proposed that to you", she wrote to him on one occasion with reference to the *Stavka* at

Moghilev. "I see that my black trousers are needed at headquarters."[1]

There was about Nicholas II some strange quality which both repelled and attracted. Some of the terrorists who assassinated his Governors and officials died upon the scaffold with a plea to "his kind heart and noble intentions", not for mercy for themselves, but for an examination of "the bad conditions of affairs in Russia". The would-be assassin of Louis XV declared that he had stabbed the king in order to discover "whether he had a heart", these murderers of Nicholas II's representatives died proclaiming themselves his faithful subjects. "What sort of a man is he?" wrote his cousin, the Grand Duke Nicholas Mikhailovitch. "He is repulsive to me and yet I love him, for he is not naturally a bad sort, and is the son of his father and mother. Perhaps I love him by reflection, but what a vile little soul he is!"[2]

The first weeks of the World War had sent a blaze of enthusiasm through Russia, as through every other country. The Tsar, "the Little Father of his People", became a revered and honoured figure to his millions of subjects, the mysticism inherent in the Slav mind was centred upon the Emperor in a renewed devotion. But the enthusiasm and the devotion soon waned. The crushing defeats inflicted upon the Russian armies in East Prussia, the growing shortage of food in urban districts, and the increasing incapacity of administration throughout the Empire produced signs of war-weariness in Russia earlier than in any other belligerent state. To the strain on the population was added the effect of the secret propaganda which had circulated throughout the country since the collapse of the abortive revolution of 1905. The Russian masses stirred again under the stimulus of additional hardships and revolutionary exhortations. The army,

---

[1] *Letters of the Tsaritsa to the Tsar* (London, 1923), p. 122.
[2] *Krasni Arkhiv* (Moscow, 1922), xlix. 102.

though it fought with the greatest gallantry, resented the peculation and corruption which deprived it of equipment and the very necessities of life. The morale of the rank and file steadily deteriorated after the first autumn campaign, and by December 1914 General Kuropatkin was noting in his diary : " They are all hungry for peace ... whole battalions, instead of counter-attacking, came up to the German trenches and raised their weapons in token of surrender. They were weary of the hardships of war." [1]

The desire for peace manifested itself even earlier in certain higher Government and Court circles. On September 10, 1914, Count Witte, recently returned from France, expressed to Maurice Paléologue, the French Ambassador, his conviction that the wisest course for Russia was to " liquidate this stupid adventure as soon as possible ", since a victory for the Allies would mean the triumph of democracy and the proclamation of republics throughout Central Europe. " That means the simultaneous end of Tsarism. I prefer to remain silent as to what we may expect on the hypothesis of our defeat." [2] This attitude was shared by the ultra-conservatives of " The Union of the Russian People " (the organization of the Black Hundreds) and the pro-German element about the Court.

Thus, by the beginning of 1915, the Tsar was faced from all sides with a growing desire for peace : from the Left because of sheer war-weariness and an increasing eagerness for constitutional reform, and from the Right because of a desire to suppress that tendency while this was still possible. A dynastic peace was urged upon the Tsar for the preservation of the autocratic principle. The problem of peace had become dominant in Russia.

Nicholas II was himself loyal to the cause of the

[1] Victor Chernov, *The Great Russian Revolution* (New Haven, 1936), p. 159.

[2] Maurice Paléologue, *An Ambassador's Memoirs* (London and New York, 1923–5), i. 123.

Entente, and he had it within his power to renew the war enthusiasm of the masses. A concession to the moderate elements of the Left and Centre during 1915 or 1916 would have had the effect of restoring confidence between the people and the throne ; but the Tsar's besetting sin of weakness, combined with a lack of confidence in his own judgement, caused him to listen to the counsel of the extreme Right rather than to that of the would-be reformers.

The result was a series of desultory and unrelated attempts to negotiate a separate peace with Germany, carried on through financial and commercial agencies, through the King of Sweden, and through the Grand Duke of Hesse, brother of the Tsaritsa.[1] These attempts were aided and abetted by the German agents who poured into Russia and sought to foster the cause of peace by playing upon the nervous sensibilities of the Conservatives, emphasizing the danger of revolution from within and of the betrayal of Russia by her Allies. Britain, it was alleged, was planning to deprive Russia of her legitimate spoils of war by keeping Constantinople for herself and creating a new Gibraltar at the Dardanelles. France and Japan were said to have agreed to this move, the latter at the price of the promise of expansion into Manchuria. This so disturbed the Russian Government that at the Inter-Allied Conference at Chantilly, in November 1915, the Russian representative advised most earnestly the abandonment of the Gallipoli campaign. Moreover, the autumn of 1915 had seen an important step towards a Russo-German understanding. The Tsar, against his better judgement and under pressure from the Empress and her circle,

[1] No German account of these secret negotiations has been published (so far as the present writer is aware) but the Russian sources of information, taken largely from the archives of the late Tsar, have been used by V. P. Semmenikov in two works, *Monarkhia pered Krusheniem, 1914–1917* (Moscow, 1927) and *Romanovyi germanskie vliyania, 1914–1917* (Moscow, 1929).

removed from the position of Commander-in-Chief the Grand Duke Nicholas Nikolayevitch, whom the German Crown Prince has described as the chief obstacle to a separate peace,[1] and himself took the supreme command of his armies.

Despite the forebodings of the Tsar's more moderate counsellors and their opposition to his replacing his uncle as Commander-in-Chief, fortune smiled upon Russian arms in the summer campaigns of 1916. General Brussilov, in his drive to the Carpathians, achieved a victory second only to that of the summer of 1914. The Austrian army dissolved like " thin clouds before a Biscay gale ", but the Russian sacrifices were appalling, and when the German divisions, hastily summoned to the support of their allies, appeared upon the broken front, the Russian attacks became increasingly costly and barren. Brussilov strove to make flesh and blood achieve the function of the artillery which he lacked. In certain divisions only three men out of ten went into action with rifles. Wire entanglements, which there were no shells to cut, were traversed on the heaps of dead which the German machine-gunners piled upon them. The Russians fought with desperate, heroic courage, but, when this last effective military operation undertaken by the Tsar's armies ended in September, the losses involved were little short of a million, and, despite the gallantry of the troops, the will to victory had forsaken them, to be replaced by an aching, overwhelming desire for peace. " Peace and Bread ", became the slogan, " Peace and Bread."

Meantime the peace party of the Right had not been idle, and their activities provide one more of those baffling contradictions which are so striking a factor in this phase of tortuous diplomacy. In the middle of July, at the moment when the troops under the supreme command of Nicholas II were winning victories, he, at the behest of the

[1] *Memoirs of the German Crown Prince* (London, 1922), p. 136.

peace party, dismissed his pro-Entente Minister for Foreign Affairs, Sazonov, and concentrated power in the hands of the President of the Council, Stürmer, a friend of the Empress and a creature of the " Man of God ", Rasputin.

The appointment at this juncture of a reactionary with pro-German sympathies, who had always opposed the idea of an alliance with the democratic governments of the West for fear that it might serve as a channel through which liberal theories might penetrate into Russia, had the most profound effect both at home and abroad. To the civilians and the army, the substitution of Stürmer for Sazonov meant the elimination of one of the last moderate influences among the Imperial advisers, and the determination of the Tsar to persist in an administrative system which, through incompetence and corruption, had deprived the civil population and the troops of the necessaries of life.

The representatives of the Entente in Petrograd felt the new appointment as a severe blow to the Allied interests. " I can never hope to have confidential relations with a man in whose word no reliance can be placed, and whose only idea is to further his own ambitious ends ", wrote the British Ambassador of Stürmer. " Though self-interest compels him to continue the foreign policy of his predecessor, he is, according to all accounts, a Germanophil at heart." The French Ambassador, Maurice Paléologue, was even more emphatic in warning his Government of the new spirit in the Russian Foreign Office : " We must expect that the secrets of our negotiations will not long be a secret to certain persons who, by their pro-German leanings, indirect relations with the German aristocracy or German finance, and their hatred of liberalism and democracy, have been completely won over to the idea of a reconciliation with Germany ".[1]

The Central Powers in turn hailed the appearance of

[1] Sir George Buchanan, *My Mission to Russia* (London, 1923), ii. 18 ; Paléologue, ii. 306.

Stürmer in control of affairs in the same sense but with different emphasis. " He was undoubtedly well-disposed towards us ", writes the German Crown Prince. " I regarded that appointment as an indisputable sign of a desire to open negotiations for peace." [1]

Too astute to make an obvious break in policy by opening direct negotiations with Germany, Stürmer nevertheless made every effort to advance the cause of a Russo-German *rapprochement*. He delayed publishing both the agreement which had been reached with England in order to banish all fear of the British designs on Constantinople, and also the manifesto on Poland which Sazonov had wrung from the Tsar on the day before his dismissal. His efforts succeeded so well that, by November, German political circles were strongly of the opinion that a separate peace with Russia was now to be regarded as a matter of course, and that this chance could be let slip only by the most clumsy diplomacy.[2]

But diplomacy of the clumsiest was forthcoming. Led away by the mirage of a Polish army under German officers contributing a much needed addition to the manpower of the Central Powers, the Supreme Command of the German army insisted upon the proclamation of a Kingdom of Poland under the joint protection of the German and Austrian Emperors. The move was opposed by the Government and the Foreign Office and by many elements in the General Staff. But, blinded by the flickering brilliance of their own delusions, the Supreme Command ignored their critics and persisted in their own policy, a policy which led inevitably to the destruction of all hopes of peace. Where Stürmer had been silent—because of the fact that Sazonov's Polish plan envisaged the possible cession of territory by Germany and Austria—Hindenburg and Ludendorff were supremely vocal in advocating a Poland which consisted of

[1] *Memoirs of the German Crown Prince*, pp. 136-137.
[2] Chernov, p. 38.

Russia's share of the country. Matthias Erzberger, who had taken an active part in pressing negotiations from the German side, declared that the Polish proclamation was " a positive political catastrophe " undermining the " only chance for peace ".

The collapse of Stürmer's plans coincided with a certain knowledge of them reaching the moderate leaders of the Left and Centre. Prince Lvov, the President of the Zemstvos Organization, declared that " tormenting, horrible suspicions of treason, of secret forces working for Germany and striving to prepare a shameful peace . . . have now passed into clear realization ". Paul Miliukov, the Cadet Party leader, went even further, and in a historic speech denounced Stürmer before the Duma as guilty of high treason. Under the irresistible pressure of events, the Tsar, with a glimmering of enlightenment, dismissed Stürmer, and would have got rid of his infamous colleague, Protopopov, but for the protest of the Empress, who visited G.H.Q. " in her black trousers " and fought fiercely for the man whom Rasputin had selected to save the destinies of the Empire. Thus, though the new Government was headed nominally by Trepov, a pronounced supporter of the Entente, the real control of affairs still remained in the hands of the same clique.

By the close of 1916 the position in Russia, exacerbated by the murder of Rasputin in December, had been clarified to the extent that a clash between the forces of the Right and the Left had become inevitable. Revolution was being planned both from above and from below, and the watchword of both revolutionary parties was Peace—Peace to save autocracy, or Peace to hasten the " dictatorship of the proletariat ".

In deadly earnest the champions of autocracy were preparing to end the struggle at the front and transfer it to the rear. At the beginning of February 1917 " The Union of the Russian People " advised the Tsar to " restore order in the state, *at whatever cost*, and be certain of the victory over the foe *within*, who long since has become both more dangerous and more relentless than the *foreign enemy* ".[1] The economic situation was rapidly deteriorating, food became increasingly scarce, and it was openly stated in Petrograd that the Government was deliberately causing the shortage in order to make the continuation of the war impossible, and to provoke strikes and disorders which would provide an excuse for strong measures against the Socialist organizations.[2] To meet this situation peace was essential.

Equally desirous of peace was the extreme Left, who realized that the final battle with autocracy was near and wished to be free for the coming struggle. Revolutionary propaganda was widely distributed, inciting the workers to strike and demand peace, and the soldiers to refuse to fight further. An addition was made to the slogan of revolution, which now read, " Peace, Bread, and Land " ; but peace came first. Commanding generals on all fronts received anonymous letters through the field-post declaring that the men were exhausted, that they would fight no more, and that an immediate conclusion of peace was imperative.[3]

Between these two groups stood the moderates of the Left, the liberal elements represented by Lvov, Miliukov, and Rodzianko, President of the Duma, who remained loyal to the cause of the Entente, and desired to see Nicholas II save himself and his country by the adoption of constitutional reform before it was too late. In vain they inveighed against the *Camarilla* which surrounded the Tsar, and besought him to listen to wiser counsellors. Their pleas were shattered against the lifeless detachment of the Emperor, and, in the face of impending disaster,

[1] Chernov, p. 36. [2] Paléologue, iii. 65.
[3] General A. A. Brussilov, *A Soldier's Note-Book* (London, 1930), p. 282.

they returned to the political salons of Petrograd, where, among civilized individuals, statesmen, soldiers, and nobles, the question was continually discussed as to who should be "removed"—the Emperor, the Empress, Protopopov, or all three.

The Grand Duke Alexander Mikhailovitch added his words of warning. "Disaffection is spreading very fast", he wrote. "Strange though it may seem, the Government itself is the organ that is preparing the revolution."[1] Finally the British Ambassador, transgressing the rules of diplomatic etiquette, spoke out bluntly : " You have, Sire, come to the parting of the ways, and you have now to choose between two paths. The one will lead you to victory and a glorious peace, the other to revolution and disaster."[2]

Enwrapped in his impenetrable mantle of apathy, Nicholas II foiled every attempt to save him from himself. Those around him at this final crisis were amazed at his " cold, stony calm ", which contrasted sharply with the prevailing depression. " What is this ? " asked General Danilov in these fatal days. " Is it a tremendous, almost incredible restraint, achieved in training, or faith in divine predestination, or is it lack of intelligence ? "[3] This spiritual pachydermity enabled the Tsar on his return to Moghilev in March 1917 to write of dominoes and patience. Later (March 16) when the storm burst, and he was confronted with the unavoidable necessity of abdication, he performed the act with a lack of emotion which embarrassed both the friends and enemies who witnessed it.

Nicholas II passed into the oblivion of exile and martyrdom, and with him vanished the Romanov dynasty

[1] *Arkhiv Russkoi Revoliutsii* (Berlin, 1922–1934), v. 333. Later, in conversation with General Brussilov, the Grand Duke confessed : " I have no influence and I am of no consequence. My cousin . . . is the slave of influence and pressure that no one is in a position to overcome." (Brussilov, p. 286.)

[2] Buchanan, ii. 43.   [3] Chernov, p. 10.

with a tradition of three hundred years of absolutism behind it. The old order fell by reason of its own weight and because of the inner weakness and decadence which had undermined it. It gave way to a popular movement, vague and confused in thought, but having three predominant desires, " Peace, Bread, and Land ". The curtain had risen upon the greatest drama of modern history.

2

But the principal actor in the drama was still in obscurity. At Zurich, in a room rented from a working-class family, themselves tenants in a sombre sixteenth-century house in the Spiegelstrasse, lived Vladimir Ilyich Ulianov, known to his revolutionary brethren, and later to the world at large, as Lenin.

The outbreak of the war had found Lenin and his wife, Krupskaya, in exile in Austrian Poland. After a brief period under arrest as a spy, he was allowed to proceed to Switzerland, where for a while they had settled in Berne. They were very poor. ("No money, no money, that is our chief misfortune", wrote Lenin; and again: "This diabolical cost of living—it has become devilishly hard to live".) For personal funds they had one hundred and sixty pounds which Krupskaya's mother had left them, and they lived on it for three years. Now finally they had moved to Zurich.

The room was small and inconvenient, the courtyard on which it opened was smelly and stifling in summer, smelly and dank in winter; the Spiegelstrasse itself is but a narrow alley. But one of Lenin's most fortunate attributes was his imperviousness to externals. It mattered not to him that his coffee was served in a cup with a broken handle, that the food, eaten in common in the kitchen, was simple to the point of poverty, that the sole furnishings of the room consisted of a table, two beds, two chairs, and a sewing machine ; these matters might irk the housewifely mind of his loving Krupskaya, but Lenin's whole soul and mind were bent upon his struggle for the soul of international Socialism.

He worked with that same untiring zest which later was to achieve the miracle of bricks without straw in Soviet Russia. His waking hours were filled with his efforts to encourage his supporters inside and outside Russia, and with literary work which aimed at the destruction of the Second International and the building up of a Third, based upon what to him was the true proletarian movement.

It was impossible to work at home. The courtyard of the house in the Spiegelstrasse adjoined a sausage factory, and its intolerable stench forced them to live with closed windows. Lenin reverted to his old battle-ground of the public library. (Had not the greater part of the plans for the creation of the Bolshevik Party been conceived in the peaceful atmosphere of the reading room of the British Museum ?) Here in Zurich the library authorities exacted a respectable appearance from their readers. Some of Lenin's fellow Bolsheviks had been refused admittance on account of their mud-spattered shabbiness, but he still owned a decent coat and a pair of sound shoes, and the haven was therefore open to him. Few frequenters of the library took much notice of this bald little Russian with his snub nose, and his big mouth and square chin covered by his red moustache and short beard, who, day after day from nine in the morning till six at night, laboured with the fierce unquenchable zeal of the revolutionary. With a pen dipped in vitriol he inveighed against the Majority Socialists in both camps of belligerents, who, in allying themselves with capitalist governments for the purpose of prosecuting the war, had betrayed the proletariat to " Imperialism ".

At the Conferences of Zimmerwald (1915) and Kienthal (1916) Lenin and his followers of the Left, a forceful minority with a definite end in view, had castigated unmercifully their fellow Socialists of the Right and Centre and had openly declared for " Civil war, not civil peace " Their manifesto at Zimmerwald had called for " the utilization of every movement of the people caused by the results of the war for the organization of street demonstrations against the governments, propaganda of international solidarity in the trenches, the encouragement of economic strikes and the effort to transform them into political strikes under favourable conditions ". [1] For Lenin the European War had but one purpose—the destruction of the capitalist system and the substitution of the " dictatorship of the proletariat ". It must be the funeral procession of Imperialism.

Though numerically an impotent minority, Lenin and his group exercised an influence altogether disproportionate to their size. Lenin's doctrines, though rejected by the International Socialist Conferences, found a fruitful soil in the extreme Left of the German Social Democrat Party. As early as January 1915, Karl Liebknecht in a speech at Neuköln had adopted the thesis of " Class War against the War " which Lenin had enunciated from Zurich, and a year later, in conjunction with Rosa Luxemburg, he began the underground circulation of the famous series of " Spartacist " letters exhorting spiritedly to revolutionary action.[2] Nor were their efforts without result. In the month of May 1916, three German officers and thirty-two privates were shot for distributing copies of these letters and of the Zimmerwald Manifesto in the trenches.[3]

In the bitter struggle in which they were involved Lenin's followers did not always share their leader's unwavering faith and singleness of vision. During 1916 there developed in Zurich the basis of those differences

[1] *Collected Works of Lenin* (London, New York, 1930), xviii. 477-478.

[2] Merle Fainsod, *International Socialism and the World War* (Cambridge, Mass., 1935), pp. 49, 79.

[3] N. K. Krupskaya, *Memories of Lenin* (London, 1930), ii. 184.

of opinion within the group which were to have such tremendous consequences later. Lenin and Trotsky were already in conflict. Trotsky's formula, "True national self-defence consists in the struggle for peace," seemed to Lenin mere sermonizing, and he wrote furiously in reply: "To assume that the imperialist war will end in a democratic peace . . . is to mislead the masses by concealing from them the essential truth that a democratic peace is impossible without a series of revolutions. Away with the parsonical, sentimental, absurd dreaming about 'peace at any price'."

To Lenin the fundamental of revolution was the dictatorship of the proletariat, a seizure of power which should ensure the leading rôle of the worker and peasant in the reconstruction of the entire social fabric, and there again he met with wavering support among his followers. His letters of the period to his friends Sklyapnikov and Alexandra Kollontai are full of protests against vacillation. "Who is wavering ? " he wrote in March 1916. " Not only Trotsky and Co. but also Pyatakov. . . . Radek is the best among them . . . but *Radek* is also *wavering. . . .* Pyatakov and Bukharin did not want to understand and could not understand." [1]

These men, obscure and unknown as yet, were to make history, and were later to be arrayed against Lenin again.

In these years, too, occurred the Battle of the Pseudonyms. Writing in the Socialist press both Bukharin, as " Nota-Bene ", and Radek, as " Parabellum ", incurred Lenin's vituperative wrath and castigation for their misunderstanding of the rôle of democracy in the struggle for Socialism. Lenin tore to pieces the arguments of his lieutenants, demonstrating his own thesis that economics were only the foundation and premise of Socialism, but that the

[1] *Letters of Lenin*, edited by Elizabeth Hill and Doris Mudie (London, 1937), p. 386.

crux lay in the fundamental rebuilding of society on the basis of revolutionary democracy.

But while these revolutionary theorists clashed and battled in the realm of ideology, not one of them—not even Lenin—was aware of how soon their theories would be put to the acid test of practical application. Communication with the comrades in Russia was slow and faulty. The Bolshevik members of the Duma had been arrested in November 1914 and the party organization had suffered accordingly. Out of touch with immediate happenings and steeped in theoretical work, Lenin himself confessed in a letter from Zurich that he felt " as if I had come here to lie down in my grave ". Unflaggingly he kept up the fight against the Second International, but it was weary work waiting for the world revolution, so long dreamed of, to happen. Though he had gauged far more correctly than any one else the enormous forces of social upheaval which unsuccessful war would release in Russia, he was unable to estimate the degree to which that upheaval had already progressed. Up to the eve of the March Revolution he was not sure whether he would live to see the realization of that fond ambition upon which his whole being was so intensely concentrated.

In January 1917, when the proximity of the Palace Revolution was a common conversational topic at the dinner table of the British Ambassador in Petrograd, the only uncertainty being whether both the Emperor and the Empress would be killed, or only the latter,[1] Lenin was dejectedly informing a youth meeting at the Zurich Volkshaus that " we of the older generation may not live to see the decisive battles of this coming revolution ".[2] Beyond the disciplining of his followers in their doctrinal wanderings there was no preparation for the great Day; no thought had even been given to a possible return to Russia in the event of revolution. Lenin, in Zurich, was as completely unexpectant of the March Revolution as was

[1] Buchanan, ii. 41.   [2] Krupskaya, ii. 198.

Lord Milner after four weeks' sojourn in Petrograd, for, at the moment when the latter was reporting to his colleagues in the British Cabinet : " I have formed the opinion that there is a great deal of exaggeration in the talk about revolution " [1] (February 1917), Lenin was writing to his sister : " Our life goes on as usual, very quietly . . . it is still very cold. . . . News from you comes very slowly." [2]

The days dragged on in weary sameness. Lenin completed the draft of a book on education which a Swiss publisher had commissioned. He needed more money. . . .

Suddenly the monotony of the exiles' life was broken. On the afternoon of March 16, 1917, Krupskaya was washing the dishes after their frugal meal, as Lenin gathered the papers into his portfolio preparatory to returning to the library. There was a sound of hurrying feet upon the stair ; their friend Bronsky broke, breathless, into the room, waving the small thin sheets of a special newspaper edition. " Haven't you heard the news ? " he panted. " There is Revolution in Russia ! "

" I don't remember how we finished the day ", writes Krupskaya.

[1] David Lloyd George, *War Memoirs* (London, 1933–1936), iii. 468.
[2] *Letters of Lenin*, p. 407.

II

KERENSKY, LENIN AND PEACE

II

KERENSKY, LENIN, AND PEACE

1

IT is ironical, in view of the general desire for peace which permeated Russia at the moment of the Revolution, that the power should have fallen into the hands of the one group which was in favour of continuing the war. Had the Tsar's Government been successful in suppressing the March Revolution, a peace with Germany on practically any terms would have followed immediately. Alternatively, had the Bolsheviks been sufficiently well-organized to seize the power at once, the policy which led to the peace of Brest-Litovsk would have been launched nine months earlier. It so happened that, when the sceptre of Russia fell from the Imperial grasp on March 16, the only people who were prepared to pick it up were those Liberal constitutionalists who favoured the prosecution of the war for democracy and freedom, regardless of the fact that the vast majority of the Russians yearned for peace and had, in fact, made the Revolution in its name.

The muddled period between the Revolution of March and the Revolution of November was complicated by this misconception on the part of the Provisional Government and the realization, too late, that it was impossible to reconcile loyalty to the Allies with acquiescence in the cry for peace at home. It was this futility of delusion which enabled the Bolsheviks to capitalize the general desire for peace and transform it into a weapon with which to destroy the Liberal-Socialist Revolution.

Of sheer political impotence and well-meaning in-

eptitude history has few more striking examples than
that of the Provisional Government which took office on
the abdication of the Tsar. Composed of ten Liberals and
one Socialist ("Ten capitalists and one hostage of
democracy", wrote Lenin) it endeavoured, pathetically
and with ever diminishing success, to walk the tight-rope
between loyalty to the Allies and the alleviation of
Russia's war-weariness. It was lacking both in all means
of enforcing its authority and in those supports of tradition which had so long buoyed up the monarchy, and it
failed signally to create any new supports of its own. It
was not so much revolutionary as idealistic, and proved
utterly incapable of interpreting or controlling the vast
forces of unrest which had brought it into power. In composition and qualifications the Provisional Government
would have been best suited to govern a long-established
democracy which had earned a period of weak government. It was entirely unequal to handling a revolution.
The majority of its members were monarchists at heart,
not revolutionaries.

The Prime Minister, Prince Gregori Lvov, well esteemed
for his work as President of the *Zemstvos* organization,
had long urged constitutional monarchy under the Tsar,
and was the obvious leader of a democratic, constitutional
régime. The study of foreign policy and international
affairs which had for so long engaged Paul Miliukov,
leader of the Cadet (Constitutional Democrat) Party in
the Duma, singled him out for the portfolio of foreign
affairs, but his intellectual gifts, brilliant though they
were, were rather those of a pedagogue than a statesman,
and the impression created by his speeches was that of
a schoolmaster lecturing a rather backward and un-
enlightened form. Alexander Guchkoff, to whom fell the
Ministry of War, was a representative of the well-to-do
business class of Moscow. His idealism had led him to
fight for the Boers in the South African War, and he had

become prominent as leader of the Octobrist (Conservative) Party in the Duma. To the very young and ardent Michael Tereschenko—one of the wealthiest men in Russia, a sugar king and a great philanthropist, who in the autumn of 1916 had been involved with Guchkoff in an abortive *révolution du palais*—fell the thankless task of Finance Minister in a virtually bankrupt and creditless state. And there was Kerensky.

Of the many strange figures thrown up by the war, Alexander Kerensky is among the strangest. The son of Lenin's former schoolmaster, he had achieved, partly by sheer ability and partly by the capitalization of nuisance-value, a position of considerable prominence on the Left benches of the Duma. Turgid and hyperbolic of speech, impetuous of character, he was a man of extravagant ambition and strange spiritual force. " He filled his sails with the breath of his own restless fantasy, letting it bear him where it would," wrote one of his former colleagues, " and at times he came very near to genuine hysteria ! " [1]

Such was the man who arose in a few short weeks from the position of " a hostage of democracy " in Prince Lvov's cabinet to be nominal ruler of All the Russias, publicly hailed by Mr. Lloyd George as " that brilliant young statesman ", and, finally, after a brief and uncomfortable sojourn upon the points of unstable bayonets, to be plunged into more complete obscurity than that from which he had emerged.

Yet there was something remarkable about that strange young man with his square head and pallid face, forever delivering his high-falutin speeches and fighting a not ungallant rear-guard action with fate. Now, in middle age, there still lingers about him a vestige of that histrionic fervour which held his audiences spell-bound but failed to bind them to him. The Girondins are inevitable in

[1] Chernov, p. 173.

revolutions. They burn with idealistic love of national resurgence, and with the best will in the world they start the avalanche which they cannot hope to control in its descent. They are most fortunate when they become the victims of the force of destruction which they themselves have loosed, for martyrdom is infinitely preferable to life in the limbo of historical " might-have-beens ".

That the Provisional Government had failed to grasp the gravity of the situation with which it was faced was clearly demonstrated in its early moves in foreign policy. One of the principal causes of the overthrow of the Tsarist régime had been a deep-seated revulsion against the prolongation of an intolerable war. The whole tone of the early days of the March Revolution had been a glad revolt against the war, a grateful relief from the nightmare of two and a half years. " Peace, Bread, and Land ", had been inscribed upon the banners which the crowds carried through Petrograd. " Peace, Bread, Land " had become the answering cry from the returning soldiery—no longer soldiers, but armed civilians, militant revolutionaries. But the anxiety for peace was even more dominant than the craving for bread and the hunger for land.

All now looked to the Minister for Foreign Affairs to vocalize this nation-wide feeling in some official statement to the Allies which might at once acquaint them of Russia's desire for a speedy peace and, if possible, exert influence upon them to follow suit.

This was precisely what Miliukov did not do.

In his first statement on March 18 to the Russian diplomatic corps abroad, acquainting them officially with the change of government at Petrograd, Miliukov showed clearly that he had failed to interpret the spirit of the Revolution and that, at least as far as he was concerned, the foreign policy of the new Government would be that of the old. " The Cabinet will remain mindful of the international engagement entered into by the fallen régime, and will honour Russia's word . . . faithful to the pact[1] which united her indissolubly to her glorious Allies. Russia is resolved, like them, to assure the world, at all costs, an era of peace among the nations, on the basis of stable national organization guaranteeing respect for right and justice. She will fight by their side against a common enemy until the end, without cessation and without faltering." [2]

Although this statement of policy was most gratifying to the Allied Governments, who were anxiously awaiting news from Russia, and still more anxiously speculating as to whether the Eastern Front was to collapse entirely, it in no way represented the general will of either the Russian army or the Russian people.

There was, however, in session in Petrograd another body of great importance and exercising, even at that time, amazing influence. This was the Soviet of Workers', Soldiers', and Peasants' Deputies, which had been elected on March 10, before the final crash of the imperial régime. From the very outset the Petrograd Soviet was the only body the authority of which was acknowledged by those who had supplied the element of physical force in bringing about the Revolution, that is to say, the garrison and factory hands of the capital. This body was at the moment under the control of Prince Tseretelli and the Menshevik Party. As yet the Bolsheviks were a very small and uninfluential faction in the Soviet, suffering greatly from lack of intelligent leadership. Stalin and Kamenev, lately

[1] This is in reference to the secret Treaty of London signed in September 1914 by Great Britain, France, and Russia, pledging themselves not to enter into any separate peace negotiations with the Central Powers.

[2] See *Russian-American Relations*, by C. K. Cumming and Walter W. Pettit, pp. 3-4. This indispensable collection of documents on Revolutionary Russian diplomatic history from 1917–1920 was published in 1920 by Harcourt, Brace Co., New York, for the League of Nations Association, now the Foreign Policy Association. The book is now out of print.

returned from Siberian exile, were their chiefs at this moment, but in these early days the future dictator of Russia showed no capacity to rule or lead.

There can be little doubt that the Petrograd Soviet represented the feelings of the great masses of the organized wage-earners far more than did the Provisional Government, or that it was trusted in a far greater degree by workers and peasants alike. But it refused to co-operate in the organization of the Government, limiting its relations to the presenting of definite political demands, and reserving to itself the rôle of critic. Moreover, in its revolutionary zeal, it added the final touch to the destruction of discipline in the army by issuing the notorious *Prikaz* No. 1, which among other things absolved the Russian soldier from the necessity of saluting his superiors.

How completely the Government realized its own helplessness and its degree of dependence upon this powerful external agency may be judged from a letter written by the Minister of War to General Alexeiev, on March 22. " The Provisional Government possesses no real power," Guchkoff confessed, " and its orders are executed only in so far as this is permitted by the Soviet of Workers' and Soldiers' Deputies, which holds in its hands the most important elements of actual power, such as troops, railroads, postal and telegraph services. It is possible to say directly that the Provisional Government exists only while this is permitted by the Soviet of Workers' and Soldiers' Deputies. Especially in the military department it is possible now only to issue orders which do not basically conflict with the decisions of the above-mentioned Soviet." [1]

Sitting independently the Petrograd Soviet carried on its own foreign policy, and interpreted to the world the Russian workers' great desire for peace. The Soviet developed its foreign policy along two distinct lines : on the one hand, it impressed upon the Provisional Government the immedi-

[1] W. H. Chamberlin, *The Russian Revolution* (London, 1935), i. 101.

ate urgency of a general democratic peace, negotiated between all the belligerent Governments, while, on the other, it appealed over the heads of all governments to the peoples. Herein lies the germ of all ensuing Soviet foreign policy and is found the explanation of the close relation which has hereafter existed between policy and propaganda.

On March 27 the Petrograd Soviet issued its Proclamation to the Peoples of the World appealing to the labouring classes to take steps to bring to an end the sanguinary struggle. " The time has come to start a decisive struggle against the intentions of conquest on the part of the governments of all countries ; the time has come for the peoples to take into their own hands the decision of the questions of peace and war. . . . The Russian democracy calls upon the peoples of Europe for concerted decisive actions in favour of peace." The proclamation continued with a special appeal to the " brother proletariats of the Austro-German coalition and first of all to the German proletariat " ; it declared at the same time, however, that Revolutionary Russia would defend her freedom against any attack from any quarter, and ended with the revolutionary exhortation of 1847 : " Proletarians of all Nations, unite ! " [1]

This was the first intimation the world received of the new force behind the Revolution and of the existence of internal conflict.

The position of the Provisional Government was further complicated by an interview given by Miliukov to the press, in which he championed the annexation of the Dardanelles as a necessary safeguard for the outlet to the Mediterranean which Russian economic development needed. This interview revealed clearly the gulf which existed between official foreign policy and public opinion, and produced a storm of criticism in the Soviet. Bolshevik

[1] Cumming and Pettit, p. 8.

and Menshevik alike joined in condemning this flagrant espousal of the old imperialist policy. Prince Lvov hastened to explain away the *contretemps*. The Foreign Minister had, he said, given his purely personal views as regards the annexation of Constantinople, views with which the Government, as a whole, were not in accord. He promised a statement on foreign policy at an early date.

But before this promise could be fulfilled an event had taken place, which, though it attracted comparatively little attention either at home or abroad, was destined to overshadow all else in importance—Lenin had returned to Russia.

2

The March Revolution was hailed by the Allies with satisfaction and relief. Though they appreciated the loyal personal efforts of the Tsar, they could not but welcome the disappearance from power of those pro-German and corrupt elements about the Imperial Court which had played so important a part in the breakdown of the military machine and, indeed, of the very life of the country. It had long been realized that there was no one in authority who had the capacity to handle the critical situation, and that those who were alleged to be competent were refused power by the prejudices of the Tsar. Under these circumstances, wrote Mr. Lloyd George, " the Revolution was not only inevitable—it was imperative ".[1] It was not yet appreciated— not even apparently by the usually so astute Sir George Buchanan—that Russia had exchanged one form of inept government for another which, by the very nature of things, could not long endure. For the moment the hopes of the Allies were concentrated on a keener participation of Russia in the eastern theatre of war.

There was a further consideration which endeared the Provisional Government to the Allies. The appearance of

[1] Lloyd George, iii. 505.

Russia as a neophyte in the ranks of democracy at this particular moment was of very real importance. It removed the last obstacle to the participation of the United States of America in the war on the side of the Allies, and, within the Allied countries themselves, it secured an even firmer degree of support from organized labour and Socialism, which had never felt entirely happy in being allied with Russian despotism. That the Revolution played an important part in President Wilson's calculations is clearly indicated in his Message to Congress recommending the declaration of war upon Germany : " For the United States the possibility that a new and liberal government in Russia may now develop is a welcome factor in removing previous American hesitation at associating with a Russian Government which we rightly judged to be tyrannical and corrupt ".

Mr. Lloyd George wrote in his telegram of congratulation to Prince Lvov on March 24 :

Much as we appreciate the loyalty and steadfast co-operation which we have received from the late Emperor and the Armies of Russia during the last two and a half years, yet we believe that the Revolution, whereby the Russian people have placed their destinies on the sure foundation of freedom, is the greatest service which they have yet made to the cause for which the Allied peoples have been fighting since August, 1914.[1]

The Governments of the other principal Allied Powers also sent messages of felicitation couched in similar terms, and all hastened to accord *de jure* recognition to the Provisional Government and to despatch their Socialist colleagues to observe a modern revolution on the spot and to watch over Allied interests under the new régime. Arthur Henderson from England, Albert Thomas from France, Emile Vandervelde from Belgium, and Charles Edward Russell from America, all hurried to Petrograd bearing fraternal greetings and urging on the unfortunate

[1] Lloyd George, iii. 507.

Provisional Government to the impossible feat of a more active prosecution of the war. The Allied Socialists returned to their respective countries convinced of the many reasons which, in spite of everything, justified young democratic Russia's belief in her future, but it is noteworthy that Emile Vandervelde closed the account of his own mission with a quotation from Nietzsche : " There must be chaos, that out of chaos may come forth new stars ; there must be chaos that new worlds may be born ".[1]

If the March Revolution was hailed with relief by the Allies, it was correspondingly a source of anxiety to the Central Powers. Though hopes of a separate peace with Russia by direct negotiation had vanished with the proclamation of the Kingdom of Poland in November 1916, the corruption and inefficiency of the Imperial régime, together with the pro-German influences at the Court, had proved an indirect but by no means a useless ally. The war on the Eastern Front had been brought virtually to a standstill, and the Supreme Command, already occupied with its preparations to meet the Allied spring offensive on the Western Front, were loath to see the Russian armies regalvanized into action.

Far better informed as to the actual state of affairs in Russia than were the Allies, the Supreme Command at once divined that the weakest spot upon which to work was the war-weariness of civilians and soldiers alike. " Orders were given for propaganda to be set on foot at once to encourage a movement for peace in the Russian Army ", writes Ludendorff ; [2] and the Russians were accordingly exhorted to desert their Allies and sue for peace. " What is it that the free Russian people desire ? " enquired one of the leaflets distributed in the trenches. " Is it the attain-

[1] Emile Vandervelde, *Three Aspects of the Russian Revolution* (New York, 1918), p. 241.

[2] Lieutenant-General Erich Ludendorff, *My War Memories, 1914–1918* (London, 1919), ii. 414.

ment of the aims of the Allies, which Russia has not yet
repudiated, or is it the conclusion of peace, murmurs of
which we seem to hear from the Russian Army ? . . . If
the new Russian Government, prompted by its Allies,
wishes to make sure whether the German divisions and
German heavy artillery are still intact upon your Western
Front—let them try. Oh, when *will* you come to realize
that your grave-digger is England ? " [1]

But this direct method of approach was too slow in
producing results. The Allied attack against the new
Hindenburg Line might develop any day now. Something
more vital must be found to sabotage the Russian Revolution which the Allies were working so hard to bolster up.
The Supreme Command cast about for some more subtle
weapon and quite unexpectedly they found one ready to
their hand. It was not until a year later that they discovered
it to be a boomerang of the most deadly nature.

3

In Zurich Lenin was almost demented with anxiety and
impatience. The Revolution, for which he had worked and
waited, had come and had taken him by surprise. He was
chained to these sordid surroundings while revolutionary
history was being made in the streets of Petrograd. The first
three days after he received the news were passed in a
frenzy. His waking hours were spent in desperate planning,
his nights in fevered delirium. He read every paper he could
lay his hands on, English, French, and German, scanning
them avidly for the least scrap of news from Russia. Every
telegram from Petrograd tore his soul with a fierce nostalgia,
a yearning to be released from these long years of labour in
the vineyard of theory and to return to the field of action.
At all costs he must escape from Switzerland ; that was his

[1] Alexander Kerensky, *The Crucifixion of Liberty* (London, 1934),
p. 281.

dominant thought, and he knew well enough that both the
Provisional Government and the Allied Secret Service
would go to any lengths to stop him. He planned fantas-
tically : he would take an aeroplane ; he would wear a wig
and travel under a forged passport as a dumb Swede.

" You might talk in your sleep ", said his practical wife.
" If you dream of the Mensheviks you will start swearing
and shout ' scoundrels and traitors '."

Very well, then, he would learn Swedish, Lenin replied.[1]

But after three days he regained his normal sense of
proportion. His letters to the faithful Kollontai in Sweden
displayed his old fierce analysis of the situation, showing
that he was under no illusion as to the ability or durability
of the Provisional Government. To her he despatched for
circulation in Russia his first theses on the Revolution,
adjuring the comrades not to be misled by the Provisional
Government into believing that it was not as imperialistic
and capitalist in its aims as the old régime it had replaced.
It could not, he declared, give the masses what they
expected from revolution—peace, bread, and freedom.[2]
" Our tactics : complete contempt, no support of the new
Government," he telegraphed to the Bolshevik faction in
the Petrograd Soviet. " Kerensky especially suspicious.
Armed proletariat, only guarantee." [3]

In the three weeks which followed (March 20–April 8)
Lenin elaborated this theme in his five " Letters from
Afar " written to the Bolshevik faction for their guidance.[4]
These letters, in which he touched upon all the fundamental problems of the Revolution and charted the course
of its further development towards the desired second
stage—the dictatorship of the proletariat—provide an outstanding example of Lenin's revolutionary genius. His

---

[1] *Letters of Lenin*, p. 416 ; Krupskaya, ii. 200-201.

[2] Lenin, *Collected Works*, xx. Book 1, pp. 19-26.

[3] Leon Trotsky, *History of the Russian Revolution* (London, 1932–
1933), i. 307.   [4] Lenin, *Collected Works*, xx. Book 1, pp. 27-63.

clarity of judgement, his acute perception of weakness and strength, and his abounding belief in the masses are displayed, the more remarkably when it is considered how imperfect were his sources of information and his channels of communication.

With devastating accuracy he demonstrated the inability of the Provisional Government to satisfy the fundamental desire of the Russian people for peace, and proclaimed as basis of the " proletarian " peace programme the publication and repudiation of the secret treaties which bound Russia to the Allies, and the immediate proposal to all belligerent parties of an armistice on all fronts. This would be the first task of the workers' and peasants' Government after it had seized power.

His advice and tactics were not wholly intelligible to his followers in Petrograd, who regarded all talk of a second revolution and the seizure of power by the proletariat as a Utopian dream. When Lenin was striving to communicate the tensity of his will to Petrograd across Europe, Kamenev, with the co-operation of Stalin, was turning sharply towards social patriotism.

Sensing this tendency amongst the Bolshevik faction, partly by instinct and partly from articles which appeared over Kamenev's name in *Pravda*, Lenin redoubled his efforts to seek a means of escape from Switzerland. At a meeting of the representatives of Russian political parties in Geneva on March 19, it was proposed by Martov, the Menshevik leader, that, since the Allied Powers were adamant in their refusal to allow passage to the exiles, permission should be requested for political emigrants to return to Russia via Germany in exchange for interned German civilians. Other members of the Menshevik Party hesitated at so bold a plan, frightened at the interpretation which would inevitably be placed upon it in Russia. Lenin, however, grasped at it without a moment's hesitation. If the alternative lay between a return to Russia via Germany and remaining in Switzerland, there was for him no question at all. He would travel through Hell, with the personal guarantee of the Prince of Darkness, if it would take him back to Petrograd. With bitter contempt he mocked the waverings of the Mensheviks and forced the adoption of the plan.

The first tentative approaches were unsuccessful. In reply to the request of Robert Grimm, the Secretary of the Swiss Social Democratic Party, that the Swiss Government should act as intermediary with Berlin for the procuring of a permit of passage, the Federal Councillor, Hoffman, who had charge of the political department, refused to take any such action, on the ground that the Entente Powers would regard it as a violation of neutrality on the part of Switzerland. The political exiles must make formal application to the Minister of Justice in the Provisional Government (at this time Kerensky) for official permission to return. Chafing at the delay, Lenin agreed *faute de mieux* and the formal application was accordingly made.

A week went by, two weeks, still no reply came from Petrograd. Lenin was again in a frenzy of impatience. At last he could wait no longer. Against the advice of the Mensheviks and others, he directed Fritz Platten, Secretary of the Swiss Socialist Party, to open direct negotiations with the German Government. Platten placed himself in communication with Dr. Helphand, known to the revolutionary world as " Parvus ", a Russian political emigrant who at the end of the 'nineties had become a member of the German Social Democratic Party. Without consulting the party executive,[1] Helphand began to explore the situation in Berlin. He sounded the Foreign Office. The Eastern European experts, Mirbach and Maltzan, were definitely interested, and an approving report was forthcoming from Brockdorff-Rantzau, then Minister in Copenhagen. He spoke a word in the Bureau of the Imperial Chancellor ;

[1] Philip Scheidemann, *The Making of New Germany* (New York, 1929), i. 365.

more important still, he talked with Erzberger and through him made contact with the Supreme Command. The success or failure of the scheme turned upon the approval or veto of Hindenburg and Ludendorff.

To them Helphand explained that if they really wanted Russia out of the war, Lenin was the man to achieve it. He would sweep away mealy-mouthed idealists, such as Kerensky and Tchkeidze, and be ready for an immediate armistice ; it would then only depend on Germany to make a reasonable peace with Russia.[1]

To the Supreme Command the game with Lenin was worth the candle. They gave their approval willingly, little realizing that in so doing they were preparing for themselves the weapon which should later effect that famous " stab-in-the-back ". As a short-term policy the Supreme Command were amply justified in their decision. The disintegration of the enemy's army by means of propaganda was entirely feasible as an indirect method of attack. What is astonishing is the confident belief of the General Staff that German troops and civilians would be immune from infection by the same political virus which they were prepared to use against the Russian military and civilian population. " At that time nobody could foresee the fatal consequences that the appearance of those men would have for Russia and for the whole of Europe ",[2] wrote General Hoffmann ; and again : " We neither knew nor foresaw the danger to humanity from the consequences of this journey of the Bolsheviks to Russia. At that time we weighed the matter with as little consideration as the Entente does now." [3] In the days to come Ludendorff was anxious to transfer the onus of responsibility from his own shoulders and Hindenburg's to those of Bethmann Hollweg. " By sending Lenin to Russia our Government

[1] Scheidemann, pp. 365-367.

[2] Major-General Max Hoffmann, *War Diaries and other Papers* (London, 1929), ii. 177.   [3] *New York Times*, December 24, 1920.

had assumed a great responsibility", he wrote in his memoirs. "From a military point of view his journey was justified, for Russia had to be laid low. But our Government should have seen to it that we also were not involved in her fall."[1] Later, in an article written for a military journal, he was even more explicit: "In sending Lenin, the Chancellor promised us more rapid development of the Russian Revolution and an increase in the desire for peace which was already noticeable in the Russian army and navy. Headquarters considered that in this way the defences of the army would be weakened. No one at Headquarters knew who gave the Chancellor his idea of sending Lenin. The Chancellor himself scarcely knew his name; but nevertheless events proved that our acceptance of the Chancellor's proposals was justified."[2]

If conditions of government in Germany at the moment be considered, this meek acceptance by the Supreme Command of the Chancellor's view on so important a subject is entertaining. Hindenburg and Ludendorff held Bethmann Hollweg in that supreme contempt which the Prussian military caste reserved for the civilian politician. A few weeks before, they had forced acceptance by the Kaiser of unrestricted U-boat warfare over the objections of the Chancellor. Within three months they were to engineer his dismissal from office and the appointment of their own creature, Michaelis. They, and not he or the Emperor, were the final arbiters of German destinies, and on them rests the onus for this historic step.

The die was cast. Instructions went forth to the German Legation in Berne to respond amicably to Fritz Platten's advances. As a result, on April 4 a most remarkable "treaty" was drawn up between the Empire of the Hohenzollerns and the editorial staff of a Swiss revolutionary paper. Lenin, in preliminary conversations with

[1] Ludendorff, ii. 510.
[2] *Militär Wochenblatt*, No. 35, (Bodin, February 26, 1921).

Platten, had worked out the details of the agreement with extraordinary care. He demanded complete extra-territorial rights for the train during the period of transit, and absolute freedom from supervision for the personnel of the party, their passports, and their luggage. Platten should accompany the party for the whole journey and he alone would communicate with German authorities and officials ; in addition, no one could leave the train during the journey, nor enter it, without Platten's per-mission. (From this last provision grew the legend of the "sealed train".) The sole obligation which the *émigrés* undertook was to agitate on their arrival for the exchange of a corresponding number of Austro-German civilians interned in Russia.[1]

On April 6 word came that this agreement had been approved and "ratified" in Berlin, and two days later the train-load of political dynamite, a party of thirty-two including Lenin, Krupskaya, Zinoviev, Sokolnikov, and Radek, steamed out of the Central Station of Berne.

The Mensheviks stayed behind, condemning to the last the action of the Bolsheviks in negotiating independently with the German Government without awaiting an answer from Petrograd. Martov and Axelrod feared the accusation of their comrades in Russia that, in obtaining the consent of the German Government to pass through Germany, they would put themselves under an obligation to the General Staff and become "German agents".[2] This in effect was

[1] Lenin, *Collected Works*, xx. Book 1, pp. 91-94, 360-361 ; Book 2, pp. 381-386. A further regulation, which proved of considerable irksome-ness to the returning Bolsheviks, was that smoking in the compartments was forbidden. The German railway officials strictly enforced the rule and the Russians, to whom a cigarette was practically a fifth finger, were forced to retire to the toilet at the end of the coach when the craving for tobacco became irresistible, much to the annoyance of those of their companions who had other legitimate uses for this convenience.

[2] A few months later both Martov and Axelrod, together with nearly 200 Mensheviks, also returned to Russia by way of Germany.

the accusation which Lenin and his companions had to
face on their arrival, not only from the Allied countries and
from the Provisional Government (which was perhaps
natural enough), not only from the Mensheviks and the
Social Revolutionaries, but from their fellow Bolsheviks
in the Petrograd Soviet. And their first action had to be to
dispose of such an allegation.

The suggestion that Lenin in travelling through Germany
to Russia was acting in any sense as a German agent is
ridiculous. No two parties ever entered into an agreement
with more brutal cynicism than did Ludendorff and Lenin.
The attitude of the German General Staff was admirably
described by General Hoffmann, Chief of Staff on the
Eastern Front, who incidentally had had no part in the
agreement and did not even know of its conclusion until
Lenin was back in Russia. " In the same way as I send
shells into the enemy trenches, or as I discharge poison gas
at him," he wrote, " I, as an enemy, have the right to use
propaganda against him. . . . I personally knew nothing
of the transport of Lenin through Germany. However, if
I had been asked, I would scarcely have made any objection
to it." [1] Nor was Lenin lacking in realism. " If Karl Liebknecht were in Russia now, the Provisional Government
would certainly allow him to return to Germany ", he wrote
at the moment of his departure. " The internationalists
of all countries have a right and a duty to utilize this
gamble of the imperialist governments in the interests of
the proletariat without changing their course and without
making the slightest concessions to the governments." [2]

If any pact existed between Ludendorff and Lenin
it was one of mutual mistrust and deception. In the game
they were playing, the German under-estimated the calibre
of the man opposed to him. For whereas Ludendorff was
saying to himself, " Lenin will overthrow the Russian

[1] Hoffmann, ii. 176-177.
[2] Lenin, *Collected Works*, xx. Book 2, p. 385.

patriots, and then I will strangle Lenin and his friends ",
Lenin was thinking, " I shall pass through Germany in
Ludendorff's car, but for his services I shall pay Ludendorff in my own way ". His farewell letter to the Swiss
workers, written on the day of his departure, leaves no uncertainty as to his intentions towards Germany. " We will
be forced to carry on a revolutionary struggle against the
German—and not only the German—bourgeoisie. This
struggle we will carry on. We are not pacifists. . . . The
future [in Germany] belongs to that tendency which has
given us Karl Liebknecht and which has created the
Spartacist Group. . . . The German proletariat is the
most trustworthy, the most reliable ally of the Russian and
the world proletarian revolutions." [1]

It so happened that Lenin's particular brand of poison
coincided with the interests of Germany ; it also so happened that the interests of Germany coincided with Lenin's
overwhelming desire to return to Russia. Either side was
prepared to betray the other. In this Machiavellian battle
of wits, Lenin was the more subtle.

It was, however, not unnatural that the Entente
countries and the Provisional Government should spread
the story that Lenin was a German agent, that he carried
with him, not only the goodwill of the German High Command and the Imperial Government, but also bulging money-
bags of gold (as well as a transfer account on the *Deutsche
Diskontogesellschaft*) wherewith to do the bidding of his
masters. It was the obvious Allied counterblast to the
German move of the " sealed train ", and the propaganda
service did excellent work. What those who were willing to
believe this story did not realize was that Lenin's promises
of peace and bread were infinitely more corrupting to the
Russian army and workers than any amount of German
gold could have been. To the very end the Allied Powers
failed to realize the war-weariness of Russia.

[1] Lenin, *Collected Works*, xx. Book 1, pp. 85, 87.

The story travelled more quickly than Lenin himself. It was in Petrograd to greet him and, in fact, it partially facilitated his return ; for, when the Provisional Government debated the question of his arrest, according to the memoirs of Vladimir Nabokov, the Secretary-General of the Provisional Government, the Ministers were convinced that the very fact of his having appealed to Germany would so undermine the authority of Lenin that they need have no fear of him.[1]

The publication by the United States Government at a later date of the famous " Sisson Documents " greatly assisted the circulation of the story,[2] and similar " circumstantial evidence " convinced many people in all parts of the world of its truth. Amongst the converts were both Kerensky and the American Ambassador in Petrograd, Mr. David Francis.[3]

But Lenin, speeding northwards across Europe to Malmö, was not greatly concerned by the prospect of the accusations. He had weighed all that in the balance before negotiating with Germany. He knew that his Russian opponents would throw mud at him, but he knew also that the masses would finally follow his lead.

The terms of the Berne Agreement were scrupulously adhered to. Lenin rebuffed with scorn an attempt of some

[1] Quoted by Trotsky in *The History of the Russian Revolution*, i. 309-310.

[2] The " Sisson Documents " were a collection of material obtained by Mr. Edgar Sisson, of the U.S. Committee for Public Information, then in Russia. The documents purported to prove conclusively the connection between the Bolshevik leaders and the German High Command, and their accuracy was vouched for by prominent Slavonic scholars in the United States. Some months before Mr. Sisson had acquired it, the collection had been offered to and refused by the British Foreign Office, who rightly suspected its authenticity. Mr. Sisson's own account of the affair is contained in his book *One Hundred Red Days* (New Haven, 1931).

[3] Kerensky, pp. 278-294 ; also Hon. David Francis, *Russia from the American Embassy* (New York, 1922), pp. 222-226.

German Social Democrats to enter into conversation with him while the train stood at a siding in Berlin. To him Kautsky, Scheidemann, and Ebert, who had voted war credits in the *Reichstag*, were as much anathema as were Ludendorff and the Kaiser. He would have no truck with those who, in his view, had betrayed international Socialism.

At the Russian frontier the police refused admission to Fritz Platten and to Karl Radek—the latter on the ground that he was still an Austrian subject and a member of the German Social Democrat Party [1]—but allowed the remainder to proceed. As the home-coming exiles crossed the border into Finland to change trains, they were welcomed by members of the Bolshevik Party who had come from Petrograd. " What's all this you've been writing in *Pravda* ? " was Lenin's first greeting to Kamenev after a separation of several years. " We saw several issues and gave it to you hot and strong."

As the train approached Petrograd on the evening of April 16, Lenin became convinced that he would be arrested on arrival. He was not afraid, but the idea of a sojourn in the Fortress of Peter and Paul irked him. He had.lost so much time already. There was so much to do. But his fears were groundless. As they steamed into the station a great throng swept on to the platform, and as Lenin stepped down he was engulfed by it. Some one thrust a bouquet of roses into his arms and, surrounded by his comrades, he was rushed into the Tsar's waiting-room. Lenin in the Tsar's waiting-room ! Here was an irony of history, but there was more to follow. The head of the reception committee was Tchkeidze, the President of the Petrograd

---

[1] Radek had settled in Germany after the abortive Revolution of 1905 in which he had played a part in Poland. He had joined the left wing of the Social Democrats and was not an original Bolshevik, though in close friendship with Lenin. He returned to Russia immediately after the November Revolution (1917) and at once became a member of the Communist Party.

Soviet ! Tchkeidze, the Menshevik, of whom the kindest thing Lenin had ever said was " scoundrel and traitor " ! Lenin stopped dead on seeing him; Tchkeidze looked abashed. In hurried tones he repeated his speech of welcome—with its note of warning :

Comrade Lenin, in the name of the Petrograd Soviet and the whole Revolution, we welcome you to Russia . . . *but* we consider that the chief task of the revolutionary democracy at present is to defend our Revolution against every kind of attack both from within and without. . . . We hope you will join us in striving toward this goal.

The whole situation must have appealed to Lenin's ever lively sense of irony. The bouquet—the Tsar's waiting-room—Tchkeidze's speech. On his words of reply might depend many things. He determined to make his position clear from the start. He waited for a few moments in silence, quite composed, a little amused, and seemingly concerned with the rearrangement of his bouquet. Then, with a gesture as it were of dismissal, he turned from Tchkeidze to the crowds outside, from the Government to the masses ; it was symbolic of his whole policy :

Dear Comrades, Soldiers, Sailors, and Workers, I am happy to greet in you the victorious Russian Revolution, to greet you as the advance guard of the international proletarian army. . . . The hour is not far when, at the summons of Karl Liebknecht, the German people will turn their weapons against their capitalist exploiters. . . . The Russian Revolution created by you has opened a new epoch. Long live the world-wide Socialist revolution !

Here in a few words was a declaration of war against Miliukov and Kerensky on the one hand, and Ludendorff and Kautsky on the other. It was a forecast of Lenin's future policy.

And he was right in his psychology. The appeal had its instantaneous effect. The crowd took Lenin to its bosom, this strange, bald-headed little man, forty-seven years old, whom few of them had ever seen before, but whose name already meant so much to them. Sweeping aside the committee of welcome, in the early dusk of a rainy evening, they brought Lenin riding triumphantly and ominously upon an armoured car to the luxurious home of the fashionable ballerina, Kshesinskaia, head-quarters of the Bolshevik Party. (This incongruity, too, must have tickled Lenin's sense of humour !) Russia was paying its first salute to its future ruler.

A few days before, at a cabinet meeting, Kerensky had exclaimed petulantly, impatient with his colleagues : " Just you wait, Lenin himself is coming, then the real thing will begin ".

4

It was, indeed, a strange Petrograd to which Lenin had returned. Life had become a tremendous gamble and an air of uncertainty overhung the events of each day. No one now believed in the stability of the Provisional Government, but they did not yet know what would take its place. Demonstrations and counter-demonstrations filled the streets, often leading to open fracas and death. Yet the night life of the capital went on as usual. Theatres and cabarets remained open ; at the " Europe ", Jimmy, the barman from the old New York Waldorf-Astoria, continued to purvey his famous concoctions. The ballet season was in full swing, with Karsavina enchanting her public, while at the opera Chaliapin had never been in better voice. There was even an appearance of a sufficiency of food in the city, though reports of scarcity still poured in from the provinces. A strange sense of unreality permeated everything.

In the political field all waited with anxiety for the Prime Minister's statement on foreign policy which should disavow Miliukov's imperialist views regarding the acquisi-tion of Constantinople. The people hoped for, and expected, a declaration which should abandon territorial aggrandizement once and for all, and which should pave the way for the negotiation of that peace for which they longed so ardently. The impossibility of reconciling peace with loyalty to the Allies did not trouble the Russian people at this moment. They desired peace above all things, and they regarded it as the primary duty of the Provisional Government to give it to them.

The promised statement was made by Prince Lvov on April 27 and bore traces of grave searchings of heart on the part of the Government to achieve the impossible. It stated that the vital interests of Russia required the

defence by all means of our own inheritance and the liberation of the country. . . . Leaving to the will of the people in close union with our Allies the final decision of all questions connected with the war and its termination, the Provisional Government considers it its right and duty to declare that the purpose of free Russia is not domination over other peoples, nor spoliation of their national possessions, nor the violent occupation of foreign territories, but the establishment of a permanent peace on the basis of the self-determination of peoples. The Russian people are not aiming to increase their power abroad at the expense of other peoples. . . . These principles will be made the basis of the foreign policy of the Provisional Government, which will firmly carry out the will of the people and will protect the rights of our fatherland, at the same time fully observing all obligations made in regard to our Allies.[1]

This statement, which in tone was in marked contrast with Miliukov's note of March 18, was a victory for the Soviet and was in accordance with its principles of foreign policy. On all sides it was acclaimed as a sign that at last the Provisional Government would take steps to persuade the other Allied Governments to restate their war aims as a preliminary to a general and an early peace.

It was in transmitting this statement to the Russian diplomatic corps in the Allied countries on May 1 that

[1] Cumming and Pettit, p. 10.

Miliukov made his final blunder. In a covering Note to each diplomat he took it upon himself to interpret the statement of Prince Lvov as being in the nature of a sop to the Soviet and purely for home consumption, his purpose being to allay the suspicions and fears which had arisen in Allied countries as a result of the Soviet proclamation of March 27. " The declaration of the Provisional Government," he wrote, " being imbued with the free spirit of free democracy, naturally cannot afford the least pretext for assumption that the demolition of the old structure had entailed any slackening on the part of Russia in the common struggle of all the Allies. On the contrary, the nation's determination to bring the war to a decisive victory has been accentuated, owing to the sense of responsibility which is shown by all in common and each one of us in particular."[1]

At once a storm of fury and criticism broke out against the Foreign Minister, and in a less degree against the War Minister, Guchkoff, who was also suspected of "imperialist" leanings. Monster anti-war demonstrations filled the streets, and clashes with the police and troops occurred. All the bitter class-hatred of revolution secured an outlet, and Lenin fanned it with an ardent zeal. Daily, almost hourly, he addressed the crowds from a raised platform before the home of Kshesinskaia, directly opposite the British Embassy, where the Troitsky bridge spans the Neva. Quietly, without the arm-waving hysteria of Kerensky, his hands buried in the side pockets of his old double-breasted blue jacket, Lenin talked with absolute assuredness of purpose. He asked one question only of the crowds: " What do you get from war ? " and he gave them the answer they knew so well—" Wounds, suffering, hunger, and death." " Will you go back to the factories and the land to work under the capitalists again ", he taunted them, " —those of you who are left alive ? " And back came the

[1] Cumming and Pettit, p. 11.

roar of thousands, " We will go back to the factories and the land to take them for ourselves ! *Doloj boorjooiev !* "

Within the Soviet, Lenin, who had now brought his own faction to heel, establishing his dominance over them, took occasion to point out that Miliukov's " duplicity " demonstrated how impossible it was to co-operate with the bourgeoisie as represented by the Provisional Government. In this he received the support of the Mensheviks, but the Soviet as a whole was not yet ready for the break. They were still scared by the ruthlessness of Lenin's ideas.

The Provisional Government bowed before the storm. On the evening of May 4 it presented to the Soviet an " explanation " of the Miliukov Note, endeavouring to bring it more into line with the Soviet Manifesto of March 27. It declared that " free Russia does not aim at the domination of other nations or at depriving them of their patrimony, or at occupying by force foreign territories, but that its object is to establish a durable peace on the basis of the rights of nations to decide their own destinies."[1] This explanation was accepted by the Soviet late in the evening, and a motion of confidence in the Provisional Government was carried, after a stormy and acrimonious debate, by a majority of only 35 in a vote of 2500. In view of this Guchkoff resigned on May 13 and Miliukov on May 17. On this last date Leon Trotsky arrived in Petrograd from America.

The part played by the Petrograd Soviet in the Miliukov affair clearly illustrated to all the amazing increase in its power, and the corresponding diminution in that of the Provisional Government. Prince Lvov, in reconstructing his Cabinet, had the choice of either following the advice of the military circles and suppressing the Soviet by force, or of allying himself with it. He chose alliance, and opened negotiations for a coalition. Participation in the Provisional Government was bitterly opposed by Lenin and the Bol-

[1] Cumming and Pettit, p. 12.

sheviks ; Trotsky, though not himself a member of the party, allied himself with them on this and subsequent issues, utilizing the occasion to make his first public speech after his return. He advocated the handing over of all power to the revolutionary people and voiced for the first time the slogan which was later to sweep the Bolsheviks into power, " All power to the Soviets ".

But, on May 18, the Soviet agreed to the entrance of Socialist Ministers into the Cabinet, and a new Government was formed under Prince Lvov, consisting of six prominent Socialists—Chernov, Tseretelli, and Skobelev, from the Soviet, among them—and nine Liberals and Radicals. Kerensky became Minister for War, and Tereschenko succeeded Miliukov as Minister for Foreign Affairs. In its ministerial declaration issued on the same day, the Government declared that " in full harmony with the entire people " it rejected the idea of a separate peace, but that its aim was " to bring about at the earliest possible moment a general peace " based upon a policy of non-annexation and self-determination. Having thus endeavoured to meet all parties, the declaration added that the question of transfer of land to the workers—the point with which Lenin had made so much play in his harangues—would be left to the Constituent Assembly, whose convocation they would make every effort to secure " as soon as possible ". The postponement of this vital point was an added weapon to Lenin's armoury, and one which he did not hesitate to use.

Three days previously, on May 15, the Petrograd Soviet had issued a Manifesto to the " Socialists of all countries ", in pursuance of its original declaration of March 27. It definitely declared against a separate peace, which " would free the hands of the Austro-German Alliance ", but urged the Socialists of the world to force their respective governments to adopt a " platform of peace without annexations or indemnities, on the basis of the self-determination of peoples." This appeal included also the Socialists of the

Central Powers, and, in order to co-ordinate their efforts with those in Allied countries, the Petrograd Soviet declared its intention of calling an International Socialist Conference at the earliest opportunity.[1]

This declaration by the Soviet had a disastrous effect on the way in which the Ministerial Statement of the new Provisional Government was received in Allied countries. British and French statesmen, unwilling to differentiate between the two bodies and falling victims to the force of their own propaganda, ended by mistrusting both Government and Soviet alike. Neglectful of the reports which were reaching them from their Embassies in Petrograd and obsessed by the idea that German influence was rampant there, Great Britain and France chose to suspect both declarations as being inspired by the evil one. " The formulae of all these declarations are ambiguous catches and cleverly laid traps, not invented in Petrograd but imported from abroad, their origin being clear ", Mr. Bonar Law informed the House of Commons on May 30.

The Allied Governments did not want to believe that Russia was out of the war, and ignored the continually increasing volume of evidence which pointed to this fact. For now both the Bolshevik and the Menshevik press were clamouring for peace. " The passionate desire for peace, peace of whatever kind, aye, even a peace costing the loss of ten governments [*i.e.* provinces] is growing ever more plainly evident ", wrote a military correspondent in the *Rabochaya Gazeta*, the leading Menshevik daily, at this time. " Men dream of it passionately, even though it is

---

[1] It was largely due to this resolution that the Dutch Socialist leader Troelstra took the initiative, in April 1917, in summoning the so-called Stockholm Conference. This gathering was barren of any concrete result, chiefly owing to the fact that the Socialists of the Allied countries were forbidden by their governments to attend it. There were present only representatives of Socialist parties of the neutral States, Germany, Austria, and Russia.

not yet spoken of at meetings and in resolutions, even though all enlightened elements of the army fight against this movement." [1]

There was only one way to counteract the growing demoralization within the army, and that was to let the soldiers know that the Provisional Government was doing everything in its power to end hostilities and to bring about the conclusion of peace. This, of course, the Provisional Government could not do as long as it remained bound by the Tripartite Agreement of September 1914, by which Great Britain, France, and Russia undertook not to make a separate peace with the Central Powers. Lacking the courage to face facts and to request the Allies for release from pledges which Russia could no longer honour, the Provisional Government staggered from disaster to disaster in a desperate and futile attempt to save its face. Thus, when Tereschenko suggested on June 16 to the Allies the summoning of an Allied conference " for the revision of the agreements concerning the final objects of the war ", he specifically stated that the agreement of September 5, 1914, " must not be a subject of discussion at this conference " ; [2] and on the following day the Duma passed a resolution in favour of carrying out the military offensive which had been agreed upon at the Inter-Allied Conference of January. Tereschenko's suggestion received no sympathetic response in London and Paris, the Allied Governments merely intimating that the summer offensive was still expected of Russia and should be launched as soon as possible. A further blow was thereby inflicted on the Provisional Government, to some extent a self-inflicted blow.

Probably the wisest course, both for the Western Powers and the Provisional Government, would have been to release Russia from her obligations, a course which was

[1] *Rabochaya Gazeta*, May 26, 1917.
[2] Cumming and Pettit, p. 26.

actually proposed by Sir George Buchanan after the
November Revolution. For practical purposes Russia was
already out of the war, and the July offensive, when
launched, added nothing to the success of Allied arms
but merely opened the way for a substantial German
advance. Peace with Germany at this moment and the
convoking of the Constituent Assembly would have removed
one of the highest trumps from Lenin's hand, and would
have done much to restore the confidence of the people in
the Provisional Government. As it was, the Provisional
Government treated the world to a performance of political
suicide.

The new offensive was bitterly opposed by the
Bolsheviks, and Kerensky, in his attempt to reorganize
the army, had to contend with their well-organized propaganda along the whole front. He put forth the whole
of his turgid eloquence. He wept in his exhortations,
pled with the troops to fight for the defence of democracy, and begged for their confidence. It was during
this campaign for reorganization that Kerensky and Lenin
met for the only time in their political careers. Before the
first All-Russian Congress of Soviets they spoke from the
same platform and Kerensky taunted his opponent with
favouring a separate peace. Lenin indignantly denied the
accusation. "It is a lie", he cried. "Down with a separate
peace ! We Russian revolutionaries will never stand for it.
To us separate peace means entering into an agreement
with the German robbers, who are quite as predatory
as the others. But an agreement with Russian capital in
the Russian Provisional Government is also a separate
peace."[1] For Lenin the only cessation of hostilities was

[1] Lenin, *Collected Works*, xx. Book 2, pp. 210-211. According to
German military sources, the Provisional Government, to hide its
military weakness and divert attention from its preparation for an
attack, initiated a " peace offensive " in the spring and early summer
of 1917. Conversations took place in Stockholm between Erzberger and
Russian agents which Erzberger at least took very seriously, for on

one brought about by, and based upon, the assumption of power by the "proletariat" in all countries.

The offensive was duly launched on July 1, and the Russian troops fought with their customary courage, despite their acute war-weariness and lack of equipment. Few events in the war were more tragic than this last Allied offensive on the Eastern Front, carried out by men whose one desire was for peace and a return home, and of whom, in many cases, only one in six or eight possessed a rifle. By sheer impetus they achieved a not inconsiderable advance, and, within the first twenty-four hours, had captured more than 36,000 prisoners.

Yet there were many units who would not attack, who flung down their rifles and stood sullenly with folded arms, while their officers, threats and prayers alike proving useless, spat at the silent men and went towards the enemy alone. The poison was already at work.

The offensive neither surprised nor discouraged the German High Command, and when they began their counter-attack on July 19 it was apparent how greatly the Russian morale had suffered. Bolshevik agents appeared in every division and the success of their work was only too clear; regiment after regiment revolted, murdered its officers, and then hesitated, not knowing what to do next. The front was paralysed. The German advance gave the last touch to the disintegration which the Bolshevik agitation had initiated. The effect was ghastly. A panic spread in the ranks of an army already in a state of dissolution. There was scarcely any question of resistance. The retreat paralysed even the will of those individual units which were

June 11 he wrote to Ludendorff that the moment had arrived for the conclusion of an armistice. Both the Foreign Office and the General Staff were warned to be in readiness for the formal opening of negotiations, but when the final preparations for the July offensive were completed these tentative feelers were speedily withdrawn. (Cf. Hoffmann, ii. 169-170; Mathias Erzberger, *Erlebnisse im Weltkrieg* (Berlin, 1920), pp. 237-239.)

prepared to take up fighting positions. The troops melted away before the eyes of their commanders. " The army voted for peace with its legs ", Lenin afterwards declared.

Tarnopol was captured at the end of July, and on September 2 the German armies crossed the Dvina, taking Riga on the following day. Only the difficulty of transport prevented a more rapid advance, and hostilities on the Eastern Front were virtually brought to an end by the middle of October with the occupation of the islands of Moon, Dagö, and Oesel, in the Gulf of Riga.

In Petrograd the Provisional Government was rocked by one catastrophe after another. On July 17, when the offensive had shot its bolt and had failed to reach its objectives, and the Cadets in the Cabinet, including the Premier, had resigned on the issue of the recognition of 'Ukrainian autonomy', the Bolsheviks engineered their first *coup d'état*, an abortive movement, lacking in preparation and proper organization. It grew spontaneously out of a mass meeting of disgruntled machine-gunners in Petrograd. Lenin was out of town, recuperating in the country after a slight illness, and in his absence his more spirited lieutenants considered that the combination of a Cabinet crisis, the meeting of the first All-Russian Congress of Soviets, and a revolt of troops was a suitable moment for a political uprising.

For two days fierce street-fighting took place and then the forces of the Provisional Government gained the upper hand, due more to the unpreparedness of the Bolsheviks than to their own efficiency. The repressive methods which followed were characterized by the vacillation of a government anxious to stamp out its enemies but uncertain of its power to do so, and were in marked contrast with those ruthless but efficient methods which Noske employed against the Spartacists in Berlin in 1918 and 1919. The Bolshevik press was silenced; Trotsky, Krupskaya, Kollontai, and others were arrested and condemned to

death, but their sentences were commuted and they were
subsequently released. Lenin, disguised as an engine-
driver, escaped with Zinoviev to Finland, where he
remained in hiding for the next three months, though
keeping in constant touch with the party by means of
secret letters.

Kerensky, relieved for the moment from the Bolshevik menace, devoted his attention to the reorganization
of the Government, and on July 22 was able to form
a Cabinet based upon all parties with the exception of
the extreme Right and Left, the Monarchists and the
Bolsheviks. General Kornilov was appointed to succeed
Brussilov and was to try to check the German advance, and
on August 1 Kerensky issued a further pathetic assurance
to the Allied Powers that Russia would continue in the war
to the best of her ability.[1] But this statement struck the
first note of that hopeless fatalism which was beginning to
envelop the Social Revolutionary movement in Russia.
Kerensky, now Premier, realized only too well that his
only chance of success depended upon an immediate peace
move by the Allies and the calling of the Constituent
Assembly ; he realized, too, the impossibility of achieving
either.

The attitude of the Allies towards the Provisional
Government had changed considerably from the bene-
volent expectation with which they had greeted the March
Revolution. The gravity and despondency of the reports
from the Embassies and missions in Petrograd, describing
the continued and increasing confusion which surrounded
the Government, had given rise to grave disillusionment
mingled with irritation and resentment. The fact that the
approval of the British Foreign Office had been requested
and given for the appointment of three different individuals as Ambassador to the Court of St. James', none of
whom had taken the trouble to come to London, had

[1] Cumming and Pettit, pp. 33-34.

soured the outlook of Downing Street not a little, and the sole reply vouchsafed to Kerensky's latest assurances, which arrived in London at the moment of an Inter-Allied Conference, was " a stern protest against the continuation of disruption and anarchy in Russia ", a protest on the despatch of which, oddly enough, the Russian Chargé d'Affaires was asked to express his views.[1]

Meanwhile the Kerensky Government continued its dismal course towards the inevitable *débâcle*. Disasters multiplied during the autumn. The capture of Riga by the Germans on September 3 brought Petrograd within raiding distance for Zeppelins. The front had virtually collapsed. In desperation at the inability of the Government to deal with the situation either at home or in the face of the enemy, the Commander-in-Chief, General Kornilov, " the man on horse-back ", attempted a military *coup d'état* (September 9–15), as fantastic as it was ill-organized. In essence it had the makings of a great patriotic movement—Lenin described it as a " formidable and a really unbelievably dramatic stroke "—but because of its immaturity of conception and inefficiency of execution, it became, in effect, an *opéra bouffe* affair, since Kornilov's Cossacks easily surrendered to the armed workers' battalions of Petrograd. Kerensky showed himself as barren of judgement in this matter as in the rising of July. Then he had had the chance of suppressing the Bolsheviks once and for all, but he had failed to take it; now, instead of reaching an understanding with the one man whom the army showed any sign of following, Kerensky antagonized him to the point of open insurrection, and to quell this it was necessary to play into the hands of the Bolsheviks by arming the populace. Once the workers had arms in their hands they would not surrender them. From this moment the fate of the Provisional Government became a matter of weeks.

[1] Constantin Nabokoff, *The Ordeal of a Diplomat* (London, 1921), pp. 128-130.

Despite the failure of the Kornilov adventure, the Cabinet fell and Kerensky was established at the head of a directorate of five. A Democratic Conference on a widely representative basis was called at Moscow on September 27. But little came of it save a further reorganization of the Government. Events now gained such momentum that the Provisional Government was hurtling to its fall. On October 3 and 8, respectively, the Moscow and Petrograd Soviets came under the control of Bolshevik majorities, with Trotsky as president at Petrograd. Meanwhile, Kerensky, in a desperate effort to evolve some temporary substitute for the Constituent Assembly, proclaimed the creation of the Council of the Russian Republic (also known as the Preliminary Parliament) in which all classes of the population were represented. This body, a consultative assembly without any legislative power, held its first session on October 20, when the Bolshevik delegates withdrew after a demonstration, proclaiming their refusal to participate in a " Government of Treason to the People " and announcing their intention of summoning the All-Russian Congress of Soviets to meet in Petrograd in the first week of November " to take over the government of Russia ".

This was the situation at the moment when it was announced that the Inter-Allied Conference on War Aims, for which Kerensky and Tereschenko had prayed so long, was to meet in Paris on November 10. It came to the distracted Government like an eleventh-hour reprieve, and it was at once proposed that Tereschenko and old General Alexeiev should represent Russia. But the Petrograd Soviet, jealous of its vastly increased power and still profoundly suspicious of the " imperialistic " aims of the Government, insisted that their representative Skobelev should be included in the delegation, and issued to him the now famous *Nakaz* for a peace based upon the principles of " No annexation, no indemnities, and the right of self-determination of peoples ".

The Provisional Government objected to Skobelev, and, on the appearance of the *Nakaz*, the Allied Governments protested vehemently through their Ambassadors against his being sent as a delegate. Finally Mr. Bonar Law administered the crowning disappointment to Russia. " As far as I know," he said, in answer to a question in the House of Commons, " the Paris Conference will not discuss the aims of the war at all, but only the methods of conducting it."

Meanwhile, General Verkhovsky, the Minister for War, declared, in a statement to the Government, that in the state of chaos prevailing in the Russian army the only hope for the Republic was to press the Allies to offer peace. At once his statement was seized upon by the Bolshevik press as a proposal for a separate peace independently of the Allies, and a vehement attack was launched. The Minister was given indefinite leave of absence, and Kerensky, for a last brief moment, became supreme military dictator of Russia.

On October 23, Lenin, who since the July rising had been in hiding in Finland, returned secretly to Lesnoye, near Petrograd. Throughout his period of exile he had poured forth letter after letter to his party, encouraging them, guiding their actions, and directing a torrent of cold and reasoned arguments against the Provisional Government. At no other time does Lenin's amazing genius for propaganda show as clearly as in these letters, classical examples of revolutionary literature.[1]

The headquarters of the Bolshevik Party had been transferred from the palace of the *prima ballerina* to equally incongruous surroundings in the former fashionable school for young ladies, the Smolny Institute, in a northern suburb of Petrograd. Here, in the rooms where, in other and happier days, had been taught deportment and the technique of the drawing-room, the party tacticians per-

[1] Lenin, *Collected Works*, xxi. Book 1, pp. 219-279.

fected their plans for that armed uprising which, they felt, alone could save the Revolution from the bourgeois influence of Kerensky and his fellow doctrinaires.

The first meetings on October 23 and 29 of Lenin with his comrades were at Lesnoye, it still being too dangerous for him to come to the capital. Here, to Trotsky, Zinoviev, Stalin, Sverdlov, Kamenev, Dzerzhinsky, Kollontai, Sokolnikov, and three others, Lenin declared that the time had come to reap the harvest of propaganda which the Bolshevik agitators had been sowing ever since the July rising. Now was the moment for the Bolsheviks to seize the power. There could be no further delay. It was now or never.

All agreed save Kamenev and Zinoviev. They considered the issue too great a gamble, too uncertain of success. They preferred to wait until their programme and their exposure of the Mensheviks and the Social Revolutionaries had become more widely known to the masses. They feared a repetition of the July days and the consequent success of counter-revolutionary movements such as Kornilov's.

Failing to make their views prevail in the Central Committee, they resigned on October 29 and took the drastic step of attacking Lenin's policy in the non-party paper, *Novaya Zhizn* (October 31). For this breach of faith, Lenin branded " this little pair of comrades " as " strikebreakers ", subjecting both them and their doctrines to annihilating criticisms, and demanded their exclusion from the party. This threat of excommunication was not enforced, and both Kamenev and Zinoviev continued their opposition to the policy of an armed uprising until the very eve of the November Revolution, but they did not again carry their dissension beyond the party circle.[1]

Meanwhile the Government, though declaring that they were fully informed of the preparations of the Bolsheviks, continued their plans for the forthcoming Allied Conference.

[1] Lenin, *Collected Works*, xxi. Book 2, pp. 106-137, 325-341.

Tereschenko in the Council of the Republic demanded the
withdrawal of the *Nakaz* to Skobelev.

> The combination of forces which unites us to the Allies is favour-
> able to the interests of Russia. . . . It is therefore important that
> our views on the question of war and peace shall be in accord with
> the view of the Allies as clearly and as precisely as possible. . . . To
> avoid all misunderstanding, I must say frankly that Russia must
> present at the Paris Conference *one point of view*.

Yet, while the Council wrangled petulantly over words
and phrases, the structure of the Provisional Government
was already being undermined. This was October 29, and
on that day the Petrograd Soviet had created its Military
Revolutionary Committee. The day following, the first
prop was struck from beneath the ramshackle administration sitting in the Marinsky Palace. The regiments of the
Petrograd garrison unanimously adopted the following
resolution : " The Petrograd Garrison no longer recognizes
the Provisional Government. The Petrograd Soviet is our
Government. We will obey only the orders of the Petrograd
Soviet through the Military Revolutionary Committee."

A third party meeting was held at Lesnoye on November
3. Lenin, who had constantly urged the necessity of swift
action, still met with opposition from those who, though
converted to the principle of an armed uprising, were yet
hesitant as to the ripeness of the moment. Plans for the
revolt were discussed on November 3, but even then Lenin
was unable to get agreement on a date. The Second Congress
of Soviets was due to meet on November 7, and he was
convinced that they must strike before that body had had
time to organize itself, preferring the certainty of seizing
power by force to the uncertainty of achieving it by popular
vote. On the evening of the 6th he wrote to the Central
Committee his final appeal for action : " It is as clear as
can be that delaying the uprising now really means death.
. . . History will not forgive delay by revolutionists who
could be victorious to-day, while they risk losing much

to-morrow. . . . It would be disaster to wait for the uncertain voting of November 7. The people have a right and a duty to decide such questions not by voting but by force. . . . To delay action is the same as death." [1]

Later that same evening, Lenin came disguised from Lesnoye to Smolny to take direct charge of the operations. His presence, though concealed, destroyed the last remnants of uncertainty, and the death-blow to the tottering provisional régime was dealt on November 7.

The Kerensky régime perished, as it had lived, ingloriously and with infirmity of purpose. Red guards had been organized on a large scale in expectation of fierce opposition, but the Provisional Government simply melted away. Kerensky on the morning of the 7th left Petrograd to look for an army. He neither found one, nor returned. A few hours later the remaining members of the Government, betrayed by their own guards, were arrested during their last session at the Marinsky Palace. Their final defenders were bewildered old Palace servants, a handful of army cadets, and some singularly ineffective military amazons.

[1] Lenin, *Collected Works*, xxi. Book 2, pp. 144–145.

III

THE DECREE OF PEACE

III

FROM THE DECREE OF PEACE TO
THE ARMISTICE

1

In the problem of peace the Bolsheviks faced a crucial test. As it had been a vital issue in the struggle against the Provisional Government, so now it was a vital issue in the activity of the Soviet régime. The great masses of the people yearned for peace, yet this was not a simple problem. Peace had to be considered in relation to the Revolution, and its negotiation had to be in accord with the new revolutionary policy. First, however, it was necessary to abandon the former policy of the Provisional Government of attempting through diplomatic channels to influence the Entente Powers. That policy had collapsed, and collapsed miserably. Vigorous action for a general peace was demanded by circumstances.

The Bolshevik Party had never included a separate peace in its platform. It was in fact completely outside the scope of the party programme, which declared for a general European peace based upon the dictatorship of the proletariat. The party had, however, from the very first, advocated an immediate peace on the lines of the Manifesto issued by the Petrograd Soviet on March 27.[1]

This had ever been uppermost in Lenin's mind during his weeks of exile between the abortive rising of July and the *coup d'état* of November. In his instructions to his followers, written from his hiding-place, he stressed the need for peace. "It is precisely in the war against the Germans

[1] See above, p. 29.

that action is now necessary: *it is necessary immediately and unreservedly to propose peace to them on definite terms*. If that is done there will be either an early peace or else a revolutionary war " (August 1917); and again: " the Bolsheviks if they take power can offer the people an immediate proposal of peace." Finally, in his article, " The Aims of Revolution ", published in mid-September, Lenin declared :

> The Soviet Government must *immediately* formulate proposals to all belligerent countries (that is simultaneously to their Governments and to the masses of workers and peasants) to negotiate a general peace on the spot on democratic terms, and to conclude an armistice at once if even for only three months . . . such a peace will not have the good fortune to please the capitalists, but it will receive such a warm welcome from the people, will evoke such an explosion of enthusiasm in the whole world, such indignation against the interminable war of plunder waged by the bourgeoisie, that very probably we shall obtain at one slide both an armistice and the opportunity to broach peace negotiations. For the workers' revolt against the war grows everywhere with undiminished vigour.[1]

It was upon this basis, therefore—a complete misconception of Western European psychology—that the first diplomatic actions of the Soviet Government took form. The theory was that only the declaration of the principles of a general peace was needed for the peoples to rise and compel the Governments to enter into the necessary negotiations. Clear from the first, this attitude became even more marked as the Brest-Litovsk Conference drew near.

Buoyed up by the memories of the German naval mutiny at Kiel in July, Lenin allowed himself to believe that the proletarian revolution in Germany was only " around the corner "—an error of judgement for which Russia had later to pay dearly. " As soon as ever the Bolsheviks are in power," he declared, " the German

[1] Lenin, *Collected Works*, xxi. Book 1, p. 259.

proletariat will compel the Kaiser to start negotiations for peace."

Little time was lost in putting Lenin's peace theories into operation. At a quarter-past five on the morning of November 8, there arrived at Smolny a telegram from the Northern Front bringing the greetings of the army to the new régime and thereby setting a seal of recognition on the *coup*. Pandemonium broke loose, men weeping and embracing each other. The burden of fatigue and tension of the past twelve hours was forgotten in this moment of success. But the breathing-space was only a brief one. A crushing anxiety descended again upon Smolny, enveloping it as though in a shroud. The Bolsheviks had seized the power ; the Petrograd Soviet had overthrown the Government and the army had felicitated the new revolution, but the Congress of Soviets, who as yet had not even seen Lenin, had still to ratify the establishment of the dictatorship. And then, what of the rest of Russia ? What of the world ?

Throughout November 8 Lenin stamped with cold contempt and fierce invective on the waverings of those amongst his followers, who, like Kamenev, frightened by the very magnitude of their success, favoured the sharing of power with the Mensheviks and the Social Revolutionaries, thereby broadening the basis of the Revolution. To these hesitants Lenin replied that he would co-operate with any one who would accept the Bolshevik programme. " We won't give way an inch ", he declared.

His intransigence was justified. As evening drew on, word came that the Social Revolutionaries would not leave the Petrograd Soviet and would continue to co-operate with its Military Revolutionary Committee.

" See, they are following ", said Lenin.

All attention was now centred upon the meeting of the Soviet Congress which, since one o'clock in the afternoon, had been waiting to receive Lenin's report on the *coup*. It became known that he would place his peace policy immediately before the delegates. Excitement ran high, the air was alive with expectancy and speculation.

It was nearly nine o'clock before the Bolshevik leaders reached the Congress hall, staggering with fatigue, having neither slept nor eaten, their faces drawn and grey, yet exultant. Here it seemed was sheer fantasy; while the success of the *coup d'état* was by no means yet assured, they were about to discuss the question of world peace.

John Reed, eyewitness of these events, left a vivid record :

A thundering wave of cheers announced the entrance of the presidium, with Lenin—great Lenin—among them. A short, stocky figure with a big head set down on his shoulders, bald and bulging. Little eyes, a snubbish nose, wide generous mouth, and heavy chin ; clean-shaven now but already beginning to bristle with the well-known beard of his past and future. Dressed in shabby clothes, his trousers much too long for him. Unimpressive, to be the idol of a mob, loved and revered as perhaps few leaders in history have been. . . . Now Lenin, gripping the edge of the reading stand, let his little winking eyes travel over the crowd as he stood there waiting, apparently oblivious to the long-rolling ovation, which lasted several minutes. When it was finished, he said simply, " We shall now proceed to construct the Socialist order ! " Again that overwhelming roar.

" The first thing is the adoption of practical measures to realise peace. . . . We shall offer peace to the peoples of all the belligerent countries upon the basis of the Soviet terms—no annexations, no indemnities, and the right of self-determination of peoples. At the same time, according to our promise, we shall publish and repudiate the secret treaties. . . . The question of War and Peace is so clear that I think that I may, without preamble, read the project of a Proclamation to the Peoples of All the Belligerent Countries. . . ."

His great mouth, seeming to smile, opened wide as he spoke ; his voice was hoarse—not unpleasantly so, but as if it had hardened that way after years and years of speaking—and went on monotonously with the effect of being able to go on forever. . . . For emphasis he bent forward slightly. No gestures. And before him, a thousand simple faces looking up in intent adoration.[1]

The Decree, a lengthy document,[2] proposed an immediate opening of negotiations for a " just and democratic peace ", without annexations and without indemnities. It declared the intention of the Government to put an end to secret diplomacy and to publish all secret treaties of the Tsarist régime. It advised the concluding of an immediate armistice for three months on all fronts to facilitate the negotiations.

When the thunder of applause had died away, Lenin spoke again. He asked that the Congress approve the Decree immediately, leaving it to the Constituent Assembly to ratify the peace treaty which should result therefrom. But he left them under no illusions :

This proposal of peace will meet with resistance on the part of the imperialist Governments—we don't fool ourselves on that score. But we hope that revolution will break out in all the belligerent countries. . . . Probably the imperialist Governments will not answer our appeal—but we shall not issue an ultimatum to which it will be easy to say no. If the German proletariat realises that we are ready to consider all offers of peace, revolution will break out in Germany, but to agree to examine all conditions of peace does not mean to accept them.

For an hour the Congress, faction by faction, recorded its approval of the Decree in varying measure. Finally Kamenev put it to the vote of the whole. For approval ? A sea of hands was raised, waving enthusiastically. Against ? For an instant a single hand rose in disapproval, but a sudden outburst of protest quickly brought it down again. The vote was unanimous.

As by a common impulse the delegates found themselves upon their feet, breaking into a hurricane of sound

[1] John Reed, *Ten Days that Shook the World* (New York, 1919), pp. 125-127.　　　　　　[2] For text see Appendix I, p. 375.

which developed into the chorus of the " Internationale ". A grizzled old soldier was sobbing like a child, a young workman, his face shining with sweat and exaltation, repeated over and over, " The war is ended ! The war is ended ! "

So peace came to Russia.

But things did not long remain in this idyllic state. The Revolution had been made but not consolidated, and the Bolsheviks had to overcome both armed and passive resistance before they could claim to be masters of the situation.

When, on the morning of November 10, Trotsky, as Commissar for Foreign Affairs, went to take possession of the Foreign Office and ordered the Decree of Peace to be translated into foreign languages, six hundred officials resigned and walked out of the Ministry. His colleague, Uritsky, who demanded the texts of the secret treaties for publication, was literally thrown out of the Archives Department, and of the Administrative Staff only one member of the Economic Section remained. The employees of the State Bank refused to pay out money to the new Government. Meanwhile, on November 11-14, occurred the Cadet Rising and Kerensky's military adventure at Gatchina.

But within a few days these efforts had been suppressed, and both Moscow and Petrograd were definitely in the hands of the Bolsheviks. Gradually the machinery of government, thrown out of gear by the *coup d'état*, was made to resume its usual functions, and, on November 20, Trotsky circularized the Allied Ambassadors, acquainting them formally with the change of government and calling their attention to the Decree of Peace. This note was to be considered in the nature of a " formal proposal for an immediate armistice on all fronts and the immediate opening of peace negotiations ".[1] On the following day a similar letter was addressed to the diplomatic representa-

[1] Cumming and Pettit, p. 44.

tives of neutral States requesting their assistance in bringing the peace proposals " in an official manner to the knowledge of the enemy Governments ".[1]

The Allied Ambassadors and Ministers agreed among themselves, at a conference on November 22, to take no notice of Trotsky's advances and to advise their respective Governments to make no reply to the communication " as the pretended government was established by force and not recognized by the Russian people ".[2] This advice was generally followed, and the Allied Governments neither recognized the existence of the new régime nor its proposals of peace.[3] They went even further, and transferred their recognition from the Council of Commissars in Petrograd to the *Stavka* (G.H.Q.) at Moghilev.

Meanwhile a very definite step towards peace had been taken on November 21, when Krylenko, the Commissar for War, had authorized troop fraternization on all fronts, and had instructed General Dukhonin, Commander-in-Chief since the arrest and disappearance of Kornilov, " to address to the military authorities of the hostile armies a proposal immediately to cease military operations with a view to opening peace negotiations ".[4]

General Dukhonin gave no indication either that he had received the orders of the Council of Commissars or that he had any intention of carrying them into effect. When taxed directly on the night of the 22nd, he declared that he could only obey the order of " a government sustained by the army and by the country ". He was at once dismissed by telegraph, Krylenko being appointed

[1] Cumming and Pettit, p. 45.

[2] *U.S. Foreign Relations, 1918 : Russia*, i. 245.

[3] Buchanan, ii. 223 ; and Mr. Balfour's statement in the House of Commons, November 26, 1917 (Hansard, col. 1614).

[4] *U.S. Foreign Relations, 1918 : Russia*, i 247 ; James Bunyan and H. H. Fisher, *The Bolshevik Revolution, 1917-1918*, Documents and Materials (Stanford University, California, 1934), p. 233; S. A. Piontkovsky, *Khrestomatiia po istorii oktobrskoi revoliutsii*, p. 265.

to succeed him, with Dybenko at the Commissariat for War.[1] Lenin, in a broadcast wireless message to all troops, made public the circumstances of the change of command :

> The matter of peace is in your hands. You will not suffer counter-revolutionary generals to destroy the great cause of peace. You will surround them with a guard in order to prevent lynching unworthy of the revolutionary army and to prevent these generals from avoiding the court that awaits them.

The election of regimental plenipotentiaries was formally authorized and the armistice negotiations left for the moment in their hands.[2]

But Dukhonin did not leave Moghilev, nor was he immediately arrested by his own troops. With his Head-quarters staff and certain of the corps of officers he stuck to his guns, and met invective with invective. Leaflets were printed at the Headquarters press and distributed amongst the troops ; they even found their way into opposition papers in Petrograd. Confident in the knowledge that he had the support of the Allied Military Missions and, tacitly, of the diplomatic corps, Dukhonin appealed widely for support from workers and peasants for a popular government " knowing neither violence, nor blood, nor bayonets. Lose no time. The Army awaits your word." [3]

The Allied Governments gave the *Stavka* a certain negative support. They had ignored the Revolution, they

---

[1] Bunyan and Fisher, pp. 233-235 ; *Dyelo Naroda* (Petrograd), November 23, 1917.

[2] *U.S. Foreign Relations, 1918 : Russia*, i. 247 ; *Izvestia*, November 23, 1917. When criticized in the Central Executive Committee for the wording of this proclamation, which was interpreted as a proposal for a separate armistice, Lenin denied this and declared : " Our Party never promised that we would give peace immediately. What we said was that we would immediately offer an armistice and publish the secret treaties. This we have done. Now begins the revolutionary struggle for peace " (*Dyelo Naroda*, November 24, 1917).

[3] *U.S. Foreign Relations, 1918 : Russia*, i. 251. A proclamation was also issued to the army [Bunyan and Fisher, p. 240].

had snubbed Trotsky, but they could not disregard the definite order of the Council of Commissars to cease hostilities. Over the heads of the *de facto* Government in Petrograd, they addressed themselves to Dukhonin. Between November 23 and December 1, the General Headquarters Staff received protests first from the Allied Military Attachés " against the violations of the terms of the Treaty of September 5th, 1914 ",[1] then from General Berthelot, head of the French Military Mission, to the effect that " France will not recognize a government of the Council of People's Commissars " and trusted that the Russian Supreme Command would " hold the Russian Army at the front facing a common enemy " ;[2] and finally from the American Military Attaché, who protested " categorically and energetically against any separate armistice which may be made by Russia ".[3]

It was generally hinted by all that the most serious consequences would ensue from any such separate action, and this hint was interpreted to mean that the Allies were about to call upon Japan to attack Russia in the rear. The policy of protests and veiled threats was unfortunate and ill-advised—a fact which was certainly appreciated by a few of the Allied diplomats in Petrograd [4]—and nothing could illustrate more abundantly the ignorance of the Entente concerning the Russian situation.

Dukhonin circulated these protests to the army and thereby drew at once an energetic reply from Trotsky, who characterized the efforts of the Allied military representatives as an attempt " to force by threats the Russian army and the Russian people to continue the war in execution of the treaties concluded by the Tsar ".[5] At the same time he issued an official warning to the heads of the Allied Military Missions that " the Government

---

[1] Cumming and Pettit, p. 49. [2] *Ibid.* p. 50.
[3] *Ibid.* p. 53. [4] Buchanan, ii. 224.
[5] Cumming and Pettit, p. 54.

cannot permit Allied diplomatic or military agents to interfere in the internal affairs of our country and attempt to incite civil war ".[1]

The full force of the propaganda machinery of the Smolny Institute was used to combat the effort of the General Staff. The troops were exhorted: " Do not obey Dukhonin ! Pay no attention to his provocations ! Watch him and his group of counter-revolutionaries carefully." They were told that around the *Stavka* at Moghilev was gathering a group of Kerenskyists who " obey the orders of the French, English, and American financiers ". Above all, the General Staff were "responsible for the offensive of July 1st and the prolongation of the war ".[2]

It was this final argument which influenced most strongly a discouraged, disorganized, and defeated army. In any event, the effect was swift and terrible. On December 2, the garrison at Moghilev mutinied and arrested Dukhonin and his staff, imprisoning them in their own special train.

Next day Krylenko arrived with a reinforcement of Bolshevik sailors. The mutinous soldiery, intoxicated with revolutionary propaganda, first demanded Dukhonin's epaulettes, and having secured these, through the mediation of Krylenko, dispersed for a while. But in half an hour they were back again, this time intent upon murder. Krylenko made a half-hearted attempt to block the entrance to the railway-coach but was swept aside. The General was dragged out, surrounded by the mob, and beaten. He fell on his face on the platform, but the beating went on. Finally one of the sailors fired two shots into his body. The crowd cheered.[3]

[1] Reed, p. 260.   [2] *Ibid*. p. 261.

[3] See Krylenko's Report in *Novaya Zhizn*, December 13, 1917, and also an eyewitness' account published in *Russkoe Slovo*, December 6, 1917 ; Reed, p. 261 ; Bunyan and Fisher, pp. 267-268 ; and Ariadna Tyrkova-Williams, *From Liberty to Brest-Litovsk* (London, 1919), pp. 311-312. Despite the fact that John Reed refers to Dukhonin as the "old General ", he was only 41 at the time of his murder. Dr. Masaryk, who

Meanwhile, on November 26, Trotsky had made formal application to the German High Command for an immediate armistice for the purpose of concluding a democratic peace without annexations and indemnities ; to the Allied diplomats he declared that the Soviet régime had never desired a separate peace and still hoped for a peace that would embrace all belligerent parties. But peace they were determined to have, and the onus would lie upon the Allies if Russia were forced to sign a separate agreement. Two days later (November 28), Krylenko carried out the original orders issued to his predecessor and ordered " firing to cease immediately and fraternization to begin on all fronts ".

The collapse of the attempts of the Allied Military Missions to prevent the Russian army from declaring an immediate armistice had convinced the British Ambassador, Sir George Buchanan, that to *faire bonne mine à mauvais jeu* was the only course now open to the Entente Powers. The situation was now so desperate that a reconsideration of the Allied attitude was essential. Though they were not prepared to accept the Soviet proposals as a basis for general peace negotiations, they must recognize that sooner or later a separate peace between Russia and Germany was inevitable. Much advantage would accrue therefrom to Germany, who hoped undoubtedly to establish an economic protectorate, and it was a matter of vital importance to checkmate this latest move. German-Russian relations must be exacerbated at all costs, even though peace existed officially between the two countries, for a Russo-German Alliance after the war would constitute a perpetual menace to Europe in general and to Great Britain in particular.

was in the neighbourhood of the *Stavka*, organizing the Czech legions, speaks of the General as " a young and vigorous officer ". He adds that the body was " barbarously profaned at Moghilev for days " (Masaryk, *The Making of a State* (London, 1927), pp. 163-164).

Sir George Buchanan therefore proposed that the Allies should formally release Russia from her obligation under the agreement of September 1914, thereby at one stroke recognizing a *fait accompli* and making a bid for continued good relations with the Soviet Government. In the separate negotiations which would follow, national resentment in Russia would turn against Germany if peace were delayed, or had to be purchased on too onerous terms.[1]

This eminently sound advice arrived in London on the eve of that fateful inter-Allied conference for which Kerensky had yearned so despairingly and which was now to meet in Paris on November 30. Mr. Lloyd George was sufficiently impressed by Buchanan's despatch to place the proposal formally before the meeting. Both he and Mr. Balfour were fully alive to the dangers of a potential Russo-German *rapprochement*. " No policy would be more fatal," wrote the Foreign Secretary in a memorandum for the Cabinet, " than to give the Russians a motive for welcoming into their midst German officials and German soldiers as friends and deliverers." Colonel House also supported Buchanan's views, though the United States had not adhered to the inter-Allied agreement of 1914.

But the Continental Allies would have none of it. Baron Sonnino violently opposed Buchanan's suggestion, and M. Clemenceau declared that " if M. Maklakoff (Kerensky's Ambassador in Paris) and all the celestial powers asked him to give Russia back her word, he would refuse ". When, however, M. Maklakoff was sent for, he concurred more definitely with the views of Clemenceau and Sonnino than with those of Lloyd George and Balfour. He opposed the acceptance of Buchanan's proposal and suggested as substitute a declaration that the Allies would " proceed to a revision of war aims together with Russia, so soon as

[1] Buchanan, ii. 225-226.

there shall be a government aware of its duties to the country and defending the interests of the country and not of the enemy ".[1]

This resolution entirely begged the point raised by Sir George Buchanan, which was the necessity of keeping some modicum of goodwill for the Allied Powers in Soviet Russia. Maklakoff's proposal, slightly modified by Colonel House, was accepted by the Conference and the last opportunity was missed of retaining any basis of co-operation with the Bolsheviks. Had the Buchanan policy been adopted, the subsequent history of the Brest-Litovsk Treaty might well have been very different.

2

In the dismal cold and stark discomfort of the Brest-Litovsk citadel, Major-General Max Hoffmann sat and waited. Beneath him lay the blackened ruins of the city emerging from their blanket of snow, and beyond them the interminable white landscape stretched out to meet the grey November sky. The city had been burnt at the time of its evacuation by the Russians in July 1916, and when that greatest of all military combinations, HLH (Hindenburg, Ludendorff, and Hoffmann), had first set up their headquarters there, they lived in the greatest discomfort in their special train. The summer sun beat down pitilessly on the steel roof and made the cramped space unendurable. There was little room to work, and such as there was, was encumbered by the big Staff maps. The citadel, the only part of the city to survive the fire, was quickly made habitable, and it was from there that HLH fought their final engagements in the struggle for the downfall of

[1] Lloyd George, v. 108-109 ; Charles Seymour, *The Intimate Papers of Colonel House* (New York, 1928), iii. 283-290. Maklakoff was formally dismissed by Trotsky on the following day for his part in the conference deliberations.

Falkenhayn and the succession of Hindenburg to the supreme command of the German armies.[1]

This end had been achieved at the close of August 1916, and from that time, for a year and three months, Hoffmann, separated from his great partners, had been in virtual command of the Eastern Front; for the actual Commander-in-Chief, Field-Marshal Prince Leopold of Bavaria, was little more than a figurehead.

In a man more highly strung, the waiting and inaction of the Eastern Front might have produced an intolerable nervous tension. But Hoffmann, composed of equal parts of steel and whalebone, was not troubled with nerves. (Had he not proved that at Tannenberg when Ludendorff had cracked under the strain ?) Within that great shaven skull reposed the most brilliant brain of the German General Staff, and patience had always been his strong suit. Ever since the March Revolution in Russia he had known that his rôle was to hold the Russian Front immobile and to allow a free hand to his colleagues in the West. This he had done with success, greatly aided by the disinclination of the Russian army to give battle, and the result had been that, in the West, Hindenburg and Ludendorff had been able to withstand the assaults of Haig and Nivelle upon the *Siegfriedstellung* and to repel them with heavy losses. " Had the Russians attacked in April and May and met with only minor successes," Ludendorff confessed later, " I do not see how G.H.Q. could have mastered the situation." [2]

When the Kerensky offensive was launched in July, Hoffmann met it with determination and success. Once the first shock of the assault had spent itself, it was not difficult to counter-attack, and before the German advance the Russian army had collapsed like a house of cards. From the beginning of October the front was quiet, and Hoffmann was content to await the effect of the virus

<hr />

[1] J. W. Wheeler-Bennett, *Hindenburg, the Wooden Titan* (London, 1936), pp. 69-71.   [2] Ludendorff, ii. 427.

which the return of Lenin had injected into the body-politic of Russia.

Of what was happening beyond the now silent front line, Hoffmann had little knowledge during these November days. The fall of Kerensky and the advent of the Bolsheviks to power were facts that so far could not be fitted into the general picture. Hoffmann could not know of the chaos which raged behind the Russian lines and within the Russian capital. He only knew that the front had become sufficiently quiet for troops to be taken out of the line and transferred to the West, to be trained and equipped for the new task awaiting them. Beyond this elementary fact General Headquarters at Brest-Litovsk were at a loss to know what to make of the situation.

Their mystification was increased when wireless operators began to pick up messages addressed " To All ", sent out by an unknown individual called Trotsky, and declaring the desire of the new Soviet Government for peace. " We cannot get a clear view of what is happening," wrote Hoffmann in his diary on November 21 ; yet he urged the Chancellor to declare Germany's willingness to negotiate.

The uncertainty persisted until November 26. " Whether they will [declare an Armistice] I cannot yet say ", recorded Hoffmann on the morning of that day. " We have no clear picture of what is likely to happen in the interior of Russia in the immediate future." [1]

But in the afternoon there arrived Trotsky's formal proposals for an armistice and Krylenko's wireless message proclaiming the actual cessation of hostilities. At last something definite had happened, and Hoffmann reported by telephone to Ludendorff at Kreuznach.

" Is it possible to negotiate with these people ? " asked Ludendorff.

" Yes, it is possible ", was the reply. " Your Excellency needs troops and this is the easiest way to get them." [2]

---

[1] Hoffmann, i. 203-204.   [2] *Ibid.* ii. 190.

That the Quadruple Alliance must gain by a separate peace with Russia was obvious. The military, political, and economic position of the four countries was anything but satisfactory. The warlike fervour of Germany had fallen to a disquietingly low level, and the spirit which was to cripple the German people in the summer of 1918 and in 1919 had become apparent. The naval mutiny at Kiel in July had given the authorities grave anxiety and had already affected the internal morale of the country. The influence of the Independent Socialists had been realized for the first time and the result was not heartening. The food supply had sunk to a low ebb and many people went hungry. Forage had become very scarce : the oats harvest had been bad, and the hay crop scanty. The stocks of oil were alarmingly low, and it was urgently necessary to increase the supply from Rumania. Lightless winter evenings were in store for the country districts.

Yet the national spirit of Germany was better than that of her Allies, and indeed the Quadruple Alliance was only held together by the hope of a victory by German arms. " Peace at the earliest moment is necessary for our own salvation and we cannot obtain peace until the Germans get to Paris—and they cannot get to Paris unless their Eastern front is free," wrote Count Czernin, the Austrian Foreign Minister, to a friend on November 17.[1] The Austro-Hungarian army was worn out. It had lost 1,800,000 in prisoners. It was short of recruits, and its fighting value was slight, but if Russia were eliminated that army might be equal to its task.

The war spirit of Vienna was at an end, indeed it had not lasted long. The shock of the assassination of the heir to the throne at Serajevo had momentarily kindled a flame of anger and resentment, but three years of war, much of it unsuccessful so far as the Austrians were concerned, had caused the flame to flicker and burn low. Now at the close

[1] Count Ottokar Czernin, *In the World War* (London, 1919), p. 217.

of 1917 there began to settle over Vienna that air of fatalistic melancholy which has never really lifted again. An amazing apathy prevailed. Other capitals of Europe were passionately demanding the return of territory and the more eager prosecution of the war ; certain national centres within the Dual Monarchy were yearning for independence ; in the midst of this clamour Vienna remained silent and hungry, asking only for peace and bread ; *une ville sans âme,* awaiting the end.

Moreover, by publishing the secret treaties concluded by the Entente Governments, Trotsky had dealt the Austro-Hungarian Government a staggering blow. Czernin now knew that the Allies were aiming at nothing less than the dismemberment of the Dual Monarchy. Peace at any price became his motto, and while he pressed for negotiations with Russia, he connived at the secret conversations which Prince Sixte of Bourbon and Count Mensdorff-Pouilly were carrying on with Allied emissaries for a separate peace. If Austria reached the end of her military power, her political structure was doomed. Nothing but the army held the Dual Monarchy together.

In Bulgaria the situation was slightly better. But Bulgaria had occupied all the territory she wanted to keep when peace came, and both the people and the army were tired of war. Germany could only count on Bulgaria remaining faithful to the Quadruple Alliance so long as all went well with the German armies. " I could believe in the steadfastness of the Bulgarian Army for just so long as I could believe in the faith of the Bulgarian nation ", wrote Ludendorff cryptically.[1]

Turkey was faithful to her Allies, but at the end of her strength. Her man power was greatly reduced and part of her army existed on paper only.

All therefore depended upon Germany, the king-pin of the Quadruple Alliance, and in that country it was

[1] Ludendorff, ii. 541.

admitted on all sides that a speedy end to the war was an imperative necessity. To bring this about there were two alternative methods : the favourable military position of Germany could be used either for concluding a peace of conciliation or for an attack in the West. The peace policy was warmly favoured by the Foreign Secretary, Baron von Kühlmann, and by Prince Max of Baden, and had the secret support of the German and Bavarian Crown Princes. But the High Command would have none of it.

Ludendorff had become convinced, even before the Bolshevik armistice proposals, that the sole hope of Germany's victory lay in " a gambler's throw ", a blow in the West, swift and terrible. At a Staff Conference at Mons on November 11, while the echo of Lenin's Decree of Peace still resounded in the corridors of Smolny, the First Quartermaster-General had taken a fatal decision. " It will be an immense struggle," he wrote to Wilhelm II, " that will begin at one point, continue at another, and take a long time ; it is difficult, but it will be successful." The Emperor, against his better judgement, agreed.

For this new manoeuvre three factors were essential : speed, troops, and, above all, tangible success at an early stage. The unrestricted U-boat warfare, upon which Hindenburg and Ludendorff had gambled so disastrously, had reached its height and had begun to wane. The pressure of the Allied blockade had established a strangle-hold on the German people ; American troops, fresh and young, were being landed in France, despite the proud boast of the Chief of Naval Staff in February that not one American soldier should reach the Continent. The blow in the West could not fall too soon. Time was the essence of the contract.

Reinforcements were a vital necessity. The termination of hostilities on the Eastern Front was a godsend. By the end of November troop trains were pouring incessantly from east to west. It was no longer a case of replacing tired divisions by fresh ones, but of adding to the number of combatants on the Western Front. The collapse of the Rumanian Front—recognized by the Armistice of Foscari on December 8—released further troops, and divisions were withdrawn from the Italian and Salonika Fronts.

Success, above all, was essential for German arms. The fate of the Quadruple Alliance hung upon this final effort. Failure now would mean the beginning of speedy disintegration and ultimate *débâcle*. Victory might silence the ticking of the death-watch already audible in the structure of the Alliance.

A fresh lease of life was therefore granted to the Central Powers by the November Revolution in Russia, and it may be imagined with what emotions Hoffmann's telephone message must have been received at Kreuznach on November 26. If negotiations in the East were successful, all would be ready in the West by the middle of March. With thankful satisfaction the Supreme Command authorized Hoffmann to treat for an armistice.

3

In the early-morning darkness of November 27 three muffled and blindfolded figures crossed the German lines before Dvinsk and were conducted to the divisional headquarters of General von Hofmeister. They were empowered to make preliminary armistice arrangements. All day they waited while authority was sought from Brest-Litovsk, and at midnight the answer came. The German armies would negotiate. Official conversations should open on December 2.

In Berlin and in Vienna the Imperial Governments formally declared on November 29 that the Russian proposals constituted a suitable basis for armistice negotiations, which, it was hoped, would soon assume the more concrete shape of a general peace. Both the German Chancellor and the Austrian Prime Minister couched their acceptances in terms nicely balanced to proclaim their readiness to negotiate, while concealing their anxiety to secure peace at the earliest possible moment.

In Petrograd, Trotsky, on November 30, acquainted the Allied diplomats with the fact that an agreement for a preliminary truce was about to be declared, and again requested them to state whether they wished to take part in the forthcoming negotiations.[1] A complete silence was the sole reply.

Meantime in Brest-Litovsk two hastily collected delegations were in process of assembling. For the Central Powers a composite group had been formed under Hoffmann, with Baron von Rosenberg representing the German Foreign Office, and, as military assistants, Major Brinckmann of the Headquarters Staff, and a young lieutenant of cavalry, Bernhard von Bülow, a nephew of the former Chancellor and himself destined in later years to become permanent Secretary of State at the *Auswärtige Amt*. Colonel Pokorny for Austria-Hungary, General Zekki Pasha for Turkey, and General Gantcheff for Bulgaria, completed the delegation of the Quadruple Alliance.

The Bolsheviks had had more difficulty in composing their group. It had to be representative of the Revolution, and yet capable of negotiation, a difficult combination in these early days of Soviet rule. Consequently the party which finally left by special train from the Warsaw station at Petrograd was both strange and varied. The head of the delegation was Adolf Joffe, a typical revolutionary intellectual, not unpolished in manner and with a soft pleasant voice. Long hair and beard framed his Semitic face, and pince-nez perched upon his Semitic nose. A similar type, though less obviously Hebraic, was Leo Kamenev, Trotsky's brother-in-law, whose tired, dreamy

[1] *Proceedings of the Brest-Litovsk Peace Conference* (U.S. State Department, Washington, D.C., 1918), p. 8.

eyes seemed always about to close in reflection or slumber. In strong contrast was Leo Karakhan, Secretary-General of the delegation. A typical Armenian, almost a cartoon type of Levantine, he was capable of changing with feline swiftness from sleepy laziness to noisy active agitation. With Sokolnikov, a man of very considerable ability, these three provided the orthodox revolutionary element of the delegation. In addition, out of compliment to their somewhat unwilling allies and in conformity with their theories of sex equality, the Bolsheviks had included the famous Social-Revolutionary assassin, Mme. Anastasia Bitsenko, but lately released from a seventeen-years' sentence in Siberia for the murder of the former Minister for War, General Sakharov.

But since the Revolution had nominally been made in the name of the soldiers, sailors, workers, and peasants, representatives of all these categories had to be included in the delegation. By an irony of fate these lesser fry were more colourful than their more revolutionary colleagues. They were produced for " window-dressing " and had no other duties than to create an atmosphere of revolutionary democracy ; the whole affair was for them an extraordinary experience which they could not entirely comprehend. Here was the soldier, Nicholas Bieliakov, a sullen old badger, short, strongly built, middle-aged, and silent, the " Old Bill " type found in all armies ; here, too, Fedor Olich, the sailor, tall and good-looking in his neat naval uniform, but seeming cramped and ill at ease in his new surroundings. In no way out of his element was the young worker, Obukhov. He appeared to look upon the whole thing almost as a joy-ride ; his dark, impish face, beneath its curly hair, was insolent and yet humorous as he lay sprawling in his railway seat, an open waistcoat over his black shirt, arrogantly unconcerned.

Lastly there was the peasant delegate, old Roman Stashkov, a good-natured, simple old fellow with yellowish-grey hair and beard, and deep wrinkles in his brick-tanned face. He was utterly and completely bewildered by the whole proceeding, and still—despite the times—addressed his revolutionary colleagues as *barin* (master). He had been a last-minute addition to the party. Not until they were on their way to the station did the leaders of the delegation realize that the peasant class was unrepresented among them, and, as their motor sped through the dark and deserted streets of Petrograd, there was consternation among them at this omission.

Suddenly they turned a corner and came upon an old man in a peasant's coat plodding along in the snow and carrying a bag. The car stopped.

" Where are you going, *tovarish* ? "

" To the station, *barin*—I mean *tovarish* ", replied the old man.

" Get in ; we'll give you a lift "—and they sped on.

The old man was mildly pleased at the unusual attention he received from his new friends, but as they neared the Warsaw station he showed signs of worry.

" This is not the station I need, Comrades ; I want the Nikolaevsky station. I've got to go beyond Moscow."

This would never do, thought Joffe and Kamenev, and they began to question the old peasant about his politics.

" What party do you belong to ? "

" I'm a Social Revolutionary, Comrades ", was the slightly disconcerting reply ; " everybody in our village is a Social Revolutionary."

" A left or a right one ? "

Something warned the old man, perhaps it was the tone of his questioner, that he had better not say " right ".

" Left, Comrades, of course, the very leftest."

No other requirements were needed for a " mandatory representative of the Russian peasantry ", and it was getting near train time.

" There's no need for you to go to your village ", the

old man was told. " Come with us to Brest-Litovsk and make peace with the Germans." A little more persuasion, a little money promised, and thus, incredibly, the lacuna in the delegation was filled. Stashkov departed for Brest-Litovsk, where later he was to be a social *tour de force*.[1]

In addition to the " mandatory representatives " there were attached to the delegation nine naval and military officers, headed by Admiral Vasili Altvater, and including Lieutenant-Colonel Fokke, whose published recollections are a valuable source of information. These unfortunates, placed by fate in a false and humiliating position, were in a purely advisory capacity, and had no voice or power of voting. Plucked arbitrarily and suddenly from their commands, they were compelled to give their technical advice to a Government which they were convinced was ready to barter away Russia's territory in pursuit of a policy of peace at any price. Like sheep to the slaughter, they came, with death in their souls, to the betrayal of their country. Subsequently the front which Joffe and Kamenev put up during the armistice negotiations brought about a change of attitude and a warmer degree of enthusiasm among these officers. Trotsky even spoke of Admiral Altvater as becoming " *plus bolchévik que les bolchéviks sur cette question de la paix* ", but this new loyalty did not save the Admiral from a cruel death during the Red Terror which followed the attempted assassination of Lenin in August 1918.[2]

Lumbering southward in their war-worn train, this strange menagerie, as Fokke called them, came at last to the Russian front lines at Dvinsk. Here they were greeted with wild applause by the troops, to the gratification of the

[1] Lieutenant-Colonel Ivan Grigoreyevitch Fokke, " Na stsene i sa kulisami brestskoi tragikomedii ", in *Arkhiv Russkoi Revoliutsii* (edited by I. V. Hessen, Berlin, 1925–1934), xx. 15-17.

[2] Captain Jacques Sadoul, *Notes sur la révolution bolchévique* (Paris, 1920), pp. 140-141 ; Fokke, p. 13.

revolutionaries and the despair of the officers. With peace
at last in sight, a new enthusiasm had awakened in the
men, and a deputation from the Congress of the Fifth
Army assured the delegation that while they carried on
the negotiations the troops would " destroy every wasp-
nest of counter-revolution ".

Accommodation was already crowded in the citadel of
Brest-Litovsk ; G.H.Q. was itself housed in a collection of
huts, and two of these were set apart for the Russians,
both delegations eating together in a common mess-room.
The problem of feeding these additional visitors was one
which taxed the commissariat department very considerably, and for the first day or two the delegates lived on
short commons, but German efficiency and organization
soon surmounted this difficulty and comparative plenty
was restored.

The armistice terms which the Central Powers were
prepared to offer to Russia had been prepared by Ludendorff as early as May and had received the approval of the
Imperial Chancellor and the other Chiefs of Staff.[1] They
were clearly dictated by the German desire to end the war
on one front, and contained no conditions that were unjust
or humiliating to the Russians. Hostilities were to cease,
and each side was to retain the position they held. On such
a basis it was hoped to settle the whole matter in a few
hours ; but it was not quite so simple as that.

The Soviet delegation had come for propaganda as
well as for negotiation. They therefore opened with a
request for entire publicity of the negotiations, and, when
this had been agreed to, Joffe delivered a long address
setting forth the Bolshevik principles of peace and concluding with a demand to all belligerents to end the
struggle and conclude a general agreement. He was
succeeded by Kamenev, who talked for an hour of his

[1] Lieutenant-General Erich Ludendorff, *The General Staff and its
Problems* (London, 1920), ii. 517.

sorrow that in the declaration of the German and Austrian Governments no evidence was shown of a real desire for a general peace on the unshakable basis proclaimed by the Russian Revolution.

After this preliminary broadside Joffe made three proposals :

(1) An armistice of six months' duration.
(2) The evacuation by German military and naval forces of the Islands of the Moon Sound in the Gulf of Riga.
(3) No German troops to be transferred from the Eastern Front to other fronts, or even to be withdrawn to rest quarters.

The first of these proposals Hoffmann countered with an offer of an armistice of twenty-eight days automatically prolonged unless a week's notice of termination was given. The second point he dismissed with the remark that " such terms could be addressed only to a conquered country ". But to the third he had no difficulty in agreeing, since, before the negotiations had begun, orders had already been given to send the bulk of the Eastern army to the Western Front. " Consequently I was able to concede to the Russians that, during the Armistice that was about to be signed, the Germans would not send away any troops from the Eastern Front, *except those that were already being moved, or that had already received orders to go.*" [1]

On the third day of the negotiations (December 5) the Soviet delegation declared categorically that they were " treating for an armistice on all fronts with the view to the conclusion of a general peace on the basis already established by the All-Russian Congress of Soviets ". But, replied Hoffmann, had they the authority of their Entente Allies to make such proposals ? He was ready to negotiate an armistice with Russia alone or with her Allies, but, as

[1] Hoffmann, ii. 194 (author's italics).

the Allies had not chosen to participate, should they not proceed to arrange a separate armistice with Russia ?

Thus cornered, Joffe lost his nerve. Though forced to admit that he had no authority to negotiate for the Entente, he confessed to Hoffmann at luncheon that he could not sign a separate armistice without further consultation with Petrograd. He must return to confer with Lenin and Trotsky. A separate agreement was utterly opposed to the scheme of things as visualized at Smolny, and he knew the cold fury of Lenin's wrath. The fear of every revolutionary diplomat lest he pay for an error with his head, was upon him. He must return.

Hoffmann agreed to the face-saving formula that the delegations concerned should " transmit to their respective Governments the proposal made by the Russian delegation to invite all belligerents to take part in the negotiations ", and the arrangement was reached to interrupt the negotiations for a week, until December 12. Thereupon the Bolsheviks departed for Petrograd, leaving Karakhan to hold the diplomatic fort.

Throughout these preliminary negotiations, and indeed eversince Krylenko's order to begin fraternization, Bolshevik agents had not ceased to make use of the time for propaganda purposes. Copies of the Decree of Peace, together with a special proclamation to the German army, were not only smuggled into the trenches but dropped by aeroplanes far behind the lines. One of Trotsky's earliest innovations in the Foreign Office had been to institute a Press Bureau under Karl Radek and a Bureau of International Revolutionary Propaganda under Boris Reinstein, among whose assistants were John Reed and Albert Rhys Williams, and the full blast of these power-houses was turned against the German army.

A German newspaper, *Die Fackel* (The Torch), was printed in editions of half a million a day and sent by special train to Central Army Committees in Minsk, Kiev, and other cities, which in turn distributed them to other points along the front.[1] " Brother Soldiers of Germany ! " cried the first issue. " The great example of your leader, Liebknecht, the struggle which you are conducting through your meetings and through the press, and finally the revolt in your navy, is a guarantee to us that, among labouring masses, the struggle for peace is ripe."

Armed with this and similarly inflammable material, Zinoviev, at the head of a delegation, was despatched to the frontier to foster revolt in Central Europe. As might have been expected, they were turned back at the German lines and a car-load of *Die Fackel* and of Lenin's appeals was burnt. " The further demand for free admission into Germany of all Bolshevik propaganda and literature, I was obliged to refuse," writes Hoffmann, " but I said I was quite willing to assist in the export of this to France and England."[2]

Meanwhile, in Petrograd, Lenin still harboured the illusion that the proletarian masses would respond to the bait of a general peace. But whether they did or did not do so, peace had been promised to Russia and peace must be achieved, whether as a separate treaty or as part of a general agreement. But even if a separate armistice was signed, the Entente might still participate later in the peace negotiations which would follow, and Joffe was there-

---

[1] The German Headquarters Staff had itself published a propaganda sheet, *Russky Vyestnik* (The Russian Messenger), for prisoners of war, but they were as children in this business by comparison with the Bolsheviks.

[2] Hoffmann, ii. 194. This willingness to make use of the new weapon of Bolshevik propaganda against the enemy was not confined to Germany. William Hard, in his record of Colonel Raymond Robins' mission to Russia, recounts that on one occasion Robins offered seventy-five thousand roubles to certain Bolshevik agents, who were about to leave for Germany and Austria, on the ground that " it might do them some good and might do the Kaiser some harm " (William Hard, *Raymond Robins' Own Story* (New York, 1930), pp. 85-86).

fore instructed to return to Brest-Litovsk and pursue the conversations.

Trotsky took the opportunity, on December 6, of informing the Allied Governments of the course of the armistice negotiations. He drew their attention to the interval designed to give them an opportunity to define their attitude, " to express their willingness or their refusal to take part in the negotiations for an armistice and peace. In the case of a refusal, they must declare clearly and definitely, before all mankind, the aims for which the peoples of Europe may have to lose their blood during the fourth year of the war." [1]

At the same time, the first hint of a threat made its appearance in the press. An inspired leading article declared that the Soviet Government might have to resort to a repudiation of Russia's debts as a means of forcing the Allies to participate in the forthcoming negotiations.[2]

No reply having been received by the morning of December 12, Trotsky issued a further declaration " throwing the responsibility for Russia's concluding a separate armistice on the Governments which refuse to present conditions for an armistice and peace ". The final paragraph of the declaration contained a warning of what was to come —though Trotsky himself was always opposed to such a policy—" a separate armistice is not yet a separate peace, but it means a danger of a separate peace. Only the peoples themselves can avert this danger." [3]

The Soviet delegation returned to Brest on December 12, and the formal negotiations for a separate armistice began next day. The main subjects of controversy were the transfer of troops, naval matters, and fraternization between the opposing armies. In the first of these the Quadruple Alliance insisted on their own terms, but they were

[1] *Proceedings*, p. 35.
[2] *Pravda*, December 6, 1917.
[3] Cumming and Pettit, p. 56.

inclined to be conciliatory in relation to naval matters. It was agreed to " organize " fraternizations.

Thus when the armistice agreement was finally signed on December 15, the duration was to be until January 14, 1918,[1] with automatic prolongation unless seven days' notice of rupture was given by either party. Article 2 provided that, until January 14, no removal of troops should take place between the Black Sea and the Baltic, " that is to say, such removals as had not been commenced before the time when the armistice agreement was signed ". Naval matters were governed by a proposed special agreement to be entered into after mutual consultation (Article 5). For the " organization " of fraternizing it was agreed that there should be two or three intercourse centres in every sector of a Russian division, but that " there must not be present at any one time more than 25 unarmed persons from each side ". The exchange of views and newspapers was permitted.[2]

It was in this provision that the Central Powers made a fatal error. Hoffmann, with his astuteness and knowledge of the Russian mind, should never have permitted the article on propaganda to be included. Admittedly it was difficult to prevent the infiltration of Bolshevik ideology, but to permit the organizing of fraternization was to play into the Soviet hands. As one historian has commented somewhat grimly, " twenty-five men was enough for the Russian anti-war propaganda purposes ".[3]

It became impossible to check the activities of the Bolshevik agents. At the official fraternization points bundles of *Die Fackel* and its successor, *Der Völkerfriede* (The Peoples' Peace), were ostentatiously carried, and were frequently confiscated by German officers. There

[1] For text see Appendix II, p. 379.
[2] *Texts of the Russian " Peace "* (U.S. Department of State, Washington, D.C., 1918), pp. 1-8.
[3] Louis Fischer, *The Soviets in World Affairs* (London, 1930), i. 30.

were many secret meetings at isolated spots at which bundles of propaganda literature were put into the hands of German soldiers. At other points such material was buried by Russians in agreed places and dug up later by Germans. The virus was spreading rapidly.

A supplement to the armistice agreement provided for " the immediate exchange of civil prisoners and prisoners of war unfit for further military service ". There were thousands of these throughout the country, and they provided a fertile field for propaganda. Through the Bureau of War Prisoners, attached to the Ministry of Foreign Affairs, emissaries were despatched to visit all prison camps in Russia and Siberia to encourage the formation of Socialist organizations. In Moscow alone, ten thousand German and Austrian prisoners were organized along Bolshevik lines and began an active propaganda among their countrymen. So effective was the work that when the prisoners of war were eventually repatriated they were confined for thirty days in " political quarantine camps " and mentally " deloused " with patriotic literature and Majority Socialist propaganda.

Hoffmann protested furiously to Krylenko and threatened to denounce the armistice, and Krylenko publicly ordered that revolutionary propaganda should cease, but privately sent word urging that the efforts should be redoubled.[1]

Already the Germans were beginning to reap the whirlwind. The Frankenstein monster which they had helped to create was no longer responding to their control, and would never return to it. Nor would they take warning. " The influence of Bolshevik propaganda on the masses is enormous ", said Admiral Altvater, in a burst of confidence to Hoffmann. " I was defending Oesel and the troops actually melted away before my eyes. It was the same

[1] John Reed, " How Soviet Russia conquered Imperial Germany ", in *Liberator*, New York, January 1919.

with the whole army, and, I warn you, the same thing will happen in your army."

" I only laughed at the unfortunate Admiral ", records Hoffmann.[1]

[1] Hoffmann, ii. 196.

IV

"PEACE WITHOUT INDEMNITIES
OR ANNEXATIONS"

IV

" PEACE WITHOUT INDEMNITIES OR ANNEXATIONS "

1

THE actual signing of a separate armistice between the Central Powers and Russia translated the whole question of affairs on the Eastern Front from the military sphere to the field of international politics. The Entente Powers preserved their attitude of aloofness and washed their hands of all further responsibility. " Since Russia has entered into separate negotiations," said Mr. Lloyd George in the House of Commons on December 20, " she must of course alone be responsible for the terms in respect of her own territories "—and this may be taken to represent the general Entente attitude.

For the Central Powers, however, the position was of considerably greater importance. They now were pledged to negotiate peace with the Entente and with Russia on a basis of " no indemnities, no annexations, and the principle of self-determination ". Superficially, at least, this coincided with the terms of the Peace Resolution which the Reichstag had adopted in July 1917. " We are not animated by any desire for conquest ", it had declared, and had demanded a peace " by mutual agreement and reconciliation " ; it had protested against all possible " acquisition of territory " and " all political, economic, and financial oppression ". But in every document of this nature it is the spirit rather than the letter which ranks foremost in importance, and more important than either is the interpretation of both. For every man is free to interpret a principle for himself, and this freedom had been emphasized by the Imperial Chancellor, Dr. Michaelis, who, in giving his support to the Resolution, had made use of the sinister qualifying phrase, " as I interpret it ".

Fully to appreciate the significance of this qualification —and indeed of the German attitude throughout the negotiations of Brest-Litovsk—it is necessary to understand the changes which had taken place in the governmental situation in Germany since August 29, 1916.

On that date Hindenburg and Ludendorff had been appointed to the Supreme Command, under the Kaiser, of the German armies in the field, and from that date a change, at first subtle but later starkly blatant, had come over the political structure of Germany. For the new High Command demanded a free hand even in the control of internal and foreign policy. In pressing this demand the leading spirit was always Ludendorff. The strangely intimate relations between the Marshal and his second-in-command, which Hindenburg himself described as " those of a happy marriage ", had already resulted in the merging of the older man's identity with that of the younger. In this strange " marriage of minds " Ludendorff was the brilliant, dominating husband, Hindenburg the placid, acquiescing, dependable wife. On the Eastern Front, in conjunction with Hoffmann's organizing genius, this combination had proved, militarily, vastly effective. Transferred, minus Hoffmann, to the West, it was still effective until applied to political problems, when it became highly unfortunate. For Hindenburg despised politics, which he did not understand and which frankly bored him. He was only too glad to leave all that to Ludendorff, who made use of his chief's name and position in the most unwarrantable manner.

The Supreme Command became an *imperium in imperio*, with Ludendorff negotiating independently with the Emperor, with the Chancellor, with the Foreign Office, with the party leaders in the Reichstag, with industrial magnates and trade-union officials, in fact with everyone who had to be subordinated to the will of G.H.Q. Gradually a complete dictatorship was built up on the interpretation which Ludendorff put upon the word "responsibility". For example, when any policy was mooted of which Ludendorff disapproved, or which he considered injurious to the conduct of the war, he declared that the Supreme Command could not assume "responsibility" for such action, and asked leave to resign. By exercise of this method of "persuasion", the First Quartermaster-General forced everyone to give way to him, from the Emperor downwards. Sometimes he obtained Hindenburg's approval for his proposals, frequently he made use of his name; always his final argument was, "The Field-Marshal and I will resign".

Thus, in November 1916, the Supreme Command wrecked Bethmann Hollweg's efforts for a separate peace with Russia, and in February 1917 forced the adoption of unrestricted U-boat warfare against his opposition. In July they insisted upon his complete elimination, and secured as his successor a poor colourless creature, George Michaelis, the former Prussian Food Controller, who was merely their mouthpiece.

With their nominee at the head of the Government, Hindenburg and Ludendorff felt in a position to dispose of the Peace Resolution which they had failed to prevent the Majority Parties from bringing before the Reichstag. Michaelis' sinister phrase "as I interpret it" was nothing less than a reservation on behalf of the Supreme Command, to whose dreams of conquest and annexation the terms of the Resolution were sharply opposed.

But the Reichstag had missed the significance of the Chancellor's phrase and had adopted the Resolution, ironically enough, at the same time that they passed huge additional war-credits. With justifiable pride could Michaelis write to the German Crown Prince on July 25, 1917 : " The hateful Resolution has been passed by 212 votes to 126, with 17 abstentions and 2 invalid votes. I have deprived it of its greatest danger by my interpretation. One can, in fact, make any peace one likes, and still be in accord with the Resolution."

Indeed one could. " You see, Your Highness," explained the egregious Erzberger, in discussing the Resolution with Prince Max of Baden, " this way I get the Longwy-Briey Line by means of negotiation." At a later date it was even asserted that the Treaty of Brest-Litovsk accorded with the terms of the Peace Resolution, " as the High Command interpreted it ".

Such, then, was the position in Germany at the opening of the negotiations with Russia. In September the Supreme Command had sabotaged a not unpromising peace offer on the part of the Pope, and Michaelis, the Chancellor of a Hundred Days, had been replaced in the last week of October by the aged Bavarian Prime Minister, Count von Hertling. Had the new Chancellor been younger, he might have put up a better fight against the daily increasing encroachment of the military upon the civil sphere. But though his ripe experience and high character rendered it impossible for him to adopt the views of Ludendorff *in toto*, his advanced age and lack of vigour made him unequal to embarking on a controversy with the Supreme Command.

Not so his Secretary of State, Richard von Kühlmann. Like Hertling, Kühlmann was a Bavarian and a Catholic; at the age of forty-four, he was the most astute of Germany's diplomats and, with the exception of Bethmann Hollweg, the most enlightened of her war-time states-men. Essentially civilized and *homme du monde*, he had travelled extensively and served widely. Born in Constantinople, he had been attaché and counsellor in half a dozen capitals, and there was that unforgettable morning in March 1905, when, green with sea-sickness and hampered by the full uniform of a Bavarian Uhlan, he had scaled a heaving rope ladder to greet his Kaiser in the open road-

stead of Tangier. The war had brought him great responsibilities. A successful Ambassador at the Hague and at
Constantinople, he had been recalled by Michaelis to take
charge of the Foreign Office, and was confirmed in that
position by Hertling, who was glad to find a fellow country-
man and a co-religionist in this unwelcome desert of
Prussian Lutheranism.

Unlike many Germans, Kühlmann understood the
art of living. He appreciated to the full the perfection of
good wine, fine *objets d'art*, and beautiful women. There
was about him a certain detachment, a certain spiritual
arrogance, which made him almost equally actor and critic.
Even in the midst of great events, he never lost entirely
that nonchalance of the onlooker, a rather sardonic onlooker,
laughing at everyone, including himself. Without being
superficial, he was never deeply stirred by any issue. He
would never risk his name or reputation on a throw, as had
Bismarck. To him it did not appear worth while. He played
for the mere charm of playing.

But Kühlmann was far-sighted as well as civilized. In
closer touch with events of the day, and having a greater
appreciation of them, he saw very much more clearly than
did the Supreme Command, who were separated from
actualities by a horde of " yes-men " and an atmosphere
of wishful thinking. Far from sharing Ludendorff's annexationist illusions, Kühlmann had already perceived the
impossibility of a victorious peace for the Central Powers.
A peace of mutual exhaustion was the best that could be
hoped for, and it was with an eye to this ultimate end,
rather than the permanent acquisition of new territory,
that the Secretary of State had directed his efforts since he
took office in August 1917. His early attempts to capitalize
the Papal Peace Offer had been nullified by the machinations
of the Supreme Command and the duplicity of Michaelis,
but he had not yet given up hope. The prospect of
negotiations with Russia gave him a second opportunity.

2

No two groups could have been more fundamentally dissimilar in outlook than those which were warring, on the eve of the Brest-Litovsk Conference, for the control of German foreign policy, and the fact that deep cleavages of opinion existed between them robbed the forthcoming negotiations of the element of speed which was so necessary an asset for success. For, throughout the conference, questions of high policy were the subject of the fiercest contention between the Imperial Government and the Supreme Command, and the German delegates were always hampered, from first to last, by the intrigues of Ludendorff in Berlin.

The chief ground of disagreement was the future status, under the peace settlement about to be concluded, of the areas already under German and Austrian military occupation, which included Courland and Lithuania, Russian Poland, and extensive territory inhabited by the White Russians and Ukrainians. This Polish question was of the greatest complexity and had involved the two senior partners of the Quadruple Alliance in not a few acrimonious exchanges.

Both groups of belligerents had used the slogan of Polish resurrection as a weapon of political propaganda. The Tsar had in 1914 proclaimed the future reunion of Poland as an autonomous unit within the framework of the Russian Empire. This was followed in the summer of 1916 by negotiations between Berlin and Vienna, which resulted in an agreement for the creation of an independent kingdom of Poland with a hereditary constitutional monarchy. The announcement of the agreement had, however, been pigeon-holed, in deference to the representations of Falkenhayn, Hindenburg's predecessor as Chief of the General Staff, who feared the effect of liberty upon a people pronouncedly anti-German and occupying an important position in the rear of the Eastern Front.

With the arrival of Hindenburg and Ludendorff to control affairs, this eminently sensible policy was reversed. Ludendorff, dazzled by the mirage of new Polish divisions contributed to the German army by a grateful Polish people, forced through the proclamation by the two Emperors of the Kingdom of Poland in November 1916, thereby completely ruining the approach to a separate peace with Russia which had been fostered by both sides with such laborious care.

The policy of the Supreme Command was completely barren of results. The Poles accepted the premise of independence as nothing more than their due, but would not place their man-power at the disposal of the Central Powers unless they were given a genuine Polish Government to control the Polish army. Ludendorff's dream of a Polish army under German officers vanished in smoke. On his terms the Poles refused to play.

The Imperial Proclamation of November 1916 had merely established the academic existence of Poland ; it made no attempt to define its status politically, and the control of the occupied area remained in the hands of the Governors-General of Warsaw and Lublin. A year later no further progress had been made, though there were three potential solutions upon the board.

The first of these, the so-called " Austrian Solution ", provided for a union of Congress Poland with Galicia, the whole to be made a partner in a tripartite Habsburg Monarchy. The solution was favoured by the Habsburgs and at times by the German Government, but was opposed by the Hungarian Premier, Count Tisza, who felt that the political structure of the Monarchy should not be changed, and that, if Poland must be added to it at all, it should much rather form an Austrian province.[1] The German General Staff also objected on the ground that, both

[1] Czernin, p. 200.

politically and strategically, such a solution would put a tax upon the strength of Germany's alliance with Austria which could not be borne in the long run.[1]

There were put forward two possible German solutions of the problem. The first, a counterpart of the " Austrian Solution ", and emanating from the ingenious brain of Erzberger, envisaged the incorporation of both Russian and Austrian Poland within the German Empire, Austria being compensated by the incorporation of Rumania. This was rejected out of hand by Vienna, wise enough not to throw away the substance for the shadow.

The second " German Solution " was one dear to the heart of the General Staff. It provided, by widening the narrow neck between Danzig and Thorn, a "protective belt " for East Prussia against an attack such as that made by the Grand Duke Nicholas in 1914, and another " belt " east of the Vistula to protect the Upper Silesian coal-fields.[2] With the remainder of the dismembered Congress Poland the General Staff were not concerned; it could either become independent, providing that it established favourable economic relations with Germany, or it could be given to Austria.

This proposal was opposed by both the Austrian and German Governments. The first objected because " Poland, crippled beyond recognition by the frontier readjustment, even though united with Galicia, would have been so unsatisfactory a factor that there would never have been any prospect of harmonious dealings with her " ;[3] and the second, because they were unwilling to see large numbers of Poles added to the Empire. To this objection the General Staff replied that " an increase of Polish population in the defensive belt, which would follow, was undesirable, but

---

[1] Field-Marshal von Hindenburg, *Out of My Life* (London, 1920), p. 232 *et seq.* ; Ludendorff, ii. 531 *et seq.*

[2] Ludendorff, ii. 520.

[3] Czernin, p. 521.

this grave objection would have to give way before military necessity ".[1]

In the case of Courland and Lithuania, the General Staff was opposed to relinquishing from German control any territory which had been won by force of arms. It was their wish to create two Grand-Duchies which should be connected with the House of Hohenzollern in the person of the Emperor himself, and so far had they impressed their views upon the local governments through the agency of the Commander-in-Chief in the East, and, in Courland, of the Baltic Barons, that elections for constituent assemblies had already taken place in both provinces, and the Diet of Mitau had actually requested the Kaiser to become Duke of Courland.

The Lithuanians had proved less tractable, and more drastic methods were necessary to ensure their compliance. The Diet of Vilna had been curtly informed by Prince Isenburg and General von Freytag-Loringhoven that, unless it voted for an independent Lithuania with support from the German Empire, the Supreme Command would insist upon the establishment of a new strategic frontier for Germany, a Kovno–Grodno–Dvinsk line cutting the country in two, and leaving the Lithuanians on the east of it to their own devices.[2]

Such was the principle of self-determination " as I interpret it ".

3

December 19, 1917. Crown Council at Kreuznach ; the All-Highest War Lord presides. Pale and nervous, he sits sunk in his chair, listening to the wrangling of his Ministers and generals. Square-headed, grey, and sphinx-like, Hindenburg remains impassive throughout the session ; near him the white-whiskered Chancellor, Count von Hertling, a sad old man, anxious to do his best but unwilling to cross the

[1] Ludendorff, ii. 521. [2] Scheidemann, ii. 101.

path of the High Command. Later in the conference, both he and the Marshal pass intermittently into the easy dozing of the old, leaving the burden of discussion to the subordinates. This is what their subordinates expect of them ; Ludendorff, his *Pour le Mérite* cross glittering at the collar of his field-grey uniform, his absurdly small mouth pursed above his bulging jaw and jowl, arrogant and contemptuous of civilians, looks with dislike across the table at Kühlmann who, a little cynical, a little nonchalant, succeeds in maintaining his dual personality of actor-onlooker.

Ludendorff presents vehemently the case of the Supreme Command. It is vitally necessary to the safety of the Empire that the " German Solution " of the Polish question be adopted and a " protective belt " established along the new frontier. In addition, Courland and Lithuania must be established in personal union with the German Crown. The Russians must be taken at their word and should be asked to evacuate Estonia and Livonia in order that the inhabitants of these provinces might exercise the right of self-determination. It is not said, but it is implied, that they will be persuaded to determine themselves in the right way.

The Kaiser till now has favoured the " Austrian Solution " for Poland, but he is always influenced by the latest speaker, and he now swings about and endorses the views of the High Command. The " German Solution " it shall be, and as for the Baltic Provinces, he will accept them in personal union with the Crown of Prussia or with the German Empire, provided the Federal Princes agree.

The Chancellor concurs in the majority opinion. Kühlmann is alone.

Alone, but not silent. With a greater issue in his mind, he repeats his dislike of the policy of the High Command and reiterates his belief that the question of the future of the Eastern Provinces should be left open. One point he concedes: " I might withdraw my opposition to hoisting the German flag in the Eastern border States, but I would energetically advise against ever nailing it to the mast there."

Ludendorff is furious, the All-Highest nervous and ill at ease (must there always be these clashes ?) ; Hindenburg is awakened and Kühlmann puts a direct question to him :

" Why do you particularly want the territories ? "

Rumblingly from that gigantic torso comes the Marshal's solemn answer : " I need them for the manœuvring of my left wing in the next war "..And Ludendorff adds that the Eastern Provinces would improve Germany's food supply and bring her additional man-power in case she should, in a future war, have to rely once more on her own resources.

Kühlmann remains unconvinced ; the Kaiser vacillates, unwilling to come down on either side of the fence. The conference adjourns without a final decision being taken, and Kühlmann leaves for Brest-Litovsk without definite instructions.

Such, then, were the circumstances of Kühlmann's departure for the Peace Conference. Regarding himself as unbound by the discussions at Kreuznach, which had ended in indecision, he was determined to pursue the policy which he believed best. Confident in his belief that all that the Central Powers could hope for was a peace by negotiation, he was equally convinced that the time for this had not yet arrived. If the Entente Powers were prepared to accept the Bolshevik proposals for a general peace, well and good ; but Kühlmann was convinced that they would not. The main problem, therefore, was to induce the Russians to make a separate peace, and it was with this purpose in view that he agreed to the drafting of a proposal for a general peace. Only after its rejection by the Entente was the door open to separate negotiations, and once the Bolsheviks realized that the Central Powers were ready for a general peace and that the Entente were not, there would be nothing left for them to do but to make a separate agreement.

So reasoned the Foreign Secretary. If general peace negotiations ensued, he was prepared to barter Courland and Lithuania against possible Allied annexations on Germany's Western frontier. These might go back to Russia, despite the dangers thus involved for the many Baltic Germans therein, provided only that Germany remained intact in the West. The Secretary of State was a man who believed in doing one thing at a time, and, though he hoped for a separate peace, for the moment he devoted himself to the work in hand, which was the negotiation of a general settlement.

With Hertling, Kühlmann met the Reichstag party leaders immediately before his departure for Brest-Litovsk. To them he unfolded the policy which the Government proposed to follow in the forthcoming negotiations, a policy based upon the Peace Resolution of July, and embodying the Soviet formula of no annexations and no indemnities. From the Centre to the Left Kühlmann's views received wholehearted support. There were many among the members of these parties who genuinely desired a just peace with Russia and who sincerely hoped that the results of the conference might be such that " no Russian will have to regard as a misfortune for his country the peace which is now being concluded ".[1]

From the jingoes of the Right, the Fatherland Party, came a more qualified form of approval. It mattered little to Westarp and Stresemann what formula of " abracadabra " was recited so long as the result was the addition of the Baltic Provinces to the Reich, and the " protective belt " required by the Supreme Command. If Kühlmann could obtain these by means of his policy, well and good, the Conservatives and the National Liberals would support him ; but they warned him frankly that " we have purchased

[1] *Vorwärts*, December 17, 1917.

our right in the East far too dearly to give it up for the sake of cheap revolutionary phrases ", [1] and it was with this warning from the " ancestral voices " in his ears that the Secretary of State departed for Brest.

4

By December 20 five delegations had assembled at Brest-Litovsk. From Berlin Kühlmann had brought Rosenberg as his assistant and, as his *chef de cabinet*, a young Saxon nobleman, Baron von Hoesch, who was later to achieve distinction as Ambassador in Paris and London. The question of the representation of the Supreme Command on the delegation had been a very vexed one. Ludendorff had originally intended to go himself to Brest-Litovsk, but wisely abandoned the idea. The antipathy which existed between him and Kühlmann would have rendered any form of co-operation impossible. Hoffmann was therefore appointed as military representative, with plenipotentiary status but having only the right of advice and protest.[2] He made good use of both. But though loyally representing the views of his chief, Hoffmann was capable of understanding the very difficult situation which Kühlmann had to handle. The Secretary of State was agreeably surprised to discover this unexpected support.

Ludendorff therefore remained in Jovian detachment, brooding above, ready to hurl his thunderbolts, even as Lenin dominated the situation from the other side. Indeed, as events progressed it became more a duel between these two gigantic figures, the delegates at the conference being but pawns upon the board. Originally Ludendorff had sped Lenin on his way, thinking him too a pawn ; now

[1] *Berliner Lokal Anzeiger*, December 21, 1917.

[2] Hoffmann's plenipotentiary status, later challenged by the Social Democrats, was clearly stated by Kühlmann in a speech in the Reichstag on February 20, 1918. See *Verhandlungen des Reichstags*, No. 130, pp. 4042-4043.

they faced each other across Europe, matching wits in a titanic contest.

At Brest-Litovsk, Kühlmann found awaiting him Czernin, General Csiscerics, and Baron von Wiesner, who in later years travelled Europe in vain as the representative of the exiled House of Habsburg. M. Popoff and Nessimy Bey headed the Bulgarian and Turkish delegations ; these were later joined by M. Radoslavov, the Prime Minister, and Talaat Pasha, the Grand Vizier.

The Soviet delegation, again led by Joffe, was practically identical with that which had negotiated the Armistice, save that Pokrovsky, the " Court Historian " of the Revolution, had been added to it, and that General Samoilo had joined Admiral Altvater as joint head of the technical advisers.

Remarkable are the tragic fatalities which over-hung many of the delegates assembled at Brest-Litovsk. Kühlmann survives, though somewhat precariously, in Nazi Germany, but both Hoesch and Bülow died in their early middle age, their will to live sapped by disgust and contempt for a régime which they continued to serve in fear of what type of men would succeed them. Talaat Pasha was destined to die at the hand of an Armenian assassin, the avenger of countless massacred victims, and Radoslavov was to be led in chains through the streets of Sofia.

Among the Bolsheviks Fate was even more thorough. Trotsky, who had not yet appeared upon the scene but who was to play so great a part, leads in his Mexican retreat a life of dynamic hatred and bitter vituperation. In his fall he carried many with him. Over 1500 Soviet citizens have been "liquidated " as Trotskyists, among them the most prominent of the figures at Brest-Litovsk. Joffe, Kamenev, Sokolnikov, and Karakhan all rose to ambassadorial rank to be hurled from their high estate with ignominy. Joffe died by his own hand, Kamenev and Karakhan by the bullets of the executioner as " Fascist " supporters of Trotsky. Sokolnikov exists in a Soviet prison on a similar charge of treason, and with him Radek, the most brilliant political commentator of the régime. Of the Russian experts Admiral Altvater and General Samoilo perished in the Red Terror of 1918.

Altogether nearly four hundred people were gathered and housed in the huts of the Brest-Litovsk citadel, living in frugality and eating at a common mess-table. The Germans were generous to the Bolsheviks in the matter of placing motor cars at their disposal (though there was nowhere to drive to) and an air of at least superficial friendliness prevailed. They were particularly thoughtful of the Russian military and naval experts, realizing to the full their invidious position and showing them sympathy.

On the evening of December 20, the Commander-in-Chief in the East, Field-Marshal H.R.H. Prince Leopold of Bavaria, gave a dinner party to the assembled delegates, and nearly a hundred persons sat down to what must have been the most unique gathering in the history of modern diplomacy. The picture was rich in contrasts. At the head of the table sat the bearded, stalwart figure of the Prince of Bavaria, having on his right Joffe, a Jew recently released from a Siberian prison. Next to him was Count Czernin, a *grand seigneur* and diplomat of the old school, a Knight of the Golden Fleece, trained in the traditions of Kaunitz and Metternich, to whom Joffe, with his soft eyes and kindly tone, confided : " I hope we may be able to raise the revolution in your country too ".[1]

According to the rules of " revolutionary etiquette " the mandatory representatives were given precedence over the experts ; thus the sailor, Olich, sat at the high table

[1] " We shall hardly need any assistance from the good Joffe, I fancy, in bringing about a revolution among ourselves ", commented Czernin in his diary that evening as he recorded the events of the day ; " the people will manage that, if the Entente persist in refusing to come to terms " (Czernin, p. 221).

while Admiral Altvater dined in the ante-room. This added a definite piquancy to the proceedings. Opposite Hoffmann the workers' delegate, Obukhov, was in considerable difficulties with the various implements beside his plate. He tried to seize the food first with one thing and then another ; " it was only the fork that he used exclusively as a tooth-pick ". But the *tour de force* was old Stashkov, the peasant. He had got over his embarrassment by now and was thoroughly enjoying himself. What a story he would have to tell when he got back to the village ! He laughed jovially, shaking his long grey hair and shovelling food through his enormous untrimmed beard. He was particularly appreciative of the wine, never refusing it and drawing a smile even from the frozen-faced German orderly by enquiring in a business-like manner of his neighbour Prince Ernst von Hohenlohe, " Which is the stronger ? Red or white ?—it makes no difference to me which I drink, I'm only interested in the strength." By the end of the meal Stashkov, not pale by nature, was upholding in his flushed, good-natured old face the reputation of a " red " delegate.[1]

On the other side of the table were Baron von Kühlmann and General Hoffmann with Kamenev and Sokolnikov, who spoke to them enthusiastically of the task which lay before them in leading the Russian proletariat to the heights of happiness and prosperity. Opposite this group Prince Ernst von Hohenlohe sat next to Mme. Bitsenko, a quiet and reserved little grey-haired assassin.

But it was not only at the dinner-table that the contrast between the two groups of negotiators was remarkable. At the conference board it became even more plain. The whim of history willed that the representatives of

[1] Czernin, pp. 219-221 ; Hoffmann, ii. 195 ; Fokke, pp. 36-37. Trotsky's comment on this incident, of which he was not a witness, is that " the peasant, an old man, was encouraged to drink more wine than was good for him " ; cf. *My Life* (London, 1930), p. 312.

the most revolutionary régime ever known should sit at the same diplomatic table with the representatives of the most reactionary military caste among all ruling classes. The spokesman of the most disciplined and apparently most firmly established Government met the leaders of a revolutionary State whose lease of life was still uncertain.

No two groups could have thought more differently. The Central Powers spoke the ancient language of diplomacy, time-honoured and crusted with tradition. They thought in terms of strategic lines, of provinces ceded, of economic advantages to be gained. Not so the Bolsheviks. Theirs was not a parlance of frontiers and concessions. This was the first contact of Bolshevism with the Western World, and it was the aim of the Soviet representatives to utilize the meetings as a sounding-board for the propagation of their doctrine. In their principles of a general European peace they were not concerned with geographical terms and expressions. They banked upon the immediate effect of their propaganda on the war-weary masses of Europe to achieve what they knew could not be achieved by force of arms, namely the World Revolution and the replacement of Imperialism by " the rule of the proletariat ".

" We began peace negotiations ", wrote Trotsky, " in the hope of arousing the workmen's parties of Germany and Austria-Hungary as well as those of the Entente countries. For this reason we were obliged to delay the negotiations as long as possible to give the European workmen time to understand the main fact of the Soviet revolution itself and particularly its peace policy." [1]

Moreover, fully to appreciate the inwardness of the Bolshevik peace proposals, they must be regarded in the light of Bolshevik philosophy. At first sight the promises of self-determination given to nationalism in the Russian peace programme would appear to weaken the Bolsheviks, for almost inevitably it meant that large areas of the former

[1] Leon Trotsky, *Lenin* (London, 1925), p. 128.

Russian Empire would elect either to become independent or to seek the protection of the Central Powers. But to the Bolshevik mentality of that time (it has become modified with years) it mattered little whether the enemy, in the form of capitalist imperialism, gained further sources of territorial and material strength. It was not upon this ground that battle was being given. The battle-ground was that of social struggle, and therein frontiers mattered little in comparison with the fight of the proletarian against the capitalist. " It made little difference to them whether Lithuania was or was not ceded to Germany. What did matter was the struggle of the Lithuanian proletarian against the Lithuanian capitalist." [1]

" He is no Socialist ", wrote Lenin, in an open letter to American workers, " who does not understand that the victory over the bourgeoisie may require losses of territory and defeats. He is no Socialist who will not sacrifice his fatherland for the triumph of the social revolution." [2]

Such was the psychological approach of the Bolsheviks to Brest-Litovsk, the policy with which they confidently hoped to convert the world. When that policy failed, something fundamental went out of Bolshevism and was replaced by compromise. It is the search for that " fundamental something " which is disintegrating the Soviet Union to-day.

5

The first plenary session of the conference was held in the afternoon of December 22, and the proceedings were opened with a speech of welcome by Prince Leopold. Kühlmann was unanimously voted first president of the conference, and when the usual compliments had been exchanged, he made a brief speech indicating the lines on which their discussions must proceed. " Our negotiations

[1] Étienne Antonelli, *Bolshevist Russia* (London, 1920), pp. 159-160.

[2] Reprinted in *Class Struggle* (New York), December 1918.

will be guided by a spirit of placable humanity and mutual esteem ", he declared. " They must take into consideration, on the one hand, what has become historical, in order not to lose our footing on the firm ground of facts, but, on the other hand, they must also be inspired by that new great leading motive (*Leitgedanke*), which has brought us here together. I may regard it as an auspicious circumstance that our negotiations should begin in sight of that festival which for many centuries past has promised peace on earth and good will towards men." [1] With this preliminary he invited Joffe to state the general principles upon which the Soviet delegation hoped to base conditions of peace.

After reciting the major portion of the Decree of Peace, Joffe formally presented the six main tenets, which had already become familiar to all present.

I. No forcible appropriation of any territories taken in the course of the war. The occupying armies to be withdrawn from those territories at the earliest moment.

II. Complete political independence to be given to those nationalities which had been deprived of it since the beginning of the war.

III. Nationalities not hitherto enjoying political independence to be allowed the right to decide by means of a referendum whether they elect to be united to other nations or to acquire independence. The referendum to be so arranged as to ensure complete freedom of voting.

IV. In the case of territories inhabited by several nationalities, the rights of minorities to be safeguarded by special provisions.

V. None of the belligerent Powers to pay any war indemnity. War requisitions should be returned, and

[1] *Proceedings*, p. 38.

sufferers by war should be compensated from a special fund levied on all belligerent countries in proportion to their resources.

VI. Colonial questions to be settled in conformity with points I, II, III, and IV.

In conclusion, the Russian delegation proposed that no restriction of the liberty of weaker nations by stronger should be tolerated, such as economic boycotts, the subjection of one country to another by means of the imposition of economic treaties, and bilateral Customs conventions hindering freedom of commerce with a third country.[1]

The delegations of the Quadruple Alliance took formal note of the Soviet proposals and requested time and an adjournment to prepare their reply, which they promised to deliver as soon as possible.

Kühlmann and Czernin had no difficulty in reaching an agreement. They had nothing to lose and everything to gain by accepting the Soviet principles for the basis of a general peace. Even Austria had little to risk, for, if the Entente endorsed these same principles, they must abandon the postulates of the Treaty of London of April 26, 1915, which aimed at the partition of the Dual Monarchy. And though it was a dangerous move for the Imperial Government to accept the principle of self-determination in view of the national ambitions of the Czechs, Croats, Rumanians, and the other half-dozen peoples who went to

[1] Among the treasured relics closely guarded in the vaults of the Lenin Institute at Moscow is a sheet of MS. entitled " Outline of Program for Peace Negotiations with Germany ". In two distinct handwritings follow the instructions for the Soviet delegation as adopted at the session of the Council of Commissars on December 10, 1917. The first part of the document is halting, almost incoherent, the page marred by many erasions and corrections. Then the handwriting changes, and with it the nature of the document, which becomes terse and direct. The first script is that of Lenin, the second of Stalin. The master had provided the formula, but the prescription was the work of the disciple.

make up the Habsburg dominions, yet this was safer than facing certain dismemberment at the hands of the Entente. If a general peace were not possible, Czernin determined to make a separate agreement with Russia for the cessation of hostilities and the resumption of commercial and economic relations on the basis of the old pre-war commercial treaty. For him it was an absolute necessity to bring home a *Brotfrieden* (Bread Peace).

The Austrian and German Foreign Secretaries therefore agreed at once to return an unqualified acceptance of the Russian thesis " if the Entente would also agree to negotiate a Peace on similar terms ". Hoffmann protested against such a decision " because at bottom it was a lie ". He urged that " it would be more correct to keep strictly to facts ", and for the Central Powers to take their stand on the Peace Resolution of the Reichstag rather than the more embracing Soviet formula. The Russians should be told frankly, as he had told them during the armistice negotiations, that, though the Central Powers were ready to negotiate a general peace, until the Bolsheviks could produce credentials entitling them to speak for the Powers of the Entente, it would be possible only to discuss a separate peace between Russia and the Quadruple Alliance.

Both Kühlmann and Czernin were opposed to this doctrine, and between them they overbore Hoffmann's objections and also those of the Turks, who wished to insist that Russian troops should be withdrawn from the Caucasus immediately on the conclusion of peace. This, of course, was inadmissible to the Germans, since it might logically entail their withdrawal from Courland and Lithuania at the same time. After much argument Nessimy Bey was persuaded to withdraw both this demand and a further objéction that the Soviet delegation had not clearly stated its intention to refrain from all interference in internal affairs. To this Czernin replied cynically that if he, in view of the perilous internal condition of Austria-

Hungary, had no hesitation in accepting, the Turks could also rest content.[1]

These obstacles to unanimity removed, other difficulties suddenly arose with the Bulgarians, who, owing to the fact that most of them, including M. Popoff, could speak no German and hardly any French, had grasped very little of what was going on at the first plenary session. Once it had been explained to them, they expressed themselves with considerable heat and demanded that Bulgaria should be exempted from the no-annexation provision. Bulgaria had come into the war on a frankly annexationist basis, and they would only agree provided that the territory which they had seized from Serbia and Rumania was not regarded as an annexation.

Kühlmann and Czernin lavished threats, cajoleries, and charms upon the recalcitrant Popoff; he would have none of them. In vain did they assure him that it was, so to speak, " all in fun " and that they were only going through the motions of accepting the Soviet formula ; that there was no danger at all, because it was impossible that the Entente Powers should agree to join in the negotiations, and that, once this was established, the assurances given now by the Central Powers would become void. In vain they pointed to the example of the more malleable Nessimy Bey—still Popoff stuck obstinately to his " NO " ; the word Dobrudja had become graven upon his heart. He would rather leave the conference than abandon one iota of his claims. The deadlock seemed complete.

But the soldiers succeeded in finding a solution where the diplomats had failed. After consultation with Hoffmann, General Gantcheff, Chief of the Bulgarian General Staff, took it upon himself to send a detailed telegram to Tsar Ferdinand, leaving the ultimate decision in his hands. Back came a telegraphic order from Sofia, somewhat peremptory in tone, authorizing Popoff to concur in the

[1] Czernin, p. 223.

views of Bulgaria's allies. Unanimity was finally achieved on the evening of the 24th.[1]

It was on Christmas Day, 1917, that the reply of the Central Powers was read by Czernin to the conference. The Quadruple Alliance, he said, found that the Soviet proposals formed a discussable basis for an immediate general peace without forcible acquisitions of territory and without war indemnities. They were, therefore, ready to begin such a peace on two conditions :

(1) All Powers now participating in the war must within a suitable period, without exception and without reserve, bind themselves to the most precise adherence to the general conditions agreed upon.

(2) With respect to point No. III of the Russian proposal, the question of self-determination for national groups which possess no political independence cannot, in the opinion of the Quadruple Alliance, admit of international settlement, but must, if necessary, be solved by each State independently together with the nationalities concerned, and in accordance with the constitution of that State.

He then replied agreeing in detail to the six Soviet points and concluded with the proposal that, although they were all ready to enter into general negotiations, in order to save time, they should begin discussion on those special points which in any event would have to be settled separately between Russia and the Central Powers.[2]

Joffe warmly welcomed the decision of the Alliance and accepted their reservations in principle, though regretting the necessity for them.[3] He agreed to examine the special

[1] Czernin, pp. 223-224 ; Hoffmann, ii. 200-201.

[2] *Proceedings*, pp. 40-41.

[3] The Soviet press, however, criticized the second reservation of the Alliance somewhat sharply, declaring that to speak of " constitutional

points referred to during the ten days' adjournment of the
formal negotiations arranged in order to allow the Entente
an opportunity of participating in them.

The Christmas Day declaration was hailed in Germany
with conflicting emotions. To the parties of the Left
and Centre, who had supported the Peace Resolution
and who were suspicious of the sincerity of the Government's adherence to its principles, Czernin's statement
came as a welcome relief and appeared to render their
doubts groundless. " The most democratic government
in the world (the Soviets) has given testimony that the
Central Powers' peace policy is entirely free from all
lust of conquest and all striving after violence ", wrote
Georg Bernhard. " These negotiations must be continued
without paying any attention to obstacles and in the spirit
of the pure love of peace." [1]

But to the annexationists of the Right the statement
was little short of treachery. In acquiescing in it, Kühlmann
had abandoned the right to dictate which the victory of
German arms had achieved, and had descended to the
level of mere negotiation on the basis of equality. The
editors of the jingo press fulminated in righteous anger
against so disgraceful a proceeding. " Never before have
we so completely given up diplomatically everything which
has been so dearly bought with the blood and lives of
hundreds of thousands, with the sweat of millions, with
the deprivation of our children, and with our own hunger ",
stormed the *Tägliche Rundschau* ; [2] and another writer
pictured his readers dropping the morning newspapers on

channels " in this connection was to nullify the principle at issue. The
Central Powers " while they agree not to apply the right of the strongest
in territories occupied during the war, nevertheless do nothing for the
small nationalities in their own territories. The war cannot come to an
end without the restoration of independence to small nationalities "
(*Pravda*, December 26, 1917).

[1] *Vossische Zeitung*, December 26, 1917.

[2] *Tägliche Rundschau*, December 27, 1917.

their breakfast-tables "with painful bitterness in their hearts when reading this news ".[1]

The ink was scarcely dry on the preliminary agreement, when there came a roar of protest from Kreuznach. The Supreme Command considered that the declaration of December 25 was a "betrayal" of the "agreement" reached at Kreuznach on the 18th. They considered the adjournment an unwarrantable delay by which nothing could be gained, since there was no prospect of the Entente's accepting the invitation. The military security of the frontiers had been sacrificed to political sophistry. Hindenburg addressed an angry telegram protesting against this "policy of renunciation", and Ludendorff telephoned furiously to Hoffmann demanding an explanation. Hoffmann very rightly replied that he had not been present at Kreuznach on the 18th, and knew nothing of what had occurred. He had, however, endeavoured to dissuade Kühlmann from his devious course.

In the midst of this outburst Kühlmann remained, true to his name, a "cool man". He spoke with the Chancellor, explaining the position in detail, and begged him to see the Kaiser. Hertling did so, and Wilhelm II, with one of his rare bursts of courage, decided in favour of the Secretary of State and against the High Command. " I am personally satisfied ", was his message to Kühlmann, who, turning to Czernin, commented, " The Kaiser is the only sensible man in the whole of Germany ".[2]

Nevertheless, this brush with the Supreme Command had the effect of stiffening Kühlmann's attitude in the next crisis, which arose almost immediately.

Jubilant at the acceptance of the Soviet terms by the Central Powers, Joffe had telegraphed enthusiastically to Petrograd. The Russians talked happily among themselves and to their colleagues on the other delegations. It was

[1] *Düsseldorfer General Anzeiger*, December 26, 1917.
[2] Ludendorff, ii. 545-546 ; Czernin, p. 228.

made suddenly clear to the Germans and Austrians that their declaration had been completely misunderstood, and that the Russians believed that a peace " without annexation " would give them back Russian Poland, Lithuania, and Courland. This manifestly was neither strategically possible nor politically desirable from the German point of view. Apart from the fact that they wished to hold the Eastern Provinces as security for the general peace negotiations, these territories formed part of their munition establishment. The railway *matériel*, the factories, and, most important of all, the grain, were indispensable so long as hostilities lasted. The German *Realpolitik* rendered withdrawal impossible.

Matters were brought to a head when, in conversation with Hoffmann's G.S.O.1, Major Brinckmann, Colonel Fokke stated deliberately that the Russians unquestionably deduced from the statements of Czernin and Kühlmann that not only would Austrian and German troops be withdrawn from all occupied Russian territory behind the frontiers of 1914, but that the return of these territories to Russia was not in itself precluded.[1] In some dismay Brinckmann reported to his chief, who in turn carried the news to Kühlmann. The Russians must be disillusioned at once, said Hoffmann, for, if they were allowed to return to Petrograd under this misapprehension—namely that the peace they were about to sign would guarantee to Russia her pre-war western frontier—their awakening at a later date to the fact that they had been wholly deceived would only result in frantic indignation, and perhaps in a rupture of negotiations. Besides, the Supreme Command, already critical of the conduct of the negotiations, would be doubly incensed if the position were not made perfectly clear.

Kühlmann and Czernin agreed, and Hoffmann was commissioned to undertake the unpleasant task. He selected the luncheon-table as his field of operations and,

[1] Hoffmann, ii. 201 ; Fokke, p. 38.

seating himself next to Joffe, came, with characteristic bluntness, directly to the point. The Russians were clearly under a misapprehension as to the interpretation of the phrase " no annexations ", he declared. The attitude of the Central Powers was that it was no forcible annexation if portions of the former Russian Empire had, of their own free will and acting through the duly constituted authorities, elected to separate from Russia and assume either an independent existence or a protected status within the German Empire. The Soviet State itself, Hoffmann indicated with some point, had, by the Decree on the Self-Determination of Nations which they had promulgated on November 15, given the right of withdrawal to the different nationalities within the State. Poland, Courland, and Lithuania had merely exercised that right. The Central Powers reserved their liberty of action to reach a direct understanding with the representatives of the States to the exclusion of Russia.

Joffe's appetite seemed to desert him (" he looked as if he had received a blow on the head ", says Hoffmann), and immediately after luncheon he asked for a meeting with Kühlmann and Czernin. The shock to the Bolsheviks had evidently been a severe one. Indignation mingled with disappointment. Joffe protested, Kamenev stormed, Pokrovsky wept. "How can you talk of peace without annexation ", he sobbed, " when nearly eighteen provinces are torn from Russia ? "

The Germans remained adamant. Joffe threatened at last to break off negotiations. Then Czernin lost his nerve. Peace he must have, peace and bread for Austria. If not a general peace, a separate peace—but peace. Desperately he sought for a compromise. He proposed that, though Germany could not evacuate the territories until a general peace had been signed and ratified, after this had been achieved plebiscites should be held, with guarantees given to the Russians that there should be no coercion in the voting. Both Kühlmann and Joffe rejected this, and, when Joffe left for Petrograd, Czernin, in considerable excitement, went to Kühlmann and told him that if a rupture occurred now he would open independent negotiations with the Russians. At the same time he sent General Csiscerics to Hoffmann with a similar statement.

Both Kühlmann and Hoffmann remained calm under this threat. Kühlmann was even able to turn it to his own advantage. He asked Czernin for a written statement of the Austro-Hungarian intentions in regard to a separate peace. It would, he thought, be a useful additional weapon in his fight with the Supreme Command, should Ludendorff push him too far. The Secretary of State was an adept at profiting from critical situations.

To Csiscerics Hoffmann behaved with brutality. The idea of separate peace, he declared, was entirely welcome to him since it would release the twenty-five German divisions now occupied in stiffening the Austrian army. By an Austro-Russian agreement Germany's right flank would no longer be open to attack and a large number of troops would therefore be released for duty in the West. He was entirely unimpressed by the General's threats.

The Austrians retired checkmated and furious, but the situation was eased by the news that no rupture would take place. It is to be more than suspected that the Bolshevik leaders in Petrograd had been less impressed with the acceptance of the Central Powers than had their representatives at Brest. " We could see clearly ", writes Trotsky, " that this was merely a piece of make-believe " ; and adds, somewhat naïvely, " but we did not expect even that, for is not hypocrisy the tribute paid by vice to virtue ? " [1] " There was no question of negotiations being broken off ", Hoffmann records with cynical clearness ; " the only chance the Bolsheviks had of remaining in power was by

[1] Leon Trotsky, *The History of the Russian Revolution to Brest-Litovsk* (London, 1919), p. 126.

signing a peace. They were obliged to accept the conditions of the Central Powers, however hard they might be . . . the only one of us who doubted this was Count Czernin." [1]

The influence of the Supreme Command and the views of the Fatherland Party could also be seen in the attitude adopted by the Germans during the negotiations which followed from December 26 to 28 on the special questions which concerned Russia and the Central Powers. The Russians presented in draft form two articles concerning the treatment of occupied territories which provided for the simultaneous withdrawal of Russian troops from Turkey and Persia, and of Austrian and German troops from Poland, Lithuania, and Courland. The local plebiscites which it was proposed to hold in these territories were to be carried out in the absence of all troops of either party, leaving the control in the hands of local or national militia. Until the holding of the plebiscites the government of these regions would " remain in the hands of representatives of the local population elected democratically ". The fixing of the date and the organization of the mutual evacuation was to be the task of a special military commission.

The Central Powers suggested making these proposals the subject of the first two articles of the preliminary peace, but they put forward an alternative text of their own, more definite in form :

Article I. Russia and Germany are to declare the state of war at an end. Both nations are resolved to live together in the future in peace and friendship. On the condition of complete reciprocity, *vis-à-vis* her allies, Germany would be ready as soon as peace is concluded with Russia and the demobilization of the Russian armies has been accomplished, to evacuate her present position in occupied Russian territory in so far as no different inferences result from Article II.

[1] Hoffmann, ii. 201-204 ; Czernin, pp. 226-228 ; Fokke, p. 130.

Article II. The Russian Government having, in accordance with its principles, proclaimed for all people without exception living within the Russian Empire the right of self-determination, including complete separation, takes cognizance of the decisions expressing the will of the people demanding full State independence and separation from the Russian Empire, for Poland, Lithuania, Courland, and portions of Estonia and Livonia. The Russian Government recognizes that in the present circumstances these manifestations must be regarded as the expression of the will of the people, and is ready to draw conclusions therefrom. As in those districts to which the foregoing stipulations apply, the question of evacuation is not such as is provided for in Article I, a special commission shall discuss and fix the time and other details in conformity with the Russian idea of the necessary ratification—by a plebiscite on broad lines and without military presence whatever—and of the already existing proclamation of separation.

It was clearly evident that these proposals disclosed a grave divergence from the declaration of December 25, and were in far greater accord with the views which Hoffmann had expressed to Joffe. The Soviet delegates in taking note of them were forced to make a reservation. Though they were beginning to understand only too clearly, they insisted upon a more precise formulation of the points raised in the two articles, but they agreed to a special commission being formed to examine the technique of such a referendum as was proposed and to fix the date for evacuation.

At last Joffe saw that the optimism which he had displayed in Petrograd after the Armistice and at Brest after the Declaration of Christmas Day had been misplaced. Kühlmann's statement of December 28 had shown beyond all doubting that the original agreement to the formula of "peace without annexations" was but a myth, and that the German and Russian conceptions of self-determination were irreconcilable. From December 28 Joffe "faded", and never recovered either his poise or his enthusiasm. It was impossible that he should continue to lead the Russian delegation.[1]

The plenary session of December 28 closed the first stage of the negotiations, and it was agreed that though the period of grace for acceptance of participation by the Entente terminated on January 4, the conference would not resume its deliberations before January 9.[2] Leaving a nucleus of experts behind them, the delegates dispersed to their capitals, Joffe and Kamenev to Petrograd, Czernin to Vienna, Kühlmann and Hoffmann to Berlin.

6

Kühlmann, in his endeavour to placate the Supreme Command, ran foul of the Liberal and Majority Socialist elements of public opinion in Germany. Those who still believed in the principles of the Peace Resolution as the basis of Germany's peace policy awoke suddenly to the fact that these principles were being used as a decoy and a cover for a programme of annexation. They realized that the German policy of equivocation would be welcomed as a god-send by the Entente, who could fasten upon Germany the responsibility for deliberately sabotaging principles for a democratic peace. Prince Max of Baden writes in his Memoirs:

On December 28, 1917, we made our irreparable mistake. We gave the impression to the whole world and to the German masses that in contrast to the Russian attitude our agreement to the national right of self-determination was insincere and that annexational designs lurked behind it. We rejected the Russian demand for a free and untrammelled popular vote in the occupied territories

[1] Fokke, p. 118.   [2] *Proceedings*, pp. 42-46.

on the ground that the Courlanders, Lithuanians, and Poles had already decided their own fate. We ought never to have claimed the arbitrarily instituted or enlarged land-councils as authoritative representative assemblies. The Russian request for a referendum should either have been accepted without reserve or replaced by a demand for a National Constituent Assembly elected by universal suffrage.[1]

Summoning the party leaders to meet him on New Year's Day, Kühlmann found himself the target of attack both from the Right and the extreme Left. Westarp, as usual, was bitter and implacable, frankly opposing recognition of the right of self-determination. " Herr von Kühlmann has not shown himself a born statesman ", he sneered, " he has gone far to reduce our glittering advantages to nothing." Haase, for the Independent Socialists, declared in favour of the Russian thesis, saying that political life in the occupied territories was obstructed by military pressure which must be removed; and Scheidemann bitterly assailed the Secretary of State for his prostitution of the principles of the Peace Resolution. Only from the Centre did Kühlmann receive support. Fehrenbach approved his policy, while, outside the conference, Erzberger took up the cudgels in his defence.

A Crown Council had been summoned for January 2, 1918, and Kühlmann was well aware of what reception he might expect at the hands of the Supreme Command. He therefore insisted on bringing Hoffmann to Berlin with him, and, proving himself a better strategist than Ludendorff, arranged for Hoffmann to be received in audience by the Emperor on New Year's Day. Wilhelm II had not seen the General since those hectic days on the Eastern Front in the summer of 1916 when HLH had been bent upon the downfall of Falkenhayn. So impressed was he now that he invited Hoffmann to luncheon at the Schloss Bellevue and asked him to give his views on the situation.

[1] *Memoirs of Prince Max of Baden* (London, 1928), i. 208.

Hoffmann was in a quandary. He did not share in their
entirety the views of the High Command and yet was
diffident in placing himself in opposition to them. Moreover, though he had not seen Ludendorff, he had every
reason to believe that the First Quartermaster-General
was seriously displeased with him. In view of these circumstances, he begged to be excused from giving his personal
opinion to the Emperor.

" When your All-Highest War Lord wishes to hear
your views on any subject it is your duty to give them to
him, quite irrespective of whether they coincide with those
of the Supreme Command or not ", replied Wilhelm II.

At that Hoffmann began to talk. He gave the Emperor
the views of a man who for the past eighteen months had
been in constant touch with the situation and who had
had practical experience of its difficulties. He pointed out
that, notwithstanding the measures taken by Prussia during
many decades, she had not been able to manage her
Polish subjects, and that consequently he could see no
advantage to the Empire from the addition of a further
two million Poles to its population, as was envisaged by
the demands of the Supreme Command. He was even more
critical of Erzberger's so-called " German Solution ". He
suggested that the new Polish frontier should be drawn
in such a way as to bring to Germany the smallest possible
number of Polish subjects. Only a small additional strip of
territory, with not more than 100,000 Polish inhabitants,
was necessary, near Thorn and Bendzin, to prevent the
enemy artillery in any subsequent war from firing straight
on to the main railway station of Thorn, or into the Upper
Silesian coal-fields.

Deeply impressed with the reasonableness of Hoffmann's
argument, the Emperor, always swayed by what he had
last heard, agreed with him, and at once had a map prepared in accordance with his proposals. This he produced
next morning at the Crown Council, to which Hoffmann

had been summoned. The latter attended with no little apprehension, for he had still been unsuccessful in getting into touch with Ludendorff, who was in ignorance of what had passed between Hoffmann and the Emperor.

Wilhelm II opened the Council by laying the map before them.

" Gentlemen ", he said, " you will find on this map the future frontier between Poland and Prussia, as I, in my capacity of All-Highest War Lord, consider that it should be drawn." He then added : " I base my conclusion on the judgement of an excellent and competent expert, namely, that of General Hoffmann, who is here ".

For a moment there was silence, and then Ludendorff, his voice hoarse with anger, all self-control abandoned, shouted at the Emperor that he had no right to ask the opinion of a General over his (Ludendorff's) head. In no circumstances could the line drawn by the Emperor be considered as final. The Supreme Command would have to consider the matter further.

" We must certainly think this matter over carefully ", muttered Hindenburg in approval.

For a moment the Emperor hesitated in indecision. Should he assert himself and provoke a joint resignation ? The Council sat about him, disturbed and uncomfortable. Finally he temporized.

" I will await your report ", he said, and brought the painful scene to a close.

It was a repetition of the scene at Kreuznach in December. Nothing had been settled definitely or decisively. Kühlmann had only obtained the Imperial approval for his policy so far and authorization to proceed along the same lines. He was still anxious to secure the separation of the border States by means of self-determination rather than open annexation ; but the whole conduct of the negotiations had been jeopardized by the attitude of Ludendorff and Hindenburg.

In the Reichstag debate on foreign affairs on January 2 and 3, the Majority Parties made a determined effort to repair the error of December 28 and to secure a return to the more definite principles of Christmas Day. A formula was proposed by which the decisions of the existing bodies in the occupied territories should only have provisional force, but that final decisions should be taken by democratic parliaments to be elected after the evacuation. Any hopes of agreement on these lines were doomed by Hertling's reply on January 4, in which he sought to placate the Supreme Command. Germany, he said, could not recede from her present position. " We cannot withdraw Articles I and II. We base ourselves upon our position of power (*Machtstellung*), upon the loyalty of our intentions, and upon the merits of our case."

The Supreme Command was not thus easily mollified. They considered that their authority had been flouted and their dignity aspersed. That the All-Highest War Lord of Germany had the right to consult one of his own generals without their knowledge and consent they vehemently denied, and they retired to Kreuznach in high dudgeon, preparing to wreak their vengeance on Kühlmann and Hoffmann. The two intended victims returned to Brest-Litovsk with the impression that from now on they lived in constant danger of Ludendorff's wrath.

Nor were they mistaken. On January 7 the Emperor received from Kreuznach not the promised report, but a letter of pontifical admonition from Hindenburg. It was one long complaint against the Emperor, the Secretary of State, and the Chief of Staff in the East.

Your Majesty has adopted a line which seriously cut down our demands and thus made the Austro-Polish Solution unacceptable to Main Headquarters. Your Majesty certainly permitted your decision to be subjected to a closer examination ; I do not know, however, whether a solution can be found which will remove our serious objections to the Austro-Polish Solution. . . .

Even the situation in Courland and Lithuania has become very uncertain as a result of the Declaration of December 25. . . . We were entirely surprised by the Declaration. I am bound to ascribe the hitherto unsatisfactory political and economic results [of the peace negotiations] to the pliancy of our diplomacy towards our allies and our enemies. . . . Judging by my impressions from Brest the German representatives appeared to be more diplomatic than resolute. . . . It was frank surrender !

In the Polish question, Your Majesty has been graciously pleased to give the opinion of General Hoffmann preference over mine and that of General Ludendorff. General Hoffmann is my subordinate and has no responsibility in political matters. The events of January 2 have made the most painful impression on General Ludendorff and myself, and have shown us that Your Majesty disregards our opinion in a matter of vital importance for the existence of the German Fatherland. . . .

It is Your Majesty's noble right to decide. But Your Majesty will not ask that honest men, who have loyally served Your Majesty and the Fatherland, should cover with their authority and their names actions in which they could not participate from inward conviction. . . . My position and that of General Ludendorff must be immaterial where exigencies of State are concerned.[1]

This letter, the origin of which lies clearly with Ludendorff, was a direct challenge to the authority of Wilhelm II, both as All-Highest War Lord and as King of Prussia. It showed to how great a degree the Supreme Command considered itself the deciding power within the Empire. They regarded their responsibility as covering every question which could remotely affect " the existence of the German Fatherland ". Supreme dictatorship could not go farther.

The Emperor dared not resist. In the main issue of responsibility he did make some feeble protest, urging the Supreme Command to leave politics to the Government and to concentrate on their own task of winning the war, but in the matter of the peace negotiations he surrendered abjectly. In answer to Hindenburg's letter the Imperial

[1] Ludendorff, *The General Staff and its Problems*, ii. 524-528.

Chancellor hastened to inform the Supreme Command that a misunderstanding had arisen and that the Emperor had taken no definite decision in regard to Poland.

But though he abandoned Hoffmann's proposals, the Emperor stood between him and the wrath of Ludendorff, who had demanded his dismissal as Chief of Staff in the East and his appointment to the command of a division. By order of the Emperor, Hoffmann remained at his post at Brest-Litovsk, but the breach with Ludendorff was permanent. The symbol HLH, so invincible in its early inception, had been irreparably shattered. It had in fact become merely a gigantic L.[1]

The dispute between Ludendorff and Kühlmann became a public issue once the news of the threatened resignation of the Supreme Command had leaked out; the newspapers of the Right and Left raged furiously together, and political orators were bitter in their denunciations. In a violent attack upon Kühlmann the *Rheinisch-Westfälische Zeitung* thundered :

If a prize had been offered for showing how a brilliant military position may be utterly ruined, Baron von Kühlmann would have won it. . . . Renunciation in the East is his watchword; renunciation in the West will follow. There is no question of the guarantees which our people needs for a peaceful future. . . . The German people have now to choose between Hindenburg and Ludendorff on the one hand, and Kühlmann and Hertling on the other. They will rally in unanimous love round their two heroes.[2]

The two heroes, however, seemed less sacrosanct to Karl Severing, the Majority Socialist deputy, who, in a speech at Bielefeld on January 11, declared that " the overwhelming mass of the German people will not shed a single tear over the General, whoever he may be, who opposes a peace

[1] Ludendorff, *My War Memories*, ii. 547-550 ; Hoffmann, ii. 205-208 ; Wheeler-Bennett, pp. 128-131.
[2] *Rheinisch-Westfälische Zeitung*, January 6 and 14, 1918.

by understanding or who would rather resign than continue
to fight for such a peace ".[1]

Against this background of conflict and uncertainty
Kühlmann resumed the negotiations.

7

When Joffe returned to Petrograd on December 29
there still remained six days during which the Entente
Powers could exercise their right to participate in the
negotiations. Trotsky, therefore, on that day, addressed to
these Governments his longest and most impassioned Note
describing the course of events and begging them not to
" sabotage the course of a general peace ". Since the
Central Powers, he contended, had, by their acceptance
of the Soviet formula, agreed to evacuate Belgium, Northern
France, Serbia, Montenegro, Rumania, Poland, Lithuania,
and Courland on the conclusion of a general peace, the
Entente could no longer claim to be fighting for the liberation of these territories. He now threatened them openly
with a separate peace between Russia and Germany which
" would no doubt be a heavy blow to the Allied countries,
especially France and Italy ". He made a desperate appeal
to their workers :

The question of compelling their own Governments immediately
to present their peace programs and to participate on the basis of
them in the negotiations now becomes a question of national self-
preservation for the Allied peoples. . . . If the Allied Governments, in
the blind stubbornness which characterizes decadent and perishing
classes, once more refuse to participate in the negotiations, then the
working-class will be confronted by the iron necessity of taking the
power out of the hands of those who cannot or will not give the
people peace.[2]

The Entente made no direct reply to these overtures.

[1] *Vossische Zeitung*, January 12, 1918.
[2] Cumming and Pettit, p. 61.

They adhered firmly to the House-Maklakoff formula of November 30. " There is no disagreement among us ", M. Pichon told the Chamber of Deputies on December 31 ; " Russia may treat for a separate peace with our enemies or not. In either case, for us the war continues. An ally has failed us . . . but another ally has come from the other end of the world." " If the present rulers of Russia take action which is independent of their Allies," Mr. Lloyd George informed an audience of British labour leaders a few days later, " we have no means of intervening to avert the catastrophe which is assuredly befalling their country. Russia can only be saved by her own people." But at the same time he took the opportunity offered by the German attitude to outline a programme of war aims on behalf of the Allies, which, while embracing the Soviet formula of self-determination and no forcible annexations or indemnities, was so phrased as to prove that the Central Powers, and not the Entente, were wrecking a peace of understanding. While refusing to be drawn himself into negotiations with the Bolsheviks, Mr. Lloyd George astutely capitalized the hypocrisy of German diplomacy at Brest.

It was made abundantly clear to the Soviet leaders in Petrograd that no hope could be entertained of the negotiation of a general peace, and, more disturbing still, that the world " proletarian revolution ", which, in the first blush of their own success, they had fondly imagined to be but " around the corner ", was in reality very far from being ripe for eruption. The workers of Europe, whom even Lenin, the genius of revolution, had trusted to rally immediately to the standard of a general democratic peace, failed completely to fulfil the rôle expected of them, and continued to give their support to the " imperialist-bourgeois " Governments.

The Bolsheviks, with their infinite capacity for believing in what they thought they ought to believe, treated it as only an error in schedule. They implicitly believed in a world revolution, therefore, even if delayed, a world revolution must come. When Kamenev reported on the peace negotiations on December 31 to a joint meeting of the Central Executive Committee of the party, the Petrograd Soviet, and representatives of the army, he criticized bitterly the hypocrisy of the German policy, but added his conviction that this same policy would lead to the downfall of German imperialism and to a peace with revolutionary Germany.[1]

It is part of the strange enigma of Lenin that, though he never failed to gauge the reactions of the Russian masses, of whose mental processes he possessed an almost uncanny intuitive understanding, he never succeeded in estimating accurately the workings of the European working-class mind. Its lack of Slav mysticism, its failure to appreciate the grandiloquencies of Marxist phraseology, seem to have created a non-receptive mentality which failed to respond to Lenin's undoubted revolutionary genius. But, though Lenin shared the early illusions of his friends, he was the first to awake to the fact that they were impossible of realization.

So at this juncture, when the majority of the party refused to believe that, even with enough time and sufficient propagandist encouragement, the Bolsheviks of Europe would fail to follow the example of their Russian comrades and establish a dictatorship of their own, Lenin was on the verge of a great reversal of policy. While the others declared that propaganda activities must be intensified in all countries in order to profit by the change and slackening of the revolutionary *tempo*, he agreed, but for different reasons.

He was perfectly willing that the Governments should be vilified and the workers " educated ", that every opportunity should be used to expose the hypocrisy and flagrant brigandage of the Central Powers, and that

[1] *Izvestia*, January 2, 1918.

revolutionary propaganda should be intensified among the troops and the prisoners of war. All these were useful adjuncts in the diplomatic game, but they were nothing more than that. Lenin was beginning to realize that the world revolution was considerably further off than he, or anyone else, had ever suspected. On the other hand, the Revolution in Russia was in actual being, but by no means consolidated. It was threatened, seriously jeopardized, both by schisms within its own ranks and by the now reorganized forces of anti-Bolshevism. The world revolution was a dream which might in time be realized, the Russian Revolution was a fact which must at all costs be defended and consolidated, and to this end Lenin bent his mental efforts, leaving to Trotsky and his fellow enthusiasts the task of turning the conference at Brest-Litovsk into a sounding-board for the advocacy of Marxism and the gospel of revolution.

For it so happened that, both for achieving a world upheaval and for securing a breathing-space for the Russian Revolution, a policy of delay was necessary at Brest-Litovsk. The peace negotiations must be protracted by every possible means. Against the might of German militarism Russia had but one remaining weapon, the incalculable capacity of the Slav for interminable conversation, and this weapon Lenin was prepared to use to its utmost capacity while he prepared in secret for a strategic retreat.

Lenin realized that to achieve this end someone of heavier calibre than Joffe was required in charge of the operations. " To delay negotiations ", he said to Trotsky, " there must be someone to do the delaying." Trotsky agreed. " You'll do it, Lev Davidovitch ? " And again Trotsky agreed.[1] The history of Brest-Litovsk had taken on a new aspect.

The opening gambit in this new phase of the game was

[1] Trotsky, *Lenin*, p. 128 ; *My Life*, p. 311.

made on January 2, when to the returning delegates of the Central Powers there came a telegram from Petrograd proposing that the peace negotiations should be transferred to Stockholm, and declaring that the text of the two articles put forward in draft on December 28 was contrary to even that qualified formula of no annexations and no indemnities which had been accepted by the Central Powers on Christmas Day.[1]

But Kühlmann and Czernin were not to be caught thus easily. In Stockholm every international Socialist would be on their necks urging the conclusion of a democratic peace. Here in Brest-Litovsk, in the rigid atmosphere of military headquarters, they could both restrict those who visited the conference out of curiosity, and control, to some degree, the course of the negotiations. Their reply therefore was to threaten to break off all *pourparlers* and denounce the armistice agreement if the Russians did not return to Brest. This they followed up on January 5 with a further telegram to Petrograd stating that as Russia's Allies, the Entente, had failed to join in the negotiations for a general peace, the Quadruple Alliance was no longer bound by its declaration of December 25 accepting with reservations the Soviet peace formula.[2]

Two things were now clear and definite to the Bolsheviks : first, that the Central Powers had every intention of rejecting the formula of " no annexations and no indemnities " as a basis of negotiations, and, secondly, that the Soviet could no longer play off the willingness of the Central Powers to negotiate against the Entente's refusal. The Soviet attitude towards the Allies, therefore, changed. Though outwardly the stream of obloquy and abuse appeared to flow unchecked, in secret Trotsky began to sound out the reaction of the Entente to the possible rupture of negotiations with the Central Powers and the resumption of hostilities.

[1] *Proceedings*, p. 46.   [2] *Ibid.* p. 47.

These secret approaches to the Allies were hampered by the curious diplomatic situation which then obtained in Petrograd. The Allied Ambassadors and Ministers remained in the Russian capital but functioned in a vacuum, since no recognition of the Soviet régime had been accorded by their Governments. The Belgian Government had, early in January, considered getting into direct touch with the Council of Commissars and had sounded the Italians on the subject, but Sonnino was absolutely opposed to such a course and even forbade the Italian consular officials to visa passports issued by the Russian Foreign Office.[1] Great Britain, France, and the United States, however, though their Embassies had little or no contact with the Government, maintained relations by means of unofficial agents. Mr. Bruce Lockhart, a former British Consul-General in Moscow, was the most directly accredited of these agents. Lockhart had been appointed by the War Cabinet, on the recommendation of Lord Milner, with the sole purpose of keeping the British Government informed as to the situation in Russia ; in addition he carried to Trotsky credentials from Litvinov, written in a Lyons' shop in the Strand after a famous luncheon party. He had as his colleagues Colonel Raymond Robins, head of the American Red Cross in Russia, and Captain Jacques Sadoul, of the French Military Mission.

These agents derived both strength and weakness from their unofficial status. Unhampered by the strict rules of diplomatic etiquette and protocol, they could say and do much that was impossible for professional diplomats. They could and did establish intimate and friendly relations with the Bolshevik leaders, relations which would have been invaluable to their respective Governments had they had the wit to utilize them ; but their weakness lay in the fact that they spoke for themselves alone, could be disowned by their Governments, and could give no assurance to the

[1] *U.S. Foreign Relations*, 1918 : *Russia*, i. 332.

Bolsheviks that their Governments would even consider
the views and recommendations which they forwarded.
Despite these difficulties all these agents, and notably
Bruce Lockhart, the youngest of them—he was only thirty
in 1917—performed prodigies of skill in unofficial negotiations, and it was not their fault that their Governments
failed to profit by the sound advice which they gave.

In these early days of January Trotsky turned to
Colonel Robins—that strange idealistic figure in American
political life in whose veins flowed Red Indian blood—and
began the first of that series of halting approaches to the
Allied Powers which became so important a part of the
Brest-Litovsk saga.

" We have started our peace negotiations with the
Germans ", he said. " We have asked the Allies to join us
in starting peace negotiations for the whole world on a
democratic basis—the Allies have refused to accept our
invitation. We still hope, of course, to compel them."

" How ? " asked Robins.

" By stirring up the comrades in France and in England
and in America to upset the policy of their Governments
by asserting their own revolutionary Socialist will. We may
fail at it, in which case we shall continue negotiations with
the Germans alone. Germany, of course, will not want to
sign a democratic peace. Germany wants a peace with
annexations. *But we have the raw materials.* Germany needs
them. They are a bargaining point. If we can keep them
away from Germany we have an argument in reserve, a
big argument, perhaps a winning argument. *Therefore I
want to keep them away.*" Trotsky looked emphatically at
Robins. " *I want to keep them away.* But you know our
difficulties at the front. It is in chaos. But if you will send
your officers, American officers, Allied officers, any officers
you please, I will give them full authority to enforce the
embargo against goods into Germany all along our whole
line."

Robins realized the importance of the proposal. It meant that if the negotiations at Brest could be drawn out for several months, Germany and her allies would be cut off for the greater part of the winter from the raw materials of Russia which she so badly needed : the hides, the fats and oils, the nickel, copper, and lead, upon which she was counting for the final winter of the war, and to assist in the manufacture of munitions for the great spring offensive. Robins approached the official Allied diplomatic and military missions in Petrograd. He begged and pleaded with them to accept Trotsky's offer. But in vain. Official opinion was divided between a horrified distrust of the Bolsheviks and a sublime conviction that they would be swept from power in a few weeks by the united forces of the White Guards and the Cossacks, then mobilizing in the North and South. The diplomats refused to consider Robins' suggestion.

Only in one quarter did he succeed. The American military attaché and head of the military mission, General William V. Judson, was convinced of the importance of Trotsky's proposal. He went to confer with Trotsky about it, and, in his later report, concluded with the phrase " the time for protests and threats addressed to the Soviet authority is over, if it ever existed ". A few weeks later, however, he was recalled to America, and the German and Austrian commissions arrived in Petrograd to arrange for the resumption of commercial and economic relations.[1]

Robins, however, succeeded in one respect in arming himself with a potential weapon in the event of the resumption of hostilities by Russia. From Ambassador Francis he obtained two draft documents to be used only in such a contingency. In the first of these, entitled a " Suggested Communication to the Commissar for Foreign Affairs ",

[1] *Raymond Robins' Own Story*, pp. 66-70; *U.S. Foreign Relations*, 1918 : *Russia*, i. 279, 282-283, 288-289, 294-295.

Francis pledged himself to recommend the fullest possible assistance to Russia and the ultimate recognition of the Soviet Government in the event of a renewal of the war with Germany. The second document was a suggested cable to the State Department urging assistance and the immediate establishment of informal relations with the Soviet Government. Neither of these documents was ever sent, but they mark a slight success of Robins' efforts to mitigate the effects of a separate peace.[1]

By this time the issue with the Allies had become so involved and uncertain, that to Jacques Sadoul—who was unsuccessfully trying to persuade his Ambassador, M. Noulens, to give a similar declaration to that which Robins had secured from Francis—both Lenin and Trotsky stated their belief that France and Great Britain had given up all hope of victory on the Western Front and were negotiating secretly with Germany at the expense of Russia.[2] But before the peace *pourparlers* reopened at Brest-Litovsk on January 9 the Allies had themselves taken steps to clarify their position.

Pressure was being brought upon President Wilson from all sides to re-state on behalf of the Allies the objects for which they were fighting and their attitude towards Russia. Those who urged this course upon the President were actuated by a desire not to have the Bolsheviks enjoy the sole monopoly of peace formulae and to profit by the false position in which Germany's policy at Brest had placed her. It was believed that a statement by the President, declaring the desire of the Allied and Associated Powers for a democratic peace, would have the double purpose of checkmating Bolshevik propaganda based upon the refusal of the Allies to enter into peace negotiations, and perhaps of persuading Russia to stand by the Allies

[1] Cumming and Pettit, pp. 65-66 ; *Hearings on Bolshevik Propaganda before a Sub-committee of the Committee on the Judiciary, U.S. Senate, 65th Congress,* 1919, pp. 1009 *et seq.*   [2] Sadoul, pp. 176, 191.

in their defence of democratic and liberal principles. At the same time it was hoped that such a statement, widely circulated in Central Europe, would appeal to the growing antagonism of the German and Austrian Socialists to a war of conquest and annexation.

" If the President will restate anti-imperialistic war aims and democratic peace requisites of America, I can get it fed into Germany in great quantities and can utilize Russian version potently in army and everywhere ", cabled Edgar Sissons on January 3 to his chief, George Creel, of the National Committee on Public Information at Washington. " Obvious of course to you ", he continued, " that disclosure German trickery against Russia in peace negotiations promises to immensely open up our opportunities for publicity and helpfulness." [1]

The Allies also, concerned beyond measure at the exposure of their secret diplomacy by the publication of the secret treaties in Petrograd, urged Mr. Wilson to make his announcement. " Should the President himself make a statement of his own views, which, in view of the appeal made to the peoples of the world by the Bolsheviks, might appear a desirable course, the Prime Minister is confident that such a statement would also be in general accordance with the lines of the President's previous speeches, which in England as well as in other countries have been so warmly received by public opinion." In such discreetly indirect, yet clearly understandable, language did Mr. Balfour on January 5 convey the desire of Great Britain for the President's message.[2]

On the specific question of Russia Mr. Wilson received support even from Kerensky's Ambassador, George Bakhmetieff, who had a far more realistic grasp of the situation than his colleague, Maklakoff, in Paris. " Any evasion on the part of the Allies in the matter of peace ", he wrote to the President, " will simply strengthen the

[1] Cumming and Pettit, p. 67.   [2] House Papers, iii. 340.

Bolsheviks and help them to create an atmosphere unfriendly to the Allies." [1]

In compliance with these and other urgent requests,
Mr. Wilson on January 8 issued his memorable peace
proposals in an address to both houses of Congress. The
keynote of the speech and the subject of its first three
paragraphs were the negotiations of Brest-Litovsk and the
Russian peace formula. The Soviet representatives, whom
he termed " sincere and earnest ", had insisted, " very
justly, very wisely, and in the true spirit of modern democracy ", on full publicity in the negotiations, but had found
themselves confronted by representatives of the Quadruple
Alliance who seemed to represent not their Parliaments or
peoples but " that military and imperialistic minority
which has so far dominated their whole policy ". The voice
of the Russian people—" a voice more thrilling and compelling than any of the moving voices with which the
troubled world is filled "—called upon America and her
associates to say what it was they desired, and in what if
in anything they differed in purpose and spirit. " Whether
their present leaders believe it or not, it is our heartfelt
desire and hope that some way may be opened whereby
we may be privileged to assist the people of Russia to
attain their utmost hope of liberty and ordered peace."

The Fourteen Points followed, of which the Sixth related
to Russia :

VI. The evacuation of all Russian territory and such a settlement
of all questions affecting Russia as will secure the best and freest
co-operation of the other nations of the world in obtaining for her
an unhampered and unembarrassed opportunity for the independent
determination of her own political development and national policy
and assure her of a sincere welcome into the society of free nations
under institutions of her own choosing ; and, more than a welcome,
assistance also of every kind that she may need and may herself
desire. The treatment accorded Russia by her sister nations in the

---

[1] House Papers, iii. 330.

months to come will be the acid test of their good will, of their comprehension of her needs as distinguished from their own interests, and of their intelligent and unselfish sympathy.

On the day following the receipt in Petrograd of the text of the President's address, the city awoke to find it placarded upon the walls. It was printed on a hundred thousand Russian posters and on three hundred thousand Russian hand-bills. The American Y.M.C.A., availing itself of Bolshevik aid, distributed one million copies throughout the Russian lines, and another million, in German, within the German lines on the Eastern Front. Every newspaper carried it in full. For though the Bolsheviks distrusted Wilson's " empty phrases ", and made no secret in the columns of *Izvestia* of their distrust, the message was an admirable weapon of propaganda and they exploited it as such.

But despite this prodigal distribution, the Fourteen Points were destined to have little or no effect upon the Brest-Litovsk negotiations. They had no restraining influence upon the Soviet Government, for, while President Wilson was addressing the crowded Congress of the United States in Washington, Lenin at Smolny was travelling a strange road to a stranger Damascus. In the depths of his own soul he had reached the conviction that a separate peace with Germany was now inevitable. The revelation that the world revolution was not yet ripe for fruition had declared itself to him, and now, alone, and with fierce searchings of heart, he was preparing the enunciation of that bitter doctrine to the party. It would entail a policy of defeatism which it would be difficult to defend and which would meet with violent opposition both within the ranks of the Bolshevik Party itself and from their unwilling allies the Left Social Revolutionaries. For what Lenin had decided upon was no less than the temporary abandonment of world revolution to save the Russian Revolution. It was that principle of strategic defeat which he had had the courage to adopt when he saw his early hopes shattered in 1905, and which he was to adopt in 1921, when, against all previous conceptions of Marxism, he declared a "truce with Capitalism" and propounded the New Economic Policy. Lenin was not a slave of revolutionary orthodoxy. Just as the voices of the Maid of Orleans would whisper to her only what she herself had decided in any particular situation, so Karl Marx confirmed to Lenin the things which he himself felt to be necessary.

V

THE STALEMATE

V

THE STALEMATE

1

A CHANGE had come over the scene at Brest-Litovsk when the delegations reassembled there in the second week of January 1918. Within the ranks of the Central Powers grave dissension had broken out between the Big Three—Czernin, Kühlmann, and Hoffmann. The General and the Austrian Minister were for an increased *tempo* in the pace of the negotiations, the first actuated by a desire for troops, the second for bread. For though Hoffmann had broken with Ludendorff personally, and thenceforward only communicated with him through the medium of the Chief of the Operations Section, Colonel Bauer, he was still in accordance with the general policy of the Supreme Command in so far as it concerned the non-evacuation of the occupied areas and the speedy release of troops for use on the Western Front.

For Czernin it was the old story of bread, bread, bread. " Peace *must* be arranged, but a separate peace without Germany is impossible ", had been the sum-total of the conversations which he had had recently in Vienna.[1] His rôle, as he saw it, was to accelerate the signing of some kind of a treaty at all costs.

Neither of these policies appealed to Kühlmann ; in direct opposition to the Supreme Command, but with the tacit approval of the Kaiser, he was preparing to follow a policy of long-term negotiation in which he hoped first to demonstrate to the world that, stripped to its essentials,

[1] Czernin, p. 230.

Bolshevism was but a new form of nationalism, and, also, to secure ultimately the eastern territories for Germany under the guise of self-determination. He hoped to entrap the Russians in their own mysterious phrases, and it is not improbable that had he been pitted against the delegation as it was originally constituted, he might well have succeeded. But he was now to meet an adversary who was to prove his equal, if not his master, in the art of debate and dialectics. Leon Trotsky had come to Brest-Litovsk.

Broad-chested, his huge forehead surmounted by great masses of black waving hair ; his eyes strong and fierce, yet with traces of much human suffering about them ; heavy protruding lips, with their little beard and moustache, Trotsky was the very incarnation of the revolutionary in caricature. Dynamic and tireless, he was consumed with the flame of his ardour, uncompromising and bitter in opposition, fearless and scornful in defeat. Versatile, cultivated, and eloquent, he could be charming in his rare occasions of good-humour, but in his more usual attitude of contemptuous anger, he was a freezing fire. Mephistophelian, diabolically intelligent, diabolically scornful, he was destined to be both the Michael and the Lucifer of the Revolution. For it was his fate to command all the armies of Red Russia, and finally to be cast into outer darkness. " A four-kind son of a bitch, but the greatest Jew since Jesus Christ ", said Colonel Robins. " If the German General Staff bought Trotsky, they bought a lemon."

And so it proved, for no better quietus could have been asked for the " German agent " legend than Trotsky's conduct at the peace conference. But it was both a mental and physical ordeal for him. Never a good mixer, and always ill at ease when meeting strange and alien people, he approached the conference " as if being led to the torture-chamber ". There was something physically nauseating to him in the atmosphere of insincere courtesy and superficial convention which was part of the old-world diplomacy. His first contact with Kühlmann was illustrative of this. They met in the ante-room, where both were hanging up their hats and coats. Kühlmann recognized Trotsky, introduced himself, and, to put his adversary at his ease, said that he was very pleased to see him since it was always better to deal with the master than the emissary. " This made me feel exactly as if I had stepped on something unclean ", Trotsky records. " I even started back, involuntarily. Kühlmann realized his mistake, put himself on his guard, and his tone instantly became more formal." [1]

Moreover, Trotsky at the outset made clear that he came to the conference not to establish friendship but only to negotiate peace—he even objected to the inclusion of the word " friendship " in the preamble of the draft treaty— and he at once put a stop to the old *bonhomie* which had existed between the delegations. The new note was struck at the moment of the arrival of his special train, when Radek, drawing down the window, immediately began throwing out newspapers and propaganda pamphlets in German to the troops on the platform. Trotsky refused to be presented to the Prince of Bavaria and demanded that the Bolsheviks should eat alone, and not as formerly with the other delegates. (" He is putting them into a monastery ", wrote Kühlmann.) When Radek had a dispute with the German driver of his automobile and Hoffmann took the soldier's part, Trotsky forbade the use of cars to the Bolsheviks ; they were forced to walk, continually encountering notices written to warn prisoners of war, " Any Russian found in this place will be shot ". He exacted the most implicit obedience from his colleagues, none of whom was allowed to speak at the conference table without first having obtained his per-mission. " They have indeed a holy fear of Trotsky ", wrote Czernin in his diary.

But Trotsky was not the only new arrival at Brest.

[1] Trotsky, *My Life*, p. 314.

Count Adam Tarnowski had appeared as representative of the Polish Council of Regency, and, more important still, there had arrived a delegation of young men, hardly past their student years, who represented the Government of the Ukrainian *Rada*.

The recognition of Ukrainian autonomy had brought about the resignation of Prince Lvov and his Cadets from the Provisional Government at the moment of the Bolshevik rising in July 1917 ; the Ukrainians exercised their right of self-determination at the earliest opportunity after the Bolshevik coup. The election at the end of November had resulted in an overwhelming victory for the liberal national forces, giving them more than 75 per cent of the seats in the Assembly, and only 10 per cent to the Bolsheviks. The Bolsheviks then had recourse to their old policy of a direct appeal to the masses, and a congress of workers and peasants was summoned at Kiev. Contrary to the expectations of Smolny, out of the 2000 delegates assembled only 80 were Bolsheviks, the remainder being overwhelmingly in support of the Central *Rada*. The Bolshevik group seceded and set up a rival government at Kharkov where they bided their time and sought help from Petrograd.

In great jubilation, and very full of their own import-ance, a delegation of three young men, MM. Levitsky, Liubinsky, and Sevruk, set off for Brest, demanding a place at the conference table ; they harboured far-reaching plans for a greater Ukraine which envisaged the annexa-tion of the Ruthenian portions of Galicia and the Buko-vina, and the surrender by Austria of the district of Cholm.

The arrival of these tempestuous young men proved a source of considerable annoyance to Count Czernin. Apart from the natural personal humiliation at being called upon to negotiate with schoolboys, he was perturbed at the prospect of having to purchase Ukrainian grain for Austria by the cession of territory—which, in the case of Cholm, would earn him the undying hatred of the Austrian Poles —instead of obtaining it from Russia as a part of the general peace treaty. For a moment he scouted the idea of a separate treaty with the Ukraine, but ever in his mind was the sad knowledge that beggars cannot be choosers. Corn and peace he must have, and at any price.

By the same token the Germans were not sorry to welcome the young Ukrainian delegation. Both Kühlmann and Hoffmann realized that here was an added means of keeping Czernin in step with themselves, and also an additional weapon against Trotsky, who would certainly wish to avoid a separate peace between the Central Powers and a bourgeois State on Russian soil. Thus, as the Ukrainians showed no desire to follow the Bolsheviks into monastic retreat, they were welcomed to the common mess-table, courted and flattered.

On January 8 Kühlmann, Czernin, Talaat Pasha, and Popoff conferred together about their plan of campaign. The plenary session had been set for the following day and, acting on the principle that attack was the best method of defence, it was agreed not to let Trotsky talk at all, but to confront him immediately with an ultimatum on procedure. It was not anticipated that any opposition would be offered. The Russians dared not risk the resumption of hostilities. The German and Austrian officers who had accompanied Trotsky from Dvinsk reported that the trenches opposite to their positions were entirely empty and that, save for an outpost or two, there were no Russians left in that sector. Trotsky, they said, had arrived in the German lines deeply depressed at the military conditions which he had seen on his journey from Petrograd. One of the escort, Baron Lamezan, added his conviction that the Bolsheviks were altogether desperate now, having no choice save between a bad peace or no peace at all. " In either case ", he concluded, " the result will be the same ; they will be swept away." "*Ils n'ont que le choix à quelle sauce ils se feront manger*", remarked Kühlmann cynically to Czernin. "*Tout comme chez nous*", was the dejected reply.[1]

According to plan, therefore, Kühlmann led off on January 9 with a declaration that, as the Entente Powers had not seen fit to take part in the negotiations, the declarations made by the Central Powers on December 25 and 28 were null and void. He formally rejected the Soviet request for the transfer of the seat of negotiations to Stockholm, stating it to be " the fixed and unchangeable decision" of the Quadruple Alliance to conduct peace *pourparlers* only at Brest-Litovsk. Czernin followed, in the same vein, saying with equal emphasis that the Russians must now confine themselves to the question of a separate peace ; he demanded the immediate setting-up of the commissions for which provision had already been made, and warned the Russians that the responsibility for the continuation of the war would fall exclusively upon them. Talaat Pasha and Popoff associated themselves with the views of their colleagues, and then Hoffmann, on behalf of the military representatives of the Four Powers, protested vehemently against the flood of propaganda and incitement to mutiny which was continually disseminated by the Soviet Government.[2]

In the face of this barrage put down by his opponents, Trotsky, who had prepared a long harangue, asked for an adjournment. He made his reply on the following day (January 10) and treated his hearers to their first taste of his bitter contempt for them. Hoffmann's objections he dismissed with the remark that " neither the armistice conditions nor the character of the peace negotiations limited freedom of press or speech ". To Kühlmann he then reaffirmed Russia's refusal to accept the German view of self-determination for the people of the occupied territories, " by which the will of the people was in reality

[1] Czernin, pp. 232-233.   [2] *Proceedings*, pp. 51-56.

replaced by the will of a privileged group acting under the control of the authorities administering the territories " He confirmed the intention of the Soviet Government to continue negotiations for a separate peace and agreed to carry on those negotiations at Brest-Litovsk, protesting, however, that the atmosphere

at the headquarters of the enemy armies under the control of the German authorities creates all the disadvantages of an artificial isolation in no way compensated for by the enjoyment of a direct telephone wire. . . . We remain, therefore, at Brest-Litovsk, so that the slightest possibility of peace may not be left unexhausted. . . . Our Government has placed at the head of its program the word " Peace ", but it has engaged itself at the same time before its people to sign only a democratic and a just peace.[1]

At the outset, therefore, both sides had stated their case with admirable clearness, and it was obvious from the first that the chasm dividing them was unbridgeable, yet for four mortal weeks did Kühlmann and Trotsky circle round each other like duellists upon a cloak, debating the ethics, forms, and principles of self-determination and its application to the border states. Trotsky demanded a full referendum taken without the presence of foreign military forces. Kühlmann refused to consider the evacuation of German troops, and claimed that the occupied territories had already declared their will through the bodies created under the auspices of *Ober Ost* (the German Administration of Occupied Territories in the East). To this Trotsky replied : " We are realists as well as revolutionaries, and we should prefer to talk directly about annexations, rather than to replace their real name with a pseudonym ". At the word " annexation " Kühlmann would recoil, and would again develop his theory of self-determination until once more brought up short before the facts by Trotsky ; *e da capó*.

[1] *Proceedings*, pp. 61-63.

Their debates travelled from Dan to Beersheba, and from China to Peru, embracing such apparent irrelevancies as the degree of dependence of the Nizam of Hyderabad upon the British Crown, and the scope and powers of the Supreme Court of the United States. In general dialectics, the two opponents were effectually matched, but in tactics Kühlmann was the better man. He headed Trotsky into recognizing the delegates of the Ukrainian *Rada* as participants in the negotiations and representatives of an independent State; and immediately took him up on his proposal to allow representatives of the border States to come to Brest and express their views without let or hindrance. He would be delighted to welcome the delegates, Kühlmann said, but on one condition, namely that Trotsky should accept their judgement, if in favour of Germany, as valid. Trotsky withdrew his suggestion, which must have given Kühlmann much secret relief; for had, for example, the Poles been allowed to speak their minds, their anti-Prussian feelings would have been embarrassing. Trotsky, however, restrained by none of the finer feelings of the professional diplomatist, scored again and again with barbed references to the violation of Belgian neutrality, unrestricted U-boat warfare, and kindred subjects.

These prolonged discussions, while engrossing to the participants, were positively infuriating to the onlookers. The Turks and Bulgarians, junior partners in the Quadruple Alliance and perhaps thus accustomed to be kept waiting, sustained with comparative equanimity the display of manœuvre and counter-manœuvre which did not affect any of their vital interests. But to Czernin and to Hoffmann the delay was insufferable. The nerves of the Austrian Foreign Minister became frayed. To have to listen day by day to these seemingly endless " spiritual wrestling matches " while the sands of his country's life were running out, reduced him to a state of almost hysterical prostration. Daily the news from Vienna and Budapest grew worse;

almost hourly the slim margin between possible victory and certain defeat shrank more and more. His attempted interventions, his efforts to effect a compromise between the German and Russian theses, were brushed aside by both Kühlmann and Trotsky, who by this time were interested only in each other. Despairingly Czernin went hunting with the Prince of Bavaria and turned for solace, somewhat strangely, to the collection of memoirs of the French Revolution which he had brought with him to Brest; he found relief in making entries in his diary such as: " Charlotte Corday said: ' It was not a man, but a wild beast I killed ' . . . who can say if there will be a Corday ready for Trotsky ? " [1]

The relationship between Czernin and Kühlmann was becoming anything but friendly. The German was contemptuous of his colleague's nervous flutterings, and could not resist giving, every now and then, a reminder of the reverses which the Austrians had received at the hands of the Russians. " *Our* German territory, thank God, is not being held by foreign troops anywhere ", he declared one day at the conference, stretching himself and giving a glance at Czernin, whose " face went green and . . . figure shrank ". Such scenes, Trotsky records, were frequent.[2]

To Hoffmann, too, the delay was intolerable. He had been opposed to these tactics from the start and had wished to go straight forward with a series of ultimata. " Give them another touch of the whip ", he urged Kühlmann at their conference on the evening of January 10, after Trotsky had accepted their preliminary conditions. Kühlmann insisted, however, upon the policy of *suaviter in modo* and Czernin at that moment agreed with him. High words passed between them and Hoffmann, and the affair seemed to emphasize the lack of harmony within the ranks of the Central Powers.[3]

[1] Czernin, p. 227.   [2] Trotsky, *My Life*, p. 314.
[3] Czernin, p. 235.

At Kreuznach, Ludendorff sat—in his own words—upon " the fiery coals of impatience ". Through Bauer he demanded an explanation from Hoffmann of the delay, and when he learned of it, he cursed Kühlmann by all his gods and ordered Hoffmann to break the deadlock. Accordingly, at their regular meeting, the next evening (January 11), Hoffmann pointed out to Kühlmann and to Czernin the impossibility of gaining any advantage from a series of debates which had wandered further and further from the original subject of discussion. It was absolutely necessary, he represented, to bring the negotiations back to a basis of fact, and he offered to make clear to the Russians what the situation really was, and why they were assembled there.[1]

Czernin, torn between his natural distrust of Hoffmann's methods, which he feared might bring about a rupture in the negotiations, and the prospect of sitting and listening endlessly to the continuous disputations, finally came down on the side of the General and gave his consent. Kühlmann had no real objections, for he was privately convinced that Hoffmann's methods would get them no further than his own, but he considered it possible that a fighting speech by Hoffmann would improve his relations with Ludendorff, and, though Kühlmann had no love for the Supreme Command, he could not but realize the unsatisfactory position of having as his colleague a man who was not on speaking terms with his own superiors. It was therefore agreed that, without preliminaries, Kühlmann would, at the psychological moment, give Hoffmann the floor.

The moment arrived sooner than any of them had expected. On the following morning, January 12, the Russians had decided to bring forward some concrete proposals, and Trotsky had entrusted the task of presenting them to Kamenev ; in a long speech, in no way compli-

[1] Hoffmann, ii. 211.

mentary to the Central Powers, he proposed a series of regulations for the evacuation of the occupied territories and the organization of popular plebiscites to be held both in them, and in the other border States outside the zone of occupation, namely in Estonia and Livonia. The scheme was to be conditional on the agreement that

Russia binds herself not to exercise direct or indirect pressure on these territories to accept a particular form of government, and not to restrict their independence by any tariff or military conventions concluded before the regions are finally established as the basis of their right to political self-determination. The Governments of Germany and Austria-Hungary, on their part, categorically confirm the absence of any claims either to annex the territories of the former Russian Empire now occupied by their armies, or the so-called frontier "rectifications" at the expense of these regions.

Germany and Austria were also to accept the same pledge as that given by Russia in respect of the territories lying outside the area of occupation.[1]

These proposals, put forward with the object of driving the enemy into a corner and forcing him to declare himself, took the conference completely by surprise. To the Quadruple Alliance it appeared as if the Russians were imagining themselves victorious before the gates of Berlin and Vienna, and dictating terms to their defeated foes. It was always a source of annoyance to them that the Soviet representatives, after Trotsky's arrival, would never realize their rôle of a country suing for peace.

Kamenev's speech was followed by complete silence. Then, without further comment, Kühlmann said quietly : " General Hoffmann has the floor."

This was Hoffmann's big moment, the moment for which he had prepared with diligence and care. He was angered by Kamenev's remarks, and his own became

[1] *Proceedings*, pp. 80-82; *Mirnye peregovory v Brest-Litovske* (Moscow, 1920), i. 92-94.

perhaps slightly harsher in reply than he had originally intended. Perfectly controlled, he spoke in short staccato tones, without any gestures to emphasize his points. We have the word of all his colleagues that the famous thumping upon the table with his fist is as mythical as the story that he frequently put his spurred boots upon it.

After protesting against the tone of Kamenev's speech, the General pointed out that, though they talked loudly of self-determination, the Soviet Government, " based purely on violence, ruthlessly suppressing all who think differently ", had themselves denied that right to the White Russians and Ukrainians, breaking up their Constituent Assemblies with bayonets and machine-guns. In addition, the Russian Government had not ceased to violate those provisions of the armistice agreement which prohibited the interference of the Bolsheviks in the internal affairs of the Central Powers. Their agents were continually disseminating propaganda. " The German High Command therefore considered it necessary to prevent any attempt to interfere in the affairs of the occupied territories. . . . Also, for reasons of a technical and administrative nature, the German High Command must refuse to evacuate Courland, Lithuania, Riga, and the Islands of the Gulf of Riga." [1]

The effect of the General's speech was anything but what he had hoped for or expected. It did not even bring about a reconciliation with the Supreme Command, for, though Ludendorff signified his approval of Hoffmann's remarks and urged upon him the necessity for greater speed, he did not abandon the method of indirect communication through the Chief of the Operations Section. [2] Kühlmann and Czernin were frankly distressed at the speech, which in brutal frankness had gone far beyond what they had anticipated, and they did not conceal from Hoffmann that he had gained nothing by it beyond exciting

[1] *Proceedings*, pp. 82-83 ; *Mirnye peregovory v Brest-Litovske*, i. 94-95.   [2] Hoffmann, ii. 213.

public opinion at home against them.[1] For, indeed, the only concrete result of the speech was a chorus of indignation in German and Austro-Hungarian newspapers reflecting the views of those who still believed in a peace of understanding and the principles of the Peace Resolution of July 1917.[2] In addition, Hoffmann had presented the propaganda agencies of the Entente with a welcome and magnificent example of Prussian militarism, naked and unadorned, of which they took full advantage.

As for embarrassing Trotsky—the Soviet Commissar had actually smiled during Hoffmann's diatribe. His brilliant dark eyes sparkled as he listened, leaning a little forward in his chair, his hands draped upon the conference table before him. For the moment he was entirely happy, for he knew what could be done with the General's sentiments both at Brest and at Petrograd. His reply was bitter and incisive. In a society based on classes, he told Hoffmann, every government rests on force. The only difference was that the General's friends applied repression to protect big-property owners, whereas the Bolsheviks applied it in defence of the workers. " What surprises and repels the governments of other countries ", continued Trotsky, " is that we do not arrest strikers, but capitalists who subject workers to lock-outs ; that we do not shoot peasants who demand land, but arrest the land-owners and officers who try to shoot the peasants."[3]

After this lesson in elementary Marxism, Trotsky proceeded to deal with the more specific of Hoffmann's charges, namely the circulation of propaganda in Germany. This he did not deny, but pointed out that German newspapers had free access to Russia, whatever their views, yet the Soviet Government did not find it possible to demand the curtailment of even that part of the press which supported the views of General Hoffmann. " There is no doubt that

[1] Czernin, p. 237. [2] Ludendorff, ii. 552.
[3] Trotsky, *My Life*, pp. 319-320.

the support which our reactionary circles are receiving by certain declarations by German official circles is doing much to continue civil war in our country, but we do not find it possible to connect this question with the conditions of the armistice." [1]

Kühlmann intervened to say that it was Germany's settled principle not to interfere in the internal affairs of Russia, and Trotsky scoffed at him for thus abandoning the moral offensive. He would regard it as a step forward, he said, if the German Government would freely and frankly express their views regarding the internal position in Russia.

Here was a challenge which Kühlmann, had he taken it up, might have used to his advantage. Had he accepted Trotsky's invitation to speak his mind on the internal affairs of Russia, he could have turned the tables on his adversary and redeemed to some extent Germany's position in the eyes of the world. Instead of allowing Trotsky to brand Germany as a hypocrite, a liar, and a brigand, he could have unmasked the Bolsheviks as the enslavers of the minds of men and the destroyers of the social fabric of civilization. Had Kühlmann taken his stand, publicly and unreservedly, on the principle that Germany conceived it to be her right and her duty to protect the peoples who had seen fit to free themselves from the chaos of revolutionary Russia, he could have capitalized the existing and steadily growing fear of Bolshevism in the countries of the Entente. Germany, as the champion of Western civilization, protecting the border States from civil war, rapine, and bloody murder, as a bulwark against the spread of Bolshevism across Europe, would have been in an infinitely stronger position, both within and without, than Germany, the apostle of *Machtpolitik*, deliberately perverting the principle of self-determination to cover a policy of annexation. The propaganda of the Entente

[1] *Proceedings*, p. 90.

would have been robbed of one of its most effective weapons, and even the objections of the Supreme Command might have been overcome, since there could have been no question of subsequently abandoning the border States to the tender mercies of Bolshevism.

But Kühlmann allowed this golden opportunity to escape him, and plunged anew into his theoretical disputations with Trotsky in which he had lost the advantage. Nothing could now possibly be expected from these protracted debates save benefit to the enemy ; for, as a result of Hoffmann's brutal frankness, the Central Powers now stood self-convicted before their opponents and before the world. The Master Voice of Germany had spoken— Hoffmann had proclaimed the fact that he represented not the German Government but the Supreme Command, and no further doubts could be entertained either as to its power or its intentions. For Germany it would have been better to force the issue from that moment and proceed with a series of ultimata.

For Trotsky, however, the position was quite the reverse. His strategy had been wholly successful. Not only was Kühlmann apparently ready to play indefinitely the Bolshevik game of delaying tactics, but Trotsky had been able to persuade the Germans to unmask themselves. Under these circumstances, even Ludendorff is forced to admit, he would have been a fool to have given way on any point.[1] From Germany and from Austria came tidings of the rapidly deteriorating internal situation. Trotsky, too, had his illusions. Surely now, with a little more delay, proletarian revolutions would shatter the empires of the Hohenzollerns and the Habsburgs. In the days that followed he kept the game in his own hands, playing it with the technique of a master, never missing a trick, never going too far. But his tone became more and more provoking. He patronized Czernin, he baited Hoffmann,

[1] Ludendorff, ii. 552.

and finally he goaded the unwilling Kühlmann into the open admission that the German Government could not undertake any obligation to recall its army from the occupied territories, even a year after the conclusion of a general peace.[1] In the intervals of these activities, this indefatigable man found time to pay a visit to Warsaw and to dictate from memory a historical sketch of the November Revolution (*The History of the Russian Revolution to Brest-Litovsk*), which, until its prohibition by Stalin in 1924, remained in all languages a standard work on the subject.

Single-handed, with nothing behind him save a country in chaos and a régime scarce established, this amazing individual, who a year before had been an inconspicuous journalist exiled in New York, was combating successfully the united diplomatic talent of half Europe.

2

Hoffmann himself realized that his contribution to the negotiations had had no practical effect and that he was unable to stem the flow of Trotsky's eloquence or of Kühlmann's argumentation. He was, however, undaunted in his efforts to speed up matters, and turned to the other device open to him—negotiation with the representatives of the Ukrainian *Rada*. Ever since their arrival at Brest on January 7, Hoffmann had recognized the potential usefulness of these young men and had taken them under his wing, though perhaps a cat protecting a canary would be a more apt description. He encouraged the Ukrainian delegates to talk to him of their plans and hopes, and, being as able a tactician at the conference board as on the field, though a poorer strategist, he gained their confidence and their respect.

The three original delegates had been joined by M. Wsewolod Holubowicz, the President of the Council of

[1] *Proceedings*, pp. 109-110.

Ministers, thirty-four years of age and full of the fervour of national and social revolution. The declaration of the *Rada*—stating its willingness to negotiate peace with the Central Powers and its independence of the Soviet régime in Petrograd—had been presented by this youthful statesman to the conferençe on January 10, and accepted both by Kühlmann on behalf of the Quadruple Alliance and by Trotsky—though the formal recognition by the Four Powers of the Ukrainian Republic as an independent State was reserved for the peace treaty.[1]

Thereafter the young Ukrainians, like the remainder of the delegates at Brest-Litovsk, merely swelled the gallery at the " spiritual wrestling-matches ", but, as they had been recognized as not forming a part of the Soviet delegation, care was taken to keep them segregated as much as possible from the Bolsheviks, a fact against which Trotsky made protest.[2]

When, however, on January 14, it became evident that these rhetorical displays were to continue *ad nauseam*, Hoffmann approached Czernin and suggested that, with the Count's authority, he should open private negotiations with the Ukrainians and discover what terms of peace they contemplated. Czernin gave his consent not unwillingly ; he was really a sick man now and in no shape to argue with hare-brained young revolutionaries; moreover he was receiving almost daily from Vienna reports of the food-crisis arising out of the incapacity of his Austrian and the egotism of his Hungarian colleagues.

The Ukrainians, who had talked at first so freely of their general plans, were uncommunicative when it came to dealing with hard facts. Hoffmann was patient, however, and with the assistance of his Intelligence Officer, Major Hey, who acted as interpreter (Hoffmann spoke and wrote Russian but not Ukrainian, and the young men

[1] *Proceedings*, pp. 56-59, 63-64, 88-89 ; *Mirnye peregovory v Brest-Litovske*, i. 44-48.   [2] *Proceedings*, pp. 84-85.

refused to talk any language but their own), he elicited
that their claims extended to the districts round Cholm,
and also the Ruthenian portions of Galicia and the
Bukovina.

Normally the Cholm district would have been included
in the Polish State when its frontiers were delimited,
though its eastern fringe is Ukrainian. But Hoffmann, with
his soldier's realism, had never entertained the idea of an
independent Poland as anything more than a Utopian
dream; certainly, the claims of a non-existent State were
not to be considered as an obstacle to a Ukrainian peace,
and, on his own authority, he promised the delegates of
the *Rada* his support in their claim to the Cholm area.

With regard to their demands of parts of Galicia and
the Bukovina, Hoffmann assumed a very different tone.
This, he let the young men know, was a piece of impudence
which was not even to be considered. They must be crazy
if they thought they were in a position to force Austria to
cede territory to them. MM. Liubynski and Sevruk were
not greatly put out at his curtness, and with considerable
amiability agreed to seek new instructions from Kiev, the
probability being that their demands for the cession of
territory by Austria had been in the nature of a "try-on".[1]

Czernin was none too pleased with the results of
Hoffmann's mission when the latter reported to him. The
cession of Cholm to the Ukraine would inevitably embroil
the Austrian Government with the Poles, and would
imperil, if not completely wreck, the "Austrian Solution"
of the Polish problem, in which certain of the diplomats in
Vienna and Berlin still had faith. But Czernin was in no
position to argue or to disagree. The attitude and policy of
the Austrian and Hungarian Prime Ministers, against
which Czernin had so often and so earnestly warned the
Emperor Karl, had now resulted in a situation where the
principal cities of the Empire were faced with actual

[1] Hoffmann, ii. 213-214.

famine. City after city sent in its tale of hunger and revolt. "The people are starving", wailed the Prince-Bishop of Cracow. "Our bread rations are reduced by half", telegraphed the Stathalter from Trieste. "Vienna has only flour enough to last till Monday", telephoned the Burgomaster.[1]

The men whose errors had brought about the crisis now appealed to Czernin for assistance (January 16). "It is only from Germany that effective aid for the capital of the Empire can arrive in time, and that only if supplies are despatched at once", telegraphed Dr. Seidler, the Austrian Premier, who only a few weeks before had stated positively that the country could hold out till the new harvest. "We have no choice but to inform Your Excellency of all this and to beg you in due course to call the attention of the German Delegation to the uncommonly critical state of affairs which unforeseen difficulties may easily turn into a catastrophe." The Prime Minister added, by telephone, that no question excited the people so much as the negotiations at Brest, the will for peace being strongly in the ascendant.

This was in fact an understatement. The strike movement round Vienna, which had begun originally as a political demonstration actuated by hunger, swiftly developed into a public demand for the speedy conclusion of peace. At first only a movement among unorganized labour, it spread like a prairie fire to the ranks of the trade unions, which the leaders were powerless to check.

Czernin rose nobly to the emergency. Racked by high fever, his nervous system already in a state bordering on collapse, the Foreign Minister did all that he humanly could to meet the crisis. He urged the Emperor Karl to

[1] Gustav Gratz and Richard Schüller, *The Economic Policy of Austria-Hungary during the War* (New Haven, 1928), p. 93. (Dr. Gratz was *chef de cabinet* to Count Czernin, and Professor Schüller Director of the Austrian Ministry of Commerce, during the Brest-Litovsk Conference.)

appeal personally to Kaiser Wilhelm ; he humbled himself before Kühlmann and begged his assistance with the German authorities ; he even performed the supreme act of humiliation and besought help from the Bulgarians. But his efforts met with scant success. Ludendorff declared that under no circumstances could he contribute anything from his army stores, and the Imperial German Food Control Office replied that they were quite unable to help since they were on the point of reducing the flour ration in Germany. The Bulgarian Government found it impossible to send even a few trucks of grain to Vienna, but took the opportunity to urge that peace with Russia, and especially the Ukraine, must be concluded immediately, even at the cost of great sacrifices. Finally there came to Czernin, on January 17, a distracted message from the Emperor Karl at Laxenburg :

I must once more earnestly impress upon you that the whole fate of the Monarchy and of the dynasty depends on peace being concluded at Brest-Litovsk as soon as possible. We cannot over-throw the situation here for the sake of Courland, Livonia and Polish dreams. If peace be not made at Brest, there will be revolution here, be there ever so much to eat. This is a serious instruction at a serious time.[1]

Was there ever such an ironically cruel situation as that in which Czernin now found himself ? The food crisis in Austria was eventually met by forced drafts of grain from Hungary, Poland, and Rumania, and by a last moment contribution from Germany of 450 truck-loads of flour, but the desperate methods to which the Austrian Government had been forced to resort had effectually destroyed its diplomatic influence in the peace negotiations. Friend and foe alike now knew the weakness of the Dual Monarchy—that it existed on the charity and largesse of its allies. Through their negligence and folly the Austrian Ministry had proclaimed to the world the final passing of

[1] Czernin, pp. 237-240 ; Gratz and Schüller, pp. 93-98.

Habsburg glory. Implored by his sovereign to accelerate the conclusion of peace, Czernin was at the same time robbed of the last bargaining factor which he possessed. Events at home had weakened him—and this at a most critical moment—both as regards his relations with his German allies and his attitude towards his Russian opponents. He was required to exert pressure upon Germany, but was deprived of his only influence in this direction—the threat of a separate Austro-Russian peace— by the fact that it would imperil the chance of further food supplies from Germany, the more so since Hoffmann had told him bluntly that it was immaterial whether Austria-Hungary made peace or not. Despite the fact that Czernin demanded not a rouble nor square mile from Russia, he was now irrevocably riveted to the wheels of the German chariot of annexation.

With the Ukrainians, on the other hand, he had to strive for a peace settlement under the most acceptable conditions in order to put an end to the food difficulties at home, well knowing that the Ukrainians were perfectly informed about the food situation and labour troubles in Vienna, and would make their price accordingly high.

Faced with this bitter combination of humiliating impotence and the necessity for great political sacrifices, and battling heroically with his own ill-health, Czernin prepared to continue, with the assistance of Hoffmann, his negotiations with the *Rada* delegates. Liubynski and Sevruk had received new instructions from Kiev which, though they abandoned the claim for the cession of any part of Galicia and the Bukovina, and merely demanded that these Ruthenian territories should be formed into an independent province under the Habsburgs, still regarded the cession of the Cholm districts as a *conditio sine qua non*.

Czernin's position was difficult. Apart from the undying hatred of the Poles which he would incur if he conceded Cholm to the Ukrainians, the handing-over of the district without consulting the population was fundamentally opposed to the principle of self-determination, to which he was nominally pledged. Conversely, by agreeing to the creation of Ruthenian provinces he would introduce the principle of self-determination into the polyglot Austro-Hungarian Empire. But, if the parlous condition of Austria weakened Czernin's hand, it also simplified the issue. He could no longer afford to debate with himself, or with anybody else, the ethics of self-determination, its wisdom or its folly. What he wanted, and what he must have, was Ukrainian grain, without which, according to the hysterical messages from Seidler, thousands would be perishing within a few weeks. On January 18, through Hoffmann, he agreed to the conditions of the *Rada* in principle, reserving the right to refer the final decision to the Austrian Cabinet in Vienna. " I cannot, and dare not," he wrote in his diary, " look on and see hundreds of thousands starve for the sake of retaining the sympathy of the Poles, so long as there is a possibility of help." [1]

But the threat of starvation was not only on one side. One of the chief reasons for the opposition of Trotsky to a separate peace with the Ukraine was that it would entail the deflection of the flow of grain from the northward to the westward. Russia was desperately short of food and fodder, not only in the hinterland but in what remained of the army. " Immediate help is necessary ", cried the official wireless from Tsarskoe Selo on January 15. " The army which is standing patiently and bravely on guard for the freedom of the country is perishing from famine. Their provisioning has ceased. Several regiments are entirely without bread ; horses are without fodder." [2] Despite the gravity of the situation, its propaganda value was not wasted by Moscow, and Radek, in a signed article, on the same day took advantage of the food shortage to

[1] Hoffmann, ii. 214-215 ; Czernin, pp. 240-241.
[2] *Izvestia*, January 15, 1918.

FIELD-MARSHAL VON LUDENDORFF

LENIN

MAJOR-GENERAL MAX HOFFMAN

Chief of Staff to the Commander-in-Chief in the East

ARRIVAL OF THE RUSSIAN DELEGATION AT BREST-LITOVSK

1, Major Brinckmann. 2, Joffe. 3, Mme. Bizenko. 4, Kamenev. 5, Karachan

From "Brest-Litovsk" by Theodor Kröger (Verlag Ullstein, Berlin)

ARMISTICE NEGOTIATIONS AT BREST-LITOVSK

1, Hoffmann.   2, Altvater.   3, Fokke.

From "Brest-Litovsk" by Theodor
Krüger (Verlag Ullstein, Berlin)

BARON VON KÜHLMANN

KAMENEV

TROTSKY ARRIVING AT THE CONFERENCE

COUNT CZERNIN AND BARON VON KHÜLMANN
AT BREST-LITOVSK

THE SIGNING OF THE UKRAINIAN PEACE TREATY

1, Hoffmann (*standing in uniform*).   2, Czernin.   3, Kühlmann.

*From "Brest-Litovsk" by Theodor
Kröger (Verlag Ullstein, Berlin)*

LEON TROTSKY

SOKOLNIKOV

KARAKHAN

A WALK-OVER?

The Kaiser. "THIS IS THE DOORMAT OF OUR NEW PREMISES."
Emperor Karl. "ARE YOU QUITE SURE IT'S DEAD?"

GENERAL SKOROPADSKY (centre) WITH HINDENBURG AND LUDENDORFF

AT SPA, SEPTEMBER 1918

RADEK

belabour the Kiev Government. " If you want food, cry
' Death to the *Rada* ! ' . . . The *Rada* has dug its grave by
its Judas-like treachery." [1]

In the meantime the doctrinal discussions between
Kühlmann and Trotsky had reached a point of exhaustion.
Trotsky realized that the progress made in the negotiations
with the Ukrainians, which he had been unable to control,
seriously menaced his position, and in addition, he was
anxious to return to Petrograd (where the Constituent
Assembly was due to open in the near future) for a more
intimate exchange of views with Lenin than was possible
over the private wire from Brest-Litovsk. He was not yet
prepared to give up the battle, but a brief interval would
delay matters still further, and he was anxious to gain
Lenin's approval for a new line of policy which should
confound the Germans and yet save the Bolshevik face.

Kühlmann also apparently thought that such use as
these discussions had ever had was exhausted, and therefore proposed to force the issue, assigning once more to
Hoffmann the task of speaking out. On January 18 the
Secretary of State, reverting to many previous arguments,
emphasized the German reservation that the people of
the occupied territories were not sufficiently experienced
politically for popular referenda to be held, and that the
institutions already in existence must be developed for this
purpose. What must be prevented at all costs was the spread
of revolution to these regions, already sufficiently devastated
by war. Trotsky sarcastically enquired as to the exact area
to be embraced by the German principle of self-determination. For answer the Secretary of State turned to Hoffmann,
who spread a great staff map upon the table. A blue line,
which the General indicated with his thumb as he explained
the position, ran north from Brest-Litovsk to the Baltic,
demonstrating the future frontier between Germany and
Russia. It separated from the old Russian Empire most

[1] *Pravda,* January 15, 1918.

of what is now Poland, all modern Lithuania, western Latvia, the city of Riga and the Moon Sound Islands.

" What principles guided you, General, in drawing this line ? " Trotsky asked ironically.

" The indicated line is dictated by military considerations ; it assures the people living on this side of the line a tranquil organization of State life and the realization of the right of self-determination ", was Hoffmann's reply.

Further explanations followed. In reply to Trotsky's question as to the delimitation of the occupied areas to the south of Brest, Hoffmann replied that this matter would be discussed with the Ukrainian delegates. Trotsky remarked that it would also require an agreement between the Soviet Government and the Ukraine. In answer to a query of Kühlmann's concerning the relations between the Caucasus and the Petrograd Government, he said : " The army of the Caucasus is completely under the command of officers unqualifiedly devoted to the Soviet of People's Commissars. This was confirmed about two weeks ago by the Congress of Delegates at the Caucasian Front."

Rather than make any expression of opinion on the merits of the case Trotsky made a general declaration to the conference :

The position of our opponents is now absolutely clear. Germany aṇd Austria wish to cut off more than 150,000 square versts from the Polish Kingdom of Lithuania,[1] also the area populated by the Ukrainians and White Russians, and further their line cuts in two the territory of the Letts and separates the Estonian Islands from the same people on the main land. Within these territories Germany and Austria wish to retain. their reign of military occupation, not only after the conclusion of peace with Russia, but also after the conclusion of a general peace. At the same time the Central Powers refuse to give any explanation regarding the time and conditions of evacuation. Thus the internal life of these lies for an indefinite period

[1] Trotsky obviously referred to the historic Grand Duchy of Lithuania, in which the upper classes were Polonized, but the vast majority of the population were White Russian and Lithuanian.

in the hands of these Powers. Under these conditions, it is clear that any indefinite guarantees regarding the expression of will by the Poles, Lithuanians, and Letts will prove illusory, and that means that the Governments of Austria and Germany take into their hands the destiny of these nations. . . .

As a parting shot he added :

It is clear that the decisions could have been reached long ago regarding peace aims if the Central Powers had not stated their terms differently from those expressed by General Hoffmann.

" If General Hoffmann expressed these terms more strongly ", replied Kühlmann suavely, " it is because a soldier always uses stronger language than diplomats. But it must not be deduced from this that there is any dissension between us regarding the principles, which are a well-thought-out whole." [1]

Faced with this new situation, Trotsky at first threatened to break off the discussions. Kühlmann meditated an ultimatum, and both possibilities nearly threw Czernin into nervous prostration. At last, however, a compromise was reached. Negotiations were adjourned to enable Trotsky to go to Petrograd, but he undertook to return by January 29. He left on the night of the 18th, taking with him Hoffmann's map as evidence.

3

On the night of January 18, while Trotsky's train sped north-eastwards towards Petrograd, an event was taking place in that capital which was to affect materially the negotiations at Brest-Litovsk. The Constituent Assembly was being dissolved.

In the days following the March Revolution, when the Bolsheviks were in opposition to the Provisional Government, they had joined with the Socialist and bourgeois

[1] *Proceedings*, pp. 113-116 ; *Mirnye peregovory v Brest-Litovske*, i. 97-130 ; Judah P. Magnes, *Russia and Germany at Brest-Litovsk* (New York, 1919), pp. 92-94.

parties in attacking Prince Lvov, and later Kerensky, for their delay in convoking the Constituent Assembly. Lenin had realized at once the popular appeal of a national democratic gathering and capitalized it as a matter of tactics. Constituent Assemblies had no place in the orthodox Marxian doctrine which recognized only the dictatorship of the proletariat, but Lenin had never any qualms as to the weapons he used. To the Bolsheviks the Assembly was a stick with which to beat the Provisional Government, and at the same time they urged the seizure of power by the Soviets, as the best way of ensuring the calling of the Assembly.

Once their own dictatorship had been established the attitude of the Bolsheviks towards the Constituent Assembly radically altered. This had become the rallying-ground of all the elements, Right, Left, and Centre, who wished to encompass the downfall of Soviet dictatorship. But the Bolsheviks were not agreed among themselves as to whether the elections for the Assembly should be held. The more extreme faction were for suspending them altogether, and leaving the Assembly a dead letter. Sverdlov and others, on the contrary, believed that the party was as yet too weak to ignore the popular demand for the Assembly, and that by its postponement the Soviet Power, of which the country as a whole was still ignorant, would be further weakened.

What Lenin thought is not known, for he left no record of his personal views, and there is only the conflicting evidence of his two great commentators.[1] According to Trotsky, he was in favour of postponing the elections, of enlarging the electorate by lowering the voting age to

[1] Lenin's theses on the Constituent Assembly, published in *Pravda* on January 8, 1918, give little clue to his private opinion regarding the advisability of convoking that body ; they merely emphasize the discrepancy between the views of the Assembly and those of the Soviet Power and indicate the inevitability of a clash between the two.

eighteen, and of making a new list of electors, which would include the workers and peasants as well as the intellectuals. He was also in favour of outlawing the Cadets and the supporters of Kornilov. In answer to Sverdlov, who opposed postponement, Lenin declared that it would be a definite step backward if the elections were held at that time with the old voters' lists and resulted in a victory for the Mensheviks, Cadets, and Social Revolutionaries of the Right.[1] Stalin, on the other hand, declares that Lenin favoured the calling of the Assembly in order to compromise it with the masses, on the principle that Bolshevik co-operation was justified in order to make it easier for the proletariat to instruct the backward masses as to why such Parliaments should be broken and " to drive another nail into the coffin of bourgeois parliamentarianism ".[2] In any case, whether Lenin's personal feelings were favourable or not, the Central Executive Committee decided to permit the elections, while preparing to maintain itself in power regardless of results.

The returns at the polls on November 25, December 2, and December 9 showed that, while the Bolsheviks had a majority in Petrograd, Moscow, and a few other cities, in fifty-four electoral regions out of seventy-nine they had received only nine million votes out of thirty-six and a quarter million cast, whereas the Social Revolutionaries had an absolute majority with nearly twenty-one million votes. The Council of Commissars acted with determination and despatch. They immediately arrested the entire All-Russian Commission on Elections and kept them locked up at Smolny for two days, appointing Uritsky as Commissar for Elections, with orders to require the presence of four hundred representatives before the Assembly could open.[3]

[1] Trotsky, *Lenin*, pp. 145-146.
[2] Stalin, *Leninism* (London and New York, 1928–1933), i. 207-209.
[3] Bunyan and Fisher, pp. 348-350.

By means of this handicap the Bolsheviks were able to prevent the Assembly from meeting, despite an abortive attempt to open it on December 11, until they had perfected their own plans for its destruction. As the Bolshevik deputies arrived in Petrograd from all parts of Russia, at Lenin's insistence and under Sverdlov's direction, they were assigned to the various factories, industrial works, and army corps. Here they developed the party " cell system ", and created an atmosphere favourable to the Bolsheviks, organizing the workers in opposition to the democratic theory.[1]

The Right Social Revolutionaries were also strengthening their position. They published a newspaper bitterly attacking the Bolsheviks, they attempted to win over two of the remaining crack regiments of the old army, they endeavoured to arm the workers, and even to bring back soldiers from the front under the guise of their attending a military university. They even worked out a plot for the kidnapping of the whole Council of Commissars, and were implicated in an attempt upon Lenin's life in the course of which Fritz Platten was wounded in the hand.[2]

By the third week of January 1918, the necessary quorum had gathered and the Bolsheviks had completed their arrangements. In any case the atmosphere of plot and counter-plot in Petrograd had become so tense that further delay would provoke an untimely outburst, and the delegates were summoned to meet on January 18. But at the same time it was made clear by the Council of Commissars that the Assembly would be immediately dissolved unless it recognized the Soviet Power, ratified the programme of the Second Congress of Soviets, and approved the measures of socialization taken by this body.

[1] Trotsky, *Lenin*, p. 148.

[2] J. Mavor, *The Russian Revolution* (London, 1928), pp. 190-191. (Based largely upon the memoirs of Boris Sokoloff, who organized these activities.)

As the deputies to the Constituent Assembly gathered in the Tauride Palace they found all approaches closely guarded by the Lettish Riflemen and Red Guards. None was allowed to enter without a pass. Dybenko, Commissar for War, was taking no chances, machine-guns were mounted on the house-tops, and the guards had been supplemented by two thousand sailors drawn from Viborg and Helsingfors. The precautions were justified. Demonstrations for and against the Assembly filled the streets and resulted in severe street fighting, which delayed the Japanese Ambassador and the British Chargé d'Affaires in their arrival at the American Embassy, where a meeting of the Chiefs of the Allied Missions was in progress. During this discussion, which terminated in general agreement among the diplomats not to attend the opening of the Assembly, rifle-fire and the sounds of conflict could be heard continually.[1]

The Session, which had been due to open at noon, was, in true Russian fashion, delayed until 4 P.M. There was endless speculation as to possible eventualities. All expected some drastic action by the Bolsheviks, and many had brought with them candles and sandwiches lest they should be called upon to stand a siege. " Thus democracy entered upon its struggle with dictatorship heavily armed with sandwiches and candles ", commented Trotsky contemptuously.[2]

The first tilt took place at the very moment of the opening. The Social Revolutionaries of the Right, as the majority party, proposed the oldest member present, one of their own number, Sergei Petrovitch Shevtsov, as temporary presiding officer, but before he had time to do more than ring his bell, Sverdlov, as President of the Petrograd Soviet, took possession of the chair and, amid cries of " Go wash your bloody hands, you murderer "

[1] *U.S. Foreign Relations*, 1918 : *Russia*, i. 350-351.
[2] Trotsky, *Lenin*, p. 149.

from the Right and Centre, read to the Assembly the declaration of the Council of Commissars concerning its duties and conduct, and the terms upon which it would be permitted to survive.

During scenes of great disorder, in which the Bolsheviks sang the " Internationale " at the tops of their voices, a vote was taken for the presidency of the Assembly. The Social Revolutionaries of the Right put forward Victor Chernov, Kerensky's former Minister of Agriculture, the Bolsheviks nominated a member of their only allies, the Social Revolutionaries of the Left, Maria Spiridonova, who had lately been liberated from an incompleted fifteen-year sentence in Siberia for the murder of the Governor of Tambov. The voting showed that Chernov, a man with a flat-nosed bespectacled face, almost beardless and with prominent cheek-bones (whom Trotsky describes vividly, if perhaps inaccurately, as " verbose, emotional, feeble, coquettish, and, above all, sickening "),[1] was elected by a large majority.

Chernov in his opening speech attacked the Bolsheviks for their failure to make good their promises both in regard to external and internal affairs, and dwelt lovingly on what democratic constitutional government would do for Russia. Bukharin followed for the Bolsheviks, and then Tseretelli for the Mensheviks, who denied the right of the Council of Commissars to demand the ratification of their actions by the Assembly as the price of its life and proposed a Social Democrat programme which would make the Constituent Assembly temporarily the highest power in the land.

Other anti-Bolshevik speakers followed Tseretelli, their remarks being frequently punctuated and often drowned by remarks shouted from the galleries, where a crowd of soldiers, sailors, and workmen, admitted to the Tauride Palace by the commander of the Red Guard, had taken possession and were making merry. The pandemonium was

[1] Trotsky, *Lenin*, p. 152.

reminiscent of the Convention in revolutionary Paris during one of its more ribald sessions.

The crucial clash came on voting the order of the day—it was then about one o'clock in the morning of January 19. The Right Social Revolutionaries wished to discuss their peace programme and measures for land reform, the Bolsheviks demanded priority for their Declaration of the Rights of the Toiling and Exploited Peoples. The voting showed 237 to 136 in favour of the Social Revolutionaries of the Right. Whereupon, among scenes of such complete disorder that a free fight seemed imminent, the Bolshevik deputies withdrew, to be followed an hour or so later by the Social Revolutionaries of the Left.[1]

Lenin had left the Tauride Palace to return to Smolny, where the Central Executive Committee of the party was in permanent session. There the news came to him of the Bolshevik withdrawal from the Assembly, and the Committee at once voted for its dissolution. The decree exists in Lenin's own hand. He wrote it on the spot and with great speed. It was a terse and peremptory document :

The Constituent Assembly, which was elected on lists made out before the November Revolution, represents the old order when the compromisers and Cadets were in power . . . [It is] carrying on an open war against the Soviet, calling for its overthrow, and in this way helping the exploiters in their efforts to block the transfer of land and of the factories to the workers. It is clear that the Constituent Assembly can be of help only to the bourgeois counter-revolutionaries in its efforts to crush the power of the Soviets. In view of the above the Central Executive Committee hereby decrees : *The Constituent Assembly is dissolved.*

Lenin himself bore the order to the Tauride Palace. To the officer of the guard he gave a written instruction, " The Constituent Assembly is not to be dissolved before the close of the present session " ; and he added verbally,

[1] Bunyan and Fisher, pp. 375-377.

" Now mind, from to-morrow no one on any account is to enter the Palace ".

It was then 4 A.M. The officer and his sailors were tired out, but the deputies showed no signs of flagging. Couldn't he close the session now, the commander asked Lenin. Without directly committing himself, Lenin smiled encouragingly, bade the officer a cheerful good-night, and returned to Smolny.[1]

Within the Chamber the atmosphere was heavy but enthusiastic. In the absence of the Bolsheviks the Assembly had succeeded in adopting the proposed Land Law of the Right Social Revolutionaries amid scenes of wild applause. As the final reading was completed, the commander of the guard entered the hall and, advancing to the President's chair, patted Chernov familiarly on the shoulder, explained that he was acting under orders of the Council of Commissars, and asked the Deputies to go home as the guard was tired.

" All the members of the Constituent Assembly are very tired," replied Chernov, " but that must not stand in the way of going ahead with the laws for which Russia waits." And, ignoring the officer, he began to read very quickly the peace declaration calling upon the Allies to define " the exact terms of a democratic peace acceptable to all belligerent nations ", exactly as if nothing had occurred since the days of Kerensky.[2]

The commander of the guard, his patience at last at an end, gave the order to his sailors to turn out the lights. In the growing darkness disorder reigned, and, amid cheers and cat-calls from the galleries, the voice of Chernov could be heard pathetically proclaiming, " The Russian State is declared a Russian Democratic Federative Republic ".

---

[1] Valeriu Marcu, *Lenin* (London, 1928), pp. 323-324.
[2] Bunyan and Fisher, p. 378.

4

Trotsky arrived in Petrograd on the morrow of these momentous events and, according to him, Lenin was still even then of the opinion that it would have been better had the Constituent Assembly not met. " It was a great risk on our part that we did not postpone the convention —very, very unwise ", he said. " But in the end it is best that it happened so. The breaking up of the Constituent Assembly by the Soviet Power is the complete and public liquidation of formal democracy in the name of revolutionary dictatorship. It will be a good lesson." [1]

This may have been true in a revolutionary sense, but in the realm of practical affairs the " liquidation " of the Constituent Assembly did serious harm to the Soviet position both at home and abroad. The Central Powers had always feared that the Constituent Assembly would prove so strong a rallying-ground for the patriotic forces in Russia that the Soviet Government would be forced to compromise and ally itself with that element. It was even believed that an attempt might be made to continue the war as a result of such an alliance. But the dissolution of the Assembly now convinced the Germans of Russia's avowed readiness to end the war at any price. Furthermore, in suppressing the Assembly the Bolsheviks had abandoned whatever moral basis they had ever had at Brest-Litovsk. Here was justification for every accusation which Hoffmann had made. No longer could they twit the Germans with refusing to admit the expression of free-will in the occupied territories.

In the countries of the Entente also, where, for example, the British Labour Party had, as recently as January 15, announced that the aim of the British people " is identical with Russia's ", there was a complete revulsion of feeling. Those who, still ignorant of the ruthlessness of Soviet

[1] Trotsky, *Lenin*, pp. 149-150.

methods, had hoped that from the Constituent Assembly would emerge a happy amalgam of all the revolutionary parties of Russia, were appalled at this act of flagrant dictatorship, and hastily revised their opinions of the Revolution. Immediately there occurred a recrudescence of the legend that Lenin and Trotsky were German agents and that the Soviet régime was " in cahoots " with the German General Staff. In view of the passages between Trotsky and Hoffmann at Brest this is not without humour. Even in Germany there were persistent rumours among the Majority Socialists that the Bolsheviks had been bought by the German Government, and that all which had happened at the peace conference was merely a well-played farce with the rôles allotted in advance. Eduard Bernstein, the Reichstag Deputy, writing in Maxim Gorky's *Novaya Zhizn* on January 24, declared that in German military circles the success of the Brest-Litovsk negotiations was openly ascribed to the fact that all whom it had been necessary to " oil " had been " oiled ". The personal honesty of Lenin and Trotsky was not in question, Bernstein averred, but it was believed that, having taken German gold at the time of Lenin's return to Russia, they had " become slaves of this heedless step ".[1]

It was with the laying of this ghost, finally and forever, that Trotsky was concerned as he plunged into the party discussions after his arrival on January 20. Cost what it might, he was convinced that before the signing of the peace the proletariat of Europe should be given some signal proof of the fundamental enmity which existed between Soviet Russia and Imperial Germany. From this conviction

[1] Trotsky, *Lenin*, p. 131 ; Bunyan and Fisher, p. 508. Kerensky declares that he was informed by Bernstein of his post-war investigations into the Lenin-Ludendorff alliance, to which he was forced to make an end under the personal pressure of President Ebert and other high officials of the Reich " in the name of the highest national reasons ". See *The Crucifixion of Liberty*, p. 288.

sprang the germ of what Trotsky himself terms " that pedagogical demonstration " which was expressed in the formula " We shall stop the war but we shall not sign the peace treaty ". It was necessary to test whether or no the Germans were able to send troops against Russia. If they were not, it would mean a definite victory with far-reaching consequences; while, if they were, it would be possible to capitulate at the point of the bayonet.[1]

Trotsky had revolved the idea in his mind for some time. He had consulted first Kamenev, then other of his colleagues ; all seemed in sympathy with the plan. Finally he had written to Lenin :

It is impossible to sign their peace, Vladimir Ilyich. They have already agreed with fictitious governments of Poland, Lithuania, Courland, and others concerning territorial concessions and military and Customs treaties. In view of " self-determination ", these provinces, according to German interpretation, are already independent States, and as independent States they already have concluded territorial and other agreements with Germany and Austria-Hungary. We cannot sign their peace. My plan is this :

We announce the termination of the war and demobilization without signing any peace. We declare we cannot participate in the brigands' peace of the Central Powers, nor can we sign a brigands' peace. Poland's, Lithuania's, and Courland's fate we place upon the responsibility of the German working people.

The Germans will be unable to attack us after we declare the war ended. At any rate, it would be very difficult for Germany to attack us, because of her internal condition. The Scheidemannites adopted a formal resolution to break with the Government if it makes annexationist demands of the Russian revolution.

The *Berliner Tageblatt* and the *Vossische Zeitung* demand an

[1] Later, during the struggle between Trotsky and Stalin for the control of the party after Lenin's death, Trotsky was accused of attempting, by his formula of " No War—No Peace ", to rouse the peasant masses for a revolutionary war. He is at great pains to refute this accusation both in his *Letter to the Bureau of Party History* and in the notes to volume xvii. of his *Collected Works*. See Trotsky, *The Stalin School of Falsification* (New York, 1937), pp. 26-27.

understanding with Russia by all means. The Centre Party favour
an agreement. The internal strife is demoralizing the Government.
Bitter controversy is raging in the press over the struggle on the
Western Front.

We declare we end the war but do not sign a peace. They will
be unable to make an offensive against us. If they attack us, our
position will be no worse than now, when they have the opportunity
to proclaim and declare us agents of England and of Wilson after his
speech, and to commence an attack.

We must have your decision. We can still drag on negotiations
for one or two or three or four days. Afterward they must be broken
off. I see no other solution than that proposed. I clasp your hand.

Yours,

TROTSKY.

PS.—Answer direct by wire : " I agree to your plan " or " I
don't agree ".[1]

But Lenin was not to be stampeded into giving a
precipitate answer. He was as supremely doubtful of
Trotsky's new formula as he was of the clamour which
Bukharin was beginning to raise in favour of resuming the
war against Germany in the guise of a revolutionary crusade.
Why were his colleagues so credulous ? What did Bukharin
think he could fight with ? Why was Trotsky so sure the
Germans would not continue the offensive ? What real
signs were there of a revolution in Central Europe ? Lenin
alone had seen the light, had plumbed the grim situation
to its darkest depths of impotency. They *could not* fight,
they *must* make peace, the least bad peace they could under
the circumstances.

Yet Lenin was driving a difficult team. He had not yet
reached that point when he could dictate his terms to his
colleagues. A breach now might mean permanent disruption of the party and the collapse of the Bolshevik
Revolution in Russia. He would summon a conclave at

---

[1] The authenticity of this letter, which has been in doubt for twenty
years, was personally confirmed to the writer by Leon Trotsky in conversation in Mexico City, in September 1937.

which Trotsky, Bukharin, and he would state their views. Perhaps he could make his arguments prevail against theirs.

For this reason he did not reply to Trotsky's letter either in the affirmative or in the negative. Instead he telegraphed : " When you come to Petrograd we will talk it over ".[1] When, therefore, on January 18, the negotiations had reached a critical point, Trotsky informed Smolny by direct wire and received, one after the other, two replies :· " Stalin has just arrived," ran Lenin's first message, " we shall discuss the matter with him and shall immediately send you our combined reply " ; within an hour came the second message above the double signature which was later to prove so fatal to Trotsky, " Request to call a recess and return to Petrograd : Lenin, Stalin ",[2] and it was in accordance with these instructions that Trotsky asked for an adjournment of the negotiations. Now he returned to Petrograd and the battle for the soul of the Revolution began.

Trotsky propounded his theory to a group of party leaders on January 21 and was supported, among others, by Stalin and Kamenev. At the same meeting Bukharin fiercely advocated the immediate rupture of the negotiations and the resumption of hostilities in " a revolutionary war ". Alexandra Kollontai, Bela Kun, Pokrovsky, Pyatakov, Radek, and Uritsky agreed with him.

Lenin listened to both sides. Things were turning out exactly as he had anticipated. Trotsky's complex mind had developed a complex formula, and the over-zealous Bukharin was advocating the physically impossible.

" It's all very attractive ", he said to Trotsky. " One could ask for nothing better if one could be certain that Hoffmann cannot send troops against us. But what if he

[1] Trotsky, *My Life*, p. 327.

[2] Trotsky, *Collected Works* (Leningrad-Moscow, 1926), xvii. Part I, p. 632.

can ? You say yourself the trenches are empty. What if the Germans resume fighting ? "

" Then we would be compelled to sign the peace, but everyone would know that we did so because we had no choice. And only in this way will we be able to destroy the legend of 'secret connection with the Hohenzollerns'"", argued Trotsky.

" No, it's too risky. For the moment our Revolution is more important than anything else ; we must make sure of it, cost what it may." [1]

Bukharin pressed his point.

" My poor friend," said Lenin fiercely, " go to the front and see if it is possible to fight."

The fiery Radek rose in his place and, glaring at Lenin, cried : " If there were five hundred courageous men in Petrograd, we would put you in prison ". With steely reserve and unconscious prophecy, Lenin replied, " Some people, indeed, may go to prison ; but if you will calculate the probabilities you will see that it is much more likely that I will send you than you me ".

He then read to them his now famous Twenty-one Theses, the fruits of his own bitter and soul-searching reflections, giving his reasons for accepting the German terms, though only after the negotiations had been delayed as long as possible.

. . . " To make a success of Socialism in Russia, a certain time, some months at least, is necessary, during which the Socialist Government can have a free hand, first to overcome the bourgeoisie of its own country and then to lay the basis for extensive and deep-rooted organizational work. . . . The Brest-Litovsk negotiations have made it clear by now that the war party in Germany has the upper hand and has sent us what amounts to an ultimatum. . . . The Russian Socialist Government is confronted with a question which requires an immediate solution :

[1] Trotsky, *Lenin*, pp. 131-132 ; *My Life*, p. 327.

either to accept the annexation peace or to start at once
a revolutionary war. No other solution is in fact possible.
We cannot put off the decision ; we have already done
everything possible and impossible to drag out the negotiations. . . . The question whether it is possible to undertake
at once a revolutionary war must be answered solely from
the point of view of actual conditions and the interest of
the Socialist Revolution which has already begun. If we
summarize the arguments for an immediate revolutionary
war, we shall find that the policy advocated in them is
capable of giving satisfaction to those who crave the
romantic and the beautiful but who fail completely to take
into consideration the objective correlation of class forces,
and the real conditions within which the Socialist Revolution is developing. There is no doubt that at the present time
(and probably during the next few weeks and months) our
army is in no condition to stop a German offensive. . . .
Under the circumstances it would be very bad policy to
risk the fate of the Socialist Revolution on the chance that
a revolution might break out in Germany by a certain date.
Such a policy would be adventurous. We have no right to
take such chances. . . .

" In concluding a separate peace now we rid ourselves,
as far as present circumstances permit, of both imperialistic
groups fighting each other. We can take advantage of their
strife, which makes it difficult for them to reach an agreement at our expense, and use that period when our hands
are free to develop and strengthen the Socialist Revolution. . . . A truly revolutionary war at this moment would
be a war between a Socialist Republic and the bourgeois
countries. . . . For the time being, however, we cannot
make this our object. In reality we should be fighting now
for the liberation of Poland, Lithuania, and Courland.
There is not a single Marxist who, while adhering to the
foundations of Marxism and Socialism, would not say that
the interests of Socialism are above the right of nations

to self-determination. . . . Peace on condition of the liberation of Poland, Lithuania, and Courland would be a ' patriotic ' peace from the Russian point of view, but it would be none the less a peace with annexationists and with the German imperialists." [1]

Few documents illustrate more succinctly Lenin's genius as a revolutionary opportunist or his understanding of the value of *Realpolitik* in statesmanship. With cold clear-sightedness he foresaw that a separate peace with Germany was essential for the salvation of the Russian Revolution. Likewise he realized that sooner or later the myth of " world revolution in our time " would be exploded. Like a good general he had prepared for the inevitable reaction, a reaction which might threaten the very existence of the party. That which he now propounded could not yet be published, but it gave to his colleagues in control the cold unvarnished facts which must ultimately be faced by all. He took not more than twenty minutes to read his Theses, speaking without gestures and without much emphasis. Clearly and brutally he stated his position— and waited.

But neither the majority of the leaders nor that of the rank and file of the party was alert enough to appreciate the wisdom of Lenin's view. It was a complete reversal of the slogans and propaganda which the party had circulated for so long. It was a compromise, and Lenin had always opposed compromises ; it was an acknowledgment of defeat, and Lenin had told them that Bolshevik diplomacy had only to whistle and the proletariats of Western Europe would sweep away their capitalistic governments. They were still being told so. " The triumph of the international revolution is near ", wrote *Pravda*; and again, "The victory of an honest peace has come ". It was too much to expect that they should suddenly accept the complete negation of what they had so long believed. The cardinal dilemma which

---

[1] For text see Appendix III, p. 385.

all dictators have to face is to make their post-revolutionary policy square with their pre-revolutionary propaganda.[1]

The struggle within the party grew daily more tense and more bitter. Trotsky maintains that the fiercest dissent was not between him and Lenin, but between Lenin and Bukharin. On the essential issue, whether Russia could carry on a revolutionary war and whether it was admissible for a revolutionary power to sign agreements with an imperialist régime, there was no difference of opinion between Lenin and Trotsky. Both agreed that the answer to the first was " no ", and to the second, " yes ". Where they differed was as to the moment and method of accepting the terms of the Central Powers.

At an informal vote of the 63 present on January 21, Lenin's policy received 15, Trotsky's 16, and Bukharin's 32. It was then agreed to canvass the views of two hundred local Soviets on the issue of war or peace. Only two (those of Petrograd and Sebastopol, the latter with reservations) voted for peace; from Moscow, Ekaterinburg, Kharkov, Kronstadt, and the rest came a full-throated cry for war.[2]

On the following day the question was carried from private discussion to the Central Executive Committee. The cleavage of opinion had become so deep that a split in the party seemed inevitable. Again Lenin made a passionate defence of his theses to sign. He called Trotsky's formula of " No War—No Peace " an " international political demonstration " which they could not afford. " If the Germans advance we will have to conclude peace in any case, but the terms will be worse if we do not sign now."

[1] Adolf Hitler found himself in precisely this difficulty. Having promised all things to all men before his accession to power, he found himself so enmeshed in his pledges after eighteen months of government that to him there appeared no other alternative than to choose the way of violence and cut the Gordian knot. This he did on June 30, 1934. Mussolini is the outstanding exception to the rule. Having made no pre-revolution promises, he was never hampered by the impossibility of fulfilling them.　　　　　　　　[2] Trotsky, *My Life*, p. 328.

Why should the Germans, once they had begun a new offensive, give quarter ? Why should they not press on and take what they would from a totally defenceless people ? Would the Russians have time to sign a treaty ? " This beast springs suddenly ", said Lenin. He saw it all so clearly. But the glory of the November days still blinded the eyes of the others. Trotsky talked of the revolution imminent in Central Europe. " We cannot put our trust in the German proletariat ", cried Lenin from the depths of his own revelation. " Germany is only pregnant with revolution. The second month must not be mistaken for the ninth. But here in Russia we have a healthy, lusty child. We may kill it if we start a war." To Bukharin and his followers Lenin declared : " The position of the Germans on the islands of the Baltic is such that in an offensive they could take Reval and Petrograd with bare hands ".

All in vain. Russia was in a revolutionary war fever. That same people who had clamoured for peace at any price now called with equal enthusiasm for a holy war. But the army was not there ; it had melted away.

Rather than surrender to this policy of sheer insanity, Lenin sought to compromise with Trotsky. He did not agree with Trotsky's plans and was convinced that they would lead to failure, with acceptance of worse terms as an inevitable consequence. But, short of a second *coup d'état* and a split within the party from which it might never recover, he could not succeed in imposing his own views upon his colleagues. Between the danger of a harsher peace and the certain disaster of a " revolutionary war ", Lenin chose the first unhesitatingly. He consented to give Trotsky's policy a trial.

" But in that case you won't support the slogan of revolutionary war, will you ? " Lenin asked as they sealed the compact.

" Under no circumstances."

" Then the experiment will probably not be so dangerous.

We will only risk losing Estonia or Livonia, and for the sake of a good peace with Trotsky," Lenin added with his deep chuckle, " Livonia and Estonia are worth losing."

The Central Committee of the party voted on January 22. Bukharin's proposal for a revolutionary war was lost by 11 to 2, with one abstention. Lenin's motion for dragging out the negotiations still further was carried by 12 to 1. Trotsky's formula of " No War—No Peace " was accepted by a close vote of 9 to 7. This decision left unsettled the question of accepting the German terms. It merely gave Trotsky a free hand to go ahead with his delaying tactics, and then at the psychological moment, of which he was to be judge, to put into operation the formula of " No War— No Peace ". The decision was declared to be binding upon the *Sovnarkom* (Council of the People's Commissars).[1]

To acquaint the workers of Central Europe with the enormity of the German demands at Brest, two wireless statements were broadcast on January 23 declaring the conditions of peace to be " nothing less than a monstrous annexation ", of the details of which the workers were being kept in ignorance because the German and Austrian Governments dared not disclose their demands. " The people of Germany and Austria-Hungary are being deceived by their own Governments before the whole world." [2]

Trotsky had not entirely given up hope of gaining the support of the Entente in the event of a possible German offensive. He was gambling on the hope that a revolution in Germany would prevent any such thing. His whole policy was based on the assumption that the Germans would not advance if negotiations were broken off, but if they did, he wished to be ensured (and reassured) by the promise of Allied assistance. As usual, he worked through the

[1] Trotsky, *My Life*, pp. 328-329; *Lenin*, pp. 133-136; Fischer, i. 48-49; Bunyan and Fisher, pp. 498-506; *Protokoly siezdov i konferentsii vsesoiuznoi Kommunisticheskoi Partii*, (v) *Sedmoi siezd, Mart 1918, goda*, pp. xxvi-xxvii.   [2] *Proceedings*, pp. 121-122.

unofficial agents in Petrograd. Two days after the vote in
the Central Committee he sent for Sadoul, and, showing
him Hoffmann's map, begged him to show it to his Ambassador and to the head of the French Military Mission.
"*Nous ne voulons pas signer cette paix-là, mais que
faire?*" Sadoul reports him as saying. "*La guerre sainte?
Oui, nous décréterons, mais à quel résultat arriverons-nous?
Le moment est venu pour les Alliés de se décider!*"[1]
Trotsky also summoned Robins, and asked what the
United States was going to do in the matter of recognition. Robins could only tell him that the Ambassador
had received no instructions.[2] Neither Robins nor Sadoul
could give Trotsky much comfort.

Trotsky did not despair, however. If the Allies would
not co-operate, he would scarify them. In any case the
Germans would not march. On the night of January 26,
just before his return to Brest, Trotsky addressed the Third
Congress of Soviets which had been summoned to succeed
the Constituent Assembly. It was a report, and at the same
time a challenge ; a fighting speech made on the eve of
great events, yet disclosing a strange ignorance of some of
the important factors in the situation. Just as the Allies
believed—or at least many among their leaders—that
Lenin and Trotsky were agents of the German General
Staff, so Lenin and Trotsky persisted in the belief that the

[1] Sadoul, p. 204. In a later letter to Albert Thomas, written on
January 29, commenting on the publication of the decree creating a
Red Workers' and Peasants' Army and Navy, Sadoul draws attention
to the lack of military experts among the Bolsheviks, and points out
that only highly technical military missions supplied by the Allies,
and particularly by France, would ensure the adequate reorganization
of the Russian fighting forces : "*Les Bolcheviks le savent, Lénine, et
surtout Trotsky . . . sont prêts à accepter cette indispensable collaboration
sans laquelle ils seront contraints de subir les conditions du vainquer et de
signer une paix humiliante pour la Russie et mortelle pour la Révolution,*"
(p. 210).
[2] *U.S. Foreign Relations*, 1918 : *Russia*, i. 358-359.

Allies were in secret agreement with the German Government in the matter of the peace negotiations with Soviet Russia. Both stories were laughably impossible ; nevertheless, they played their part in the tangled drama of the peace.

" The Allied Governments are responsible for these [the peace terms]," Trotsky informed the assembled delegates, pointing to Hoffmann's map which hung before them. " London gave its tacit approval to Kühlmann's terms ; I declare this most emphatically. England is ready to compromise with Germany at the expense of Russia. The peace terms which Germany offers us are also the peace terms of America, France, and England ; they are the account which the imperialists of the world are making with the Russian Revolution. . . .

" Comrades, we are leaving to-night for Brest-Litovsk . . . we make no triumphal boasts . . . but we will fight together with you for an honest democratic peace. We will fight against them [the Central Powers] and they cannot scare us by their threats of an offensive. They have no assurance that the German soldiers will follow them. We shall proceed with our programme of demobilizing the old army and forming a Socialist Red Guard. If German Imperialists attempt to crush us with the war-machine . . . we shall call to our brothers in the West, ' Do you hear ? ' and they will answer ' We hear '." [1]

To Lenin, sitting with the Presidium on the platform behind Trotsky, watching the leonine head and muscular shoulders, and the occasional gestures of the curiously small hands, all this must have sounded the greatest bunkum. He knew well enough that Germany was unripe for revolution ; Liebknecht lay in jail ; Rosa Luxemburg also ; nothing could be looked for there.

And yet—and yet— It almost seemed as if the revolutionary miracle, so long looked for, was about to be

[1] Bunyan and Fisher, p. 506.

fulfilled. Scarcely had Trotsky departed from Petrograd than a wave of strikes and outbreaks spread through Germany and Austria. Soviets were formed in Berlin and Vienna. Hamburg, Bremen, Leipzig, Essen, and Munich took up the cry. " All power to the Soviets " was heard in the streets of Greater Berlin, where half a million workers downed tools. In the forefront of the demands were the speedy conclusion of peace without annexations or indemnities, on the basis of the self-determination of peoples in accordance with the principles formulated by the Russian People's Commissars at Brest-Litovsk, and the participation of workers' delegates from all countries in the peace negotiations.[1]

To the disappointment of those who, from Petrograd, watched with feverish hope these developments in Central Europe, the Austro-German strike movement was but a flash in the pan, a false dawn. Though partly of revolutionary origin, it was caused primarily by the nervous exhaustion of the working class ; and though it showed the extent to which the influence of the Independent Socialists and the Spartacists had developed in Germany, it could not legitimately be called a protest of the working classes against the peace terms of Brest-Litovsk. It was rather a protest of a mentally and physically exhausted people against the German High Command, whose grip on the industrial life of the country demanded the imposition of ever-increasing burdens and privations.

The strikers themselves were dealt with in a most ruthless and efficient manner. Striking in time of war was tantamount to high treason, and strikers were therefore subject to severe treatment. A state of siege was proclaimed in the cities, the labour press forbidden, and all strike meetings broken up by the police. In Berlin one leader was arrested and sentenced to five years' detention in a fortress. Thousands of workers on the Army Reserve were called to

[1] *Vorwärts*, January 29, 1918.

their regiments, and finally seven of the great industrial concerns in Berlin were placed under military control and the men ordered to resume work on pain of punishment in accordance with the utmost rigour of martial law.

By February 3 the whole strike movement had collapsed, but the effect in the country was so serious that, in a letter to the Minister for War on February 18, Ludendorff recommended that in future industrial disputes should be settled " in general without the employment of force ". " Nevertheless ", he added, " it is necessary to be prepared for all eventualities, and it is for this reason that I have consented to leave the desired troops in Germany." In reality he was so much disturbed that he sent a secret order to each army commander instructing him to keep two battalions ready for use against the civilian population.

To the watchers in Petrograd and in Brest the mirage faded, the hopes of an infant revolution in Germany and Austria again burned low. Lenin had been right. One should never mistake the second month for the ninth.

5

While Trotsky thus fought for his principles at Petrograd, Kühlmann and Czernin were wrestling with " principalities and powers " in their respective capitals. Count Hertling took advantage of Kühlmann's presence in Berlin to make, in the course of a full-dress debate on foreign affairs on January 24, his reply to Wilson's Fourteen Points. His acceptance of the formula " open covenants openly arrived at " was illustrated by his reference to the fact that at Brest the negotiations were being conducted with complete publicity, and that Germany was fully prepared to accept publicity of negotiations as a general political principle.

But with regard to Russia, the Imperial Chancellor

was evasive and discreet. He denied the right of the Allied
and Associated Powers to concern themselves in what,
owing to their refusal to participate in the peace negotiations, had become an affair between Russia and the Central
Powers alone, a fact which had been virtually admitted
by Mr. Lloyd George on January 5 when he publicly and
Pilatically washed his hands of Russia, should she persist
in separate peace negotiations.

Now that the Entente has refused [to participate]. . . . I must
decline to allow any subsequent interference [said Hertling]. We are
dealing here with questions which concern only Russia and the Four
Allied [Central] Powers. I adhere to the hope that with recognition
of self-determination for peoples on the western frontier of the
former Russian Empire, good relations will be established both with
these peoples and with the rest of Russia, for whom we wish most
earnestly a return of order and peace and of conditions guaranteeing
the welfare of the country.[1]

Though on the whole the Chancellor's speech was one
of acceptance, with qualified enthusiasm, of the Wilson
principles, the tone of the debate in the Reichstag was in
the main one of nationalistic excitement. Kühlmann came
in for some very hard knocks both concerning the Brest
negotiations and also his whole conduct of foreign affairs,
which many of the Left believed to be Machiavellian and
insincere, while the Right attacked him for his lack of
acquisitive tenacity. Some frankly advocated a policy of
wholesale annexation, not only in the East but in the West,
and foremost amongst these were the National Liberal
leaders, Stresemann and Fuhrmann. " The statesman who
returns from the war without Longwy-Briey, without
Belgium in his hand, without the Flanders coast freed
from England's power, and without the line of the Meuse
in our control, will go down to history as the grave-digger
of German prestige ", cried Fuhrmann, turning as he

[1] *Verhandlungen des Reichstags*, January 24, 1918.

spoke to where Kühlmann sat on the bench of the Secretaries of State.

But the opinions of Herr Fuhrmann and his fellow jingoes were the least of Kühlmann's worries at that moment. On the previous afternoon he and the Chancellor had held conference with Hindenburg and Ludendorff, and the usual acerbity had prevailed. The situation at Brest, declared the First Quartermaster-General, was undermining the position of Germany both at home and abroad. The tame submission which Kühlmann had made to Trotsky's arrogance would cause the Entente leaders to think that Germany was running after the Bolsheviks begging them to make peace. How could they expect to intimidate men like Lloyd George and Clemenceau when Kühlmann allowed himself to be treated thus by unarmed Russian anarchists, putting up with open propaganda against his country and the German army ?

Hindenburg followed with a demand that the situation in the East should be cleared up as soon as possible, if only on military grounds, for until peace was signed it was necessary to retain in the East good divisions fit for employment in the West. There must be no more shilly-shallying, said the Marshal ; if the Russians delayed matters any further, hostilities must be reopened. This would bring down the Bolshevik Government, and their successors would be only too anxious to make peace.[1]

By way of concession the Marshal and Ludendorff produced a new plan for the boundaries of the " protective belt " of territory on the German-Polish frontier, which expressed their minimum demand. The new line ran approximately mid-way between that which they had originally demanded at Kreuznach in December, and that which the Kaiser, on Hoffmann's advice, had authorized at the opening of the Bellevue Conference on January 2. It was the last gesture of compromise on the part of the Supreme

[1] Ludendorff, ii. 553-554.

Command, and they demanded that Kühlmann be authorized to negotiate on this basis.[1]

But Kühlmann was not to be thus browbeaten by the
Supreme Command. His position was stronger than appearances would tend to show. When Hindenburg and Ludendorff had endeavoured to secure his dismissal by the Kaiser,
the Austrian Government, in a brief moment of courage,
had insisted that he be retained, and Wilhelm II had decided in his favour. In return the Supreme Command had
demanded their pound of flesh, and though Kühlmann had
remained in office, the German Emperor had been forced
to dispense with the head of his Civil Cabinet, Count von
Valentini, an official devoted to the Imperial service but who
had incurred the wrath of Ludendorff by his earlier support
of Bethmann Hollweg and his fearless criticism of the
ever-increasing encroachment of the Supreme Command
upon the prerogatives of the Emperor and the Government.

In discussions with the Marshal and Ludendorff, therefore, Kühlmann, supported by Hertling, refused to accept
their dictates, and after a severe struggle he succeeded in
gaining a further reprieve for his policy of negotiation, in
opposition to their demands for barefaced annexation.
The final agreement was in the nature of a compromise, in
which the Secretary of State secured permission to continue
his policy in the East, but not to extend it to any negotiations which might be opened in the West.

Inevitably there was growing upon Kühlmann the
realization that somehow the stalemate at Brest must be
broken. He still hoped that the negotiations with the
Ukraine would force Trotsky's hand and would compel
him to terminate the condition of stagnation by agreeing
to a peace which would not display too openly the annexationist policy imposed by the Supreme Command.

[1] *Die Ursachen des deutschen Zusammenbruches im Jahre 1918*
(Berlin, 1925–1929), i. 136-139.

6

Czernin, on his return to Vienna, had found matters even worse than he had feared. The situation was disastrous and was not alleviated by the almost pathetic incapacity of the Austrian Mihistry to meet either crisis or emergency. The obvious lack of co-operation between the Austrian and Hungarian Prime Ministers had complicated the situation still further, and had resulted in the threat of a second famine panic.

At a Crown Council presided over by the Emperor Karl on January 22, Czernin made his report on the negotiations with both the Russians and the Ukrainians of the *Rada*. With the language of a tragedian, yet maintaining a scrupulous if surprising fairness, he drew for them a picture of the long weary days at Brest-Litovsk. The dialectical acrobatics of Kühlmann and Trotsky, the brutal but realistic intervention of Hoffmann, the days of prolonged anxiety, the diminution of his own authority and influence as a result of the troubles at home, all were depicted before the Emperor and his advisers with the restraint and deference of a diplomat of the old school. But beneath it, not entirely concealed, was all the poignant anguish which Czernin had suffered during the tragedy of Brest. Spiritually he was scarred, and he could not hide completely the marks of the ordeal.

Two issues must be decided by the Council; should Czernin proceed to negotiate with the Ukrainians on the basis which Hoffmann had developed and which would provide a million tons of foodstuffs for hungry Austria ? And, in the event of the stalemate continuing between Kühlmann and Trotsky, should Czernin make a separate peace for Austria-Hungary with the Russians ?

The Austrian Prime Minister, Seidler, supported Czernin in his conduct of the negotiations and emphasized the necessity of an immediate peace with the Ukraine on the best terms obtainable. Those which Czernin had outlined were severe—they meant the cutting of Galicia into two and would involve the fiercest opposition by the Poles in the matter of Cholm—but he believed that even without the votes of the Poles he would have a two-thirds majority in the House for the acceptance of such a treaty.

The Hungarian Prime Minister, Count Wekerle, opposed the conditions of the treaty with the Ukraine. Unable to appreciate the fact that desperate conditions necessitate desperate measures, he quailed before the danger to the basic structure of the Dual Monarchy which would result from outside interference in its affairs. Some other way must be found.

Forgetting the august presence of the Emperor and the ancient usage of the council table, Czernin turned upon the man whose refusal to send grain into Austria had aggravated the recent crisis:

What is a responsible leader of foreign policy to do when the Austrian Prime Minister and the Austrian and Hungarian Food Ministers unanimously tell him that Hungarian supplies will only suffice to help us over the next two months, after which a collapse will be absolutely unavoidable, unless we can secure assistance from somewhere in the way of corn ? Do you think that I am ignorant or unaware of the danger of this step ? It is true that it will bring us to the down-grade, but from all appearances we have been in that position for a long time. If you will bring corn into Austria, I will be the first to agree with your point of view. But so long as you refuse to do this we are like a man on the third floor of a burning building. He won't stop to calculate whether, if he jumps, he will break one leg or two, he prefers the risk of death to its certainty.

Brushing aside such other opposition as there was, the Foreign Minister appealed directly to Caesar, laying the responsibility squarely upon Kaiser Karl, whose mentor he had been since the accession. The Emperor was not a man of strong will nor of quick decisions, but he acted in this moment with commendable firmness and precision.

He gave unhesitating support to Czernin, authorizing peace with the Ukraine on the lines described and deciding in principle in favour of a separate peace with Russia.[1]

It was therefore with a greater composure of mind that the Foreign Minister turned to the preparation of the speech which he was to make before the Austrian Delegation in reply to Wilson's Fourteen Points. But his moment of minor consolation was short-lived. On January 23 there came from Wiesner, whom he had left at Brest, a telegram reporting news from Joffe to the effect that the Soviet Ukrainian Government at Kharkov had decided to send two delegates to take part in the negotiations with the Central Powers. These gentlemen would form part of the Russian delegations and would not consider themselves bound by any agreements concluded by the representatives of the Kiev *Rada*, who represented only the propertied classes and were therefore incapable of acting on behalf of the whole Ukrainian people.[2] Even as Czernin read Wiesner's report, the President of the *Rada* had resigned and the Soviet Red Guards, already in possession of Poltava, the industrial district of Ekaterinoslav, and the coal basin of Donets, were advancing upon Kiev. It was Trotsky's counter-move to the threat of a Ukrainian peace. An agreement concluded with the *Rada* would no longer be an agreement with the Ukraine.

Czernin, in his speech on January 24, replied to Wilson in detail, declaring that there were among his proposals some which he could accept " with great pleasure ". He repeated that from Russia he demanded " not a square metre nor a penny " and that the principles of his negotiations had been strictly those of no annexations and no indemnities. From Poland too, " we want nothing at all . . . Poland's people shall choose their own destiny free and uninfluenced ". Personally he would have liked to see

[1] Czernin, pp. 241-245, 316 ; Gratz and Schüller, p. 101.
[2] Czernin, pp. 300-303.

Poland as an active participant at Brest, but the Russians had refused to recognize the present Polish Government as a competent representative of the country.

He reviewed for his colleagues the divergencies between the German and the Russian theses, emphatically stating that a compromise must be found, and passed to a passionate defence of his negotiations with the Ukraine :

The question is not one of imperialist or annexationist plans, but of assuring to our population a finally deserved reward for steadily holding out and of giving it those foodstuffs for which they are waiting. . . . If you wish to ruin peace, if you wish to renounce the supply of grain, then it would be logical for you to force my hand by speeches, revolutions, strikes and demonstrations. . . . If behind the front you arrange strikes . . . you are cutting your own flesh and all those who think that such means hasten peace are in awful error. . . . You must help me or you must bring about my fall ; there is no other way.

Three days later he left for Brest with a heavy heart but with his mind made up. The stalemate must be broken.

VI

"NO WAR—NO PEACE"

VI

"NO WAR—NO PEACE"

1

ONCE again the resumption of the negotiations was marked by a perceptible change in tone and *tempo*. For, though the Bolsheviks had derived a brief moment of encouragement from their military successes in the Ukraine and in Finland, where the Red Guards had seized Helsingfors, and from the transitory strike movement in Germany and Austria, they were well aware that the "liquidation" of the Constituent Assembly had laid bare before the Central Powers both their internal dissensions and their need of an early peace. Both Kühlmann and Czernin, on the other hand, had returned from their capitals with the confirmed intention of breaking the deadlock at all cost.

Trotsky, returning from Petrograd with the Ukrainian Bolsheviks as an ace in hand, was at once aware of the new note of firmness in Czernin's voice, the disinclination of Kühlmann to re-enter the dialectical ring, the grim determination of Hoffmann. For the first time since the conference opened, the delegates of the Central Powers were at one in their desire to achieve a decision with all decent speed and to bring finally to an end the tragicomedy of the past six weeks.

The opening gambit of the new phase on January 20, 1918, was the introduction of new delegates. The Bavarian Government, exercising treaty rights of 1871, had sent a former premier, Count von Podewils-Durnitz, to represent them in the discussions, his appointment being due in some measure to the opposition of the Munich press to Kühlmann's policy. The Count formed an integral part of the Imperial German delegation.

Trotsky then presented his protégés, M. Medvjedev, President of the Executive Committee of the Soviet Ukrainian Republic, together with his Commissars of Education and War, M. Satarisky and General Shachray, who in their turn would form part of the Russian delegation and who alone were qualified to speak for the Ukrainian masses. Trotsky confirmed the victories which the Bolshevik forces had won over the troops of the *Rada*, and warned both Kühlmann and Czernin that a peace concluded with the Kiev Government could in no way be regarded as a peace concluded with the Ukraine.

The representatives of the Central Powers were not going to allow themselves to be drawn by Trotsky into a lengthy discussion as to which government represented the Ukraine. They had determined upon peace with that region, and had decided upon the *Rada* as the agency with which to negotiate. Even if the Bolshevik hordes were at the very gates of Kiev, no matter ; if the *Rada* fell, they would restore it. " The difficulties were transitory," wrote Hoffmann in his diary, " in so far as at any time we could support the Government with arms and establish it again."[1]

Kühlmann therefore postponed further discussion until the return of the full *Rada* delegation from Kiev, but reminded Trotsky that, on January 12, the Russians had recognized the Ukrainians of the *Rada* as representatives of the people. On the following day (January 31), when Czernin presided, he asked Trotsky point-blank whether he admitted that the Ukrainians, of whichever Government, Kharkov or Kiev, had the right to treat alone with the Central Powers on questions dealing with their frontiers. Trotsky replied with an emphatic denial. He had always denied the right of any Ukrainians to treat separately, and had insisted that even between Kiev and Petrograd there

[1] Hoffmann, ii. 216-217.

must be some common agreement as to Ukrainian frontiers. Now that the lawful Ukrainian representatives were part of the Russian delegation, this was all the more essential. " If in the past an agreement was necessary between our delegation and the Ukrainian delegation, then at this present moment such an agreement is much more obligatory, since it is imposed by the Federal Constitution of the Russian Republic." He then read to the conference a telegram from the officer commanding Bolshevik troops in the Ukraine stating that the greater part of the Kiev garrison had passed over to the Soviet Government and that the further existence of the *Rada* was consequently likely to be of very short duration.[1]

Undeterred by this prospect, Kühlmann and Czernin staged at the next plenary session on February 1 a three-sided gladiatorial combat between the two Ukrainian delegations and the Russians, their object being to play off one against the other in the hope of making peace with at least one of them. " I tried to get the Ukrainians to talk over things openly with the Russians," records Czernin, " and succeeded almost too well." [2] This was for the young Ukrainian liberals their brief period of glory, and, fully realizing the precariousness of their position, they determined to enjoy it to the full. Before a delighted audience of the Quadruple Alliance—even Talaat kept awake and nodded his scarlet, befezzed head in solemn enjoyment—a battle-royal raged.

The *Rada* leader, Sevruk, led off by re-emphasizing the complete independence of his State from any ties, physical, spiritual, or political, with Soviet Russia. This was fiercely denied both by Trotsky and by the Ukrainian Soviet leader, Medvjedev, who declared that Kiev, in so far as it still represented anything, represented only the intellectuals and the landed classes, who sought separation from Russia for the better preservation of their privileges. There-

[1] *Proceedings*, pp. 122-131.　　　　[2] Czernin, p. 246.

upon the second *Rada* spokesman, Liubynski, retorted with
an hour-long speech which for pure vitriolic opprobrium
far exceeded anything that had been heard at this strangest
of peace conferences. He reviled the Bolsheviks without
restraint, recounting a catalogue of their sins only surpassed
by Gibbon's famous list of charges preferred against Pope
John XXIII, " the more serious of which had been
suppressed ".

A strange, wild figure in his ill-fitting Victorian frock-
coat, the young man raged at his enemies :

The noisy declarations of the Bolsheviks regarding the complete
freedom of the people of Russia is but the vulgar stuff of demagogy.
The Government of the Bolsheviks, which has broken up the Constituent Assembly, and which rests on the bayonets of hired Red
Guards, will never elect to apply in Russia the very just principle of
self-determination, because they know only too well that not only
the Republic of the Ukraine, but also the Don, the Caucasus, Siberia,
and other regions do not regard them as their government, and that
even the Russian people themselves will ultimately deny their right ;
only because they are afraid of the development of a National
Revolution do they declare here at the Peace Conference and within
Russia, with a spirit of demagogy peculiar to themselves, the right
of self-determination of the peoples. They themselves are struggling
against the realization of this principle and are resorting, not only
to hired bands of Red Guards, but also to meaner and even less legal
methods.[1]

To Czernin, sitting enthralled among the spirits which
his strategy had conjured up, the scene appeared
" grotesque ", but he obtained satisfaction from watching
Trotsky, who sat with a chalky face, nervously drawing on
his blotting-pad, staring fixedly before him, great drops
of sweat trickling down his forehead. " Evidently he felt
deeply the disgrace of being abused by his fellow citizens
in the presence of the enemy." Trotsky admits his mental
discomfiture, but attributes it to the distressing spectacle

[1] *Proceedings*, pp. 136-143.

of " the frantic self-humiliation of what after all was a
representative body of the Revolution before vain aristo-
crats who only despised them . . . it was one of the vilest
scenes I have ever witnessed ".[1] However, by the end of
the diatribe he had sufficiently recovered his composure to
offer his ironic congratulations to the presiding officer,
General Gantcheff, in that, " in harmony with the dignity
of this assembly, he has not opposed in any way the free-
speaking of the last orator, nor has he intervened in the
exact translation except to make some improvements in
expression ". He added that the delegation of the *Rada*,
being without a government, represented no greater
territory than the rooms they occupied at Brest-Litovsk.
(" Judging by the reports from the Ukraine that I had
before me, Trotsky's words seemed unfortunately not to
be without foundation ", is Hoffmann's comment.) [2]

At the conclusion of the session Czernin, despite
Trotsky's protests, declared on behalf of the Central
Powers that they recognized " immediately the Ukrainian
People's Republic [the *Rada*] as an independent, free and
sovereign State, which is able to enter into international
agreements independently ".

This prolonged manœuvre, though it had successfully
trumped Trotsky's ace, had also taken up three precious
days. An important conference on Austro-German affairs
was scheduled for February 4 in Berlin, and there was
little time for delay. Thus, when Trotsky endeavoured to
lure Kühlmann into one of their old discursive bouts on
the question of Polish representation, tempting him with
the remark that the Kingdom of Poland, having neither a
king nor frontiers, was not a State, the Secretary of State
somewhat surprisingly retorted that " the delegates of the
negotiating Powers have not come here to indulge in
intellectual combat ". Brushing aside the Polish question,

[1] Czernin, p. 246 ; Trotsky, *My Life*, p. 323.
[2] *Proceedings*, p. 145 ; Hoffmann, ii. 216.

he abruptly adjourned the conference until February 7,
and departed with Czernin for Berlin.

2

The conversations which took place in Berlin on
February 4 and 5 between the two Imperial Governments
and the German High Command were not devoted exclusively to the Brest-Litovsk negotiations. They covered
a variety of points, political, economic, and military, which
were outstanding between the two senior partners of the
Quadruple Alliance, and marked the climax in the relations
between the German and Austro-Hungarian Empires which
had been strained since the early defeats of the Austrian
armies. The Germans assumed an air of contempt for their
weaker partner who had continually to be helped out of
embarrassing situations ; while the Austrians entertained
for the Germans the inevitable feeling of dislike for anyone
to whom a sense of obligation is due.

In addition the Austrians were frankly frightened by the
effects of the annexationist paranoia of the German High
Command, not only upon Russia but upon Germany's
allies. Austria recently had had occasion to learn that not
even those allies were safe from the depredations of the
German General Staff, when in January, under the pretext
of securing a strategic frontier for Poland, Ludendorff had
demanded that the Dombrowa coal-field, then in Austrian
occupied territory, should be incorporated within the
frontiers of the German *Reich*. So great was the opposition
raised in Vienna and Budapest over this aggressive attitude
that Count Stephan Tisza, the veteran Hungarian statesman who had so vehemently opposed the declaration of
war in 1914, now proclaimed openly that, if the price of
German friendship was the surrender of the Dombrowa
coal-field, he was prepared to sacrifice the alliance with
Berlin and refuse to evacuate the district. " Let the

Germans give the order to fire, if they wish to push matters to extremes ", he declared.[1]

In Berlin, Czernin again was forced to some extent to restrain his natural feeling of resentment, as Austria once more was appealing to Germany for supplies. This, however, did not prevent Czernin from expressing himself with considerable point, both as to the annexationist policy of the Supreme Command in general and the Dombrowa affair in particular; and, finally, he declared in writing and by word of mouth that Austria-Hungary was only obliged by her pledges of alliance to fight for the pre-war possessions of Germany, which, in his reply to Wilson of January 24, he had declared that Austria would defend " equally with her own ". With the subsequent conquests and acquisitions by German arms Austria-Hungary was not concerned, nor would she expend a man or a krone in their defence.

To this Ludendorff replied that " if Germany makes peace without profit, Germany has lost the war ", and the discussion became so heated and acrimonious that Hertling, fearing some outburst on the part of the General which might have incalculable repercussions, urged Czernin to cease baiting him. " Leave him alone ", he begged. " We two will manage it together afterwards without him." This they did.

As regards the peace negotiations Ludendorff expressed himself as satisfied with the terms of the proposed Ukrainian treaty—it was not German soil that was being ceded— and agreed that the *Rada* must be supported by force of arms if need be. Czernin replied that he was far from sharing the satisfaction of the General, but that the Ukrainian peace was vitally necessary for Austria. In view of the inevitable opposition of the Poles to the cession of the Cholm district, he asked that the terms of the treaty should be kept secret for the time being.

In the most emphatic terms Ludendorff warned both

[1] Gratz and Schüller, pp. 235-240.

Kühlmann and Czernin that the Supreme Command could brook not a week's further delay on the Eastern Front. Troops *must* be transferred to the West, and therefore Trotsky must be confronted with an ultimatum. Either he must accept the peace terms or hostilities must be resumed. With profound reluctance Kühlmann finally agreed to break with Trotsky twenty-four hours after peace had been signed with the Ukraine. But Czernin gave notice, on the advice of Dr. Gratz, his *chef de cabinet*, that after the conclusion of the Ukrainian peace he would make a last attempt to effect, through personal negotiations with Trotsky, a compromise between the German and Russian points of view. Kühlmann agreed to this also, but Ludendorff remained silent.[1]

3

The fourth act of the tragi-comedy of Brest-Litovsk opened on February 6 with the return of the delegates of the Central Powers. Czernin found that in his absence Wiesner, with the assistance of the Austrian Ruthenian leader, Nicolai Wassilko, had made great strides in the elucidation of the technical details in the Ukrainian treaty. The text was virtually completed, the claims of the *Rada* delegates regarding the Ruthenian districts of Galicia having been refused. With this card in hand the Austrian Foreign Minister embarked on his final effort to achieve the impossible, to reconcile the German and Russian theses on self-determination.

Czernin had a special reason for endeavouring to prevent a peace too flagrantly annexationist on the part of Germany. At that moment his emissary, Skrzynski, was negotiating with the British Minister in Berne, Sir Horace Rumbold, for a secret meeting between Czernin and Lloyd George in Switzerland, at which it was hoped to evolve a basis for a

[1] Czernin, pp. 247-248 ; Ludendorff, ii. 555-556 ; Gratz and Schüller, p. 239.

general peace on the formula of " no annexations ". Encouraged by the British Premier's speech of January 5,
which had stated that the Entente was not fighting for the
destruction of Austria-Hungary, Czernin hoped thus to
stave off the break-up of the Dual Monarchy from within.[1]
It may be imagined therefore with what anxiety he pursued
the negotiations which he carried on with Trotsky during
the ensuing three days.

The fundamental issues which separated Germany and
Russia in their interpretations of the principle of self-
determination were four in number. First, had the occupied
territories declared their will in this matter ? If so, should
this be regarded as binding, or should a further referendum
be taken ? Secondly, if such a vote was necessary, should
it be for election to a constituent body or be in the form of
a referendum ? Thirdly, should such a consultation be
held before or after evacuation ? And fourthly, how should
it be organized ? By general franchise, by a vote of the
nobility, or what ? The Russians had proposed that the
decision of all these questions should be left to a "temporary
self-administrative body ", and, if the Germans would
agree to this, the whole issue could be narrowed down to
one single point : the question of composition of this
temporary body. (For this they had been disputing in the
discomfort of a Russian winter for eight weeks !) Here
Czernin's proposed compromise was that the Russians
should admit that the provincial land organizations, etc.,
which the Germans considered as basic, were competent
to express a part of the popular will; while the Germans

---

[1] As a result of these negotiations a meeting actually took place in
Berne between Skrzynski, General Smuts, and Lloyd George's private
secretary, Phillip Kerr, now Lord Lothian, from March 9 to 14, 1918.
But by this time the situation had become so complicated by the
German advance into Russia and the proximity of the offensive on the
Western Front that Czernin was forced to temporize and the discussions
came to nothing. (Lloyd George, v. 48-49.)

should agree that these bodies should, during the period of occupation, be supplemented by elements, chosen in accordance with the Russian principle, by popular election.[1]

Czernin's first move on February 6 was to send Dr. Richard Schüller, of the Austrian Foreign Office, to sound Trotsky as to the possibility of such a compromise and to threaten him with an ultimatum if he maintained an attitude of intransigence. To this Trotsky replied that he had not been intransigent at all, it was Kühlmann who had kept the discussions throughout on a theoretical basis by pretending that annexations were not annexations. According to the Germans the terms of the treaty would be—first, the right of self-determination of the people is recognized, and there will be no annexations; secondly, Germany annexes everything. Schüller pointed out that Trotsky himself had attached more importance to the solution of particular questions than to formulae and qualifications. " These too are of importance to us," answered Trotsky, " for we are convinced that the conditions now being created will be but temporary, and will be dissolved by the universal revolution. It would be possible for me to conclude a peace by which Russia would be violated, but in that case this intention would have to be openly acknowledged by the other side. We cannot be asked for a moral testimonial to the violation."

Count Czernin would consider this as a basis, said Schüller.

" Czernin is wholly in German leading strings ", remarked Trotsky contemptuously.

" Nevertheless he honestly desires peace and that without annexations ", was the reply.[2]

On the following morning, at a conference with the Germans, Czernin reported the result of Schüller's inter-

---

[1] Czernin, pp. 316-317 ; Gratz and Schüller, p. 103.

[2] *Ibid.* pp. 103-104.

view and asked Kühlmann for his view on the compromise. The Secretary of State was not unsympathetic ; he agreed to Czernin's proposals as a basis of negotiations, but Hoffmann, on behalf of the Supreme Command, protested violently against further delay and cried aloud for an ultimatum at the earliest moment.

Accordingly that evening (the evening of the 7th), Czernin, accompanied by Dr. Gratz, visited Trotsky in his lodging. Earnestly he told the Commissar of the danger of a rupture and offered his services as mediator between Russia and Germany. Trotsky replied with frankness that he was not such a fool as they appeared to think. He fully realized that the Central Powers were perfectly capable of annexing the Eastern Provinces. He was not greatly concerned as to what they took, but rather as to how they took it. Russia could bow to force but not to sophistry. He would never repudiate his principles nor admit German possession of the occupied territories under the cloak of self-determination, but let the Germans come out brazenly with their demands, as indeed Hoffmann had done, and he would yield, appealing to world opinion against an act of brutal brigandage. A solution could be found on the basis of annexations, but this must be openly admitted. Dr. Gratz suggested a qualification. " It would be possible ", he said, " not to touch on this at all in the treaty. The terms might simply say that such and such territorial changes will be carried out. You would then be at liberty to qualify these changes as annexations, while the Germans could say that the people in question had attached themselves to Germany by the exercise of the right of self-determination."

" I believe this way can be followed ", said Trotsky.

On this highly unethical and Machiavellian basis the theoretical side of the argument was allowed to rest, and the conversation turned to practical details. Here Trotsky appeared not so entirely disinterested as his earlier remarks would have suggested—his great weakness in debate was always that he could never resist the temptation of a quip or a gesture, no matter how much it might embarrass his basic argument. He now declared that the Hoffmann Line of January 18 was unacceptable on three points. Russia could not cede the Islands of the Moon Sound, as this would mean a permanent threat to Petrograd ; the cession of Riga was also impossible ; and there must be an alteration in the Lithuanian frontier. Above all, there must be no separate treaty with the Ukraine. On this note the interview closed.[1]

Not a great deal of progress—thought Czernin, as with Gratz he paced back to his quarters across the snow-covered courtyard of the citadel—perhaps a little further forward, though. At any rate there would be no more of the theoretical conflict about self-determination, that was over, *Gott sei Dank* ; they had got down to practical terms at last. Well, well, to-morrow he would talk it over with Kühlmann. If only that damned Hoffmann—

But on the morrow " that damned Hoffmann " did exactly as Czernin feared he would. The General had almost reached the end of his patience in this play-acting nonsense. He had been thrown into a passion on the previous day by the remarks of Radek, who, with that rare versatility which has always characterized him, was now appearing in the rôle of expert in Polish affairs, a rôle which he was admirably qualified to fill. In this capacity he had claimed to speak for the Polish troops in the German and Austrian armies and appealed on their behalf to their fellow soldiers to agitate for Polish independence. Hoffmann had protested against Radek's right to speak in the name of anyone belonging to the German army, and resented his efforts to undermine discipline in the Polish companies. The incident had enraged him perhaps unduly. (He had been particularly

[1] Czernin, pp. 248, 317; Gratz and Schüller, pp. 104-105; Fokke, p. 189; Trotsky, *History of the Russian Revolution to Brest-Litovsk*, p. 140.

annoyed by Radek's habit of leaning across the table with an impish grin and puffing tobacco smoke at him.) Even his nerves of steel were beginning to fray in the unreal atmosphere of the conference. The situation was becoming intolerable, and then, on top of it all, came Czernin with a further proposal of delay. Kühlmann was not above accepting the face-saving formula regarding annexations, and would certainly have considered the question of the territorial concessions, had not the General, in one of the worst scenes which had passed between the three of them in this stormy period, flatly refused even to discuss the frontier corrections, and demanded the immediate signing of the Ukrainian treaty to clear the way for an ultimatum to the Russians.

All hope of an agreement was therefore destroyed by the insistence of the German Supreme Command on advancing into Russia and compelling the Soviet Government to surrender unconditionally. A final effort to persuade Trotsky to accept the Ukrainian treaty was equally unsuccessful. He refused to recognize any agreement with a government which, he claimed, not only did not represent the people of the Ukraine, but which in reality no longer existed. This both Kühlmann and Czernin denied, saying that they had other information, but they refused Trotsky's offer to send a staff-officer to Kiev to find out. It is not clear, in view of Hoffmann's admission in his diary at the time of Trotsky's reply to Liubynski's tirade on the 3rd, whether the two statesmen were deliberately lying for diplomatic purposes, or whether they really believed, as Czernin stated, that, though the Government of the *Rada* had been driven out of Kiev on the 5th, it had since re-established itself. In any case it did not greatly matter, for such a pitch of fantasy had the negotiations now attained that the signing of the still-born agreement with a non-existent government seemed to be almost in character.

The final touches were put to the Ukrainian treaty on

the evening of February 8. Cholm went to the *Rada*, the Ruthenian districts of Galicia and the Bukovina were to become a Ukrainian province within the Monarchy, and linguistic rights were guaranteed to the Ruthenians of Western Galicia. In return the Ukraine undertook to place its surplus of foodstuffs and agricultural produce, computed to be at least a million tons, at the disposal of the Central Powers, who agreed to co-operate with the grain producers in the exchange of wares of which they stood in need, and in the improvement of the transport organization.

The main difficulty lay in devising means by which the execution of the territorial and political concessions on the part of Austria-Hungary would be made dependent upon the grain deliveries from the Ukraine. After some argument, the following involved method was agreed upon : In the event of non-fulfilment of the grain deliveries, Austria-Hungary would be released from her obligations. As soon as the treaty had been signed a commission was to meet at Kiev to determine the amount of surplus in the Ukraine, which the *Rada* had guaranteed to be not less than a million tons ; a supplementary treaty would then be signed.[1]

Such was the Peace with the Ukraine, that *Brotfrieden* for which Czernin laboured for so long. The effect of it was to leave the Ukraine theoretically a neutral State in the world, while actually it became a political granary and store-house for the Central Powers. From eggs to manganese, the long list of supplies required read like the inventory of a sublimated " mail order " house. But the Germans and Austrians were to find it more of a " cash and carry " establishment. As became the first peace treaty of the war, it was signed with some ceremony at two o'clock in the morning of February 9, the birthday of Prince Leopold of Bavaria, in the glaring lights of a cinema apparatus.[2]

[1] Gratz and Schüller, pp. 108-110; *Texts of the Ukraine " Peace "* (U.S. Department of State, Washington, D.C., 1918), pp. 12-13.

[2] For text see Appendix IV, p. 392.

" I wonder if the *Rada* is still really sitting at Kiev ", is Czernin's entry for the day.[1]

4

Events followed with dramatic swiftness during the next two days at Brest-Litovsk, moving crescendo to the final *dénouement*. News of the signature of the Ukrainian treaty was flashed at once to Kreuznach and, with the dawn, came the voice of Ludendorff, like the breath of destiny, claiming from Kühlmann the fulfilment of his promise to break with Trotsky. In this strange farce of self-delusion, this game of blindman's-buff, in which all the players were blindfold, Kühlmann believed himself upon the verge of a possible agreement with Trotsky, despite the fact that the Russian had made the abandonment of the Ukrainian treaty a *conditio sine qua non* of continued negotiations. The Secretary of State therefore ignored his undertaking to Ludendorff and prepared to enter the lists with Trotsky for the last time.

But now there occurred something which Kühlmann could not disregard as easily as he could the wishes of Ludendorff. Military operators at the great wireless station of Königsberg had intercepted radio-telegrams from Tsarkoe Selo inciting the German troops to mutiny, to murder the Emperor Wilhelm, the Generals of the High Command and their own regimental officers, and to conclude an independent peace with the Bolsheviks. Evidently Smolny, misled and dazzled by the prospect of revolution in Central Europe, had considered this a psychological moment for such a stroke. The effect was dramatic, but not what they had anticipated.

It so happened that, just previous to this incitement to murder, delegations of land-owners from Livonia and Estonia, still nominally part of Russia, had appeared before

[1] Czernin, p. 249.

the Kaiser and begged his protection against the depredations of Bolshevik terrorists. The Kaiser was sympathetic
to the petitioners, most of whom were of German origin,
and he was supported by Hindenburg and Ludendorff,
who were delighted to find so easy a way of completing their
programme to annex the Baltic littoral. Hertling, who
knew and approved Kühlmann's views on further annexations, opposed the Supreme Command. Once more the
Kaiser sat upon an iron-spiked fence.

The news of the Bolshevik incitement to murder turned
the scale. The Emperor was furious at this deliberate
attempt upon his person and, at the urgent request of the
High Command, telegraphed imperatively to Kühlmann
ordering him to issue a twenty-four-hour ultimatum to
Trotsky demanding the complete renunciation by Russia
not only of her claims to Courland and Lithuania, but to
Estonia and Livonia as well.

Again, in a moment of major crisis, Kühlmann justified
his name. He remained cool, and considered the matter in
all its aspects. His relations with the Supreme Command
were already so bad that they could scarcely be worse ;
he therefore left them out of his calculations. His duty to
the Emperor was, however, a different matter. Kühlmann
was fully aware—no one had better reason to be—of the
grip in which the Supreme Command held Germany at
that moment, how completely and detrimentally they
dominated throne, Government, and Parliament alike. He
realized, too, the effect abroad of such an action as that
which he was now urged to take. The whole affair at Brest-
Litovsk had damaged Germany enormously in the eyes of
all neutrals and had whetted the antagonism of the Allied
and Associated Powers. The effect of the reply of the Central
Powers to the Wilson proposals had been nullified by the
demands of the Supreme Command at Brest. This was
eloquently reflected in the announcement of the Allied War
Council on February 2, which had commented on " the

contrast between the professed idealistic aims with which the Central Powers entered upon the present negotiations at Brest-Litovsk, and the now openly disclosed plans of conquest and spoliation ". The impression made by this contrast had deepened the conviction that the replies of Hertling and Czernin to Wilson contained no " real approximation to the moderate conditions laid down by all the Allied Governments ".[1]

If this was the effect which had been produced by the demands already disclosed, how much worse would be the reaction abroad if it became known that Livonia and Estonia had been added to them ? Besides, that very moment had brought Kühlmann a slender ray of hope. Trotsky had sent Admiral Altvater to ask if it would not be possible by some means to arrange that Riga and the Islands of the Moon Sound should be retained by Russia. It seemed, therefore, that not every prospect of a settlement had vanished.

In view of all these considerations, Kühlmann, to his lasting credit, determined to sacrifice himself for what he believed to be right. To the Kaiser's command, he telegraphed a reply that the moment seemed ill-chosen to send an ultimatum with so short a time-limit, and that he urgently advised that it should not be sent at all. If, however, His Majesty insisted upon its delivery, Kühlmann begged him to find another Secretary for State. He would await the Emperor's reply until four-thirty that afternoon, and if none had arrived by that time he would consider the order for the ultimatum as rescinded.[2]

The morning of February 9 passed in an atmosphere of suspense. The conference met in commission, and the Ukrainian treaty was formally announced by Kühlmann and Czernin and formally protested against by Trotsky.

[1] Lloyd George, v. 47.
[2] Ludendorff, ii. 556-557; Hoffmann, ii. 217-218; Czernin, pp. 248-249 ; Fokke, p. 190.

A desultory discussion on the Aaland Islands followed. Sub-commissions were set up. A sense of unreality was everywhere. All knew that the fate of the conference hung on the private negotiations outside its ⅃oors, and Kühlmann knew that it rested upon whether he heard from Berlin by half-past four or not. Noon passed and still no word. The sub-commissions bickered and got nowhere.

At last the zero hour came and went without further word from the Kaiser, and Kühlmann with relief sent Rosenberg to Trotsky with the suggestion that he should put in writing that Russia was prepared to negotiate on the basis of Riga and the islands. Kühlmann had decided in his own mind that, if Trotsky was really in earnest, he would flout the High Command in the matter of these territorial concessions, if not to the extent of leaving them in Russian hands, at least by agreeing to their neutralization. In any event, a statement in writing from Trotsky would be a valuable addition to his armoury in the final battle with the Supreme Command which he felt could not be long postponed.

Alas for his hopes! Rosenberg returned with the news that, faced with a direct request to state his claims clearly, Trotsky had refused.[1] So, thought Kühlmann, it had all been in vain. He had risked his resignation to no purpose. He had incurred the ire of the Supreme Command, and probably that of the Emperor as well, only to have to agree with them after all, for now it would have to be the ultimatum. They could not delay longer. Well, anyway, it would be a relief to have it all over at last.

The Germans believed that Trotsky had refused to put his wishes in writing because he was not prepared to make a direct claim for Riga, a city of which the majority of the population was indisputably German. To violate the sacred principle of self-determination for the sake of a Russian

[1] Hoffmann, ii. 218.

strategical position was, they thought, too much even for Trotsky.

But it is by no means certain whether he ever intended to negotiate seriously. The moment was rapidly approaching beyond which negotiations could not so usefully be drawn out. Already the Scandinavian press had discovered the intention of the Russians to make a demonstration of not signing the peace treaty.[1] For the success of this manœuvre the element of surprise was essential, and Trotsky had decided that the moment had come with the signing of the Ukrainian treaty to play his trump card. On the night of the 9th, he and Karakhan conferred over the wire with Lenin and Stalin at Smolny, and it was agreed that Trotsky should deliver the Soviet declaration next day.

" I shall demand that peace be made with all Russia ", he told Schüller, who had come to him on the following morning, that fatal February 10, in a last effort to persuade him to sign. " By the Ukrainian peace you wish to secure for yourselves supplies of grain, but we too draw grain supplies from the Ukraine. I am convinced that the intention is to give military support to the Ukraine against us."

" The best way to avoid that is to make peace ", said Schüller. " If you do not make peace, you will risk the Germans advancing on Petrograd and driving you out, and presumably you wish to remain in power."

" The Germans would not dare to advance on Petrograd ", replied Trotsky ; " it would cause a revolution in Germany."

" You cannot rely on that with any certainty," was Schüller's answer, " and if the revolution does come, it is a question whether it would come in time for you."

In a final appeal to sign, Schüller again emphasized the danger of a resumption of hostilities. Trotsky replied that he would give his reply only at the session of the conference which was to meet that afternoon.

[1] Trotsky, *My Life*, p. 329.

" Beware of a breach ", warned Schüller.

" I have not said it would come to a breach ", Trotsky replied oracularly.[1]

And so, as the grey Sunday afternoon of February 10 drew to its early close, the delegates met for the last time, each, unbeknown to the other, prepared to end the struggle. They had advanced very little since they had first sat down together on December 22; a few reputations had been tarnished, a few new names added to history, that was all. Barren of achievement, negative and void in every aspect, this strangest of conferences was about to end.

Kühlmann moved to the attack with a direct accusation against the Bolsheviks of inciting the German army to mutiny and to the murder of its Emperor, Generals, and officers. Trotsky, in reply, denied all knowledge of such an order. " But ", he declared dramatically, " the decisive hour has struck."

This was his great moment, the scene which he had rehearsed for so long, and he enjoyed it hugely. After a bitter indictment of imperialism, which many of his hearers took for the prelude to capitulation, he continued :

We are removing our armies and our people from the war. Our peasant soldiers must return to their land to cultivate in peace the fields which the Revolution has taken from the landlord and given to the peasants. Our workmen soldiers must return to the workshops and produce, not for destruction but for creation. They must, together with the peasants, create a Socialist State.

We are going out of the war. We inform all peoples and their Governments of this fact. We are giving the order for a general demobilization of all our armies opposed at the present to the troops of Germany, Austria-Hungary, Turkey, and Bulgaria. We are waiting in the strong belief that other peoples will soon follow our example.

At the same time we declare that the conditions as submitted to us by the Governments of Germany and Austria-Hungary are opposed

[1] Gratz and Schüller, pp. 111-113.

in principle to the interests of all peoples. These conditions are refused by the working masses of all countries, amongst them by those of Germany and Austria-Hungary. . . . We cannot place the signature of the Russian Revolution under these conditions which bring with them oppression, misery and hate to millions of human beings. The Governments of Germany and Austria-Hungary are determined to possess lands and peoples by might. Let them do so openly. We cannot approve violence. We are going out of the war, but we feel ourselves compelled to refuse to sign the peace treaty.

In connection with this I give to the Allied [Central Powers] Delegates the following written and signed declaration :

> In the name of the Council of People's Commissars, the Government of the Russian Federal Republic informs the Governments and peoples united in war against us, the Allied and neutral countries, that, in refusing to sign a peace of annexation, Russia declares, on its side, the state of war with Germany, Austria-Hungary, Turkey, and Bulgaria as ended.

The Russian troops are receiving at the same time an order for a general demobilization on all lines of the fronts.[1]

During the early stages of the speech the delegates of the Central Powers had sat and listened contentedly. This, they decided, was Trotsky's swan-song, a concession to principles to be followed by a declaration of willingness to sign. Kühlmann sighed with relief. It might not be necessary to present that ultimatum after all. But, as Trotsky proceeded from invective to policy, and the true import of the announcement broke upon them, their satisfaction vanished and they listened incredulously. " The effect was more startling than a streak of lightning in a clear sky." When the last echoes of Trotsky's powerful voice died away, no one spoke. The whole conference sat speechless, dumbfounded before the audacity of this *coup de théâtre*. The amazed silence was shattered by an ejaculation from Hoffmann : " *Unerhört !* " (" Unheard of ! "), he exclaimed,

[1] *Proceedings*, pp. 172-173 ; *Mirnye peregovory v Brest-Litovske*, i. 207-208.

scandalized. The spell was broken. Kühlmann said something about the necessity for calling a plenary session of the conference, but this Trotsky refused, saying that there remained nothing to discuss. With that the Bolsheviks left the room ; and in gloomy silence, still scarcely believing what they had heard and wholly at a loss as to what to make of it, the delegates of the Central Powers dispersed.[1]

Late that night, under a frosty sky, with none to see them off but a handful of aides-de-camp, the Soviet delegates entrained for Petrograd. They behaved with confidence, almost with gaiety, congratulating one another on the trick they had played on the Germans. Pokrovsky was in especially good humour. Once he had wept and pled before Hoffmann, and now he derived much pleasure from the General's scandalized amazement. " *Unerhört !* " he kept repeating in imitation of the General's high-pitched staccato, " *Unerhört!* "[2]

5

The bewilderment which had descended upon the remainder of the delegates after Trotsky's dramatic departure from the conference hall remained with them, and was not easily dispelled. The situation appeared to be without parallel until the indefatigable Ministerial-Director Kriege, the German legal expert, after exhaustive researches, reported that a similar case of a unilateral declaration of peace had occurred several thousand years before, after a war between the Greeks and the Scythians.

While the Bolsheviks were departing from the station in high fettle, a still somewhat bemused group of Austrian and German diplomatists, together with Hoffmann, gathered in Kühlmann's quarters in the citadel. What was the next step, they debated. Had peace with Russia become an actual

[1] Hoffmann, ii. 218-219 ; A. A. Joffe, " The Fight for Peace ", in *Illustrated History of the Russian Revolution* (London, 1928), ii. 501.
[2] Fokke, p. 207.

fact, by virtue of Trotsky's astounding declaration, or were they still nominally in a state of war ? The unanimous voice of the diplomatists was in favour of accepting the situation as one of peace, and of evolving some manner of bringing it into line with international law and diplomatic practice. Both Kühlmann and Czernin were relieved that the presentation of an ultimatum had been unnecessary, and as the Russians, by their declaration, had tacitly agreed to the occupied territories remaining in German hands, there seemed nothing further to fight for.

But against these councils of peace there was raised one dissentient voice. Hoffmann had at once telephoned to Kreuznach and had informed the Supreme Command of the incredible situation which had arisen. He was now acquainted with their views, and their views were un-compromisingly for war. One of the most vital points in the armistice agreement, argued Hoffmann, had been the undertaking to arrive at terms of peace. As peace had not been concluded, the object of the armistice had not been attained, and therefore the truce came automatically to an end. To him Trotsky's declaration was no more than a denunciation of the armistice, and hostilities must there-fore reopen after the lapse of seven days.

Hours passed in argument, but this time Hoffmann was unable to gain his point. The statesmen were all for peace, and Wiesner, in one of those excesses of enthusiasm which had led him once before, at Serajevo in 1914, to send a remarkably ill-informed and self-contradictory telegram, had already wired to Vienna that peace had been con-cluded, with the result that the Imperial capital was even now dressing itself *en fête*.[1]

With the sincere hope of peace in his heart, Kühlmann brought the conference proceedings to a formal conclusion on February 11, and departed for Berlin. On his arrival he was summoned, with the Chancellor and the Vice-Chancellor,

[1] Czernin, p. 318 ; Hoffmann, ii. 219.

the Great Twin Brothers of the Supreme Command, and the chiefs of the Naval Staff, to the little watering-place of Homburg, where the Kaiser was taking a February cure. There, throughout the 13th, raged a battle-royal on the issues of peace and war, with the Emperor flitting in and out like an unhappy ghost. Poor Wilhelm, only a few days before he had informed his loyal Homburgers that " Our Lord God means to have peace, but a peace in which the world endeavours to do what is right and good ". It was the Omnipotent Will that Germany should be the agency for bringing such a peace into the world, and the Emperor rejoiced that with the Ukraine they had " managed it in a very friendly fashion." [1] He was now called upon to consider war.

From the moment of Hoffmann's report on the evening of the 10th. Hindenburg and Ludendorff had bombarded the Emperor and the Chancellor with demands for the denunciation of the armistice agreement, and now, confronted with Kühlmann, the object of their spleen and hatred, they redoubled the emphasis of their demands. To Ludendorff there appeared now a way both to encompass the fall of the Secretary of State and to complete, on the widest scale, his scheme of conquest in the East.

The First Quartermaster-General desired clarity in the East and proposed to achieve it by means of inflicting a short but sharp blow upon what remained of the Russian armies. Peace must on no account be signed until the German line had been advanced to include both Livonia and Estonia, thereby creating a sanitary cordon between the Teutonic peoples in Eastern Europe and Bolshevik Russia. In addition, it was apparent to the Supreme Command that if they wanted the grain, for which they had made peace with the Ukraine, they must go and get it. There was no longer any pretence that the *Rada*, at that moment appealing desperately for German assistance from

[1] *Norddeutsche Allgemeine Zeitung*, February 11, 1918.

its insecure temporary capital at Zhitomir, had any control over the country ; but as Ludendorff said : " We need the Ukraine as an auxiliary against the Bolsheviks, so it must not on any account be surrendered to them ".

This argument was undoubtedly valid. Without assistance from the Ukraine, Germany and Austria-Hungary could not survive the winter of 1918–1919. The conquest of Rumania had failed to provide the anticipated supply of grain, and the prospects of the coming harvest in Central Europe were already poor. Therefore the Ukraine must be rescued from Bolshevism in order to supply the Central Powers with food. In addition there was, from the German point of view, the danger (though the contingency was not a practical one) that the Entente might give aid and assistance to the Russians in order to re-establish the Eastern Front. " It was a military absurdity ", wrote Ludendorff, " to sit still and watch the enemy increase his strength ; it was necessary to act . . . it would then be certain that we should obtain peace." [1]

Despite these strategic considerations the civilians remained opposed to the High Command. They feared the effect on the internal condition of Germany if hostilities were resumed. Both the Majority Socialists and the Independent Socialists would be opposed to it, and the influence of the latter on the masses was steadily increasing. They advanced these counter-arguments in vain. Kühlmann, in addition to his general principles, warned them that a new war in the East would strain the alliance with Austria-Hungary almost to the breaking point, and that no support from that source could be looked for in a new offensive. Czernin had made it abundantly clear on a number of occasions that the alliance with Germany did not entail the co-operation of Austria-Hungary in the defence of anything but the pre-war German possessions. Austrian divisions

[1] Ludendorff, *War Memories*, ii. 557-559 ; *The General Staff and its Problems*, ii. 548-551.

might be brought to the West to fight against France and England, but they would not fight again in the East.

The Supreme Command remained adamant, the more so because they hoped to drive Kühlmann to the point of resignation. Gradually Count Hertling and Vice-Chancellor von Payer were won over to the military point of view. Kühlmann was isolated. But he stuck to his guns ; though defeated and deserted by his governmental colleagues, he was not going to give Ludendorff the satisfaction of in-veigling him into political suicide. A few days before, on a matter of principle, he had not hesitated to offer his resigna-tion to the Kaiser, but now, when the responsibility for capitulation to the military clearly rested not upon him but upon his superiors, the Chancellor and Vice-Chancellor, he refused to sacrifice himself. " I am against the proposal of resuming hostilities," he declared, " but I do not consider the question important enough for me to withdraw from the Cabinet." And he remained. It was to be another four months before the Supreme Command would hang Kühl-mann's scalp on the flap of the G.H.Q. wigwam. Until that time he retained his dual rôle of actor-onlooker, playing the game for the mere charm of playing.

Though balked of the victim of their personal spite, the High Command had won a signal victory. They had brought the Government to heel, and it required but little effort to secure the approval of the All-Highest War Lord. Orders were issued to Hoffmann to denounce the armistice on the 17th and to begin the advance forthwith, and the announcement of resumed hostilities was greeted in Germany with school holidays, street rejoicings, and in some towns with the ringing of bells.[1]

6

How accurate Kühlmann had been in his views re-

[1] Georg Bernhard in the *Vossische Zeitung*, February 18, 1918.

garding the co-operation of Austria-Hungary in further hostilities in the East, was quickly confirmed from Vienna. The news of the signature of the Ukrainian treaty on February 9, followed by Wiesner's despatch announcing peace with Russia, had sent the city into transports of wildest celebration. In an hour the streets of the city—so long *une ville sans âme*—blossomed with flags and bunting ; all business was at a standstill and huge crowds poured into the streets. Everywhere were signs of relief and emotion, women weeping for joy, men embracing and crying, " Now at last we shall have enough food ".

The rejoicings lasted throughout the following days until stilled by the fateful tidings of the decision taken at Homburg. The whole Empire revolted in horror against resuming hostilities with Russia, and the anti-German sentiment, never deeply hidden in these days, flared up with dangerous rancour. Austria-Hungary had suffered much from her overbearing ally in the four years of war, and the realization of her own military inferiority to Germany did nothing to soften the antagonism, which was rapidly increasing. Particularly resented was Germany's assumption that Austria-Hungary would have to collaborate in her annexationist adventures, and the entire Dual Monarchy cried out against further sacrifice.

There was no immediately apparent reason why Austria-Hungary should resume hostilities with Russia, since, by virtue of the Ukrainian treaty, she had ceased to be a contiguous State. "Conditions for successful negotiations have never been disturbed by us. We wish that they had never been disturbed by the other side ", asserted *Die Zeit* on February 16, meaning by " the other side " Germany ; and the *Arbeiter-Zeitung* was even more emphatic : " Everything must be avoided which, even against our will, may drag us again into war with Russia." Ministerial circles shared the public aversion to a renewal of hostilities, and on February 17 Dr. Seidler informed

Count Hertling that Austria-Hungary would take no part in the resumed hostilities.

Indeed, the Austro-Hungarian Government had difficulties enough internally without incurring further external complications. The apprehensions of Czernin with regard to Polish opposition to the cession of Cholm to the Ukrainians had been fully justified. The Poles, who had claimed representation at the negotiations and had been refused it, now vehemently denied the right of the Austrians to carve out and give to the Ukrainians " a piece of Polish land from our nation's living body ". The province of Cholm had been separated from Russian Poland by the Tsar's Government in 1912 and incorporated in Russia proper, and the treaty thus renewed one of the last wrongs inflicted on Poland by Imperial Russia.

While Vienna was beflagged and rejoicing at the signature of the Ukrainian Peace, the Polish press in Warsaw and Lublin appeared with heavy black borders in mourning for the rape of Cholm. A general strike was declared in Warsaw, Cracow, and Lemberg on February 14 ; the Polish Council of Ministers resigned and the three Regents, Prince Lubomirski, Archbishop Kakowski, and Count Ostrowski, issued a manifesto in language savouring of the mediaeval : " Before God and before the World ; before men and the tribunal of history ; before the German people and the peoples of Austria-Hungary, the Polish Council of Regency now raises its protest against the new partition of Poland, refuses to give its recognition, and brands the step as an act of violation ". The Polish Club in the Vienna Parliament, comprising the six Polish political parties, protested as vehemently. The Polish legions demonstratively left the Austrian front and marched into the midst of the welter of revolutionary violence in the Ukraine. Many perished there, others escaped and fought for Polish liberty on the side of the Entente.

Public feeling for and against the treaty rose fiercely

until it reached boiling point in the Lower House of the Austrian Reichsrat on February 19. The appearance in the gallery of the young Ukrainian leader Sevruk, who had signed the treaty, was the signal for an outburst from the Polish and Czech deputies. " A youngster of twenty-nine like that to conclude peace ! It's a scandal ; let him clear out of the House ! " cried an enraged Czech. Whereupon the Ukrainian members shook their fists at him, shouting : " You're a fine free people, you Czechs ; what a way to treat a distinguished guest ! You ought to be ashamed of yourselves ! " At this moment the youthful object of these demonstrations, who, in complete ignorance of the German language, had no knowledge of what had been said, was led diplomatically from the Chamber.

The sitting was further enlivened by the Social Democrat deputy Winkler, who, in support of his defence of the treaty in the interests of avoiding famine, produced and waved before his colleagues an unappetizing sample of maize bread, crying, " This is the sort of stuff we are expected to eat ".

In the face of the united opposition of the Poles, Czechs, and Slovenes, the Austrian Government gave way, and Seidler, bowing before the storm, announced at the close of the sitting that the province of Cholm would not automatically revert to the Ukraine, but that a supplementary agreement would be entered into whereby a Commission should be appointed consisting of representatives of the Quadruple Alliance, the Ukraine, *and* Poland, which should determine the future destiny of the province in accordance with the expressed wishes of its population.[1]

But this palliative could not restore the confidence or regain the support of the Poles. They accepted it only with an ill grace, and from that time onwards their

[1] The agreement with the Ukraine setting up this Commission was signed at Brest-Litovsk on March 4, 1918. See *Texts of the Ukrainian " Peace "*, pp. 27-28.

support of the Central Powers was at an end. The dreams of an independent Polish State, fostered by President Wilson's reference thereto in the Fourteen Points, caused their sympathies to drift more and more to the side of the Entente. They regarded themselves as unpardonably betrayed by the Habsburg and Hohenzollern Monarchies, and found themselves forced to look elsewhere for the realization of their national aspirations.

Such were the first of the crop of " Dead Sea apples " which was the fruit of Brest-Litovsk.

7

In Petrograd the fools' paradise still persisted. The atmosphere of elated optimism in which the Soviet delegation had left Brest-Litovsk remained with them on their return to the capital ; the *leitmotif* of their satisfaction was the simple belief, " The Germans cannot attack us after we have declared the war ended ". Nor were they entirely unjustified in their confidence. Before their departure from Brest, Herr Kriege had assured Joffe, with whom he was on the best of terms, that under the present conditions there could be no question of a new German offensive ; and on their arrival at Petrograd, Count Mirbach, who since the armistice had been in the capital negotiating agreements for the resumption of commercial relations and the exchange of prisoners, and who was now about to leave for Berlin, was equally reassuring.[1] Moreover, echoes of the decision of Kühlmann and Czernin to accept the *de facto* condition of peace quickly reached Smolny.

There was almost a love-feast of reconciliation with the Social Revolutionaries of the Right, who could not but applaud the strategy of Trotsky who, with craft and sagacity, had extracted Russia from an intolerable position. The Bolshevik press continued to build upon the old myth of

[1] Trotsky, *The Russian Revolution to Brest-Litovsk*, p. 143.

Austro-German proletarian solidarity. " The Central Powers are placed in a quandary ", exulted *Pravda*. " They cannot continue their aggression without revealing their cannibal teeth, dripping with human blood. For the sake of the interests of Socialism, and of their own interests, the Austro-German working masses will not permit the violation of the Revolution." [1] But the Central Powers did not in the least object to " revealing their cannibal teeth ", and the Austro-German working masses remained passive.

Trotsky himself may have had some lingering doubt as to the impossibility of renewed hostilities. He reported at great length on February 13 to the Central Executive Committee, giving a detailed account of the negotiations and explaining fully the reasons for his own policy. In conclusion he said :

Comrades, I do not want to say that a further advance of the Germans against us is out of the question. Such a statement would be too risky, considering the power of the German Imperialist Party. But I think that by the position we have taken up on the question we have made any advance a very embarrassing affair for the German militarists.[2]

This statement, though far from the truth, was considerably nearer to it than the unqualified optimism of the rest of the delegation, which infected the Executive Committee. On the motion of Sverdlov a resolution was passed unanimously approving " the action of its representatives at Brest-Litovsk ",[3] a sentiment which was shared and affirmed by every political party and Soviet local organization.

In the midst of the welter of enthusiasm one man remained unmoved and sceptical. To Lenin the whole

[1] *Pravda*, February 12, 1918.

[2] Trotsky, *The Russian Revolution to Brest-Litovsk*, p. 142.

[3] Bunyan and Fisher, p. 511 ; *Protokoly siezdov i konferentsii vsesoiuznoi Kommunisticheskoi Partii*, (b) *Sedmoi Siezd, Mart 1918, goda*, p. 284.

situation appeared artificial, a dream from which there must in time come a horrible awakening. He granted that outward appearances were in favour of Trotsky's case, but he felt in his bones that all was not what it seemed. He voted for Sverdlov's resolution in the Central Executive Committee, but he sensed the unreality of the position. He had no faith in the power of the German workers to restrain their Government and above all their actual rulers, the Supreme Command, from any chosen course of action, and he could not be convinced that such action would not take the form of a demonstration in force against a defenceless enemy.

" Won't they deceive us ? " he kept on asking Trotsky, and when the answer came that it did not appear so, Lenin would shake his head but little reassured. " Well, if it is so, it's all to the good. Appearances are saved and the war is over."

There was plenty to occupy his attention. The problems of creating a Socialist State were assuming gigantic proportions. Famine and civil war threatened the very existence of the régime. There were times when even Lenin believed that the Revolution would be overwhelmed. He turned his mind to grapple with them anew, comforting himself that, even if the Germans deceived them, a week's notice of the termination of the armistice agreement must be given before hostilities could begin.

The shattering of the Bolshevik dream of peace came with dramatic suddenness.

On February 16, at noon, Lenin and Trotsky sat in conference at Smolny with Karelin and another Left Social Revolutionary. A folded paper was brought to Lenin, and, without interrupting his remarks, he glanced at it. It was a telegram from General Samoilo, who had been left behind at Brest :

General Hoffmann to-day gave official notice that the armistice concluded with the Russian Republic comes to an end on February 18 at 12 o'clock, and that war will be renewed on that day. He therefore invites me to leave Brest-Litovsk.

GENERAL SAMOILO.[1]

Lenin's face remained immobile. By not so much as a flicker of an eyelash did he betray the ill news. He passed the paper to Trotsky without comment, but flashed him a glance which implied that the news contained was important. He did, however, cut short his conference with the Social Revolutionaries, and as soon as they were gone his calm left him.

" So they have deceived us after all ", he cried. " And gained five days. This wild beast lets nothing escape it. There is nothing left for us now but to sign the old terms at once if the Germans will still agree to them."

" We should wait until Hoffmann has actually opened his offensive ", said Trotsky.

" But that means losing Dvinsk and a lot of artillery."

" It means new sacrifices of course, but they are necessary so that the Germans actually enter our territory fighting, so that the workers in Germany and the Entente countries may understand our position."

It was the old myth to which Lenin had listened unbelievingly for so many weeks, the fairy-tale which he himself had outgrown. He had allowed the others to go their way, to play with the toys of revolution, and it had brought them to disaster. Now, these *svolochi* must and should listen to him.

" No," he decided, " there is not another moment to lose. Your test has been tried and it failed. Hoffmann can and will fight. It's not a question of Dvinsk, but of the Revolution. Delay is impossible. We must sign at once. This beast springs quickly." [2]

The fiction of " No War—No Peace " was at an end.

[1] *Pravda*, February 19, 1918.
[2] Trotsky, *Lenin*, pp. 137-138 ; *My Life*, pp. 331-332.

VII

"THE TILSIT PEACE"

VII

" THE TILSIT PEACE "

1

ON the night of February 17, 1918, there was no better
satisfied man in Europe than Major-General Max Hoffmann,
as he sat in the citadel of Brest-Litovsk. He had a refreshing
sense of relief from the crowded conditions and political
exasperations of the last eight weeks. The citadel had
returned to its austere appearance of a military headquarters, purged at last of the horde of procrastinating
statesmen and provoking Bolsheviks. With them had
vanished the atmosphere of false sincerity which pervaded
the negotiation period. Hoffmann was heartily sick of all
that play-acting and rapier-work, and was immensely
satisfied that Germany was now about to do what he
believed should have been done weeks before—dictate
peace at the point of the bayonet.

That morning the General had received a telegraphic
protest from Trotsky against the alleged violation of the
time-limit clause of the armistice agreement, assuming
ironically that the communication to General Samoilo
had not been " issued by those persons by whom it was
signed ", and requesting an explanation of the "misunderstanding ".[1] To this Hoffmann had not seen fit to
reply.

" To-morrow we are going to start hostilities against
the Bolsheviks ", he was writing in his diary. " No other
way out is possible, otherwise these brutes will wipe up
the Ukrainians, the Finns, and the Balts, and then quietly

[1] *Proceedings*, p. 174.

get together a new revolutionary army and turn the whole of Europe into a pig-sty. . . . The whole of Russia is no more than a vast heap of maggots—a squalid, swarming mass." [1]

This, then, was the watchword of the new offensive. In reality it was being undertaken to complete the annexation programme of the Supreme Command and to secure the concessions obtained under the Ukrainian treaty, but to the world its object was the destruction of Bolshevism in non-Russian lands. Accordingly a proclamation was issued to the Russian people by Prince Leopold of Bavaria explaining that the German armies were advancing in the interests of civilization and against the Bolshevik Government. They were coming as saviours not as conquerors, sworn to put down the tyranny " which has raised its bloody hand against your best people, as well as against the Poles, Lithuanians, Letts, and Estonians ". [2]

German aircraft had made reconnaissance persistently over the Russian lines throughout the 17th, and at dawn on the 18th the field-grey hosts went forward, capturing Dvinsk in the north, and Luck in the south. The advance could not in the military sense of the term be called an offensive, for the Russian troops made no resistance whatsoever. They were more demoralized than the Germans had even expected. The bulk of the troops had already gone home. The remainder, already in a state of disintegration, fled or surrendered wholesale ; on one occasion a lieutenant and six men received the surrender of six hundred Cossacks. The old Russian army, long ago wounded to the death, was falling to pieces, blocking the railways, roads, and by-ways ; the new Red Army was as yet rising but slowly from the appalling chaos of dissolution. [3]

[1] Hoffmann, i. 204-205.
[2] *Tägliche Rundschau*, February 19, 1918 ; *Pravda*, March 2, 1918.
[3] Hoffmann, i. 206, ii. 219 ; Trotsky, *The Russian Revolution to Brest-Litovsk*, p. 143.

On the 19th German Headquarters received a telegram from Lenin and Trotsky accepting the conditions of peace offered at Brest. This was altogether too rapid for the Germans, who were anxious to complete the advance to Lake Peipus before reopening negotiations. Hoffmann, following instructions from Kreuznach, employed delaying tactics. He replied to the Bolshevik acceptance with a demand that it be confirmed in writing to the " German Commandant at Dünaburg (Dvinsk) ". By the night of the 20th came a reply from Petrograd that a courier was on his way.

" He [Trotsky] seems to be in a devil of a hurry—we are not ", wrote Hoffmann that night. Despite the absence of resistance, his advance, owing to lack of transport, had not been as swift as he had hoped. Yet the achievement of the German troops was not without merit. Hoffmann had not expected to " run a victorious express train to Petersburg ", yet in 124 hours his men covered 150 miles over practically non-existent roads and in the bite of a Russian winter, capturing over two thousand guns, many thousands of prisoners, as well as a goodly haul of motor-cars, locomotives, and trucks. And, above all, the General was enjoying himself. " It is the most comical war I have ever known ", he wrote. " We put a handful of infantry men with machine-guns and one gun on to a train and push them off to the next station ; they take it, make prisoners of the Bolsheviks, pick up a few more troops, and go on. This proceeding has, at any rate, the charm of novelty." [1]

Thus the German hosts moved forward. The Bol-shevik formal acceptance reached Berlin on February 21, and by the 23rd the German reply, consisting of new and harsher terms presented in the form of an ultimatum, was in Lenin's hands at Smolny. Still the Germans advanced. There had been nothing to compare with this since the

[1] Hoffmann, i. 206-207.

" break-through " at Gorlice in the summer of 1915, when the Russian army had been in full flight and Russian fortresses were falling like houses of cards. Cities which had been the scenes of historic events in the early days of the Russian Revolution passed into German hands ; Pskov, where the Tsar had signed his act of abdication in his special train with so strange a lack of emotion, and Moghilev, where Dukhonin had been butchered for his attempted loyalty to the Allied cause. In Livonia and Estonia the Germans were greeted by the middle and upper classes as deliverers from the Bolshevik terror, not only by Baltic Germans but even by Letts and Estonians. The peasants and workers who had experienced a brief taste of the sweets of unlicensed power remained dumb and sullen.[1]

On February 24 the Bolsheviks signified their acceptance of the German terms and Krylenko enquired of Hoffmann by radio whether conditions of armistice similar to those which had existed before the 18th would now come into force.[2] To this Hoffmann replied :

The old armistice is dead and cannot be revived. According to Article 10 of the German terms submitted on February 21 peace must be concluded within three days after the arrival of the Russians at Brest-Litovsk. Until then the war is to go on . . . for the protection of Finland, Estonia, Livonia, and the Ukraine.[3]

Two days later the German advance in the north, having reached Lake Peipus and Narva, was halted and the Russians were informed that they might send to Brest-Litovsk a delegation authorized to sign a peace. " Whether Trotsky will take the road to Canossa in person, or will send someone else, is not yet certain ", wrote Hoffmann, " but this time the Comrades must simply swallow what we put before them."[4]

[1] Hoffmann, ii. 220 ; Joffe, p. 502.   [2] *Proceedings*, p. 178.
[3] *Pravda*, February 28, 1918.   [4] Hoffmann, i. 207-208 ; ii. 220.

In the south the Germans and Austrians were still advancing into the heart of the Ukraine.

2

Meanwhile Lenin was fighting his historic battle alone. Nothing in the new situation was favourable to his point of view, for the reaction from exalted optimism was towards a revolutionary war rather than to an immediate peace. The working class quarters of Petrograd and Moscow were ablaze with indignation at the new German offensive, and their anger was in no way directed against those who had told them that such a thing was impossible. The workers were ready in those tragic days and nights which followed February 17 to enlist in their tens of thousands for the defence of the Revolution, but there was no organization for such a movement.

Lenin was unmoved by this revolutionary hysteria. The crisis had justified his worst apprehensions and he took drastic steps to meet the emergency. Never in his career did he display greater courage than in the ensuing weeks; never had he stood out so pre-eminently above his revolutionary contemporaries.

His first step was to remind Trotsky of their compact of January 22. In return for a free hand to try his experiment of "No War—No Peace", Trotsky had agreed not to vote for a revolutionary war under any circumstances. Even now he would not concede that he had been wholly wrong, nor would he pledge his support to Lenin until the German offensive had become an accomplished fact. At the meeting of the Central Committee of the party on February 17, Lenin's motion to accept at once the German terms was lost by 5 to 6, while Trotsky's proposal to delay until the enemy advance had actually begun and its effect on the labouring masses of Russia, the Entente countries, and the Central Powers could be judged, was carried by 6 to 5. Lenin then put the crucial question : " If the German offensive becomes a fact and no revolution takes place in Germany and Austria, are we then to sign peace ? " Bukharin and his followers, the protagonists of a revolutionary war, together with Krestinsky, evaded giving an answer to this vital query by not voting. Joffe voted against peace, Lenin and the majority voted for it.

The position of Trotsky in this vote is one of the mysteries which surround that strange individual. According to his own account, repeated in many works, he voted with Lenin and the majority for peace, and he is so shown in the contemporary account of the meeting.[1] In 1928, in a reprint of these documents, Trotsky was, however, alleged to have abstained, and this was listed among the heresies for which he was excommunicated in that year.[2]

Whether he voted or not, it is certain that at this juncture Trotsky was still the victim of his own " wishful thinking ". He could not rid himself of the belief that in the last resort the German troops would not march, and the German masses would rise in protest, and he made a desperate appeal to the *Feldgrauen*.

Throughout February 16 and 17 the propaganda bureau of the Foreign Commissariat worked at double pressure. Trotsky and Radek excelled themselves in a forlorn hope. Thousands of leaflets in German and copies of a special edition of *Die Fakel* were printed and despatched to the German trenches. Surely, he thought, the common soldiers could not resist the fervour of this last appeal ? [3]

February 18 dawned grey and sullen, and with it came the confirmation of Lenin's worst fears. News came of the capture of Dvinsk and Luck, and of the advance into the Ukraine. The last faint hopes of mutiny and revolution

[1] Trotsky, *My Life*, p. 332.

[2] Bunyan and Fisher, p. 512.

[3] M. Philips Price, *Reminiscences of the Russian Revolution* (London, 1921), p. 240.

were shattered. The issue now had narrowed down to peace or war.

The Central Committee of the party again conferred. Lenin repeated his proposal for the immediate acceptance of the terms already offered. Trotsky again opposed him urging that the Central Powers should be asked to re-state their terms. Stalin for the moment deserted Lenin and swung to Trotsky's side. " It is not necessary to sign," he said, " but we can begin negotiations." Then Lenin spoke :

We cannot joke with war. . . . If we meant war, we had no right to demobilize . . . the Revolution will surely collapse if we pursue a half-way policy. To delay is to betray the Revolution. . . . To write notes to the Germans now is a waste of paper ; while we write they go on seizing warehouses and railway cars. . . . History will condemn us for betraying the Revolution when we had a choice of signing peace ; it is too late to send out " feelers ". . . . The revolution in Germany has not begun, and we know that it takes time for a revolution to triumph. If the Germans seize Livonia and Estonia we shall have to surrender them in the name of the Revolution. They may have revolutionary Finland too. All these sacrifices will not ruin the Revolution. . . . All the Germans are after is the grain [from the Ukraine]. After they have taken that they will depart. . . . I move that we notify the Germans that we are ready to accept their peace.

He did not carry them at once with the sanity of his plea. For three hours the discussion raged round the proposal. Finally reason triumphed. Late at night Trotsky shifted from opposition to support, and by 7 votes to 6 the motion was carried. Lenin, Trotsky, Stalin, Sverdlov, Sokolnikov, Zinoviev, and Smilga voted for the motion, and Bukharin carried with him Joffe, Lomov, Krestinsky, Dzerzhinsky, and Uritsky.[1] About midnight a radiogram was despatched to Hoffmann acquainting the Government in Berlin that, although protesting to the last, " under the

[1] Bunyan and Fisher, pp. 512-513 ; *Protokoly siezdov i konferentsii vsesoiuznoi Kommunisticheskoi Partii, (b) Sedmoi Siezd, Mart 1918, goda,* pp. 197-201.

circumstances the Soviet of People's Commissars finds itself forced to sign the treaty and to accept the conditions of the Four-Power Delegation at Brest-Litovsk ".[1]

For four days the Bolsheviks had no indication as to whether their surrender would be accepted or not. The first reaction to their radiogram was the peremptory reply from Hoffmann that it must be confirmed in writing to the " German Commandant at Dünaburg ".[2] A courier was despatched immediately, but after his departure there was silence from the Germans.

There was anything but silence in Petrograd. The whole city was in an uproar, both actual and political. It was now accepted that the inexorable German advance would not be halted until it had taken Petrograd. The bourgeoisie were enchanted at the prospect and openly declared themselves for the Hohenzollerns. The Allied Embassies hastily prepared for a hurried evacuation. The press of the Mensheviks and the Social Revolutionaries of the Right bitterly attacked the Bolsheviks for the supineness and cowardice of their policy. An influential group of Moscow Bolsheviks dissociated themselves from the actions of the Central Committee, resigned their party offices, and declared their freedom of action to agitate in favour of a revolutionary war. Even the Social Revolutionaries of the Left assailed their Bolshevik allies in their press and in the Petrograd Soviet. Never was speech freer in Russia than at this moment.

All semblance of order had left the city, which presented a strangely anomalous appearance. The population were starving, but the rich still had money. Restaurants and cabarets were open and well filled, and trotting-races were still held on Sundays. Yet the streets at night were infested with bands of robbers armed with rifles and hand-grenades, who terrorized rich and poor alike. On one occasion Uritsky, a member of the Central Executive

---

[1] *Proceedings*, p. 174.   [2] *Ibid*. p. 175.

Committee and later head of the Petrograd Cheka, was dragged from his sleigh as he returned from Smolny, stripped naked, and left to continue his journey in that embarrassing condition. He was lucky to escape with his life.[1] The prudent never went abroad alone after dark. In pairs or in groups they walked in the middle of the road, their fingers gripping the automatic pistols in their pockets.

In the midst of this bedlam the Bolsheviks sought to meet the emergency. The continued silence of the Germans was taken to mean that only complete and unconditional surrender on the part of Russia was intended. Because of this assumption Bukharin and his followers came into the ascendant. The Bolshevik press became clamorous with martial spirit against Germany, and Trotsky once more began his contacts with the Allied Embassies.

This time the situation was even more complicated than before. The Bolsheviks had done nothing to endear themselves to the Entente. They had arrested the Rumanian Minister and confiscated the Rumanian gold reserve of which he had been the guardian. As a result of vehement protests by the Diplomatic Corps, M. Diamandi had been released—but the gold was retained. Following on this had come, on February 10, the repudiation by the Soviet Government of Russia's external debts incurred before the November Revolution amounting to some fourteen milliards of roubles (pre-war and war debts), of which twelve were owed to the Allied and Associated Powers ; and no attempt had been made to reply to the protests which this action had called forth. Lenin and Trotsky, on their side, were both convinced that the Germans had reached an agreement with the Allies regarding the crushing of the Soviets and that " peace at the Western Front was to be built up on the bones of the Russian Revolution ".[2]

---

[1] Bruce Lockhart, *Memoirs of a British Agent* (London, 1932), p. 242.   [2] Trotsky, *My Life*, p. 332.

Yet Trotsky realized that in the renewed offensive in the East was a bridge which might span the gap between the two irreconcilables. For the Entente, the Bolsheviks might prove an instrument against German militarism, while for the Bolsheviks the Entente would provide a weapon against the mortal enemy of the Revolution. He therefore asked of Lockhart, of Robins, and of Sadoul, what co-operation their Governments would give to the Soviets if they declared a " holy war " against the Germans.

The result was more encouraging than might have been expected. As a result of Sadoul's representations, Noulens, the French Ambassador, took the initiative. " *Dans votre résistance contre l'Allemagne* ", he telephoned to Trotsky on February 21, " *vous pouvez compter sur l'appui militaire et financier de la France* ", and his lead was followed by the American, Japanese, and Italian Ambassadors, and by the British Chargé d'Affaires. The French and British engineer officers gave immediate assistance in destroying the railways to impede the German advance.[1]

It seems that for a moment even Lenin wavered from his determination. He was deeply moved by the news on the 21st that German troops had landed in Finland, routing the Red Guard detachments and suppressing the Soviet Government at Helsingfors. He first decided that armed resistance was now unavoidable, and then, with almost desperate self-discipline, he declared that it was impossible to depart from their policy of surrender.[2] None realized more acutely than he how precarious was the position of the Government at this moment. " Yesterday we still sat firm in the saddle ", he remarked to Trotsky, " and to-day we are only holding fast to the mane. It is a lesson which cannot fail to have an effect on our cursed

[1] *U.S. Foreign Relations, 1918 : Russia*, i. 383, 386 ; Sadoul, pp. 241-243 ; Lockhart, p. 229 ; Noulens, i. 223.

[2] Trotsky, *Lenin*, pp. 138-139 ; *My Life*, pp. 332-333.

negligence. . . . It will be a very good lesson if—if only the Germans, along with the Whites, do not succeed in over-throwing us." Then, with a grim little laugh, he added, " If the White Guards kill you and me, do you think that then Bukharin will come to an understanding with Sverdlov ? " [1]

The 21st passed and still no word from Berlin, only the steady, unstemmed advance of the German army. Panic and despair gripped the hearts of the Bolshevik leaders. It seemed that there was nothing left for them but to die fighting. They issued a manifesto to the Russian people declaring— somewhat anomalously—" the Socialist Fatherland " to be in danger, and authorizing the mobilization of the whole able-bodied population, a *levée en masse*, for the defence of the Revolution. No exemptions to this conscription were admitted. " In case of refusal or opposition, shoot them down ", read the order.[2]

On the following day, February 22, the Central Com-mittee of the party met to consider plans for resistance. " It is now clear ", declared Sverdlov, the president, " that the German imperialists will not reply to us, and that if they do, their answer will be completely inaccept-able. . . . There remains nothing for us to do but to save the Soviet Republic." Trotsky laid before them the fruits of his negotiations with the Ambassadors of the Entente for assistance in resisting the German advance. He asked that the offer be accepted, on the understanding that no political obligation was involved and that the Soviet Government retained its independence in foreign policy. The majority were in favour, but again there arose opposi-tion from Bukharin, who had developed into a species of " revolutionary Tory ". You could not touch pitch and remain undefiled, he maintained ; it was absolutely in-admissible for them to make any compromise with imperialism of any sort ; to accept assistance from the

[1] Trotsky, *Lenin*, pp. 165-166.   [2] *Pravda*, February 22, 1918.

Entente was as treasonable to their revolutionary principles as to negotiate with the Germans.

Lenin was not present at the meeting; he was working near by. But, when they reported the course of the discussion to him, he snorted. Here was Bukharin clamouring for a revolutionary *jehad* and refusing the only means by which it might conceivably be waged successfully. Lenin was opposed to resistance, but if they were ultimately driven to it and the imperialists of the Entente were prepared to help them against the imperialists of the Central Powers, by all means let them accept the offer. Unshakable in his fundamental revolutionary creed, Lenin never allowed himself to become the victim of his own revolutionary phrases. Unscrupulous in his code of political ethics, to him the end justified the use of any weapon. Above all he was never above " spoiling the Egyptians ". Had he not accepted a free train-journey from the military imperialist Ludendorff in order the better to destroy the bourgeois-imperialist Kerensky ?

He sent a slip of paper written in ink in a scarcely legible hand, recording his vote in favour of the following resolution: "That Comrade Trotsky be authorized to accept the assistance of the brigands of French imperialism against the German brigands ", and this uncompromising motion was carried against the almost frenzied protests of Bukharin. " We are turning the party into a dung-hill ", cried the little man, his hands clawing at his short red beard, and burst into a storm of hysterical weeping.[1]

This was Trotsky's last performance as Foreign Commissar. He now told Lenin privately that he considered he should resign in order to convince the Germans of " a radical change in our policy " and to strengthen their belief in the sincerity of Bolshevik willingness to sign a treaty. This argument had so much sense in it that

[1] Trotsky, *My Life*, p. 333 ; Isaac Don Levine, *The Man Lenin* (New York, 1924), p. 147.

Lenin agreed, though he deprecated the introduction of " parliamentarian methods " into revolutionary politics.[1] But there was no doubt that in the minds of the Germans Trotsky had become a symbol of duplicity and " slick dealing ", and his disappearance from the diplomatic arena would certainly indicate a change of heart. So to the tireless, dynamic Trotsky was allotted the thankless and herculean task, as Commissar of War, of reorganizing the defence forces of the Soviet State.

On the morning of the 23rd the suspense was ended. The courier who had been despatched on the 20th now returned with the German reply. At 10.30 he handed it to Sverdlov, who read the new peace terms to the Central Committee of the party :

Germany is ready to resume negotiations with Russia and conclude peace on the following conditions : (1) The German Empire and Russia declare the state of war ended. Both nations are resolved henceforward to live together in peace and friendship. (2) The territories which lie west of the line communicated to the Russian representatives at Brest-Litovsk, and which belonged to the Russian Empire, will no longer be under the territorial sovereignty of Russia. In the vicinity of Dünaburg (Dvinsk) the line is to be shifted to the eastern frontier of Courland. No obligations of any sort toward Russia will arise from the former allegiance of these territories to the Russian Empire. Russia renounces all interference in the internal affairs of these territories. Germany and Austria-Hungary intend to determine the future lot of the territories in agreement with their populations. Germany is ready, as soon as a general peace has been concluded and Russian demobilization has been completely carried out, to evacuate the territory situated east of the line mentioned above, in so far as nothing else results from Article 3. (3) Livonia and Estonia will without delay be evacuated by Russian troops and Red Guards and occupied by a German policing force until the country's institutions guarantee security and political order is restored. All the residents of the country arrested on political grounds are to be immediately released. (4) Russia shall immediately conclude peace with the Ukrainian People's Republic. Russian

[1] Trotsky, *My Life*, p. 333 ; *Lenin*, p. 138.

troops and Red Guards shall be withdrawn without delay from the Ukraine and Finland. (5) Russia shall do everything in her power to guarantee a speedy and orderly return of the East Anatolian provinces to Turkey. Russia shall recognize the abolition of the Turkish capitulations. (6) (a) The complete demobilization of the Russian army, including the portions of any army newly formed by the present Government, is to be carried out without delay. (b) The Russian warships in the Black Sea, Baltic, and Arctic are either to be taken to Russian ports, there to be left until the conclusion of a general peace, or immediately to be disarmed. The warships of the Entente in the Russian sphere of power are to be treated like Russian warships. (c) Commercial navigation in the Black Sea and the Baltic shall be resumed as provided in the armistice treaty. The clearing-away of mines for this purpose must begin at once. The barred zone in the Arctic shall remain in existence until the conclusion of a general peace. (7) The German-Russian Commercial Treaty of 1904 shall again come into force as in Article 7, Section 2a, of the Peace Treaty with the Ukraine, with the excision of special preferences for Asiatic countries provided in Article II, Section 3, Subsection 3, of the Commercial Treaty. In addition the whole of the first part of the final protocol is to be restored. To the above are added the guaranteeing of freedom of export and freedom from export duty for ores, speedy negotiations and conclusion of a new commercial treaty, the guaranteeing of the most-favoured-nation treatment until the end of 1925 at the earliest, and also Section 3, Section 4a, Subsection 1, and Section 5 of Article 7 of the Peace Treaty with the Ukraine. (8) Politico-legal affairs shall be regulated on the basis of the resolutions in the first version of the German-Russian Legal Convention in so far as those resolutions have not yet been adopted, e.g. in particular the indemnification of civil damages on the basis of the German proposals and the indemnification of expenditure for prisoners of war on the basis of the Russian proposal. Russia shall admit and support, according to her ability, German Commissions for the protection of German prisoners of war, civilians, and those returning home. (9) Russia shall undertake to cease all official or officially supported agitation or propaganda against the Four Allied Governments and their State and army institutions, also in the territories occupied by the Central Powers. (10) The foregoing conditions are to be accepted within forty-eight hours. The Russian plenipotentiaries must immediately proceed to Brest-Litovsk and there within three days sign the Peace Treaty, which must be ratified within a further two weeks.[1]

As Sverdlov finished reading it seemed as if a wave of passionate fury swept through the room, so fierce, so bitter, that it could almost be felt. Then there broke out a babel of indignation. If the terms which had been refused at Brest-Litovsk were harsh, these were Draconian, cutting into the very body-politic of Russia. Bukharin blared forth a call to war. Trotsky, though agreeing in principle, believed it would be impossible to wage a revolutionary war with a divided party. He was for submitting to German dictation, hoping that if capitulation failed to bring peace it would be possible to straighten out the party difficulties in an armed defence of the Revolution imposed upon them by the enemy. Still Bukharin remained unconvinced.

Alone among them Lenin remained cold and unmoved. The worst, the very worst, had happened. All that he had dreaded and warned against had come true. There was no more time for talking. The ultimatum expired at seven o'clock on the morning of the following day. " It is time to put an end to revolutionary phrases ", he said, " and to get down to real work. If this is not done I resign from the Government.[2] To carry on a revolutionary war, an army, which we do not have, is necessary. It is a question of signing the terms now or of signing the death sentence of the Soviet Government three weeks later."

Backwards and forwards the question was debated. Precious hours were lost in futile discussion. There could be no solution other than Lenin's, yet Bukharin would not

[1] *Pravda*, February 24, 1918 ; *Berliner Tageblatt*, February 27, 1918 ; *Proceedings*, pp. 176-177.

[2] Lenin repeated his threat to resign in a signed article in *Pravda* : " Only an unrestrained policy of phrases can drive Russia in the present moment into war, and I personally would not remain for a second in the Government or in the Central Committee of our party should the policy of phrases gain the upper hand " (*Pravda*, February 24, 1918).

yield. Finally a vote was called for. The fatal decision lay
with Trotsky. Lenin had failed to convince the majority.
His success or failure depended on the number of abstentions.
Trotsky could not agree whole-heartedly with either Lenin
or Bukharin. In this crucial test he was found to be a
waverer, as which Lenin had branded him before the March
Revolution. His sympathies were with Bukharin, yet his
common sense inclined him towards Lenin. In order to give
Lenin the majority he abstained from voting and the
momentous decision was taken by seven to four, with four
abstentions.[1] Immediately Bukharin and his three supporters resigned from the party.[2]

So far Lenin had scraped through by a hair's-breadth,
but, though the decision of the Central Committee of the
party bound the Council of Commissars, it had yet to be
ratified by the Petrograd Soviet and the Central Executive
Committee of the Congress of Soviets. Both these bodies
were in session in the Tauride Palace and the members
of the Central Committee drove immediately there from
Smolny.

It was already past eleven o'clock at night when they
reached the Palace, and as they entered the hall, Krylenko,
the former Commissar for War, was reporting on the
military situation. " We have no army," he was saying,
" our demoralized soldiers fly panic-stricken before the

[1] Eight months later, before a joint meeting of the higher organs of
the Soviet Government, Trotsky, on October 3, had the courage to
admit his errors in not supporting Lenin : " I deem it my duty to say
that at the hour when many of us, including myself, were doubtful as
to whether it was admissible for us to sign the Brest-Litovsk peace, only
Comrade Lenin maintained stubbornly, with amazing foresight and
against our opposition, that we had to go through with it to tide us
over until the revolution of the world proletariat. And now, we must
admit that we were wrong " (*My Life*, p. 337).

[2] Bunyan and Fisher, pp. 519-520 ; *Protokoly siezdov i konferentsii
vsesoiuznoi Kommunisticheskoi Partii*, (*b*) *Sedmoi Siezd, Mart 1918,
goda*, pp. 204-209 ; Trotsky, *My Life*, p. 333.

German bayonets, leaving behind them artillery, transport, and ammunition. The divisions of the Red Guard are swept away like flies. Only the immediate signing of peace can save us from ruin."

" Down with him ! " cried the belligerent Social Revolutionaries of the Left. " Down with the traitor ! "

" Where is our fleet ? " shouted someone.

A sailor from Kronstadt mounted the platform : " We haven't a fleet any more ; it's a wreck ", he said. " The sailors have left, and the ships are there for the enemy to take."

Radek poured out his eloquence in support of Bukharin's faction. " We don't want a war. We want peace but not a shameful peace, not a peace of traitors and blacklegs. The whole of the working masses will support us in a fight for the honour and salvation of the Revolution."

To Lenin, sitting quietly and awaiting his turn to speak, came Alexandra Kollontai, possibly his oldest revolutionary comrade. At the reading of the Declaration of Peace on November 7 she had wept with joy, but now her eyes flashed the anger and bitterness of her contempt. " Enough of this opportunism ", she cried to him. " You are advising us to do the same thing which you have always accused the Mensheviks of doing—compromising with imperialism." Calm and unmoved Lenin made no reply ; he only rubbed his chin and stared at the ground. Then he mounted the rostrum.

He was greeted with jeers and cries of " Traitor ! " These men who had cheered his Declaration of Peace now hissed him for his consistency. Long and gloomily he looked out over the meeting, a sea of faces, soldiers in green tunics, workers collarless or in jerseys, peasants in belted shirts and high boots, and, as he looked at them in silence, their jeers faded, and he seemed to tower above them, this strange little man with his wide mouth and his biting tongue. He said :

Let us beware of becoming the slaves of our own phrases. In our day wars are won not by mere enthusiasm, but by technical superiority. Give me an army of 100,000 men, an army which will not tremble before the enemy, and I will not sign this peace. Can you raise an army ? Can you give me anything but prattle and the drawing up of pasteboard figures ? . . . If we retire to the Urals we can resist the pressure of the Germans for two or three weeks, then after a month's delay we shall sign conditions which are a hundred times worse. You must sign this shameful peace in order to save the world Revolution, in order to hold fast to its most important, and at present, its only foothold—the Soviet Republic. . . .

They were listening spellbound now. All the passion of the phrases about " revolutionary war " had disappeared. What fate awaited the Soviet State, humiliated, driven to its knees ? But Lenin was still speaking :

You think that the path of the proletarian Revolution is strewn with roses ? That we will march from victory to victory with waving flags, to the strains of the " Internationale " ? Then it would be easy to be a revolutionary ! The Revolution is not a pleasure trip ! The path of revolution leads over thorns and briars. Wade up to the knees in filth, if need be, crawling on our bellies through dirt and dung to Communism, then in this fight we will win. . . .

He had conquered their antagonism now. From a pack of baying hounds they had become docile, frightened, bewildered, anxious not to criticize, but to ask questions.

" What of the World Revolution ? " asked one.

" We shall see the World Revolution, but meanwhile it is just a very good fairy-tale ; a very pretty fairy-tale ", was the reply.

" But we must bind ourselves to put a stop to agitation against the imperialists, to stop making propaganda for the Revolution."

" I did not think I had to deal with political children, here but with hardened revolutionists ", was the brutal answer. " You know well enough how we carried on agitation under the Tsar. Wilhelm is no cleverer than Nicholas."

" But we must not publish articles against the imperialists in the party press ; it is prohibited in the peace
terms."

" The Central Executive signs the peace, the Council
of Commissars signs the peace, but not the Central Committee of the party. For the behaviour of the latter the
Soviet Government is not responsible." [1]

And so step by step Lenin forced his opponents from
their position. For every question he had an answer, for
every criticism a retort, showing how manifold were the
ways and weapons which still remained to them as revolutionaries. His exposition had removed the hesitation of
many. The Petrograd Soviet voted to sign.

But there was no rest for Lenin. There remained a bare
four hours before the German ultimatum expired, and then
war. The Central Executive of the Congress had yet to be
faced. In the teeth of an even fiercer opposition, he repeated
his arguments, the naked facts, the bitter truth. At the
end of three hours he had won. The Central Executive voted
to sign the peace by 116 to 85 with 26 abstentions. But he
had not captured the loyalty of his opponents, and he left
the hall amid shouts and howls of " Traitor ! " . . . " Judas ! "
. . . " You have betrayed your country ! " . . . " German
spy ! " [2]

It was six o'clock on the morning of February 24 when
Lenin left the Tauride Palace. He had just signed the

[1] True to his word, Lenin, after the Treaty of Brest-Litovsk had
been signed, suppressed the Bureau of International Revolutionary
Propaganda which had been established in the Commissariat for
Foreign Affairs under Boris Reinstein (of Buffalo, N.Y.), assisted by
John Reed and Albert Rhys Williams. With amazing rapidity, how-
ever, there appeared a Bureau of Foreign Political Literature under the
same direction and with the same personnel. (*The Liberator*, N.Y.,
January 1919.)

[2] Leo Stupotshenko, " The Fight for Peace ", in *Illustrated History of
the Russian Revolution*, ii. 505-509 ; Philips Price, pp. 247-249 ; Marcu,
pp. 339-340 ; *Pravda*, February 23, 1918.

telegram to the German Government agreeing to the
terms of peace.[1] He was exhausted, physically worn-out
with the titanic struggle of the day. Yet he knew that in
the weeks to come there would be no slackening of the
fight, no moment of rest. He had already taken the battle
a stage further. In the issue of *Pravda*, which was now
upon the streets, Petrograd would find those famous
Twenty-one Theses on Peace which he had read to his
colleagues in January. Now was the psychological moment
to make them public, now when all Russia would be seeking
the answer to the question, " Why have they signed ? "[2]

Lenin went out to his sleigh. He looked up ; it was still
dark and very cold, but here and there in the East there
were streaks of light in the sky.

3

It is a significant illustration of the degree of sub-
servience to which the Supreme Command had reduced the
German Government, that the terms of peace to be forced
upon Russia were not officially made known to the Reichstag until after they had been communicated to, and
accepted by, the Soviet Government. In Kühlmann's
absence at the negotiations with Rumania at Bucharest,
all opposition to Ludendorff had apparently collapsed, and
the Wilhelmstrasse had become the willing handmaiden
of Kreuznach. " It must be admitted that the Foreign
Office and G.H.Q. have worked well together ", is Hoffmann's satisfied comment.

The Russian acceptance of the German peace terms was
received in Berlin at half-past seven on the morning of
February 24,[3] but it was not until two days later that
Kühlmann's Under-Secretary of State, Freiherr von dem
Bussche, announced the fact to the Reichstag and read

[1] *Pravda*, February 26, 1918 ; *Proceedings*, p. 178.
[2] *Pravda*, February 24, 1918.   [3] *Proceedings*, p. 178.

to them the terms of the ultimatum, that same document
which Sverdlov, under such vastly different circumstances,
had read to the Central Committee at Smolny. The event
was the signal for an outburst of enthusiastic jingoism and
self-congratulation, Cheers from the Right ; hisses from
the Left. " Never yet perhaps in history has the Aristotelian
dictum that we must resolve on war for the sake of peace
been so strikingly confirmed ", declared the Imperial
Chancellor beaming at the deputies through his heavy-
lensed glasses. " In order to safeguard the fruits of our
peace with the Ukraine, our High Command drew the
sword and peace with Russia will be the happy result."
Erzberger, from the Centre, demonstratively welcomed the
peace and affirmed that its conditions were in conformity
with the Peace Resolution of July 19, 1917 ! But the palm
was reserved for Stresemann. " It is not the negotiations
with Trotsky, nor the Reichstag Peace Resolution, nor
the reply to the Pope's Note," exulted the future Nobel
Peace Prize winner and negotiator of Locarno, " but the
advance of the unbroken military might of Germany
which has brought us peace in the East." [1]

From the Left Scheidemann's voice was raised in
condemnation : " It was not the intention of the German
Social Democratic Party to bring about the present state
of things in Russia ", he said, his little white goatee
bristling with indignation. " We fought to defend our
country from Tsarism but we are not fighting for the
partition of Russia. . . . The policy pursued towards
Russia is no policy of ours. . . . We do not wish in the
circumstances to attain a dominating position which would
force us to conclude a peace with the Entente on such
terms as those on which Lenin and Trotsky are now
concluding peace with the Quadruple Alliance." [2] And
he sat down amid the jeers and hisses of the Right.

[1] *Verhandlungen des Reichstags*, February 26 and 27, 1918.
[2] Scheidemann, ii. 123-124.

But many of the Socialists could find only contempt for the Russian surrender. " One shudders to think how lightly they [the Bolsheviks] gave up Russian territory ", wrote Friederich Stampfer. " Under similar circumstances the German Social Democrats would never have acted likewise."[1] Little more than a year later, at Versailles, German Social Democrats were offered an opportunity to refuse their signatures to a peace treaty which they condemned. They, too, signed.

Once again Prince Leopold and Hoffmann were hosts at a peace conference at Brest-Litovsk. In the absence of Kühlmann and Czernin at Bucharest, the German and Austro-Hungarian Foreign Offices were represented by Ambassador von Rosenberg and Baron von Merey. The Bulgarian Minister to Vienna was assisted by General Gantcheff, and the former Grand Vizier, Hakki Pasha, reappeared with General Zekki Pasha. But how different was the spirit of this gathering as compared with the last. This, thought Hoffmann, was a conference as it should be ; no more uncertainty, no more delay, no more nonsense. It was with a feeling of complete assurance that the representatives of the Central Powers came to Brest.

They had all arrived by February 26, but there was still no sign of the Russians. The Soviet delegation, composed of Sokolnikov, Joffe, Petrovsky, Karakhan, and Vassili Chicherin, destined to become Trotsky's successor as Foreign Affairs Commissar, together with Admiral Altvater and his fellow hostages, had left Petrograd on the night of the 24th and reached Pskov in safety. Here a shattered railway bridge, destroyed by their own troops in an attempt to check the German advance, rendered their further progress by rail impossible. A telegram to Brest announced the continuation of their journey " by coach ", but there was considerable delay in finding any form of

[1] *Vorwärts*, February 24, 1918.

conveyance. Nor was Pskov a pleasant locality in which to be stranded. It had but recently been taken by the Germans, and the bourgeoisie were still celebrating their release from the Bolshevik Terror, having not yet had time to experience the severity of German military occupation. Sokolnikov and his colleagues, as they chafed at the delay and feared that the High Command would take advantage of it to make their terms yet harsher, were insulted and reviled by the Russian population and treated with cold contempt by the German officials. As they waited they saw a military aeroplane rise from the flying-field outside the city. It disappeared eastwards towards Petrograd and that afternoon (February 27) dropped bombs on the Fontanka Embankment.[1]

Finally, however, they reached Brest on the afternoon of the 28th, and at once insisted that their arrival should mark the close of hostilities. A firm refusal was the only response from Hoffmann. War must continue until the peace treaty was signed.[2] A further unpleasant surprise awaited them. The Turks had made a last-moment bid for Ardahan, Kars, and Batum, which were already occupied by their troops. An additional demand was therefore made of the Russians that the fate of these districts should be settled on the basis of the right of self-determination. " For the Turks wished to retain these territories." [3]

The three days' space which the German ultimatum had allowed for " negotiation " began on March 1, and on that day the delegations met for the first time in plenary session. Rosenberg, presiding, was determined that there should be no risk of a repetition of the scenes of the previous conference, and at once appealed to the Russians to avoid unnecessary speeches and to concentrate on practical business. He outlined a detailed plan for the setting up of

---

[1] Philips Price, p. 250.
[2] *Proceedings*, pp. 179-180 ; *Pravda*, March 2, 1918.
[3] *Proceedings*, p. 181 ; Gratz and Schüller, p. 114.

political, legal, and commercial commissions to determine the actual terms of the treaty in its technical aspects. To his surprise, and not a little to his dismay, Sokolnikov proved embarrassingly accommodating in his reply to the appeal for brevity. He was, he said, entirely in agreement that the negotiations should be kept as concise as possible, and for that reason he would object to the unnecessary delay which the setting-up of special commissions would involve. There was in effect nothing to discuss. The Central Powers had presented an ultimatum and Russia had accepted the terms which Germany had dictated. He was here to sign a treaty, not to discuss it. The Russian delegation wished all the negotiations to be in plenary session.

To Rosenberg and Merey this attitude of the Russians was highly distasteful. It made what they had to do appear even more barefaced than before. Antiphonally they denied that the Central Powers had dictated the terms and declared that Russia was perfectly free to accept or reject them at will. They again appealed to Sokolnikov to cooperate in the discussion of technical details in commission. But the Russians were not to be drawn into abandoning their attitude of martyrdom. They had come to sign, not to negotiate. Discussion of the terms of peace would imply at least partial condoning, and this they wished to avoid at all costs. " If the German Emperor had demanded Moscow as his capital and a summer residence in the Ural Mountains, the Russians would have signed without winking an eyelash." [1] They asked that the texts of the main treaty and its auxiliary agreements should be handed over to them at once for study.[2]

With these in their possession the Russians retired to their quarters, but the study of the peace documents did not give them much trouble. With the addition of the new Turkish demands, they resembled too closely the terms

[1] *Münchener Post*, March 5, 1918.
[2] *Proceedings*, pp. 181-182 ; Gratz and Schüller, pp. 114-115.

of the ultimatum to require a thorough examination and the delegation was not long in agreeing on their future course of action. " As we expected, it was absolutely useless to discuss the peace terms ", Karakhan telegraphed to Lenin. " They are worse than the ultimatum of February 21. . . . We have decided to sign without discussion and leave at once." In a second telegram he asked for a special train and body-guards.[1]

It so happened that, in the chaos into which the whole system of communication had fallen, the second despatch arrived at Smolny before the first. The Central Committee and the Council of Commissars were thrown into a tumult. A special train and body-guards could mean but one thing —war. Negotiations had broken down and the German advance on Petrograd was being resumed with increased vigour. Plans, already on foot, for the evacuation of the Government to Moscow were pushed forward, and all possible means for the defence of the Revolution were considered in a frenzy of despair. In the midst of this excitement Karakhan's other telegram arrived announcing the cold comfort of the intention to sign the treaty and depart.[2]

When the conference reassembled on March 2, Sokolnikov once more rejected the proposal to set up com-

[1] *Proceedings*, p. 180 ; *Pravda*, March 3, 1918.

[2] *Proceedings*, pp. 180-181. It would appear, however, that Lenin had little hope that the signature of peace would end hostilities. On March 2 he issued this very definite order : " We believe that to-morrow, 3/III, the peace will be signed, but reports from our agents make us expect, taking into consideration all circumstances, that in Germany the military party desiring war with Russia will win within the next few days. Therefore I issue this absolute order : to delay the demobilization of the Red Army ; to intensify the preparations for blowing up of railways, bridges, and roads ; to gather and arm detachments ; to continue the evacuation rapidly ; to transport arms into the interior of the country." (Leonid I. Strakhovsky, *The Origins of American intervention in North Russia* (Princeton, N.J., 1937), p. 7 ; " Novy Dokument Lenina ", *Krasnaia Lietopis* (Leningrad, 1929), No. 1/28, pp. 5-6.)

missions for the discussion of details. In view of the fact that the treaty was a dictated peace and accepted by Russia only under the pressure of the German armies, which even now were still advancing, the Soviet delegation, although it had not had sufficient opportunity to examine the documents thoroughly, were prepared to sign them on the following day if the delegations of the Central Powers were like-minded, but they would not negotiate in an atmosphere of force.

Again Rosenberg and Merey intoned their threnody of exculpation. How could the Russians say that the terms of peace had been forced upon them when for six weeks, during the previous period of negotiation, all the issues involved had been thoroughly threshed out ? If they insisted upon implying that they were signing blindly and under duress, the Central Powers could not accept this view for a moment.[1] The Russians did insist.[2]

Once again it was a Sunday—Sunday March 3. Three weeks before, Trotsky had thrown his bomb-shell into the conference and left before the smoke had cleared ; now Sokolnikov, with greater dignity, bowed to the inevitable. But in so doing he spoke his mind as eloquently as Trotsky.

This peace is no peace of understanding and agreement, but a peace which Russia, grinding its teeth, is forced to accept. This is a peace which, whilst pretending to free Russian border provinces, really transforms them into German States and deprives them of their right of self-determination. This is a peace which, whilst pretending to re-establish order, gives armed support in these regions to exploiting class warfare, putting the working class again beneath the yoke of oppression which was removed by the Russian Revolution. This is a peace which gives back the land to the land-lords and again drives the workers into the serfdom of the factory owners. . . . Under the present conditions the Soviet Government . . . is unable to withstand the armed offensive of German Imperialism and is

[1] These arguments were repeated by Freiherr von dem Bussche during the Reichstag debate on the ratification of the treaty.

[2] *Proceedings*, pp. 183-184 ; Gratz and Schüller, pp. 115-116.

compelled, for the sake of saving Revolutionary Russia, to accept the conditions put before it. . . . We declare . . . that we are going to sign immediately the treaty presented to us as an ultimatum but at the same time we refuse to enter into any discussion of its terms.[1]

It was just five o'clock on the afternoon of March 3, 1918, when the ceremony of signing the treaty of Brest-Litovsk was completed.[2] By this agreement [3] Russia lost 34 per cent of her population, 32 per cent of her agricultural land, 85 per cent of her beet-sugar land, 54 per cent of her industrial undertakings, and 89 per cent of her coal mines.[4] " The significance of the treaty with Russia lies in the fact that the German Government has worked only for a peace of understanding and conciliation ", was the editorial comment of the *Norddeutsche Allgemeine Zeitung*.[5]

A year had elapsed since Nicholas II had signed his act of abdication. The Revolution had placed the achievement of peace at the head of its ambitions, and now at last peace had been achieved—a peace that passed all understanding.

4

An examination of the instruments signed at Brest-Litovsk on March 3 indicates the haste with which the peace terms were finally drawn up. The chief anxiety of the German General Staff was to conclude a formal settlement

[1] *Proceedings*, pp. 185-187 ; *Mirnye peregovory v Brest-Litovske*, i. 229-231.

[2] Both Kühlmann and Czernin affixed their signatures to the treaty at Bucharest on March 7.

[3] For text see Appendix V, p. 403. The only addition to the terms of the ultimatum of February 21 were the provisions for the immediate evacuation by Russia of the districts of Eastern Anatolia, which were to be returned to Turkey, and the regions of Ardahan, Kars, and Batum, and the recognition by all parties of the political and economic independence of Persia and Afghanistan.

[4] *U.S. Foreign Relations, 1918 : Russia*, i. 490.

[5] *Norddeutsche Allgemeine Zeitung*, March 4, 1918.

with Russia and to turn their attention to their great offensive on the Western Front. This was the gambler's last throw on which he had staked all ; if the battle were won and the Allies sufficiently defeated to discuss peace, the Germans could take up the matter of their eastern acquisitions at their leisure ; while if the battle were lost, they might still find a possibility of exploiting Russia. The matter of immediate importance was that they had successfully broken through the steel ring with which the Allied blockade had encircled Germany, and were no longer in danger of defeat by starvation. The very fact of freedom from any military threat in the East was a sufficient " interim dividend ", provided that the ordinary commercial relations were re-established.

It is for this reason that the economic and commercial agreements signed at Brest-Litovsk appear at first sight to be less harsh than the political sections of the treaties. Germany, having staked out her claim to territorial aggrandizement by the simple process of declaring that certain extensive areas under her occupation were no longer part of the Russian State, could afford to wait until the issue in the West had been decided, before going more deeply into the problem of how best to exploit the rich treasures which now lay open to her. With the Allies safely disposed of, the political and territorial settlement of the vast regions which Germany now controlled could be shaped to pay the cost of the three and a half years of war. Such, at least, was the reasoning of the Supreme Command at the moment the treaty was signed. Moreover, having already reached a seemingly satisfactory agreement with the Ukraine whereby the rich lands of south-western Russia passed under their control, they could, for the time being, afford to hold their hand in the development of their plans for the economic exploitation of Great Russia.

But the political clauses of the treaty could scarcely

be excelled in Draconian severity. Since Bulgaria had never been, and Austria-Hungary had ceased to be a territorial neighbour of Russia, the cessions of territory were made to Germany and Turkey. The much discussed fate of Poland, Courland, and Lithuania was disposed of in Article 3 : " The territories lying to the west of the line agreed upon by the contracting parties, which formerly belonged to Russia, will no longer be subject to Russian sovereignty. . . . Germany and Austria-Hungary purpose to determine the future status of these territories in agreement with their populations." [1] Thus the fiction of self-determination was maintained. Moreover, by Article 6, Russia recognized the Ukrainian treaty with the Central Powers, and therefore also the independence of the Ukraine from the Russian Republic. All Ukrainian territory, together with Estonia and Livonia, was to be evacuated by the Russians, the latter to be occupied by a German police force " until security is ensured by proper national institutions and until public order has been established ". Finland [2] and the Aaland Islands were also, under the same article, to be cleared of Russian troops, and the islands were to be permanently neutralized under an agreement

---

[1] *Texts of the Russian " Peace "*, pp. 15-16.

[2] The independence of Finland had been recognized by the Soviet Government in December 1917, and Red Guards had been sent to assist in the formation of a " Finnish Socialist Republic of Workmen ". With this Government the Bolsheviks signed their first international treaty, ironically enough on March 1, at which time the Reds had been driven out of Helsingfors by the Whites, with German assistance. The only point of interest in this agreement—which was legally as valueless, at that moment, as the treaty signed between the Central Powers and the Ukrainian *Rada*—was the provision that all disputes arising out of it should be settled by an arbitration court of which the president should be appointed by " the administration of the Democratic Socialist Party of the Swedish Left, except if otherwise stipulated ". On March 7 an elaborate treaty of peace, with commercial provisions, was signed between the Central Powers and the Whites. (See *Texts of the Finland " Peace "*, U.S. Department of State, Washington, D.C., 1918.)

between Germany, Russia, Sweden, and Finland.[1] The Russian army was to be completely demobilized and the navy, together with any Allied warships which might be in Russian waters, either disarmed immediately or detained in Russian ports until the conclusion of a general peace (Article 5).[2] When this process of disarmament had been completed and a general peace concluded, the Germans graciously agreed to evacuate all the remaining Russian territory occupied by them for which provision had not already been made in the treaty (Article 4).[3]

By the same article Russia promised to " ensure the immediate evacuation of the provinces of Eastern Anatolia and their lawful return to Turkey ", and likewise of the Sanjaks of Ardahan, Kars, and Batum, which were to determine their own future status " in agreement with the neighbouring States, especially Turkey ". (Again the Banquo ghost of self-determination at the feast !) A supplementary agreement between Russia and Turkey regulated the execution of this provision, and by it Russia was forbidden to concentrate more than one division, even for drill purposes, on the borders of the three Sanjaks or in Caucasia without previous notice to the Central Powers, until the conclusion of a general peace. On the other hand, Turkey was permitted to keep her army on a war footing.[4] The importance of this retrocession of the three Sanjaks—for they had been annexed by Russia in 1878 as a reprisal for the non-fulfilment of treaty obligations—lay not so much in the return to Turkey of the great fortress of Kars, which in past wars had been the Verdun of the Caucasus, but in the fact that Batum was the key and the port of the rich oil-fields of Baku and Azerbaizhan, which thus lay open to the exploitation of the Central Powers.

The formula of " no indemnities " was adhered to theoretically in Article 9 of the Russian treaty whereby the

[1] *Texts of the Russian " Peace,"* pp. 17-18.
[2] *Ibid.* pp. 16-17.   [3] *Ibid.* p. 16.   [4] *Ibid.* pp. 167-171.

Central Powers waived all claims to compensation for war costs and reparation payments, but these materialized in a disguised form under Article 8 (and Article 16 of the Legal-Political Treaty), which regulated the exchange of prisoners of war.[1] By this provision " each contracting party will reimburse the expenses incurred by the other party for its nationals who have been made prisoners of war ". Now the number of Russians captured by the Germans and Austrians was considerably larger than those taken by the Russians from the Central Powers, particularly if from the latter were subtracted those Czechs who were being formed by Dr. Masaryk into legions to fight against Germany. The burden which would fall upon Russia under this provision would therefore be considerably heavier than the costs incurred by the Central Powers. They had protested during the negotiations against its inclusion, arguing that the employment of prisoners of war at low wages led to profits which exceeded the expense of their maintenance.[2] According to Russian computations the sum payable by Russia under this arrangement would amount to between four and five milliards of gold roubles, but the Germans swept the estimate aside as " a great exaggeration " and the provision stood in the treaty.[3] So much for " no indemnities ".

The commercial agreements annexed to the general treaty [4] did not renew Russia's former commercial treaties

[1] *Texts of the Russian " Peace "*, pp. 19, 127.

[2] Nor was this provision universally popular in Germany. On the publication of the peace treaty the German agrarian press was filled with letters from Junker landlords, protesting against the exchange of Russian prisoners of war on grounds that, without their assistance, German agriculture would suffer an inevitable catastrophe. Some writers suggested the postponement of exchange till September, when the harvesting would be over ; others proposed that the entire male population of the occupied territories ceded by Russia should be transported to Germany in order to furnish cheap agricultural labour.

[3] Gratz and Schüller, p. 119.

[4] *Texts of the Russian " Peace "*, pp. 25-28.

with Germany (1904) and with Austria-Hungary (1906), but they maintained the Russian tariff of 1903, even in cases not provided for in the pre-war treaties, while the Central Powers in this respect kept a free hand. The Germans had wished to keep the treaty of 1904 in force until the end of 1930, though with a number of amendments in favour of Germany, but the Russians were opposed to this [1] and the Austrians but half-hearted in support of their allies.[2] Therefore, because time pressed and the Germans believed that they would have plenty of opportunity later to arrive at a favourable commercial arrangement with Russia, a provisional agreement was concluded which should stand until the conclusion of a general peace, or at any rate till the end of 1919. In the meantime each country was to enjoy most-favoured-nation treatment in the territory of the other, but Russia was not to prohibit the export of, nor to levy an export tax on, lumber or ores (Clause 3). Apart from this restriction, the agreement was entirely reciprocal, and Russia was allowed to retain certain unilateral privileges such as the right to tax foreign commercial travellers, while Russian commercial travellers in Germany and Austria-Hungary remained untaxed. The magnanimity of this concession may be gauged from the obvious lack of opportunities for Russia to exercise this right.

Finally, there was the important provision contained in Article 2 of the general treaty, the prohibition of propaganda.[3] All the contracting parties undertook reciprocally to refrain from any agitation or propaganda against each other's Government or public or military institutions,

---

[1] The German-Russian tariff treaty was originally negotiated in 1894 after a tariff war in which Russia was defeated. In 1904, owing to the Russian defeats in Manchuria and the incipient revolution, the Germans succeeded in negotiating a renewal of the treaty on terms still more advantageous to themselves.   [2] Gratz and Schüller, p. 122.

[3] *Texts of the Russian " Peace "*, p. 15.

TERRITORIAL CHANGES AT BREST-LITOVSK

The line shown x—x—x indicates the Eastern Front at the date of the Armistice of Brest-Litovsk, December 15, 1917.

The treaty signed between the Central Powers and the Ukraine on January 9, 1918, recognized the latter's independence and established the frontier line in the west, between Pruzhany and the Galician border at Tarnograd. - - - -

The final treaty signed with the Russians on March 3, 1918, left the German army holding the front shown above by the solid black line from Narva to the Ukrainian border beyond Homel. The dotted line in Ukrainian territory indicates the starting point of the German invasion of the Ukraine and of the Don territory after the capture of Kiev and Odessa, when the Crimea was also occupied. The solid black line denotes the fullest extent of German occupation in this area. ▮▮ ● ● ● ●

The "agreed" line, west of which Russia renounced all territorial rights, runs west of Reval through the Gulf of Riga to a point just above that city, which it embraces; there it follows the Dvina to the extreme eastern point of Courland above Dvinsk, whence it curves south-west to the east of Vilna, and across the Niemen down to the northern Ukrainian frontier near Pruzhany. ▬·▬·▬

Russian claims to Livonia and Estonia were abandoned under the supplementary treaty of August 27, 1918.

Light dotted lines indicate frontiers of 1914. ...·..

See map overleaf

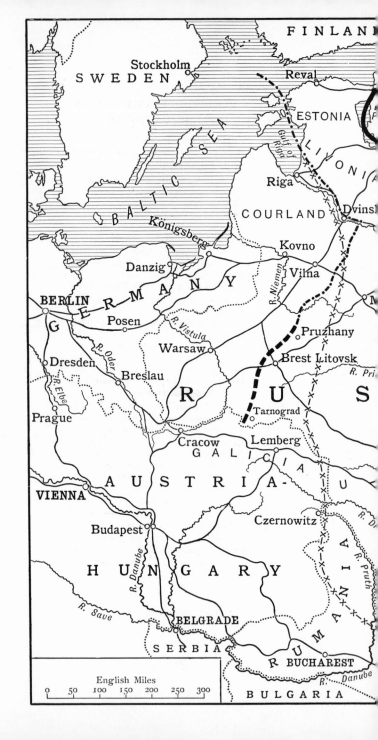

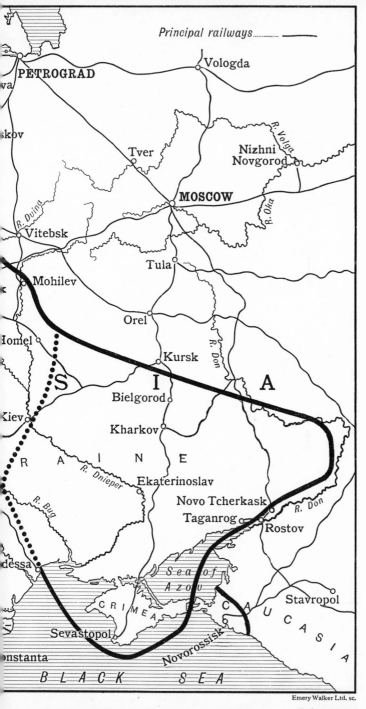

Principal railways .... ——

PETROGRAD

Vologda

va

skov

Tver

Nizhni
Novgorod

R. Volga

R. Dvina

Vitebsk

MOSCOW

R. Oka

Tula

k

Mohilev

Orel

Iomel

Kursk

S

I

A

R. Don

Bielgorod

Kiev

Kharkov

R

A

I

N

E

R. Dnieper

Ekaterinoslav

R. Bug

Novo Tcherkask

Taganrog

R. Don

Rostov

dessa

*Sea of
Azou*

Stavropol

C

R

I

M

E

A

C

A

U

C

A

S

I

A

Sevastopol

Novorossisk

nstanta

B L A C K   S E A

To face page 274

and a special obligation devolved upon Russia to extend this prohibition to the territories occupied by the Central Powers. By this flimsy formula did Germany hope to protect herself against contagion from the effects of the virus which she herself had introduced into Russia. How lightly this undertaking rested upon the Soviet authorities may be guessed by the promises which Lenin had already made to the Petrograd Soviet.

These, then, were the provisions of the Treaty of Brest-Litovsk. At one stroke Germany had extended her control of Eastern Europe to the Arctic Ocean and the Black Sea, and had acquired the undisputed arbitrament of the fate of fifty-five million inhabitants of Russia's western fringe— so much for the doctrines of " no annexation " and " self-determination "; while by the agreements with Rumania (signed on March 5)[1] and with the Ukraine, and the Turkish agreement with Russia, she had gained access to vast resources of wheat and petroleum. Such was the prospect unfolded before the avid eyes of the Supreme Command ; such was the price which Lenin paid for the salvation of the Russian Revolution.

5

If the capacity to withstand criticism be the criterion of greatness, then upon this score alone Lenin's place among the great ones of the earth would have been assured. From the moment that the terms of the treaty became public, there was no more vilified man in Russia or in Europe. Old enemies, their former hatred revived and confirmed, denounced him publicly, and old friends who had suffered and triumphed with him now forsook him and joined the ranks of his traducers. Again the accusation was flung at him that he had been bought with German

[1] *Texts of the Rumanian " Peace "* (U.S. Department of State, Washington, D.C., 1918), pp. 3-6.

gold ; again the circumstances of his return to Russia were adduced as evidence of his connection with the enemy ; again the epithet " traitor " was hurled at him when he appeared in the streets. Alone but steadfast, deserted by many whom he had trusted, Lenin continued to pursue the policy of national sacrifice which he believed to be essential for revolutionary salvation.

His enemies lost no time in organizing against him. The Social Revolutionaries of the Left were now joined by Bukharin's Left Communists, those Bolsheviks who had seceded from the party on the night that the German ultimatum was accepted. This group included Radek, Krestinsky, Alexandra Kollontai, and the ferocious Commissar of the Navy, Dybenko (with whom Kollontai had contracted a revolutionary and apparently an exhausting marriage)[1] and also Uritsky, Pokrovsky, and Pyatakov, those same whom Lenin, even before the Revolution, had castigated as " waverers ". Now they founded a new paper, the *Kommunist*, devoted to the sabotaging of the peace treaty and the denunciation of the " obscene " policies of Lenin.

Lenin's own attitude towards the treaty was clear in his own mind, yet difficult to define. It must be ratified, yet it must be violated. " I don't mean to read it," he declared when the delegation returned from Brest for the last time, " and I don't mean to fulfil it, except in so far as I'm forced." [2] The apparent contradiction of this dual policy may be explained only by an understanding of Lenin's revolutionary psychology. To save the Revolution in Russia, the peace treaty must be ratified. White armies were massing in the North, East, and South,

---

[1] " *Les deux derniers mois l'ont vieillie de dix ans* ", wrote Sadoul of Kollontai at this time. " *Sont-ce les soucis du pouvoir ou les mauvais traitements qui lui ont été infligés récemment par les Suédois ou son mariage avec le farouche Dybenko qui l'ont fatiguée à ce point ?* " (Sadoul, p. 270).

[2] William C. White, *Lenin* (New York, 1936), p. 144.

and to meet them the new Red Army, which under the spur of Trotsky's energetic spirit was being painfully and creakingly evolved from the old armed forces of the Tsar, must have a free hand. But the treaty must be violated not so much in its political and territorial clauses, for to the revolutionary the shifting of territorial frontiers was not so vital, but in its undertaking to refrain from propaganda in the territories of the Central Powers and those which they had recently acquired from Russia. Though Finland, Estonia, Livonia, Courland, Lithuania, Poland, and the Ukraine had ceased to be part of Great Russia, it was not for one moment the intention of Lenin to abandon the proletariat of these countries to their new masters. The forces of the propaganda machine, and of the Third International which it was his object to create, would be directed to all these peoples and to those of Germany and Austria-Hungary as well, despite the treaty pledges which had been given.

There was, in addition, a further consideration in Lenin's mind, and one which carried its own complications. There was no guarantee that the Germans would observe the treaty provisions any more than he himself intended to do. Their advance, which had been temporarily halted at Lake Peipus, might be resumed at any moment and on the slightest pretext. In the South it had never stopped. The Ukraine was rapidly becoming an occupied province. Moreover it was not impossible that the general sense of outrage at the peace terms might, fanned by the continual inflammatory zeal of the revolutionary patriots, result in some outburst which would precipitate the resumption of hostilities with the Germans ; and if this should prove the case Lenin wished to be sure of the assistance of the " brigands of the Entente " against the " brigands of the Central Powers ".

It was here that the complication arose. In the Far East there was steadily growing as great a threat to the

Russian Revolution as that of Germany in the West. Almost from the moment when the Tsar's Empire had fallen into chaos, Japan had manifested an increasing interest and activity in Siberia, and with the signature of the treaty of Brest-Litovsk there came to Petrograd the persistent report that the Japanese meditated an invasion of the maritime province and that such a move would be countenanced by the Governments of the Entente. If, therefore, Allied assistance was to be gained against Germany it must be on the strict understanding that any form of intervention should be confined to the West and South, and that territorial acquisition in the East on the part of Japan should be clearly excluded. For if Siberia passed out of Soviet control, not only would the new republic be shorn of a large part of those natural resources which the Treaty of Brest had left to her, but the Siberian peasants and workers would be deprived of the " benefits " of the Revolution; moreover, territory occupied by Japan would become a hotbed of White Russian activity.

With only the two weeks allowed by the German ultimatum for the ratification of the treaty, Lenin turned his dynamic and unflagging energy to the solution of these problems, and perhaps his only asset was his complete freedom from any inhibitions imposed by the necessity of playing the game according to the rules. The game that he was playing had no rules, and his guiding star was the opportunism of dictators.

His loins girded for battle, Lenin convened the Seventh Congress of the Bolshevik Party on March 6, and at the same time replied to the bitter attacks which appeared in the first issue of the *Kommunist* (March 5). " No conscious revolutionary ", wrote Bukharin and Radek, " would agree to such dishonour " ; and again : " we should die in a fine pose, sword in hand, crying ' Peace is dishonour, war is honour!' "[1] To these ravings Lenin replied with

[1] *Kommunist*, March 5, 1918.

conscious irony, treating his opponents like a pack of cheeky schoolboys. " He who wishes to learn lessons from history ", he wrote, " should study the wars of Napoleon. . . . At various times Prussia and Germany concluded treaties with France ten times more humiliating than the one we have just made with Germany. . . . We have signed a Tilsit Peace just as the Germans did, and just as the Germans freed themselves from Napoleon, so we will get our freedom. It will probably not take so long, for history moves more rapidly now than then. Let's cease the blowing of trumpets and get down to serious work." [1]

The " serious work " began that very day at the Party Congress. Not more than fifty delegates were present, for Lenin had been careful to exclude the more recent Bolshevik recruits—" the November crop ", as he ironically called them—who, *volant au secours de la victoire*, had been so precipitant in their conversion as to recall the incident of that Byzantine prelate whom Gibbon records as being " obliged to delay the ceremony of his consecration, till he had previously dispatched the rites of his baptism ". Even with this group of zealous epigones excluded there was a sharp division of opinion between the partisans of ratification and their opponents, still determined on provoking a new outbreak of hostilities. They moved for the rejection of the treaty as nullifying the importance of the Russian Revolution by the prohibition of international propaganda, converting the disarmed Soviet Republic into a tool of imperialistic politics, and cutting off Russia's revolutionary centre from the producing areas which feed her industry.

These terms not only give no breathing-space, but place the proletarian struggle in a worse position than before. . . . The signing of the peace, so far from giving us a breathing-space, demoralizes the revolutionary will of the proletariat and retards the development of the international revolution. Under the circumstances

[1] *Pravda*, March 6, 1918.

the only proper course to pursue is to wage revolutionary war on imperialism.[1]

Lenin was in a recriminatory mood. These fools talked of the dishonour and the " obscenity " of the peace terms, but if they had followed his lead earlier, the terms would not have been so harsh. " All that I foresaw has come to pass ", he cried at them.

In place of the original treaty offered at Brest-Litovsk we have one that is far more crushing. The blame lies with those who refused it [the original treaty]. By this refusal you are helping German imperialism by handing over to it millions of tons of our resources —guns, ammunition and food. . . . We had to do it [sign the peace] nevertheless, to gain a breathing-space. . . . But the *Kommunist* makes light of the *peredyshka* [breathing-space].[2]

For three days of interminable and passionate debate the battle raged and flamed. At last, late in the afternoon of March 8, Lenin put forward his resolution. Its purpose was contained in the opening paragraph :

In view of the fact that we have no army, that our troops at the front are in a most demoralized condition, and that we must make use of every possible breathing-space to retard imperialistic attacks on the Soviet Socialist Republic, the Congress resolves to accept the most onerous and humiliating peace treaty which the Soviet Government signed with Germany.[3]

Here before the Congress was the crux of the whole situation. They *could* not fight, they *must* have peace. The inexorable argument of cold and sober truth cut through the froth and glitter of revolutionary belligerency. Faced with the facts, the meeting did what Lenin believed they

[1] Bunyan and Fisher, pp. 528-529 ; *Protokoly siezdov i konferentsii vsesoiuznoi Kommunisticheskoi Partii*, (b) *Sedmoi Siezd, Mart 1918, goda*, pp. 226-229.   [2] *Ibid.* pp. 20-21.

[3] Bunyan and Fisher, p. 527 ; Chamberlin, i. 499 ; *Protokoly siezdov i konferentsii vsesoiuznoi Kommunisticheskoi Partii*, (b) *Sedmoi Siezd, Mart 1918, goda*, p. 180.

would do ; they passed his resolution by a vote of 30 to 12, with four abstentions, among them Trotsky.

In these struggles within the party organization, Lenin, to achieve the success of his policy, showed himself great in the sense that, though intolerant of the stupidity and blindness of his opponents, he did not deny them the right to express their views. The views themselves might goad him to pitiless irony and searing wit, but not to the suppression of those who held them. There was nothing petty about Lenin in this conflict ; he was a more magnanimous foe than Stalin at a later period. At a moment when the whole future of the Bolshevik Revolution was at stake, Lenin did not deny his opponents a hearing though he fought them tooth and nail, destroying them with the sheer force of his arguments. Stalin, with far less at stake save his personal position and the dictatorship which he had built up since Lenin's death, replied to his critics with the executioner's bullet and the penal settlement. Lenin never flinched from meeting dialectics with dialectics, either on the platform or in the press, but Stalin's nearest approach to his enemies was, like some mediaeval Valois or Romanoff, to watch their trial from a concealed window behind the judge's chair. When Bukharin and his Left Communists rebelled against Lenin, he treated them like naughty schoolboys, and in time they returned to their allegiance, chastened and humbled ; when twenty years later the same group opposed Stalin, they were given no opportunity for repentance.

Though Lenin had triumphed in the Party Congress, he knew well enough that this had been but a preliminary skirmish compared with the battle ahead of him in the All-Russian Congress of Soviets. The first of these congresses had precipitated the rising of July 1917, the second had fathered the November Revolution, the third had replaced the Constituent Assembly, and now the fourth stood

convened for March 12, to pass upon the ratification of
the Brest Peace. No methods would be spared by the Left
Communists and the Social Revolutionaries of the Left
to secure the rejection of the peace terms. They might
even succeed in doing so, and with a certain weariness
Lenin prepared to join battle a last time for the treaty
which in his heart he loathed.

The first step was to complete the arrangements, which
had been originated by Kerensky, for the removal of the
capital from Petrograd to Moscow. This presented some
little difficulty. When first mooted by the Provisional
Government the plan had been savagely attacked by the
Bolsheviks in the Petrograd Soviet, who had declared in no
uncertain terms that the proposal was actuated by bourgeois
cowardice. Trotsky had been particularly caustic. Now,
however, the Bolsheviks had forsaken the pleasant ways
of opposition for the bitter fruits of government, and they
were to find how unpalatable a diet their own words could
make. In point of fact, however, the case for transferring
the seat of government was now much stronger than when
Kerensky had first proposed it. Petrograd lay an easy prey
to the German armies and the White Guards of Finland.
Enemy planes had dropped bombs on the city, and could
do so again. The Allied diplomatic missions evacuated it
on February 27 to meet after varied adventures at Vologda,
where they led an uncomfortable existence in a special
train. Yet there was a sentimental objection to abandoning
Petrograd, which had seen the birth of the Revolution and
where Smolny had become the symbol of the Soviet Power.

With his usual realism, Lenin faced the situation
squarely and arrived at his decision in accordance with
the facts. " Can you cover the question of the fate of the
Revolution with that kind of sentimental stupidity ? "
he asked. " If the Germans at a single bound take
possession of Petrograd with us in it, the Revolution is
lost. If on the other hand the Government is at Moscow,

then the fall of Petrograd would only mean a serious part-blow. How is it possible that you do not see and com-prehend that ? . . . What is all that stupid talk about the symbolic meaning of Smolny ? Smolny is only Smolny because we are in it, and when we are in the Kremlin all our symbolism will be transferred to the Kremlin." [1] Result—the Council of Commissars was installed in the Cavalier wing of the Kremlin on March 11, leaving Trotsky behind in Petrograd the better to organize the defence system of the country.

6

Yet Lenin, while he fought for peace, sought to re-insure himself against war, a war which might result either from an unprovoked attack by the Germans or from the refusal of the Congress to ratify the peace treaty. Seriously concerned as to the prospect of Japanese aggression in the East, Lenin was prepared to reverse his policy and throw the weight of his influence against ratification, if from the "imperialist" Governments of the Entente and the United States could be wrung a pledge of support against the imperialists of Germany and Japan.[2]

[1] Trotsky, *Lenin*, p. 168.
[2] Japanese intervention in Siberia was not entirely frowned upon by the German Foreign Office, who had never abandoned the hope of reaching an agreement with Japan. The common exploitation of Russia appeared to provide a possible basis for *rapprochement*, and it was rightly believed that any such move by Japan would effectually prevent any re-establishment of friendly feelings between Russia and the Entente. Two important advantages would thus be achieved by indirectly encouraging the Japanese. Those in Germany with Far Eastern experience were strongly opposed to such a policy, realizing the vital importance of Japan's expansion being deflected from the South to the West. " It is a mystery how some people can pro-fess to see a prospective advantage for Germany in the present happenings in north-eastern Asia, unless it can be explained by Ger-many's systematic habit of seeing everything through rose-coloured spectacles ", wrote so experienced an observer as Colonel von Salzmann

Late in February Lenin had agreed with Trotsky to
the despatch of Kamenev on a secret mission to London
and Paris, with a message urging the Powers to give
assistance to the Bolsheviks in resisting the Germans and
in refusing to sign the peace, provided such assistance were
confined to the West and excluded Japanese participation.

The mission was a signal failure. On receiving his
credentials from Trotsky, Kamenev presented himself at
the French Embassy, where his passport was stamped with
a special diplomatic visa. Cheered at receiving this small
measure of recognition, he proceeded to a Norwegian port
and sailed for England. So far he had had no hint from
either French or British authorities that exception would
be taken to his presence, and it was not until he arrived at
Aberdeen that he became aware of the hostility which his
mission had aroused. On landing he was treated by British
officials in a manner which left no doubt in his mind that
powerful forces were at work against him. Despite the
agreement for the immunity of diplomatic couriers which
had been arrived at with the Bolsheviks on the appointment of Bruce Lockhart, Kamenev was searched and
deprived of most of his possessions, including his diplomatic
bag and a cheque for £5000 ; and his claim to be regarded
as diplomatic agent of a foreign state was ignored.[1]

---

in the *Vossische Zeitung* on March 8. " The Japanese press makes it
quite clear that the break-up of Russia will be Japan's task. That this
can be to Germany's advantage will be believed only by the most limited
intelligence. 1918 will be the most fateful year in the world's history.
Germany so disintegrated Russia that Japan changed the whole line of
her former policy and turned from south to west ". The *Frankfurter
Zeitung* of the same date was equally explicit, declaring roundly that
Germany had no hope of conducting a Far Eastern policy except in
conjunction with England and Russia. " This is what makes it unlikely
that the break-up and continued weakness of Russia will contribute to
the ultimate welfare of Germany."

[1] *House of Commons Debates*, Hansard (February 28, 1918), coll.
1605, 1626.

He was allowed to proceed to London, however, where he learned, by an announcement in the House of Commons on February 27, 1918,[1] that the French Government would not permit him to land in France. The British Foreign Office was torn between distrust and fear of anything labelled Bolshevik and a natural curiosity to learn at first hand of the events at Brest-Litovsk. Eventually a compromise was reached. While Kamenev was not allowed to enter the portals of Whitehall, two experts connected with the Foreign Office were designated to meet him privately and converse with him. One of them received his protests against the violation of his diplomatic bag, and another drew from him his impressions of the delegates of the Central Powers at the Brest Conference. Lest any misapprehension might remain, a Member of Parliament, on whom Kamenev called, explained to him that the statement made in the House of Commons must be interpreted as meaning not only that the French Government refused to recognize him as a diplomatic agent, but that Britain, too, would have nothing to do with him, and that he must return whence he had come without delay.

Thus ended the first Bolshevik diplomatic mission abroad. Kamenev departed, leaving behind him a diversity of impressions. To one of those who talked with him, he resembled " a somewhat sinister teddy-bear " ; while to a lady he had the appearance of a " cinquecento Christ ". All agreed, however, that he was a man of considerable powers of fascination. But these powers stood him in poor stead during his return journey to Russia. He was arrested on the Finnish frontier, on the initiative of the German military authorities, and remained under detention until July, when, as a result of an agreement signed between the Soviet Government and the German Embassy acting on behalf of Finland, he was released in exchange for certain Finnish citizens who had been arrested in Petrograd.

[1] *House of Commons Debates*, Hansard (February 27, 1918), col. 1494.

He returned to Moscow a disappointed and embittered man.[1]

In the meantime Bruce Lockhart had established cordial and intimate relations with Trotsky, who talked to him with the greatest frankness of the dangerous repercussions of any Japanese invasion in Siberia and of the possibilities which existed for Allied co-operation with the Bolsheviks against the Germans. If, as Lenin and Trotsky believed, it was the object of Ludendorff to destroy the Soviet Government and to replace it by one which would be purely subservient to Berlin, it was to the immediate interest of the Allies to assist the Bolsheviks in their resistance. Deeply impressed and convinced that by this means alone could large numbers of German troops be detained in the East at a moment when the spring offensive was momentarily expected on the Western Front, Lockhart cabled the Foreign Office accordingly, urging the rejection of all Japanese proposals for intervention and the active support of the Soviet Government in the event of German aggression. It was the view of the man on the spot, with inside information and the trained mind of an honest observer.[2]

But Great Britain had as yet no clearly defined policy toward Russia ; she was still groping in a tangle of conflicting ideas. Understandably bewildered by the development of the Russian Revolution, justly fearful of the extension westward of Communist theories and practice, and still not entirely convinced that Lenin and Trotsky

[1] *Texts of the Finland " Peace "* (U.S. Department of State, Washington, D.C., 1918), p. 53 ; George Chicherin, *Two Years of Foreign Policy* (New York, 1920), pp. 19-20. This mission of Kamenev's is among the many mysterious incidents arising out of the Brest-Litovsk treaty. Apart from passing references in memoirs (*e.g.* Fokke, p. 161, and Sadoul, pp. 262-263), little of its history is on record. The present writer's information was gained from the participants in the conversations.

[2] Mr. Lockhart has most generously allowed the present writer access to his personal diaries of the period.

were not in the pay of Germany, she had compromised with her own intelligence by supporting any tendency that could be labelled " anti-German ". Because the Japanese maintained that they were actuated solely by a desire to prevent the economic domination by Germany of Asiatic Russia, the British Government approved Japan's activities in Siberia ; because the White armies of Alexeiev and Kornilov represented the old Russia who had fought with the Allies against Germany and had the double advantage of being both anti-Bolshevik and anti-German, Great Britain gave them both moral and material support ; now, when the Soviet Government asked for assistance in meeting further German aggression, the British Cabinet were disposed to grant it, but without ceasing their other Russian activities, apparently unaware of the anomalous position in which they were placing themselves. Moreover they entertained the naïve belief that Lenin and Trotsky would be more inclined to accept the *bona fides* of the great capitalistic States than these States had shown themselves to accept that of the Bolsheviks.

This confusion of thought was apparent to Bruce Lockhart from a despatch written in the stately English of Mr. Balfour and dated February 21 :

In so far as they [the Bolsheviks] are opposing or embarrassing our enemies, their cause is our cause. In so far as they endeavour to foment revolution in this, or any other Allied country, we shall thwart them to the best of our ability. In so far as they are dealing with the internal politics of those parts of the country where they are *de facto* rulers, we have no desire to interfere. The very principles which induce us to co-operate with the Bolsheviks urge us to support any forces in Russia which seem likely to offer resistance to our enemies, or aid to our friends. But we cannot pledge ourselves to abstain from such action in other parts of Russia as may in our opinion help to win the war : though we have not the slightest intention of indulging in any anti-revolutionary propaganda.[1]

[1] Blanche E. C. Dugdale, *Arthur James Balfour* (London, 1936), ii. 257-258.

It was with this depressing knowledge of the lack of appreciation by the British Government of the situation that Lockhart went to his first interview with Lenin at Smolny on March 2. His first impression was of a plump, red-faced, snub-nosed little man, " more like a provincial grocer than a leader of men ", but his attention was instantly arrested by Lenin's quizzing, half-contemptuous, half-smiling look which spoke of boundless self-confidence and conscious superiority.

They talked frankly. Lenin said that to him Anglo-American capitalism was as abhorrent as German militarism, but for the moment the latter was the immediate menace. The peace which was about to be signed might not last a week and, if the Germans insisted on installing a bourgeois government in Petrograd, the Bolsheviks would fight, retiring to the Volga and the Urals if need be. In so doing they would accept Allied assistance, but only on their own terms : they were not to be made a cat's-paw for counter-revolution.

Frankly, admitted Lenin, he saw very little possibility of co-operating with the Allies—

Our ways are not your ways. We can afford to compromise temporarily with capital. It is even necessary, for if capital were to unite, we should be crushed at this stage of our development. Fortunately for us it is in the nature of capital that it cannot unite. So long, therefore, as the German danger exists, I am prepared to risk a co-operation with the Allies. . . . At the same time I am quite convinced that your Government will not see things in this light. It is a reactionary Government. It will co-operate with Russian reactionaries.

Now that peace with Russia was a certainty, replied Lockhart, Germany would be able to throw all her forces against the Allies in the West. She might overwhelm them, and where would the Bolsheviks be then ? More serious still, as a result of the peace terms the Germans would be able to relieve their starving population with grain forcibly exported from Russia.

Lenin smiled at this.

You ignore the psychological factor. This war will be settled in the rear, not in the trenches. . . . As a result of this robber peace Germany will have to maintain larger, not fewer, forces in the East. As to her being able to obtain supplies in large quantities from Russia, you may set your fears at rest. Passive resistance—and the expression comes from your own country—is a more potent weapon than an army that cannot fight.[1]

Lockhart telegraphed the sense of this conversation to London, but that same afternoon of March 2 there occurred a new development in the situation. The Soviet Government received definite news that Japan, as the mandatory of the Allies, was about to occupy Vladivostok. Trotsky telephoned furiously to Lockhart demanding how he could explain his mission in face of this meditated act of open hostility.[2] Together Lenin and Trotsky despatched Sadoul on March 4 to Vologda to beg Ambassador Francis to secure the opposition of the United States to Japanese intervention, and to discuss with him the possibility of Allied co-operation in organizing a new Russian army in the Nijni-Novgorod area, not purely a class army, but one in which all Russians might enlist for service against Germany. Before leaving, Sadoul sent off a passionate appeal to his own Government for practical military assistance in reorganizing the Russian army to oppose a further German advance. To this he received no answer, but from Francis he obtained a definite promise of action and support, and departed for Petrograd with Captain E. Francis Riggs, the American military attaché, and Colonel James A. Ruggles, chief of the American military mission.[3]

---

[1] Lockhart, pp. 239-240.   [2] *Ibid*. p. 240.

[3] Sadoul, pp. 250-254 ; Strakhovsky, pp. 8-9.

It was now March 5. The treaty of peace had been signed at Brest and the terms thereof had been broadcast throughout Russia. Indignation and war fever were spreading on all sides, fanned by the Social Revolutionaries of the Left and Bukharin's group, in the columns of the *Kommunist*. Lockhart's appeal of the 2nd had elicited from the British Government a further qualified statement of willingness to aid the Bolsheviks, but coupled with the reminder that thus far the Soviet Government had done nothing but issue proclamations which had " not caused the Germans to withdraw or the Russians to fight ".[1] Over Petrograd were brilliant blue skies ; the air was crisp and sparkling, but at Smolny the atmosphere was tense with impending danger.

Trotsky conferred with Raymond Robins. " Do you still want to beat the peace ? " he asked. " The time has come to be definite. We have talked and talked about help from America. Can you produce it ? Can you get a definite promise from your Government ? If you can, we can even now beat the peace. I will oppose ratification, at Moscow, and beat it."

" You have always opposed ratification ", replied Robins. " The question is, what about Lenin ? He is on the other side, and, frankly, it is he, not you, who is running this show."

" You are mistaken ", cried Trotsky. " Lenin realizes that the threat of the German advance is so great that if he can get economic co-operation and military support from the Allies, he will refuse the Brest peace, retire, if necessary, from both Petrograd and Moscow to Ekaterinburg, re-establish the front in the Urals, and fight with Allied support against the Germans."

" Will he say so ? "

" He will."

" In writing ? "

[1] *U.S. Foreign Relations, 1918 : Russia*, i. 290-291.

Trotsky bared his teeth in a savage grin. "You want us to give you our lives, don't you?"

"No," said Robins, "but I want something specific. I don't ask you to sign it, but put your enquiry to the United States Government in a written statement and that with affirmative response these things will take place; then get Lenin to say that he will agree with what you have written and give the document to me and my confidential secretary and interpreter, Alexander Gumberg. I will act on that."

Trotsky hesitated for a moment. Then, with an expressive movement of his small white hands, he said, "Be back at four o'clock".

At the appointed hour Trotsky, Robins, and Gumberg sat together at a long table in the Hall of the Council of People's Commissars. Gumberg took a paper from Trotsky, translated it into English and read it aloud : [1]

In case (a) the All-Russian Congress of the Soviets will refuse to ratify the peace treaty with Germany, or (b) if the German Government, breaking the peace treaty, will renew the offensive in order to continue its robbers' raid, or (c) if the Soviet Government will be forced by the actions of Germany to renounce the peace treaty—before or after its ratification—and to renew hostilities—

In all these cases it is very important for the military and political plans of the Soviet Power for replies to be given to the following questions :

1. Can the Soviet Government rely on the support of the United States of North America, Great Britain, and France in its struggle against Germany ?
2. What kind of support could be furnished in the nearest future, and on what conditions—military equipment, transportation supplies, living necessities ?
3. What kind of support would be furnished particularly and especially by the United States ?

Should Japan—in consequence of an open or tacit under-

---

[1] *U.S. Congressional Record*, January 29, 1919, p. 2336.

standing with Germany or without such an understanding—attempt to seize Vladivostok and the Eastern Siberian Railway, which would threaten to cut off Russia from the Pacific Ocean and would greatly impede the concentration of Soviet troops towards the East about the Urals, in such case what steps would be taken by the other Allies, particularly and especially by the United States, to prevent a Japanese landing on our Far East, and to ensure uninterrupted communications with Russia through the Siberian route ?

In the opinion of the Government of the United States to what extent—under the above-mentioned circumstances—would aid be assured from Great Britain through Murmansk and Archangel ? What steps could the Government of Great Britain undertake in order to assure this aid and thereby to undermine the foundation of the rumours of the hostile plans against Russia on the part of Great Britain in the nearest future ?

All these questions are conditioned with the self-understood assumption that the internal and foreign policies of the Soviet Government will continue to be directed in accord with the principles of international Socialism and that the Soviet Government retains its complete independence of all non-Socialistic Governments.[1]

Robins turned to Trotsky. " Does that translation give your understanding of the meaning of the document ? " he asked. The other nodded.

" I have one more question to ask ", said Robins. " If the United States Government answers this document affirmatively, will you oppose the ratification of the Peace of Brest-Litovsk at the All-Russian Congress of Soviets at Moscow on the 12th ? "

" Yes ", replied Trotsky. " I have talked with Lenin about that and he agrees ; if you give us this support we shall not ratify."

Bruce Lockhart also saw Trotsky on March 5, but to him the War Commissar, still suspicious of the attitude of France and Great Britain regarding Japanese intervention, was less explicit. He did tell him, however,·

---

[1] *U.S. Senate Documents, 66th Congress, 1st Session, 1919*, iv. 800-801 ; *Raymond Robins' Own Story*, pp. 134-138.

that the Congress of Soviets would probably take such action as would make a declaration of war on Germany's part inevitable. For the success of this policy, however, it was necessary to have at least some semblance of support from the Allies. He would not say friendly relations, for that would be hypocritical on both sides, but suggested that some working arrangement should be arrived at. If, however, the Allies were to allow the Japanese to enter Siberia, the position would be hopeless ; Russians of every class would prefer the Germans to the Japanese.

Lockhart went to confer with Robins and Harold Williams of *The Daily Chronicle*. They were completely agreed as to policy. None of these men was pro-Bolshevik in the sense of being pro-Communist. But they were convinced that Japanese intervention in Siberia would destroy all possibility of an understanding with the Bolsheviks as against the Germans. Even to attempt to render the pill more palatable by limiting the number of troops to be used by Japan, as Francis had suggested to Sadoul at Vologda, and by a declaration that the manœuvre had nothing anti-Russian in its character, was fantastic and futile. " Limited intervention " was impossible. As Lincoln Steffens was to inform President Wilson some months later, " You cannot commit rape a little ". Common sense seemed to indicate that as a measure for reconstructing an Eastern Front against Germany it was ludicrous, and all three were certain of the genuineness of the offer of Lenin and Trotsky to oppose ratification of the peace treaty if Allied assistance was assured.

Robins hastened to send the Bolshevik offer to Vologda for transmission to Washington, leaving Lockhart and Williams to approach London. Lockhart repeated Trotsky's conversation to Mr. Balfour and added his own appeal :

If ever the Allies have had a chance in Russia since the Revolution, the Germans have given it to them by the exorbitant peace terms they have imposed on Russia. And now when Germany's aims have been unmasked to the whole world, the Allies are to nullify the benefits of this by allowing the Japanese to enter Siberia. If H.M.G. does not wish to see Germany paramount in Russia, then I would most earnestly implore you not to neglect this opportunity. The Congress meets on March 12. Empower me to inform Lenin that the question of Japanese intervention has been shelved . . . that we are prepared to support the Bolsheviks in so far as they will oppose Germany. In return for this, there is every chance that war will be declared.[1]

In support of Lockhart so eminent a Russian expert and so strong an anti-Bolshevik as Harold Williams wrote confidentially to Mr. Lloyd George :

The peculiar revolutionary tactics of the Bolsheviks forbid them to accept this peace as final. At the Congress convened to ratify the treaty there will be a strong agitation in favour of revolutionary war with Germany. . . . This movement may supply the nucleus of a real national resistance. . . . It should be our business to foster this revival. . . . Rumours of intended Japanese intervention in Siberia embitter the sense of humiliation in all classes and divert resentment from the Germans to the Allies and endanger the future of our interests in Russia.[2]

But the British Government, who had already acquiesced in the refusal of Sir George Buchanan's plea to maintain a modicum of goodwill in Russia by releasing her from her pre-revolutionary engagement not to make a separate peace,[3] now remained as purblind and adamant as ever. Balfour, though he gave courteous consideration to Lockhart's views, listened more attentively to the advice of the British War Office. Lockhart was a civilian, they said, and knew nothing of military matters. Russia was powerless to make any sort of resistance against a German penetration of Western Siberia. The situation was lost unless Japan acted, and acted at once.

[1] Cumming and Pettit, pp. 83-84.
[2] *Raymond Robins' Own Story*, p. 142.
[3] See above, p. 76.

To Lockhart, discouraged and depressed in Petrograd, seeing the issue so clearly, yet helpless in the face of expert opposition, came Balfour's reply on March 6. The only result of a holy war, it was believed in London, would be a further surrender and further dismemberment of Russia ; " an army cannot be made of fine words, though they can easily destroy it. The Bolsheviks have with complete success endeavoured to shatter the fighting spirit of Russia, and they can hardly revive it in the same way." The Soviet Government was advised to appeal for aid to the Rumanians [with whom they were virtually at war] and to make a " working agreement with the Japanese " [whom they wished to keep out of Siberia at all costs]. " The British Government ", concluded Mr. Balfour with unconscious irony, " have clearly and constantly repeated that they have no wish to take any part in Russia's domestic affairs, but that the prosecution of the war is the only point with which they are concerned." [1]

In desperation Lockhart repeated to the Foreign Office a conversation which he had had with Chicherin on March 7 in which the Foreign Affairs Commissar had said that the German terms had raised a feeling of resentment in Russia

[1] Cf. *U.S. Foreign Relations, 1918 : Russia*, i. 393. On the same day (March 6) Mr. Balfour cabled to Colonel House, who shared Mr. Wilson's dislike for the policy of Japanese intervention : " Up to the moment when the Bolshevik Government decided to accept the peace terms, I was opposed to Japanese intervention, as I hoped Bolshevik resistance to German aggression might continue. When the Bolsheviki surrendered unconditionally, it became of the utmost importance to prevent the rich supplies in Siberia from falling into German hands, and the only method by which this could be secured was by Japanese intervention on a considerable scale." He added, " I have telegraphed to our agent [Lockhart] to suggest to the Bolshevik Government that they should invite Japanese and Rumanian co-operation for this purpose [resistance to German aggression]. I fear, however, that there is little chance of the proposal being entertained, nor do I know how the Japanese and Rumanian Governments would regard such an appeal " (*House Papers*, iii. 397-398).

similar to that in France in 1870, and that now was the most favourable moment for a demonstration of Allied sympathy.[1] His warning was ignored, and the sole reply was a somewhat testy telegram from the Foreign Office displaying even more clearly the grave lack of understanding. To add to Lockhart's discomfiture there arrived carefully worded messages from his wife and friends in London, warning him that there was no sympathy for him in official circles there and that persistence in his present policy would ruin his career. To his eternal credit Lockhart stuck to his guns at this time. Once again on the 10th he resumed his Cassandra strain :

By sheer logic of events the working classes are the only force in Russia which does not welcome German intervention. Already, as in the Ukraine, there are several bourgeois combinations which are plotting to form a government under the Germans. If, by permitting Japanese intervention at the present moment, we destroy the only force in Russia which will oppose Germany, we must take the consequences.[2]

This warning, too, was ignored, but in commenting on it marginally, Mr. Balfour displayed a note of genuine, almost petulant, annoyance : " I have constantly impressed on Mr. Lockhart that it is *not* our desire to interfere in Russian affairs. He appears to be very unsuccessful in conveying this view to the Bolshevik Government." [3]

Robins had also had his disappointments. As a result

---

[1] Mr. Lockhart's diary entry for March 7, 1918. This statement was repeated by Chicherin to Sadoul and Captain Riggs, the American Military Attaché, on March 10, and he added : " All Bolshevik leaders are convinced that war with Germany is inevitable. Some think a few weeks—others a year." (Strakhovsky, p. 10.)

[2] Dugdale, ii. 258.

[3] Dugdale, ii. 259. Mr. Balfour also knew how to be magnanimous. When a high official of the Foreign Office annotated one of Lockhart's despatches with the marginal advice: "Let us recall this impudent young man ", Mr. Balfour at once added " Certainly not " as his comment.

of unavoidable but infuriating mischances, the Bolshevik message to the United States was delayed in transmission. Robins went to Lenin on the 6th to explain the delay, and asked for an extension of time to get a reply from Washington. Lenin would give no direct answer, but on the following day *Izvestia* carried the announcement that, at the request of the President of the Council of the People's Commissars, the opening of the Congress of Soviets had been postponed from March 12 to March 14.[1] Lenin was keeping faith, but his scepticism of the possibility of Allied co-operation was growing day by day and it appeared less and less as a factor in his plans.

Meantime Sadoul, Riggs and Ruggles had returned from Vologda to Petrograd and had so satisfactory an interview with Trotsky on the 8th that Sadoul wrote that night to Albert Thomas : " The support of the United States has been officially promised.[2]

The message from Lenin and Trotsky was despatched from Vologda on March 9, and with it went an endorsement from Ambassador Francis : " I cannot too strongly urge the folly of intervention by the Japanese just now ", he cabled. " It is possible that the Congress of Soviets may ratify the peace, but if I receive assurance from you that the Japanese peril is baseless, I am of the opinion that the Congress will reject this humiliating peace." [3] Two days later he received the text of a message of goodwill from President Wilson to the Congress of Soviets. It was the attempt of Colonel House to induce the Congress not to ratify the treaty of peace and to intimate, without indicating an open breach between the United States and her Allies, the American disapproval of Japanese intervention. Unfortunately it went little further than an expression of sympathy and regret that the United States was not " now in a position to render the direct and

---

[1] *Raymond Robins' Own Story*, p. 149 ; *Izvestia*, March 7, 1918.
[2] Sadoul, p. 259.　　　　　　　　[3] Cumming and Pettit, p. 86.

effective aid it would wish to render ".[1] In acknowledging its receipt, Francis made reference to the Lenin-Trotsky message and asked whether the questions contained therein required any reply in addition to the President's message.[2] Neither then, nor at any later date, did the State Department reply to this enquiry.

As the date for the opening of the conference drew nearer, the special agents waited in despair for the answers of their Governments, but none came ; from Washington nothing, from London nothing, from Paris nothing. Their policies rejected, their hopes destroyed, their worst fears on the eve of realization, the three men were all but discredited in the eyes of the Soviet Government. The Allies at this moment were more afraid of Bolshevism than of Germany, yet it is more than probable that adequate intervention at this moment would have materially hampered the mighty concentration of troops which Ludendorff was preparing in the West and which was so soon to be loosed against the British Fifth Army.

And now all eyes were turned to Moscow, where the Soviet Government was established within the walls of the Kremlin, still bearing the scars of the Bolshevik bombardment of November, and with the gilded eagle of Imperial Russia still surmounting every steeple. With them from Petrograd had come the machinery of propaganda. The official Bolshevik press, *Izvestia* and *Pravda,* still defended the action of the Government in signing the treaty ; the Left Communists and the Social Revolutionaries of the Left persisted in the campaign for rejection of the peace and the proclamation of a holy war, and in this they were joined, though less enthusiastically, by the Mensheviks. The bourgeoisie of Moscow—and Moscow is essentially a bourgeois city—voiced their impatience at the delay of the arrival of the German deliverers, and the Cadet Party laid

[1] Cumming and Pettit, pp. 87-88.
[2] *U.S. Foreign Relations, 1918 : Russia,* i. 397-398.

the foundations of a conspiracy with the advancing invader.

In the midst of this political welter Moscow was gay with an abnormal gaiety that was almost shocking, for it savoured of dancing in a burial vault. Cabarets flourished, restaurants were nightly filled with a motley throng who paid the exorbitant price of champagne with apparent equanimity. Yet many of the finest houses in Moscow, deserted by their owners, had become the lairs of Anarchist bands whose outrages were even more daringly executed than in Petrograd.

It was against this bewildering background that the twelve hundred delegates to the Congress of Soviets were assembling from every corner of Russia. There was something which distinguished this Congress from its three predecessors. It was essentially representative of the wage-earners and peasants of the country, some 93 per cent of the population, and it was not, as the others had tended to be, composed of Soviet specialists and professional revolutionaries. The other seven per cent of the total population, the aristocracy and the bourgeoisie, were conspicuously absent, but the delegates who came, from Irkutsk and Vladivostok and Smolensk, from Murmansk in the north to Odessa in the south, represented the effective mass of Russia, the Russia in whose name the Revolution had been made.

Nor was there the aspect of the bear-garden which had characterized the earlier congresses. Perhaps a little awed by their surroundings—the Congress sat in the resplendent Hall of the Nobles—or perhaps realizing for the first time their mighty collective responsibilities as the highest political organ of the Soviet régime, the delegates showed an obvious self-conscious desire to conform to the dignity of a body which was to usher in a new social order. Whenever a tumult arose, which was not infrequently, the leaders appealed to this motive. "Remember, comrades", they cried above the uproar, "you are not in your village now, but in the All-Russian Congress of Workmen's, Soldiers' and Peasants' Deputies, the sovereign power of all Russia." And this appeal was never without immediate response. There was an odd amalgam of independence and vanity and simplicity, which was exploited to the full, for the mass of the delegates was entirely without qualification to reason deeply, and its ignorance was grossly imposed upon by the leaders of all sections of opinion. " Never was there a congress ", wrote an eyewitness, " in which the many were so patently the tools of the few." [1] It was a proletarian assembly at its best and worst.

Lockhart had not come to Moscow with the Government. Depressed beyond words at the negative attitude of his superiors, he did not wish to see the final act of the tragedy, for he knew now that ratification was inevitable. Instead he remained in Petrograd with Trotsky, whose virile action he preferred to the subtle vagueness of Chicherin, who now presided over the Foreign Commissariat. Indeed his close relations with Trotsky were among the causes of suspicion which his colleagues in Whitehall harboured against Lockhart. " He treats him [Trotsky] like a Bismarck or a Talleyrand ", they observed scornfully.[2]

Sadoul also remained in Petrograd for a while, battling against the intransigence of his Ambassador, Noulens, pouring out his heart almost daily to Albert Thomas, in a bitter record of defeat.

But Robins was in Moscow, hoping against hope for some reply to his cable, telegraphing constantly to Lockhart in Petrograd, and to Francis at Vologda, refusing to the last to believe that his Government would fail to grasp the importance of this opportunity. When the Congress opened on the afternoon of March 14, he sought out Lenin. " Have

[1] William Adams Brown, Junr., *The Groping Giant* (New Haven, 1920), p. 111.

[2] Dugdale, ii. 258.

you heard from your Government ? " he was immediately asked.

" No, I've not heard yet."

" Has Lockhart heard from London ? " [1] Lenin asked again.

" Not yet ", answered Robins, and then, greatly daring, he added, " Couldn't you prolong the debate ? "

Lenin looked at the tall, aquiline American agent, who realized so well the position and was so helpless to interpret it to others ; he had almost pity for Robins, his practical sense of reality, his heavy burden of disappointment. Lenin had gone a long way to meet the views of the Allied Governments and it had been against his better judgement to do so. As with Trotsky's experiment of " No War— No Peace ", he had been willing to give the efforts of Robins and Lockhart and Sadoul a fair trial. They had failed as Trotsky had failed. In both cases Lenin's sceptical forebodings had been justified. Now he could do no more. He would not accelerate the discussion of the peace treaty, but he would not prolong it. He simply said : " The debate must take its course ".

With this cold comfort Robins withdrew ; there was still an eleventh-hour possibility.

[1] Unknown to either Robins or Lockhart, on the same day, in London, Mr. Balfour was informing the House of Commons that if the Japanese did intervene in Siberia it would be as the friends of Russia and the enemies of Germany, to preserve the country from German domination. He was at great pains to repudiate any suggestion that Japan was moved by any selfish or dishonourable motives. " . . . Now Russia lies absolutely derelict upon the waters and . . . has no power of resistance at all, there can be a German penetration from end to end of Russia, which, I think, will be absolutely disastrous for Russia itself, and certainly will be very injurious to the future of the Allies. . . . The House will feel, I am sure," he concluded, " that the decisions which the Allies may have to come to . . . are neither ungenerous nor unfair nor hostile to Russia nor hostile to the Russian revolution ; but on the contrary that our one object is to see that Russia should be strong, intact, secure, and free " (Hansard, March 14, 1918, coll. 549-554).

The debate on the treaty began on the morning of March 15 and continued throughout that day and the next. Most of the speeches were against ratification and there was no attempt to curtail or to gag the opposition.

Bukharin, Kamkov, and Martov eloquently implored their respective followers[1] to spurn the peace terms, which were " a death-blow to Russia and to the international revolution ". They were answered by members of the Bolshevik party, who, well coached, argued skilfully and carefully the case for ratification. But no more telling speech was made than that of a burly red-headed peasant who followed a long series of opposition speakers. " Comrades," he cried in his harsh, uneducated voice, " we fought four years ; we're exhausted. We have no army. We have no supplies. The Germans have an army. It is only a few miles away from Moscow and Petrograd. It is ready to advance. We are helpless. Do you want war or do you want peace ? " He was greeted with vociferous applause, for he had put the issue in a nutshell. Without Allied assistance Russia could not fight. She must make peace.[2]

By the evening of the 16th six resolutions had been tabled for rejection of the treaty and one for ratification.[3] Wearily the debate proceeded. From the applause it was difficult to say which way the Congress would vote, much would depend on the closing speech—and Lenin had yet to make his final appeal.

A little after eleven o'clock, a stir passed through the assembled delegates. Lenin had come quietly on to the platform behind the presiding officer's chair. He spoke a word in the chairman's ear and sat down. A whisper went through the hall like the wind through a bed of reeds, " That's him —that's Lenin ". There was no demonstration, but the

[1] The Left Communists, the Social Revolutionaries of the Left, and the Mensheviks.

[2] Brown, p. 112.   [3] Bunyan and Fisher, p. 533.

personality of this one man could be felt by all, friend and foe alike. This little, unimpressive man, with his cold unemotional features, dominated the assembly by his very presence.

Raymond Robins was sitting on the steps of the platform. Lenin beckoned to him.

" What have you heard from your Government ? "

" Nothing. What has Lockhart heard from London ? "

" Nothing ", answered Lenin.

There was a pause filled by the staccato voice of an orator addressing the Congress and the murmurs of the tired delegates. Then Lenin said :

" I shall now speak for the peace. It will be ratified."[1]

He spoke for an hour and twenty minutes, coldly, starkly, without unnecessary vehemence or emphasis.[2] He spoke for a necessary peace, a preparatory peace, but he made no attempt to minimize the harshness of the German terms. " We were compelled to sign a ' Tilsit ' peace. We must not deceive ourselves. We must size up in full, to the very bottom, the abyss of defeat, partition, enslavement, and humiliation into which we have been thrown. The clearer we understand this, the firmer, the more hardened and inflexible will become our will for liberation, our desire to arise anew from enslavement to independence, our firm determination to see at all costs that Russia shall cease to be poor and weak, that she may become truly powerful and prosperous." To understand fully the reasons why the Soviet Government signed this peace of humiliation and why it now offered it for ratification, Lenin said, it was necessary to realize the meaning of the November Revolution, the main phases of its development, and the causes of the present defeat. " The main source of disagreement among the Soviet parties is to be found in the fact that our opponents are completely

[1] *Raymond Robins' Own Story*, pp. 151-152.
[2] For text see *Pravda*, March 16 and 17, 1918.

overwhelmed by a feeling of justified indignation and cannot analyze the facts objectively." Russia could still become great, " for we still have left sufficient expanse and natural resources to supply all and everyone, if not with abundance, at least with sufficient means of subsistence. We have the material in natural resources, in the supply of human energy, and in the splendid impetus which the creative spirit of the people received through the great Revolution." But to achieve this, time and peace were necessary, and Lenin repeated the arguments which the Bolshevik peasant had put forth earlier in the debate. " Revolutionary phrases will not do. One fool can ask more questions in a minute than twelve wise men can answer in an hour. We have no army ; we could not keep the army at the front. We need peace to gain a breathing-space to give the masses a chance to create new forces of life. In all probability that breathing-space will be of short duration. . . . We must prepare for the struggle. Victory is certain. . . . After we have rested, then, together with the international proletariat, we shall start a new November Revolution, but this time on a world scale."

The battle was over at last. The very simplicity of his case, presented without hyperbole or theatrical effect, had compelled for Lenin first silence, then acquiescence, and, finally, a preponderating majority. The resolution for ratification was put to the Congress as he sat down. Red cards were raised in favour and lowered, other red cards were raised in opposition. The resolution was carried by 784 votes to 261, with the Left Communists abstaining. The count was cried through the house ; it was the voice of a revolutionary assembly confident in their leader.

7

It was in almost festive mood that the Reichstag interrupted its scheduled order of the day on March 18 to

begin discussion of the Brest-Litovsk treaty. The parties
of the Right and Centre were openly jubilant at having
achieved peace in the East on their own terms, and
expressed enthusiastic hopes that the great offensive in
the West, which was about to be launched, would shortly
result in a similar peace with the remainder of the Allied
and Associated Powers. The parties of the Left were
critical in a varying degree, but only the Independent
Socialists appeared to have the courage of their convictions.

The formal case for ratification was put by the
Chancellor and the Under-Secretary of State for Foreign
Affairs, von dem Bussche, who defended the peace terms
as a whole, as containing "no conditions whatever dis-
honouring to Russia, no mention of oppressive war
indemnities, and no forcible appropriation of Russian
territories". The old fiction of the self-determination of
Courland and Lithuania was repeated, while in respect of
the other occupied territories Hertling stated expressly:
"We are not thinking of establishing ourselves permanently
[*uns festsetzen*] in Estonia or Livonia, we wish only to live
on good friendly terms after the war with the political
forces which are coming into existence there, in such a
way that will not exclude peace and friendly relations
with Russia ".[1]

That this was not the view or intention of the Supreme
Command was made clear by the words of their usual
mouthpiece, Gustav Stresemann, who viewed with apprehension the proposal to separate Courland, with Riga, from
Livonia and Estonia. " Here the right of self-determination
does not apply ! " cried the man who was later to lead
Germany to Geneva, and added, " I do not believe in
Wilson's universal league of nations ; I believe that after
the conclusion of peace it will burst like a soap-bubble ".[2]

[1] *Verhandlungen des Reichstags*, March 18, 1918, pp. 4425-4427.
[2] *Ibid.* March 19, 1918, pp. 4453, 4462. How accurately Stresemann
interpreted the view of the General Staff may be judged from the fact

Scheidemann, in a speech lacking his usual fire, decried the treaty as not being a peace of understanding and therefore incompatible with the Peace Resolution of July 1917,[1] to which Grober, the Democrat leader, replied that it was not a question of whether it was or was not a peace of understanding, but whether a peace treaty could have been obtained in any other way. This question he himself answered in the negative, adding somewhat inconsequently, " We have every reason to ask in all humility where we should have been without the merciful help of God ". At which the deputies of the Centre gave " lively applause ".[2]

The real opposition to the treaty was voiced by the Social Democrat, David, and the Independent Socialist leader, Haase, who spared no one in their attacks. " My party has only one feeling, that of shame that a peace of the sword should have been ruthlessly forced upon our eastern neighbours ", cried Haase. " Things in the East have been arranged in accordance with the mad wishes of the annexationist politicians." [3] " At Brest-Litovsk not only the Bolsheviks but also our own diplomatists have given in to the representatives of armed force'", corroborated David.[4] Together they laid bare, amidst the enraged interruptions of the Right and the nervous embarrassment of the official Social Democrat *Fraktion*, the pusillanimity and hypocrisy of the governmental policy during the negotiations. Together they flayed the jingo policies of the High Command and the *Vaterlandspartei*, and in conclusion David struck at the sacred caste of

that on April 9, at the opening of the Estonian Diet, the German Commanding General, Freiherr von Seckendorff, announced that " German troops will not leave Estonia ; they will stay here for permanent protection " (*Texts of the Russian " Peace "*, p. 225).

[1] *Verhandlungen des Reichstags*, March 22, 1918, p. 4536.

[2] *Ibid.* March 22, 1918, pp. 4636-4639.

[3] *Ibid.* March 22, 1918, pp. 4540-4544.

[4] *Ibid.* March 18, 1918, pp. 4431-4440.

privilege itself. " A peace resting on the power of the sword is the weakest peace known. Germany cannot solve the problem presented in its general policy by the methods and ways of the old Prussian ruling class. Peace at home, peace abroad can be won only through right and freedom."

But the result of the debate had always been a foregone conclusion. It mattered little to the Reichstag that Clemenceau had written on behalf of the Allies : " Peace treaties such as these we do not and cannot acknowledge. Our own ends are very different ; we are fighting, and mean to continue fighting, in order to finish once for all with this policy of plunder." [1] What did matter was that while the debate was proceeding the *Kaiserschlacht* had made its brilliant opening, and that when the final vote was taken, the British Fifth Army was reeling back in retreat before the hammer-blows of Ludendorff.

With the news of victory in their ears, the deputies ratified the treaty on March 22. Only the Independent Socialists opposed. The Social Democrats abstained from voting and thereby forfeited their right of protest when later they themselves were forced to submit to a dictated peace. Lacking the moral courage to oppose that which they had publicly declared to be wrong, they displayed both that lack of political flair and that infirmity of purpose which was to bring them to destruction some fifteen years later.[2]

[1] Cumming and Pettit, pp. 92-94.

[2] The effect of Brest-Litovsk upon the psychology of the Social Democrats was peculiar in every way. They opposed the treaty in debate but refused to vote against its ratification. They were deeply perturbed by the storm of protest which arose from the outside world, yet they continued until the breakdown in October and November to follow the dictates of the High Command. Finally, they were so greatly impressed by the rapidity with which Russia had got rid of a " victor's peace " that they placed their signatures to the Treaty of Versailles in the sublime hope that the public opinion of the world would demand a revision of its terms within a very short time. It took twenty years and cost the Social Democratic Party its life before the treaty was revised —unilaterally.

The remainder of the deputies was swept forward on the wave of military success, with the false dawn of victory before their eyes. The might of German arms had achieved so much, it must now triumph completely. The good sword which had brought them peace in the East would also hack its way to peace in the West. They voted with the sublime faith of dupes. Yet, even in this moment of ephemeral triumph, there could almost be heard the voice of Nemesis crying through the Chamber the gibe that Radek had hurled into the indignant face of Hoffmann, " It is your day now, but in the end the Allies will put a Brest-Litovsk treaty upon you ".

VIII

THE AFTERMATH

VIII

THE AFTERMATH

1

THE exchange of ratifications of the Treaties of Brest-Litovsk which took place on March 29, 1918,[1] and the subsequent appointment of Ambassadors established, at least nominally, normal diplomatic relations between the German Empire and the Russian Federal Soviet Republic, but it did not terminate the activities of German troops on Russian soil. "In the Ukraine", Hoffmann wrote in his diary, "we are still advancing."[2]

The German advance of February 17 had been undertaken almost entirely with the idea of protecting and consolidating the advantages gained under the treaty with the Ukraine of February 9. Twenty-four hours before the treaty with the Central Powers had been signed, the Red army of General Muravev expelled the Government of the *Rada* from Kiev and established there a Ukrainian Soviet Republic in communion with Moscow. The *Rada* retreated to Zhitomir and appealed in pitiful terms to the German Government for aid in resisting "this barbaric invasion of our northern neighbours".[3] It became indisputably clear that if the Central Powers, who had made peace with the Ukraine for the sake of bread, wanted to get it, they would have to go and fetch it. As Kipling once wrote of a' similar military adventure, "If you take the first step, you will take the last".

Originally the Supreme Command had been anxious to

---

[1] *Texts of the Russian " Peace ",* p. 139.   [2] Hoffmann, i. 208.

[3] *Izvestia,* February 19, 1918.

transfer the eastern army to the West for a final offensive against the Allies, and to gain access to the rich granary of the Ukraine, which would supply the wants of both Germany and Austria. Now these two objects were found incompatible. The dire necessity of bread forced the German General Staff to maintain an army in the East capable of enforcing its will upon the reluctant peasants of the Ukraine, who bitterly resented the efforts of the *Rada*, the Soviets, and the German High Command, to wrest their grain from them.

The advance which Hoffmann directed into the Ukraine met with considerably more opposition than that encountered by the German divisions in Russia proper. The Bolshevik troops defended themselves with some skill, and further hampered the German progress by destroying the railways and bridges in their retreat. Here too were met for the first time those Czechoslovak legions which Dr. Masaryk had laboured so long in forming out of the Austrian prisoners of war; [1] they gave a good account of themselves, fighting side by side with the Bolsheviks, whom they were later to encounter as opponents during their heroic anabasis through Siberia.

When the expedition into the Ukraine had been ordered by the German Supreme Command it had been fully expected that the Austro-Hungarian troops would participate in the advance. But here a rift appeared in the harmony of the Central Powers. The Dual Monarchy for political reasons, both internal and external, was anxious to avoid any appearance of continuing war-like operations. Peace in the East was earnestly desired in order to impress the Allied and Associated Powers with the fundamental honesty of the feelers which Vienna was at that moment extending, and also to restore at home something of the solidarity of the Empire which had become severely shaken by the food crisis and the continued hardships of war.

[1] Hoffmann, i. 208 ; ii. 222.

When, therefore, Ludendorff consulted with General Arz von Straussenberg, the Chief of the Austro-Hungarian General Staff, as to joint action in the Ukraine, he met with a refusal to move, which emanated directly from the Emperor Karl.[1] The reply of the German Supreme Command was simple and effective. If the Austrians would not co-operate in the Ukraine, Germany would refuse to allow the agreements for the sharing of foodstuffs to become operative in the areas occupied by German troops.[2]

This policy of pressure had the desired effect, for the independent action of the Germans and their subsequent requisitions upon the country threatened the food supply of the Dual Monarchy. Ardently as Austria-Hungary desired peace, she needed bread even more, and needed it by April; whereas the Germans did not want theirs before June.[3] On February 24 the Emperor Karl capitulated and ordered Arz von Straussenberg to send troops into the Ukraine.[4] He surrendered even more abjectly, for he accepted German domination in a new military treaty, the essential clause of which provided for the employment of troops " according to one common principle, the initiative of which shall be left principally to Germany ".[5]

So complete an abnegation was quite unnecessary. Had the Austrian Government played their cards better they could have answered blackmail with blackmail and sold their co-operation in the Ukrainian adventure at their own price. The news of the ultimate participation was received at Spa with the greatest relief, for Ludendorff was well aware—and subsequently admitted—that the Germans could not possibly have solved the problem by themselves.[6] He had, however, counted upon the nervous

[1] Ludendorff, ii. 465 ; Gratz and Schüller, p. 131 ; Hoffmann, ii. 222.
[2] Gratz and Schüller, p. 131.   [3] Hoffmann, i. 211.
[4] Gratz and Schüller, p. 131.   [5] *House Papers*, iii. 423.
[6] Ludendorff, ii. 566.

debility of Vienna and had bluffed his ally into submission with a threat of starvation.

The advent of the Austrians brought with it many minor complications. Late in the field, they found the Germans established in the best positions. Kiev had fallen to them on March 1, and the Austrians were only able to play a minor rôle in the capture of Odessa on March 12, yet they claimed this port for themselves. Some circles in Vienna, notably that round Czernin, irked by the spectacle of numerous German princelings receiving grand-ducal thrones in the Baltic Provinces and Finland, conceived the idea of a Habsburg as King of the Ukraine, and urged the Emperor Karl to send either the Archduke Eugen or the Archduke Friedrich to Odessa in order to secure the chief command for the monarchy. The Austrian General Staff protested that it was impossible to give an Archduke a command unbefitting his rank merely " on account of a few corn-cobs ". The Emperor agreed with them, but refused the demand of the Emperor Wilhelm that Germany should exercise the Supreme Command in the Ukraine and the Crimea. Much wrangling continued between the two High Commands, the Germans resenting the avaricious manner of their tardy allies. " Endless troubles with the Austrians in the Ukraine ", runs Hoffmann's record. " They . . . are behaving with their usual meanness when the knife is not at their throat. . . . It is a pity the Italians do not attack. One can deal with the Austrians only when they are in difficulties." [1]

After much acrid correspondence between the two Emperors and between German and Austrian G.H.Q., a compromise was reached. On the Black Sea Austria retained Odessa and Kherson, while Germany received Nikolaev and Sebastopol, and in the Ukraine the northern sector remained under German influence, leaving the south

[1] Hoffmann, i. 210.

to the Austrians.[1] This meant that the German army command, now separated from Hoffmann and controlled by Field-Marshal von Eichhorn, dominated the seat of government at Kiev where the *Rada* had been re-installed. Both Germany and Austria sent diplomatic representatives to Kiev, Baron Mumm von Schwartzenstein and Count von Forgach ; but these gentlemen played a very secondary rôle, and for the next few months the uncrowned king of the Ukraine was Eichhorn.

Even with the re-established *Rada* the position was highly unsatisfactory. The country was abundantly supplied with everything, but it proved almost impossible to collect supplies. The bulk of the land had been held as large estates. These had been confiscated and the land distributed among the peasants, but the new owners refused to cultivate because they did not know whether they would be left in possession of either land or crops. Nor would they sell what they had for paper money, of which there was an almost unlimited supply. The peasant would only exchange grain for goods ; otherwise he buried his surplus stocks of food and blandly refused to disclose their whereabouts. Up till March 2, instead of the 300 truck-loads of grain per day which had been promised to Austria under the agreement, but one truck-load had reached Vienna and one truck-load Budapest, and these had only been seized from captured stores and sent off to the capitals " in order to convince the people by ocular demonstration of the advantages of peace with the Ukraine ".[2]

Transport problems increased the difficulties of collecting supplies from a sullen and passively resisting peasantry. The Ukrainian railway system had to be radically reorganized and rendered self-supporting. The frontiers of the Ukraine did not embrace coal-fields, and it was decided that those of the Donets Basin must be incorporated

[1] Ludendorff, ii. 623 ; Gratz and Schüller, p. 132.
[2] Gratz and Schüller, p. 132.

therein.[1] Thus the German and Austrian armies, which had captured the grain centre of Kharkov on April 8, were drawn even further eastward and by May had penetrated willy-nilly into South-eastern Russia.

In Kiev the *Rada* existed in a welter of ineptitude. " The difficulty in the Ukraine is simply that the Central *Rada* has only our rifles behind it ", admitted Hoffmann frankly. " The moment we withdraw our troops their authority will collapse at once." [2] The separatist movement had no roots in the country, and the people as a whole were completely indifferent to national self-determination ; this had been thrust upon them by a group of political dreamers whose power derived from the presence of German bayonets.

But despite the ramshackle nature of their puppet creation, the Central Powers proceeded to conclude further agreements with it. The *Rada* was as anxious as they were to lay its hands on the hidden grain, which, they claimed, the peasants had taken unlawfully from the Government storehouses, and which it was now proposed to requisition with the help of German and Austrian arms. The German military command cared little whence the grain came so long as it was produced and eventually found its way to Berlin, Vienna, and Budapest ; and in this amicable spirit an agreement was finally reached on April 9 for the furnishing of sixty million poods [3] of bread cereals, fodder grain, podded grain, and oil seeds between April and July.[4]

The unwelcome task of executing this agreement was entrusted to Eichhorn's Chief of Staff, General Wilhelm Gröner, who had been brought specially from the West because of his brilliant record as Chief of the Transport Section of the General Staff in the first year of the war,

---

[1] Ludendorff, ii. 622.   [2] Hoffmann, i. 209.
[3] 1 pood = 36 English pounds.
[4] *Texts of the Ukrainian " Peace "*, p. 143.

and later as head of the *Kriegsamt* in Berlin, where he had achieved an unparalleled success in persuading the organized employees and trade unions to co-operate under the so-called " Hindenburg Programme " for the intensification of production.[1] Tasks of such magnitude had qualified Gröner to face the difficulties of the Ukrainian problem and, through the Germano-Ukrainian Trading Organization at Kiev (*Deutsche-ukrainische kaufmännische Wirtschaftstelle*), he developed a highly efficient plan, the success of which depended, however, on some measure of co-operation from the peasantry.

But even Gröner's persuasive qualities could not break down the sullen opposition of the Ukrainian peasant farmer. The organization, brilliant in conception, had depressingly meagre results, for, in addition to the attitude of the peasants, the delegates of the *Rada*, in their enthusiastic dreams, had over-estimated the stocks of grain in the country. Hoffmann thought that Gröner was mistaken in creating a large central organization, and that he would have been more successful if he had engaged a number of Jewish dealers to buy corn in the open market,[2] but then Hoffmann was at Kovno and not entirely conversant with the facts, whereas Gröner was in every sense the man on the spot ! Whatever the reasons for failure, the fact remained that very little corn could be procured. Only 42,000 truck-loads in all were exported from the Ukraine during the whole period of German and Austrian occupa-

---

[1] Two men came with Gröner among his assistants who were destined to play an important part in German history : Rudolf Nadolny, who was to become Ambassador to Angora and Moscow and Germany's representative at the ill-fated Disarmament Conference, and Otto Meissner, later to become the most distinguished political chameleon of his time—he found it possible to serve Ebert, Hindenburg, and Hitler as Secretary of State to the Presidency ; having begun as a Social Democrat, Meissner in 1937 was received into the National Socialist Party as a Member of Honour and holder of the Golden Badge.

[2] Hoffmann, ii. 225.

tion (March–December 1918), and of these but 30,757 were handled officially, the rest being smuggled ; [1]—a singularly poor return for a military expedition involving nearly half a million men who could have been far more usefully employed elsewhere.[2]

The passive resistance of the peasantry did not stop at the non-delivery of the grain which they had already gathered. In planning for the forthcoming harvest they proposed to cultivate just sufficient land to supply their own needs and no more, and in those districts where landlords still existed—and the landlords were almost to a man the allies of the Germans whom they looked upon as their sole bulwark against Bolshevism—the peasants gave notice that they would prevent additional cultivation.

This prospect spelled additional defeat for the Germans. Not only had they failed to secure the surplus of the 1917 harvest, but there was now every prospect that the spring sowing, already threatened by the lack of labour and agricultural implements, would be so curtailed that the harvest of 1918 would also elude them. To prevent this catastrophe Marshal von Eichhorn took immediate and energetic measures. On April 6—three days before the agreement with the *Rada* was signed—he issued a general order to the Ukrainian peasantry without the knowledge of the Central *Rada*. Cultivation, he declared, must be proceeded with to the fullest possible extent, and the harvest would belong to the cultivator, be he landlord or peasant. If the peasants in certain places were unable to sow all the land, the landlord was required to attend to the sowing, and the peasants were forbidden to interfere with his activities. Moreover, contravention of these orders

[1] Gratz and Schüller, p. 136.

[2] It was common gossip in Berlin at this time that, in order to camouflage the failure of the Ukrainian expedition, workmen in Poland were ordered to paint the word " Ukraine " on every bag of Polish flour sent to Berlin. (Lubov Krassin, *Leonid Krassin* (London, 1929), p. 88.)

would be punished not by the Ukrainian courts (whose jurisdiction extended over a very limited area) but by the military tribunals set up by the army of occupation.[1]

The issuing of this order is illustrative of the domination which the German military command exercised in the Ukraine at this time, and which was to be increased in the near future ; while the fact that the *Rada* remained ignorant of the existence of this order until a fortnight after it had been circulated to the villages is in itself indicative of the extent of their contact with the country. They were told what the military command considered fit, and further news only leaked in to them by degrees. They were the puppets of the German occupation, dependent for their very existence on their masters, who were rapidly becoming tired of their growing tendency to assert themselves. There was still in the *Rada* a spirit of national independence, especially in the Social Democrats and the Social Federalists, parties which had their representatives in the Government. These Ministers, including the youthful Minister for Foreign Affairs, Liubinsky, who had signed the treaty of January 9, resentful of the increasing interference of the military with internal administration, were continually urging a policy of resistance upon the invertebrate president of the *Rada*, M. Holubowicz.

For these elements the news of Eichhorn's order was the last straw, and, stampeding their more timid colleagues, they forced the *Rada* to declare it illegal and therefore invalid. This challenge, thrown down on April 26, was immediately answered by Eichhorn with the proclamation of martial law and the delivery of an ultimatum which demanded the rescinding of the *Rada* resolution. In effect, he had already determined upon more drastic action.

The combination of vapid idealism and resentful national

[1] Gratz and Schüller, p. 135 ; James Bunyan, *Intervention, Civil War and Communism in Russia, 1918* (Baltimore, 1936), pp. 3, 6 ; D. Doroshenko, *Istoriia Ukraini, 1917–1923* (Uzhgorod, 1930–1932), ii. 2-35.

feeling, which went to make up the mentality of the *Rada*, had for some time been considered incompatible with the realization of German aims in the Ukraine. It was now clear that the *Rada* was unable, and perhaps even unwilling, to fulfil the obligations of providing food for the Central Powers. Of the nine million poods which were to have been delivered during April, only three millions had been sent by the third week of the month, and there was little prospect of the remainder being made up. " We readily believe the declarations of the Ukrainian Government that the Ukraine has plenty of bread, but up to now we have not seen it ", remarked one German commissioner.[1] What was wanted was a pronounced pro-German leader who would not hesitate to fulfil the orders of his masters, and who would be more easy to control than a nebulous collective council. Such a man had presented himself to Eichhorn ; General Pavlo Skoropadsky, a former Tsarist officer of Ukrainian descent, whose suitability for the position may be judged from Ludendorff's dictum that he was " a man with whom it was possible to work well ".[2]

With Skoropadsky Gröner had concluded an agreement as early as April 24—two days before the *Rada* resolution repudiating the land edict ; in return for the recognition of the Treaty of Brest-Litovsk, the *Rada* would be dissolved, new elections would only be held with the permission of the German Command, and Skoropadsky was charged with the task of restoring order in the country. The right of private property in land was to be re-established and, in the interests of agriculture, the large estates were to be restored, the peasants paying for the land they had received during the partition. The laws of the Central Powers on compulsory military service were to obtain in the Ukraine until her own national law had been promulgated, and she was to compensate the Powers for the military

[1] Bunyan, pp. 19-20. [2] Ludendorff, ii. 624.

assistance accorded her.[1] In addition there was a further agreement with Austria-Hungary in which Skoropadsky released the Dual Monarchy from the agreement into which Czernin had entered with the *Rada* for the creation of a separate province from the Bukovina and that part of Galicia which was preponderantly inhabited by Ukrainians.[2] The moment for producing Skoropadsky as the Ukrainian god from the German machine was left unspecified, the military command preferring to hold him as a trump card, yet knowing that the time to play it was fast approaching.

In the meantime Holubowicz had tried to placate Eichhorn by offering to dismiss his recalcitrant colleagues and by ordering peace to be made with Soviet Russia as soon as possible, but on the fundamental question of the land edict he remained evasive.[3] It seems that the German Ambassador, Baron Mumm, who had been kept in ignorance of the pact with Skoropadsky, was inclined to regard the concessions of Holubowicz as satisfactory, and urged Eichhorn to meet the *Rada* half-way. But the Marshal was not going to allow such an opportunity to get rid of the *Rada* to escape him, and Mumm's objections were either ignored or satisfactorily demolished, for in what followed the military command is expressly stated to have acted with the approval of the Imperial Envoy.[4]

The indefinite, and therefore unsatisfactory, nature of the *Rada*'s reply to the German ultimatum of April 26,

---

[1] Bunyan, p. 6 ; Doroshenko, pp. 31-52.

[2] *Texts of the Ukrainian " Peace "*, p. 141. When later it became known that Skoropadsky had made this surrender on his own initiative and without the knowledge of any of his supporters, such excitement was caused that he was forced to declare to Vienna that his step was illegal, whereupon Count Burian, Czernin's successor, replied that he was unable to recognize these new arguments. See *The Times*, August 6, 1918.   [3] Gratz and Schüller, p. 135.

[4] Ludendorff, ii. 624 ; Bunyan, p. 8 ; *Svoboda Rossii*, April 1918. (This last was the organ in Moscow of the Cadet Party.)

together with the arrest of the banker Dobryi, who as director of the Bank for Foreign Trade had been of value and assistance to Gröner's trading commission, provided Eichhorn with the pretext for which he had been waiting. On the afternoon of April 28, the Ministers for War, Foreign Affairs, and Agriculture were arrested as the *Rada* was in full session, and the Minister for the Interior only escaped by jumping through a window. By what was later described officially as " an excess of zeal on the part of the troops employed ", the other members of the *Rada* were first made to stand with their hands above their heads, then relieved of any arms they were carrying, and, finally, forcibly dispersed. On the following day Skoropadsky was proclaimed Hetman of the Ukraine before the Congress of Landowners.[1]

Violent protests against this action were made by Holubowicz both to Baron Mumm and to the Imperial German Government, and Eichhorn was bitterly attacked in the Reichstag ; but all to no purpose, for, as Hoffmann noted with satisfaction, " everything done in the Ukraine is the result of the most careful consultation between the Chancellor, the Foreign Office, and G.H.Q."[2]

The appearance of the Hetman as a new political factor should have materially improved the position of the Central Powers in the Ukraine. In some respects it did so. The early months of Skoropadsky's régime were marked by a substantial economic revival, the land-owners, industrialists, and bourgeoisie being only too anxious to co-operate with the new Government and the agencies of Germany and Austria-Hungary. The deliveries in kind began to attain almost schedule standards ; meat became once more available in Central Europe, and 140,000 badly needed horses made up deficiencies in the German Army. Even

[1] Gratz and Schüller, pp. 135-136 ; Bunyan, pp. 9-17 ; *Svoboda Rossii*, May 9, 1918 ; *Pravda*, May 9, 1918.
[2] Hoffmann, i. 215.

the raising of a few Ukrainian military formations was begun, though this was not a success.[1]

The Ukraine became for a short time a bourgeois Mecca, and thither flocked thousands of refugees from Soviet Russia, eager to join in the riot of speculation which was sweeping Kiev.

Having refused to lend money to the *Rada*, the Central Powers at once gave the Hetman's Government a loan of 400,000,000 *karbovantsi* ($1\frac{1}{3}$ marks = 1 *karbovanets*), though the notes of the new Ukrainian bank of issue were not covered by bullion but by marks and kronen supplied by Berlin and Vienna.[2] However, the degree of confidence placed by the man in the street in these new *karbovantsi* may be judged from the fact that they at once became popularly known as *skoropadki*, a word which, both in Russian and Ukrainian, means " rapidly falling ".

But the régime of Skoropadsky did not bring peace to the Ukraine, nor did it materially ease the position of the occupying Powers. The advent of the Hetman, with his new social and agricultural policies, inaugurated a period of violent insurrections on the part of the peasants, who resented and opposed the restoration of the land to the great estate-owners and the intensified system of requisitioning food stocks. Passive resistance in certain districts was coupled with acts of sabotage in others. In Odessa an aeroplane factory was set on fire ; numerous munition dumps were exploded and trains wrecked ; and bands of partisans ambushed isolated units of soldiers. The peasant risings, bloody in themselves, were met with bitter repression at the hands of the land-owners and the German and Austrian troops, who supported the Hetman's police. Conflicts were frequent and the spirit of discontent seethed throughout the country, where it soon became apparent that the Skoropadsky Government was even more dependent

[1] Ludendorff, ii. 625.
[2] *Texts of the Ukrainian " Peace "*, pp. 153-154.

upon the foreign bayonets than the *Rada* had been.

Moreover, the policy of Eichhorn in the Ukraine was having exactly the opposite effect to that which had been originally intended. The object of the separate treaty at Brest-Litovsk had been to keep the Ukraine permanently estranged from Soviet Russia, and to create in that country an economic protectorate of the Central Powers through which they might threaten and influence the Government at Moscow. Now, as a result of the Eichhorn-Skoropadsky régime, the ground had been well prepared for a *rapprochement* between the Ukraine and Greater Russia. The peasantry, who had at first eschewed Bolshevism, now turned to it as a protection against the exploitation and repressive domination of the Central Powers, and the abortive peace negotiations which were conducted throughout the summer between Kiev and Moscow were utilized by the Soviet delegates, led first by Stalin and later by Christian Rakovsky, as a fruitful opportunity for Bolshevik propaganda. Rarely, save in the attempts of the French to separate the Rhineland from the German *Reich* in 1923, has there been a more flagrant example of how not to woo a conquered people.

At Kovno, now the headquarters of Prince Leopold of Bavaria, Hoffmann saw only too clearly the disastrous trend which events in the Ukraine were taking. He had learned, perhaps too late, the truth of the Russian proverb which warns against spitting in a well from which one may wish to draw water. From Major Brinckmann, his representative at Kiev, and from such trained observers as Colin Ross, the journalist, and Dr. Rohrbach, the well-known political writer, he learned of the effects of Eichhorn's policy. " The efforts of G.H.Q. and Eichhorn are, though they do not know it, driving the Ukraine back into the arms of Great Russia " is a constantly recurring entry in his record of the period ; and again and again he communicated his fears to the Supreme Command, but with

no effect—" my political insight is no longer esteemed as
it used to be "—Ludendorff was now beyond the point where
the reasoning of others could influence his judgement.[1]
Paranoia had him in its grip. He was supreme, omnipotent,
god-like, and his opinions must rest unquestioned. Even
the assassination of Eichhorn in July did not convince
him that his policy was mistaken, and he maintained his
grip upon the Ukraine until defeat in the West forced him
to loosen it and abandon Skoropadsky to his fate.[2]

The Germans were now paying the price for the
Napoleonic complex which had inspired Ludendorff in
the negotiations of Brest-Litovsk. He saw himself bathed
in the sunlight of victory, creating and distributing
kingdoms as had the Emperor of the French after the
Peace of Tilsit. Lenin had been more accurate than he
had dreamed when he described the peace terms of Brest
as a Tilsit peace. It was true of both victor and vanquished.[3]

[1] Hoffmann, i. 217-218.

[2] When an acute shortage of man-power in the West finally obliged
Ludendorff in the late summer of 1918 to withdraw half a million men
from the East, the power of Skoropadsky automatically declined. He
abandoned all pretence of Ukrainian independence in November and
declared the country an integral part of Greater Russia. But this could
not save the Hetman ; his enemies united against him and proclaimed
in December a People's Republic under a Directory presided over by
Petlura. This in turn was overthrown after a brief duration by the
Bolsheviks, who occupied Kiev in February 1919. After some furtive
adventures with the Poles, Petlura fled to Paris, where he was assassinated in 1927. Skoropadsky returned to Berlin, where he remained
in retirement until the Revolution of 1933, since when his hopes of
return to Kiev have been revived by the Ukrainian schemes of certain
powerful elements in the National Socialist Party.

[3] This phase of Ludendorff's Napoleonic complex had a curious and
detrimental effect upon the federal structure of Germany ; it opened up
too many possibilities for monarchical advancement, and aroused all too
many dynastic hopes of territorial aggrandizement.   In Württemberg
the Duke of Urach strove, with Erzberger's help, to become crowned king
of Lithuania ; Prince Friedrich Karl of Hesse, the Kaiser's brother-in-
law, aspired to the throne of Finland ; Wilhelm II reserved for himself

Ludendorff despatched an expeditionary force to Finland to crush a Bolshevik rising ; another expedition penetrated to Baku ; a third occupied the Crimean ports. An army of occupation was maintained in Rumania ; grand-ducal governments were in process of creation in Courland, Lithuania, Livonia, and Estonia ; and the German colonies in the Crimea were urged to appeal to the Kaiser for annexation. Ludendorff's conception of *Deutschtum* had become all-embracing (a conception later to be revived by Hitler). " German prestige demands that we should hold a strong protecting hand, not only over German citizens, but over *all* Germans ", he was writing at this moment.[1] In addition, the problem of the Polish Regency demanded constant care and supervision, and in the Ukraine the Hetman had proved a liability rather than an asset. But the plans of the· Supreme Command did not stop short there. Wilhelm II, in a message to the Hetman of the Don Cossacks, outlined plans for the ultimate partitioning of Russia into four independent states—the Ukraine, the Union of the South East, Central Russia, and Siberia—thereby eliminating the Russian state as a political threat to Germany.[2]

the title of Duke of Courland. In retaliation, the Emperor Karl sought the Ukrainian crown for the Archduke Eugen, and in the West there were also demands for compensation. Bavaria desired the partition of Alsace-Lorraine—Lorraine to go to Prussia, Alsace to Bavaria. William of Württemberg declared that in this event he would claim the Sigmoringen district, while Saxony, not to be out-done, intimated that Upper Alsace could very well be governed from Dresden. The passion of dynastic avarice let loose by the contemplated spoils of Brest-Litovsk engrossed, at this most critical moment in their histories, the interest and attention of the German princes to the exclusion of other and more vital considerations. In their ambitious dreams they shared out lands and titles in advance just as, in Schiller's *Piccolomini*, Wallenstein's captains distributed princely coronets among themselves in rosy anticipation.

[1] Ludendorff, *The General Staff and its Problems*, ii. 562.

[2] Bunyan, pp. 39-42.

But a victor's peace must be enforced. A million troops immobilized in the East was the price of German aggrandizement, and half that number might well have turned the scale in the early stages of the battle of giants which was raging in the West. According to both Sir Douglas Haig and General Mangin, only a few cavalry divisions were necessary in March and April 1918 to widen the gap between the French and British, thus severing the two armies. These were not available on the Western Front, but at that moment three cavalry divisions were propping up successive puppet governments in Kiev. The man who defeated Ludendorff the Soldier was not so much Marshal Foch as Ludendorff the Politician.

2

The events which followed the ratification of the peace treaty proved that Lenin's demand for a breathing-space for the consolidation of the Revolution was more than justified. Indeed the "breathing-space" proved rather to be a series of short, sharp gasps as the Soviet Government vainly tried to keep its head above water. During the spring and summer of 1918, the Bolshevik régime was assailed both from without and within. The Allies, though with a purpose contrary to the hopes of Lockhart, Robins, and Sadoul, attempted intervention from Archangel, Murmansk, and the eastern Maritime Province. The Czechoslovak legions fought their way across Russia to Vladivostok, and White Armies threatened from Siberia under Admiral Koltchak, from the Baltic Provinces, with German assistance, under General Yudenitch, from the Cossacks of the Don under their Hetman, and from the Crimea, with Allied aid, successively under Generals Kornilov, Alexeiev, and Denikin.

Within, the Soviet State was attacked by all its many enemies. The Cadets intrigued with the Germans in the Ukraine and at Kovno ; the Social Revolutionaries of the

Right made contact with the Entente forces; the Left Communists and the Social Revolutionaries of the Left still preached their gospel of a holy war and sought to embroil the Government with the Central Powers. And beyond them, dominant, penetrating, contemptuous, assertive, were the troops of Germany, enforcing a victor's peace upon the vanquished. "From the cold rocks of Finland to sunny Colchis", from Kiev to the Donets Basin, resounded the tramp of the *Feldgrauen*, the bark of staccato Prussian commands.

This in itself was an unfavourable atmosphere for the resumption of diplomatic relations between Russia and Germany, which, with the exchange of Ambassadors on April 23, were put on a formal footing. There was little reason for either side to respect or trust the other, and throughout the seven months preceding the denunciation of the Treaty of Brest-Litovsk by both parties, the fiction of friendly relations was barely maintained.

To Berlin Lenin had sent as his Ambassador the suave, mild-spoken Adolf Joffe; while as their representative in Moscow the Germans had selected Count Wilhelm von Mirbach-Harff, who had had experience of Russia as a Counsellor of Embassy before the war, and who, from the armistice of December 15, 1917, to the eve of the German advance in February 1918, had been resident in Petrograd as German Commissioner for the re-establishment of commercial relations and the exchange of prisoners of war. As such he had gained an intimate knowledge of many of the leading Bolsheviks and become familiar with the atmosphere of revolutionary Russia.

There is no more difficult diplomatic mission than that of ambassador from a victorious nation to a vanquished, and Mirbách's task was rendered even more complicated by reason of the peculiar situation which obtained in his own country and in Russia. The German Foreign Office was anxious to avoid a breach with the Soviets at all costs, and cautioned Mirbach to have an almost inexhaustible stock of patience ; but, on the other hand, the High Command, the supreme power in Germany, had not excluded from their plans the possibility of a further advance into Russia and the expulsion by force of the Bolshevik Government from Moscow. The mission, then, of the German plenipotentiary was anything but easy. His subordinates, however, had confidence in him. " Mirbach is a cute fellow ", said Rietzler, who was to accompany him as Counsellor, to Scheidemann on the eve of his departure for Moscow, " and when up against Radek and his comrades, it is wise to choose somebody who won't throw over everything at once, but will go on parleying and keep his head. Mirbach can do that excellently." [1]

Soon this was to be required of Mirbach. His arrival in Moscow was the signal for a series of studied insults which might well have provoked a less well-balanced diplomat. On the occasion of his reception at the Kremlin, on April 26, for the presentation of credentials, the Ambassador was received not by Lenin, the supreme power of the Soviet régime, but by Sverdlov, who, as President of the Central Executive Committee, was theoretically the highest ranking Soviet official. Just a year ago Lenin had returned to Russia as the " protégé " of the German Government; now the German Ambassador entered Moscow and Lenin did not receive him. To Mirbach's formal speech of greeting Sverdlov made the curt rejoinder, " We greet in your person the nation with whom we concluded the Treaty of Brest-Litovsk " ; and, lest there should be any misunderstanding, Radek made the position perfectly clear two days later in *Izvestia* :

The representatives of German Imperialism have entered Moscow, but to get a ticket for Moscow they have to admit the Red Embassy of revolutionary Russia to Berlin. Our comrades go there as the representatives of a country which is the weakest of

[1] Scheidemann, ii. 132.

all countries in the military sense ; but they go there as the representatives of a country morally victorious. Not one workman in Berlin will greet the Ambassador of the Russian Socialist Republic with the hate with which every workman in Moscow to-day greets the representative of German capital.[1]

Such was the spirit which inaugurated a period of almost chronic mutual recrimination, and the position was still further complicated by the presence of the special agents of the Allies in Moscow and of the Allied Ambassadors at Vologda. Lockhart had refused to be turned out of his rooms in the Élite Hotel to provide accommodation for the Germans,[2] and Mirbach, on the very day of his arrival (April 23), was forced to enter a protest against the statement issued by the French Ambassador that the continuation of the German advance might compel the Allies to intervene in Siberia in order to stop German aggression in Russia.[3] Chicherin replied on April 27 with an omnibus protest against the general policy of violation of the peace terms by Germany, instancing the invasion of the Crimea and the Donets Basin, the penetration of German-Ukrainian forces into Central Russia, and the seizure by White Guards and German landing-parties of Russian war material in the north of Finland. He concluded with an enquiry : " If the German Government thinks that it can no longer observe the terms of the peace treaty which was ratified by both States, it becomes absolutely necessary that it should state clearly the new demands for the sake of which it directs the Ukrainian, Finnish, and German forces against the Russian Soviet Republic ".[4]

This note, one of many, had neither the effect of stopping the German military activities nor of clarifying

[1] *Izvestia*, April 28, 1918. [2] Lockhart, pp. 267-268.
[3] *Svoboda Rossii*, April 23, 1918.
[4] *Ibid.* April 28, 1918; *U.S. Foreign Relations, 1918 : Russia*, ii. 512-513.

relations with Germany, and repeated protests of Joffe in Berlin, and of Leonid Krassin made personally to Ludendorff, were equally fruitless.[1]

The Germans, in their turn, with equal justification, lodged complaint against the action of the Soviet Government in forming international legions in the Red army for the defence of the Soviet régime. Mirbach's first public appearance in Moscow had been at a military review in the Red Square, where to his amazement he had seen a detachment of Germans, in German military uniforms and responding to German words of command, goose-stepping under a banner which bore, in German lettering, the legend, " German comrades, throw off your Kaiser as the Russian comrades have thrown off their Tsar ".[2] In response to Mirbach's protests, Trotsky issued an order forbidding the violation of the agreement reached in Article 2 of the Brest Treaty regarding propaganda, announcing the disarmament of all prisoners of war, and restricting the admission into the Red army to only those foreign volunteers who had become Soviet citizens.[3]

But Trotsky was not always so accommodating in his relations with the Germans. In the matter of the Black Sea Fleet, he completely outwitted them. Under the terms of the treaty, Russia had undertaken to disarm her warships immediately, or to keep them within her ports until a general peace had been concluded. Accordingly the Black Sea Fleet had been interned at Sebastopol, but with the advance of the German troops into the Crimea its transfer was ordered to Novorossisk, and the ships left Sebastopol on April 27, three days before the Germans occupied the city. Their return was promptly demanded by the Germans: Trotsky, however, procrastinated. To Bruce Lockhart and the British naval attaché, the ill-fated Captain Cromie, he proposed that British naval officers should take control

---

[1] Krassin, pp. 87-88.   [2] *Raymond Robins' Own Story*, p. 182.
[3] *U.S. Foreign Relations, 1918 : Russia*, ii. 131.

of the fleet, saying, " If they find they can do nothing else, they can at least sink the ships before the Germans get them ".[1] When this was found impracticable, the Council of Commissars ordered the fleet to return to Sebastopol, but Trotsky informed Lockhart that he had secretly arranged for its destruction. The fleet was scuttled on June 8, 1918,[2] a manœuvre which the Germans were themselves destined to emulate at Scapa Flow less than a year later.

Early in May a further crisis arose—the Soviet Government was confronted with a German demand for the cession to Finland of Fort Ino, the key position in the strategic defence of Petrograd, lest it be seized by the British, and was also required to expel the Allied forces, which had landed in Murmansk early in March, in co-operation with the Soviet authorities.[3] This demand for the cession of further territory by Russia brought to a head the opposition of the other political parties to the policy of retreat which

---

[1] Edward Alsworth Ross, *The Russian Soviet Republic* (London, 1923), p. 48. This proposal of Trotsky's was one of six instances, listed in a letter from Lockhart to Robins, in which the Commissar had offered to co-operate with the Allies. (See Cumming and Pettit, pp. 202-203 ; Ross, pp. 47-48.)

[2] Bunyan, p. 55 ; Lockhart, p. 279.

[3] The welcome extended by the Soviet authorities to the British forces, which had been sent to the Murman coast in order to prevent the Murmansk–Petrograd railway line, and also large supplies of military stores, from falling into German hands, was a direct consequence of the Brest-Litovsk negotiations. The enquiry of the local Murmansk Soviet as to whether the British were to be allowed to land arrived at Smolny on March 2, in the midst of the consternation caused by Karakhan's first telegram from Brest asking for a guard and a train. Under the impression that negotiations had been broken off and that the German advance would be immediately resumed, Trotsky telegraphed to Murmansk, " Yes, permit Allied troops to land without resistance ". Had the enquiry from the local Soviet arrived an hour or two later, when the panic had subsided on the receipt of Karakhan's second telegram, the welcome accorded to the British landing-force might not have been so warm. (See Francis, pp. 264-265.)

the Government was pursuing, and the charge of pusil-lanimity was pressed so warmly that on May 14 a joint conference of the Central Executive Committee and the Moscow Soviet was held in the Kremlin to receive Lenin's report on the situation.

Lenin remained unswayed from his original philosophy of strategic retreat. It appeared that the fortunes of the Revolution had touched bottom and that every avenue of escape from disaster was closed. Yet he would not surrender to the popular policies of his opponents. He repeated his theses on foreign policy in a long speech, of which the core was contained in a single paragraph :

Our task consists in strengthening the Soviet Power against the capitalist elements which are striving to swallow it up. From the experience of the Revolution we have learned that it is necessary to follow tactics of relentless advance whenever the situation per-mits it. But when there is no possibility of offering unsparing resist-ance, one has to apply tactics of waiting and of slow accumulation of forces.[1]

This stubborn adherence to the policy of national im-molation was bitterly attacked by the Opposition groups. The Left Social Revolutionaries demanded the abrogation of the peace treaty and the termination of the " breathing-space " : " There are only two ways open to us. One is the revolutionary way ; the other is the way of shameful re-treat, of shameful concession and manœuvring, the way of death." The Right Social Revolutionaries favoured the resumption of the war on the side of the Allies : " The interests of the Allied democracies imperatively require that Russia remain strong, independent, and capable of resisting German designs in the East ". The Mensheviks likewise stressed the necessity of fighting against German imperialism, but maintained that a prerequisite condition of Russia's salvation was the re-establishing of the Con-stituent Assembly and the substitution of a democratic

[1] *Izvestia*, May 18, 1918.

form of republican government for the Communist dictatorship.[1]

The parties of the Opposition were thus united in advocating war; Lenin replied with his old argument: "With what will you fight until the army is reorganized?" Baffled, disgruntled, yet unable to answer him, his opponents grudgingly and ungracefully gave Lenin a vote of confidence, and retired with their anger unabated and their resentment burning within them. It was realized now, particularly by those female leaders of the Left Social Revolutionaries, Spiridonova and Mme. Breshko-Breshovsky, the "Grandmother of the Revolution", that there was no hope of influencing the Government. Lenin's spell, though weaker than at first, was still strong enough to command a majority; if the treaty was to be abrogated and Russia saved from humiliation, more drastic means must be employed; and, while they publicly proclaimed their hatred of Germany, they plotted in secret for a *coup d'état*.

Having won the battle and a free hand, Lenin compromised with fate. He ceded Fort Ino to the Finns, but he did not attempt the impossible task of evicting the British and French troops from Murmansk; and with these half measures the German Foreign Office had to be content.

By the summer Russo-German relations had become so exacerbated that the Supreme Command at Spa and the headquarters staff of the Commander-in-Chief in the East were at one in their conviction that no co-operation in fulfilling the terms of the peace treaty could be expected from Russia so long as the Bolsheviks remained in power. Somewhat appalled at the Frankenstein monster which they had helped to create, the Supreme Command began to be uneasy as to the effects of Bolshevik propaganda on Germany. When they had accommodated Lenin in the matter of the "sealed train" in April 1917, they had not foreseen that a year later a Bolshevik Ambassador with full diplomatic privileges

[1] Bunyan, pp. 121-125.

and immunities would be in residence in Unter den Linden. Already it had begun to dawn on them that the severity of the terms of peace signed at Brest was defeating their own ends. They could no longer afford to have a fierce and vengeful Russia in their rear waiting for their weakening moments to take toll for an historic humiliation. Moreover, since the re-establishment of diplomatic relations, the Russians had adopted the same tactics as during the first period of negotiation at Brest-Litovsk. They were alternately defiant and procrastinating. The German score of complaints against the Soviet Government was rapidly mounting ; the treatment of prisoners of war, the support given to the Finnish Red Guards, the scuttling of the Black Sea Fleet, the welcome accorded to Entente troops in Murmansk, and the daily insults in the press which Mirbach had to swallow, convinced both Ludendorff and Hoffmann that nothing could be expected from the Bolshevik régime save a permanent danger.

The alternative course was to denounce the treaty, make a swift advance upon a Petrograd–Smolensk line, and declare the overthrow of the Soviet régime and the re-establishment of the monarchy. This could have been accomplished with the troops remaining on the Eastern Front—the military attaché at Moscow, Major von Schubert, told Hoffmann that, once Petrograd was in German hands, two battalions would be sufficient to overthrow the Bolsheviks in Moscow and restore order—and to the new Government the Central Powers would grant better terms of peace and make an offer of an alliance. Even the return of Poland to the new monarchy was contemplated.

The plan progressed so far that, on June 9, 1918, Ludendorff sent a long memorandum to the Imperial Chancellor advocating such a policy, and Hoffmann got into touch with representatives of the old Russian régime and of the Provisional Government. These elements, working through Miliukov in the Ukraine and through the

Centre of the Right in Moscow, had agreed upon a constitutional monarchy as the most desirable form of government for Russia, and the discussion of candidates for the throne was even in progress, Miliukov favouring the Grand Duke Michael Alexandrovich, while Hoffmann preferred the Grand Duke Paul.[1]

But the pace of history was swifter than the pace of intrigue. In the West it was realized even by Ludendorff that a crushing defeat of the Entente in the field was now impossible. More and more troops were withdrawn from Hoffmann to fill the gaps which the fearful carnage of the *Kaiserschlacht* had wrought in Germany's man-power. No longer could Ludendorff threaten Russia with the might of a conqueror ; the time had come for retrenchment in military adventures, and the inability of Germany to assert herself even diplomatically was to be shown with startling suddenness.

Since the conference of the Moscow Soviet and the Central Executive Committee on May 14, when Lenin had won his hard-fought victory, the internal situation of the Soviet Republic had rapidly deteriorated. The opponents of the Bolsheviks, defeated in their attempt to persuade the Council of Commissars to change their foreign policy, resorted to their old revolutionary tactics and went underground. The Cadets and the parties of the bourgeoisie were already in secret negotiation with the Germans. The Social Revolutionaries of the Right, on May 26, agreed to ask the Allies for assistance in combating both German penetration and Bolshevik oppression. The Mensheviks declared themselves in favour of armed opposition to the Soviet dictatorship, but were against inviting foreign intervention of whatever nature. The Left Social Revolutionaries decided to force the hand of the Council of Com-

[1] Ludendorff, ii. 658, and *The General Staff and its Problems*, ii. 571-575 ; Hoffmann, ii. 228-229 ; Bunyan, pp. 177-179 ; Denikin, *Ocherki russkoi smuty* (Berlin, 1924-1926), iii. 82-83.

missars by confronting it with an act of hostility against Germany, and to make an end of the " breathing-space " by organizing " a series of terroristic acts against the outstanding representatives of German imperialism ".

Though these decisions were reached in secret conclave, the efficiency of the new-old secret police, the Cheka (which had replaced the Okhrana of Tsarist days) discovered some of the plotters and arrested them. Martial law was proclaimed in Moscow, and the Mensheviks and Social Revolutionaries of the Right were expelled from the Central Executive Committee.

It was in this atmosphere of excitement and intrigue that the Fifth All-Russian Congress of Soviets met on July 4. The air seemed pregnant with foreboding ; not even in the debates on the ratification of the treaty had feeling run so high and hatred appeared in so naked a form. In spite of the Bolshevik manipulation at the elections, the Left Social Revolutionaries had succeeded in securing about a third of the eight hundred delegates present, and for the first time since the Revolution the Soviet Government was confronted in its own hand-picked Parliament with an official Opposition.

The Congress met in the Bolshoi Theatre on a sultry, humid day ; storm was brewing within and without. In the *fauteuils* sat the delegates, the green-and-khaki clad soldiers and worker followers of the Bolsheviks on the right, flanked by the brawny peasant adherents of the Left Social Revolutionaries. On the stage sat the officers of the Congress, and behind them in serried ranks the Central Executive Committee. In the boxes and galleries were the privileged spectators of this strange drama ; here were the representatives of the Allied Missions, Lockhart, Sadoul, Lavergne, Romei ; and above them the Ambassadors of the Central Powers, Mirbach with his Turkish and Bulgarian colleagues. The Imperial box, where the Tsar had received the plaudits of many a bejewelled and decorated throng, had been given over to the representatives of the press.

From the first it was evident that both the Council of Commissars and the German Ambassador were the targets of the Opposition. The note was struck by the delegate from the Congress of Ukrainian Peasants, Alexandrof, who in a speech moving in its simplicity described the lot of his countrymen under the German rule. All the Ukraine, he cried, was in insurrection against Eichhorn and Skoropadsky, and he closed with a passionate appeal : " Come to our aid, comrades; only when we have chased from Kiev our Mirbach, Baron Mumm, will you be able to chase from Russia the Mumm of Moscow, Count Mirbach ". From the seats of the Left Social Revolutionaries came a roar of fury and applause. " Down with Mirbach ! " " Down with Brest ! " " Down with the lackeys of Germany ! " they howled, shaking their fists at the Bolsheviks and in the impassive face of the German Ambassador.

That day and the next dragged on. The Bolsheviks were on the defensive. Neither the sardonic Sverdlov nor the caustic Trotsky appealed to the Congress as strongly as the bitter assaults of the Social Revolutionaries. They attacked the Bolsheviks for their foreign policy, for their use of the death sentence, and for their neglect of the peasants, but it was their relations with Germany that had put iron into the soul of the Opposition.

Spiridonova, who had achieved a crown of living martyrdom through her survival of rape by a guard of Cossacks after her assassination of an Imperial governor, whipped her audience into hysterical passion by her denunciation of the Government. Trotsky, in an attempt to answer her, was howled down. Sverdlov rang his presidential bell in vain. The minority were out of hand. Suddenly Lenin appeared on the platform, pushing his way between the members of the Central Executive Committee. As he passed he gave a pat on the shoulder to the distraught Sverdlov. He faced the roaring delegates with a smile. To their jeers and cat-calls he replied with a good-humoured shout of laughter from that great mouth. The roaring was suddenly stilled ; before he had uttered a word, Lenin had tamed his hearers. At the close of his speech the delegates even applauded him. For the moment he restored order and a modicum of dignity to the proceedings, but only for a moment. Kamkov was on his feet and was lashing himself and the Congress into a fury with a fighting speech. He spared no one, and his peroration was tremendous in its dramatic emotion :

> The dictatorship of the proletariat has developed into a dictator-ship of Mirbach. In spite of all our warnings the policy of Lenin remains the same, and we are become, not an independent Power, but the lackeys of the German Imperialists, who have the audacity to show their faces even in this theatre.

Like a pack of howling wolves the Left Social Revolu-tionaries turned as one man to the diplomatic *loge*. " Down with Mirbach ! Away with the German butchers ! Away with the hangman's noose from Brest-Litovsk ! " they screamed. They could at that moment have torn the Ambassador limb from limb. They were fanatical, distraught, crazed with anger and humiliation. In the face of that howling mob, Mirbach remained unmoved, and with a superb courage maintained complete self-possession. Hurriedly Sverdlov declared the session closed.[1]

July 6, 1918, was a day momentous in Soviet history. The congress was due to reconvene at four o'clock, and throughout the morning Lenin and his colleagues were in conference as to their plan of action. Sverdlov was dispirited. Trotsky was in favour of taking action against the Opposition. Lenin pondered. Suddenly in the early afternoon the telephone rang in Lenin's room ; a breathless

[1] Lockhart, pp. 295-299 ; Sadoul, pp. 392-397 ; Bunyan, pp. 199-212 ; *Piatyi Vserossiiskii Siezd Sovetov Rabochikh, Krestianskikh, Soldat-skikh ; Kazachikh Deputatov. Stenograficheskii otchet* (Moskva, 4-10 iiulia, 1918, g.).

voice gave him the news. Two Left Social Revolutionaries had assassinated Mirbach.

Trotsky and Sverdlov were summoned to the Kremlin. Lenin feared that the assassins had done their work only too well and that the Germans would take the excuse for military intervention. " There is ample occasion for it ", he declared. " Now at any price we must influence the character of the German report to Berlin ", and at once prepared to go personally to the Embassy.

Sverdlov, but not Trotsky, was selected to accompany him, and the question of phraseology arose. " I should like to say ' *Mitleid* '," said Lenin, " but we had better ask Radek what the proper word is." After consultation it was agreed that *Beileid* was the formal expression, and with apprehension in their hearts Lenin and Sverdlov left the Kremlin.[1] It was not an easy task to offer condolence on the death of the German Ambassador, but Lenin had other problems to occupy him as he drove to 5 Denejni Pereulok. In his mind he decided on the outlawry of the Left Social Revolutionaries. After a long silence he turned to Sverdlov : " In future we Bolsheviks must carry the burden of the Revolution alone ".[2]

[1] *Mitleid* is " sympathy ", *Beileid* " condolence ", in German.

[2] Trotsky, *Lenin*, pp. 183-184 ; Marcu, pp. 353-354. The assassination of Mirbach was the signal for risings planned by the Left Social Revolutionaries in Moscow and Petrograd. At the same time, though unconnected, similar revolts by the Right Social Revolutionaries occurred in Yaroslavl and Murom. These were all suppressed with comparative ease, but the campaign of terror continued. On July 30 Marshal von Eichhorn was assassinated in Kiev by a Left Social Revolutionary youth, and on August 30 attempts by the Right Social Revolutionaries in Petrograd and Moscow succeeded in the murder of Uritsky and in wounding Lenin very severely. The plot, which aimed at the murder or arrest of all the outstanding Bolshevik leaders, was alleged to have been hatched in complicity with the Entente Powers, and particularly the British. Reprisals were immediately taken. In Petrograd the British Embassy was broken into and the naval attaché, Captain Cromie, shot down as he stood on the stairs defying the raiders.

Contrary to Lenin's worst fears, the Germans did not take the opportunity provided by Mirbach's assassination to destroy the Bolshevik régime by military intervention. The truth was, the day had passed when Germany could take reprisals for the murder of her Ambassadors as she had in the case of Baron von Kettler during the Boxer Rising.[1] Things were going radically wrong on the Western Front, and the German Government was inclined to accept the apologies and condolences of the Bolsheviks, especially as the political party to which Mirbach's assassins belonged had been dealt with so faithfully. The affair resolved itself into a series of diplomatic exchanges in which the Soviet Government, sensing a weakening in the German attitude, stiffened their own. They refused to

Lockhart was arrested in Moscow and lodged in the death-cells of the Kremlin, where he had as fellow prisoners Spiridonova, General Brussilov, and Dora Kaplan, who had made the attempt on Lenin. Lockhart was ultimately released and exchanged for Litvinov, who had been arrested in London. The attempted assassination of Lenin was the signal for the outbreak of the Red Terror, with its systematic massacres and private murders, which resulted in the " liquidation " of many hundred thousand victims.

It is not without irony that, having originally been made the excuse for the " liquidation " of the Right Social Revolutionaries and the bourgeoisie in 1918, the attempt of Dora Kaplan on Lenin should have been attributed, at the Treason Trial of 1938, to the instigation of Bukharin and the Left Communists.

[1] At the beginning of the siege of the Peking Legations in 1900 Baron von Kettler, the German Minister, was shot on his way to the Foreign Office, and it was reported that the Empress Dowager subsequently had a chair covered with his skin. The German Emperor in turn exhorted his punitive expeditionary force to emulate Attila and his Huns. Tragedy has stalked the family fortune of the Kettlers. In April 1938, shortly after the German annexation of Austria, the son of the murdered Minister, who had been serving as personal assistant to Herr von Papen, the German Ambassador to Austria, met death suddenly and under mysterious circumstances. It was never established whether he had committed suicide or had been murdered because he knew too much of the plans which had preceded the march into Austria.

allow a battalion of German troops to act as an Embassy guard which the Wilhelmstrasse had demanded as a preliminary to the appointment of a new Ambassador, but they agreed that the staff of the Embassy should be increased to 300, and that additional forces should come to Moscow in groups of thirty, but without arms and without German uniforms. A promise was given that an adequate guard would be provided for the Embassy building by the Soviet Government.[1]

On these conditions there arrived in Moscow on July 28 as Mirbach's successor, Karl Helfferich, a former Vice-Chancellor and Minister of Finance. Though his record was one of pronounced opposition to the Soviet régime, Moscow descried in his appointment a desire on the part of Germany to strengthen her economic ties with Russia, and it was certainly true that he had received instructions to pursue a conciliatory policy of commercial *rapprochement*. He had little opportunity to display his gifts for diplomacy, however, as he only remained ten days in the capital. On August 7 he was summoned back to attend a fateful Crown Council at Spa, and he never returned. The whole Embassy staff went with him as far as Petrograd, leaving only a Consul-General in Moscow. Their sojourn there was equally short, for in less than a fortnight the Embassy was transferred to Pskov, in occupied territory.[2]

[1] Chicherin, pp. 15-17.

[2] According both to Louis Fischer, who offers Chicherin as his authority, and to Helfferich himself, the latter's stay in Moscow was sufficiently long for an amazing offer to be made to him by the Bolsheviks. This was nothing less than an invitation to the Germans to march an army into Russia through a corridor which the Bolsheviks would open up from the Finnish border and which, while avoiding such cities as Petrograd and Petrozavodsk, would enable them to advance against the Allied penetration south from Archangel and Murmansk; at the same time German forces in the Ukraine would resist the efforts of General Alexeiev to extend the sphere of influence of the Volunteer Army northwards to the Don. This proposal was not apparently trans-

With the departure of the German Embassy from Moscow begins the penultimate chapter of the story of Brest-Litovsk. It was still some months before the final words could be written, but from the month of August there was a perceptible stiffening in the Bolshevik attitude and a corresponding tendency of the Germans to assume the defensive.

No better example of this change of attitude could be found than in the supplementary treaties signed on August 27. Through the summer conversations had been proceeding in Berlin in accordance with Article 35 of the Legal-Political Treaty of Brest, which provided for further negotiations within four months of ratification. These had been carried out on the part of the Soviet by Joffe and Leonid Krassin, and on the German side by Kühlmann and Kriege, the permanent head of the Foreign Office. But at the end of June the Supreme Command at last took their revenge on Kühlmann. An unguarded but perfectly truthful speech in the Reichstag delivered him into their hands, and their importunities forced the Kaiser to dispense with the services of German's ablest and most far-sighted war statesman, with the exception of Bethmann Hollweg.

His successor was Rear-Admiral Paul von Hintze, a man who had raised himself from the position of an obscure and impecunious naval lieutenant by the indomitable force of his social ambitions. He had acquired notoriety as the messenger who had carried the ill-advised remonstrance of the German commander to Admiral Dewey at Manila, and, when naval attaché to the Court of St. Petersburg during the abortive revolution of 1905, had had experience in dealing with Russian revolutionaries. He had become an intimate adviser of the Tsar and was

mitted immediately to Berlin, but traces of it may be found in the exchange of notes which accompanied the signature of the supplementary treaties on August 27. (See Appendix VIII, p. 435; Fischer, i. 128-129; and Karl Helfferich, *Der Weltkrieg* (Berlin, 1919), iii. 466-467.)

credited with having persuaded Nicholas II to abandon the policy of appeasement in favour of more rigorous methods of suppression. His career at the Imperial Court was cut short in 1911 when a careless remark about "Hessen" reached ears not intended to hear it, and for a while he suffered eclipse. The war, however, gave him an opportunity to regain the Kaiser's favour when, disguised as a stoker, he made his way to China on a secret mission, evading the vigilance of the British Secret Service ; later his efforts as Minister at Christiania successfully kept Norway among the neutral nations with a bias in favour of the Central Powers. Favoured for the Foreign Office when Zimmermann was forced to resign in 1917, Hintze, on grounds of suspected Pan-Germanism, was rejected by the majority parties in favour of Kühlmann ; now when Kühlmann fell, Hintze, who had taken pains to " liberalize " his views in the interval, was declared acceptable by the parties of the majority. Not a distinguished-looking man—when in naval uniform he was said to look like the Kaiser's state coachman —Hintze was clever, industrious, and ambitious, but his attitude towards Joffe was certainly tinged by his former close relations with the martyr of Ekaterinburg, whose murder by local Bolsheviks occurred during the height of the negotiations.

Despite the obstacles raised by the assassinations in July of Mirbach and Eichhorn, the negotiations progressed slowly but satisfactorily. Early in August Joffe returned to Moscow to gain the approval of the party Central Committee and the Council of Commissars for the terms, and on his return to Berlin the agreements were signed on August 27.[1] The provisions, when contrasted with the original treaty of Brest-Litovsk, are of great interest, being in some respects harsher and in others more lenient. All pretence of adhering to the doctrine of " no indemnities " having been abandoned, Germany demanded, and Russia agreed

[1] For text see Appendices VII and IX, pp. 427, 439.

to, the payment of six billion marks in goods, bonds, and gold, " as compensation for the loss to Germans caused by Russian measures ".[1] In addition Russia was forced to renounce all claims to sovereignty over Livonia and Estonia, which the original treaty had recognized as still being a part of the Russian State.[2] She also undertook to expel the forces of the Entente from Murmansk and Archangel,[3] sell to Germany 25 per cent of the yield of the Baku oil wells,[4] and agree to Germany's recognition of the independence of the Caucasian State of Georgia.[5]

On her part Germany agreed to evacuate White Russia, the Black Sea territory, Rostov, and part of the Don Basin area ;[6] not to occupy any more Russian territory or to encourage the activities of separatist movements on Russian soil ;[7] to give Russia access to the sea via Reval, Riga, and Windau ;[8] and to surrender Baku to Russia on condition that 25 per cent of the oil supply be sold to Germany. In order to protect the oilfields, Germany agreed not to give any assistance to a third Power conducting military operations in the Caucasus outside Georgia and the districts of Kars, Ardahan, and Batum, ceded to Turkey under the original treaty, and promised to oppose the attempts of any third Power to carry military operations into the country immediately surrounding Baku.[9]

Such were the terms of the agreements of August 27, 1918, as published in the official German Gazette.[10] But immediately after the ceremony of signature had been

---

[1] *Texts of the Russian " Peace "*, pp. 192-194 (Financial Agreement, Articles 2 and 3).   [2] *Ibid.* p. 182 (Political Treaty, Article 7).

[3] *Ibid.* pp. 181-182 (Political Treaty, Article 5).

[4] *Ibid.* p. 188 (Political Treaty, Article 14).

[5] *Ibid.* p. 187 (Political Treaty, Article 13).

[6] *Ibid.* pp. 180-181, 186-187 (Political Treaty, Articles 2, 3, 11 and 12).

[7] *Ibid.* p. 181 (Political Treaty, Article 4).

[8] *Ibid.* p. 184 (Political Treaty, Article 8, § 4).

[9] *Ibid.* p. 187 (Political Treaty, Article 14).

[10] *Deutscher Reichsanzeiger*, September 7, 1918.

completed, two notes of even date with the agreements
passed between Hintze and Joffe, the contents of which
remained secret until published in the German press some
eight years later.[1] These documents contained certain
interpretations of the terms of the agreements, and also
additional undertakings. Russia agreed in advance to a
specified frontier east of Livonia and Estonia, for the determination of which machinery had been provided in the
political agreement. Germany expressed a willingness to
prevent armed support being given from the Ukraine to
separatist movements in Russia. In the event of the Soviet
Government being unable to carry out the undertaking to
expel the Allied troops from Northern Russia, Germany
reserved the right to do so herself with the assistance of
Finnish troops if necessary, but agreed to evacuate all
territory occupied in the course of such operations after
their termination and the conclusion of a general peace.[2]
Germany also undertook to demilitarize permanently the
fortress of Reval. In addition she promised aid to Russia
in suppressing the military activities of General Alexeiev's
Volunteer Army and of the Czechoslovaks; to use her influence with the Ukraine and with Georgia to obtain for Russia
one-third of the iron ore exported by the first, and one-
quarter of the manganese exported by the second; and
to speak a word in favour of the release from prison and
from Finnish citizenship, and of the return to Russia, of
Finnish Red Guards on condition that Russia would not
employ them again in military operations against Finland.

Taken together the instruments signed on August 27
were considerably more favourable to Russia than those
of Brest-Litovsk. Yet, in consideration of the rapidly

[1] For text see Appendix VIII, p. 435. Cf. *Europäische Gespräche*,
March 1926.
[2] Traces may be seen here of the alleged offer by Chicherin to Helfferich. It is conceivable that Joffe may have repeated this proposal to
Hintze after his return from Moscow in August.

deteriorating military position of Germany—a deterioration which had been disclosed to Hintze at the Crown
Council at Spa on August 14—a better bargain might have
been struck. It is difficult to understand how Joffe, whose
knowledge of the internal situation of Germany was so
intimate, could have been so completely deceived as to her
military strength. The very life in Berlin at that moment
should have warned him of Germany's inability to insist
on the terms proposed. Food was scarce and expensive—
being largely of the *Ersatz* variety—and the whole appearance of the city and its inhabitants was shabby and desolate.
House windows once broken remained unmended, pave-
ments had fallen in, and rubbish and refuse remained
uncollected in the streets. People and horses collapsed
through lack of nourishment ; the very street cars constantly
broke down and the passengers dejectedly alighted to the
muttered command of the conductor, "*Alle aussteigen; der
Wagen ist krank*". Moreover, Krassin's visits to General
Headquarters had convinced him that things at the front
were going badly, and he so reported in letters to his wife.[1]

It is therefore extraordinary that Joffe should have
advised Moscow to accept further demands by Germany,
especially that of reparations to amount to six billion
marks, and, still more, that the Soviet Government, whose
general views on treaty fulfilment were actuated by their
power to resist, should have made instalment payments on
this sum totalling 120,000,000 gold roubles in August
and September.

The explanation lies, in all probability, in the internal
situation of Russia, where foreign intervention and civil
war threatened the existence of the Soviet régime so
acutely that it was unable to risk the refusal of the German
demands. Moreover, the news of the " black day " (August
8) did not leak through to Berlin for some considerable
time.

[1] Krassin, p. 80.

In point of fact there was little attempt by either side
to fulfil the terms of the new agreements other than the
instalment payments by the Russians and the dilatory
evacuation of White Russia by the Germans. Through the
remainder of the summer and autumn the various commissions provided for functioned spasmodically, and there
appeared to be a lessening of the tension between the two
Governments in matters of territorial adjustment. But the
tide was setting steadily against the cause of German
arms. It could no longer be concealed that the gambler's
throw in the West had lost and that the Allied offensives
in August and September were driving the German army
ever backward. More and more troops were being withdrawn from the East, until a bare 400,000 men were left
with Hoffmann and Gröner. Their departure encouraged
the Bolsheviks to stiffen their attitude towards Germany
and towards her partners in the now tottering Quadruple
Alliance. On September 30, after a period of acrimonious
exchanges and remonstrances, the Soviet Government took
the first step to free itself from the toils of Brest-Litovsk.
In a note to the Ottoman Government it declared the
treaty with Turkey to be null and void.[1]

3

Adolf Joffe, if he failed to make the best bargain possible
in the supplementary treaties of August 27, left little to be
desired, from the point of view of Moscow, in his general
conduct as Soviet Ambassador and Bolshevik agent. For
Lenin was true to the pledge which he had given the
Petrograd Soviet on the night of February 23 : " The
Central Executive Committee signs the Peace ; the Council
of Commissars signs the Peace, but not the Central Committee of the Party, and for the behaviour of the Party the

[1] For text of Note see *Class Struggle* (New York), vol. ii. December
1918 ; Chicherin, pp. 22-23.

Soviet Government is not responsible ". Propaganda and diplomacy, therefore, went forward hand-in-hand, and Joffe's rôle was of a dual nature, diplomat and agitator. Though he may not have achieved all he had hoped in the first rôle, his performance in the second was one of considerable success.

He arrived in Berlin in the last days of April 1918, with a staff of three hundred, and hoisted the hammer-and-sickle flag above the former Russian Embassy. He refused to present his credentials personally to the Kaiser, and, instead of starting on a round of official visits in the usual manner of an incoming Ambassador, at once got into touch with the Independent Socialists and the Spartacus group. In the printed list of those invited to his first dinner-party there appeared the names of Karl Liebknecht and Rosa Luxemburg, both of whom were at that moment serving prison sentences for sedition and treason.[1]

The General Staff had foreseen the danger of allowing a Soviet Embassy to be established in Berlin, or consulates to be opened in Germany, which would serve as centres for Bolshevik propaganda. The High Command in the East had become too well acquainted with the Bolsheviks to doubt for a minute their sincerity in promoting world revolution, or that the undermining of the Imperial German Government was the first step towards it. Hoffmann, therefore, recommended, and Ludendorff agreed, that no Soviet Embassy should be allowed in Berlin until after the conclusion of a general peace, and that, as long as a state of war lasted, the two Ambassadors, both German and Soviet, should have residence in the Headquarters of the Commander-in-Chief on the Eastern Front, where a check could be kept on the excessive activity of the Bolshevik representatives.[2]

Had this advice been followed there is little doubt that the course of the friendly diplomatic relations between the

[1] *The Liberator, loc. cit.*   [2] Hoffmann, ii. 223 ; Ludendorff, ii. 644.

two Powers would have run much more smoothly. There would have been no murder of Mirbach, and Joffe would have been prevented from having any very close connection with German extremists. But both the Imperial Chancellor and the Foreign Office refused to heed these warnings against admitting the Trojan Horse of Moscow. Dr. Kriege, who had taken a great liking to Joffe during the negotiations at Brest, swore to his sincerity. Kriege was doubtless influenced by the traditions of his training, for he was deeply imbued with those policies which had guided Germany until the 'nineties. Following these he felt that for Germany it was essential to return permanently to Bismarck's policy of close friendship and understanding with Russia. Count Hertling also assured the Reichstag that the Government believed sincerely in the intention of the Soviet Government to carry out the provisions of the treaty prohibiting the dissemination of Bolshevik propaganda in Germany, and emphasized his confidence in the personal integrity and trustworthiness of the Soviet Ambassador.[1]

Joffe, however, attached greater importance to his functions as a revolutionary agent than as an Ambassador. Acting in perfect bad faith—which he publicly admitted in January 1919 [2]—he worked with tireless energy for the overthrow of the Imperial German Government. It was now the turn of Russia to repay her revolutionary debts. In former years the Socialist Party in Germany had aided and financed revolution in Russia. Now the Bolsheviks could return the favour. The Soviet Embassy became the

[1] Helfferich, iii. 495. According to Ludendorff, the Government were even prepared to supply Joffe with arms and ammunition for use against the Whites. (Ludendorff, ii. 659.)

[2] In a memorandum published in the *Vestnik Zhizni* he declared: "It is necessary to emphasize most categorically that in the preparation of the German revolution, the Russian Embassy worked all the time in close contact with the German Socialists ". (See also Trotsky, *Terrorismus und Kommunismus* (Hamburg, 1920), p. 104 ; and Fischer, i. 75.)

headquarters of the German revolutionary element. More than ten Independent Socialist newspapers were directed and supported from 7 Unter den Linden. The Embassy bought information from German Government officials and passed it on to Radical leaders for use in their Reichstag speeches, in their addresses to workers' meetings, and in the press of the Left. Anti-governmental literature found its way to all parts of the country, and leaders of the Independents and Spartacists discussed matters of revolutionary tactics with Joffe, himself an experienced conspirator.[1]

Again and again the Supreme Command drew the attention of the Imperial Government to the danger of Joffe's work and his presence in Berlin—the reply was always the same : it was better that he should be in Berlin then anywhere else. They had their eyes on him there. " Unfortunately ", writes Ludendorff, " those eyes were blind." [2]

Apart from the activities of the Soviet Embassy and the Independent Socialists, there were two other channels through which the poison of Bolshevism worked back into the body-politic of Germany. Prisoners of war released under the treaty began slowly to return to the ranks after long leave, bringing with them the infection bred of the revolutionary propaganda to which they had been subjected in Russian prison camps since the November Revolution. They had drunk deeply of the heady wine of freedom and sedition, they had seen an army melt away before their eyes, and now they returned to their depôts speaking a new language of peace and bread,—and bringing with them a spirit of general insubordination. The effect on the army was one of marked deterioration in morale, but this was due rather to direct influence from Russia than to the machinations of the Independents or the Spartacists.[3]

[1] Fischer, i. 75.   [2] Ludendorff, ii. 644.
[3] *Ibid.* p. 642. The acting G.O.C. in Allenstein (East Prussia) reported

The views of Bolshevism also infected the German divisions retained on the Eastern Front after the conclusion of peace. The conditions under which they lived rendered them an easy prey. Though fraternization was forbidden it was impossible to prevent it, and propaganda, by leaflet and word of mouth, spread quickly among the troops. " Immediately after conquering those Bolsheviks, we were conquered by them", Hoffmann admitted after the war to an American journalist. " Our victorious army on the Eastern Front became rotten with Bolshevism. We got to the point where we did not dare to transfer certain of our eastern divisions to the West." [1]

Here indeed was irony. Not only were large numbers of German troops retained in the East to gather in the fruits of Brest-Litovsk, but, at the moment when they were desperately needed in the West, it was discovered that their transfer would prove both useless and even dangerous. According to Prince Max of Baden, the Supreme Command was prepared, towards the end of October 1918, to evacuate the Ukraine altogether, but Ludendorff and Hoffmann agreed that these troops were so impregnated with Bolshevik ideas that they would be of no real service in attack, and would threaten the morale of the jaded divisions which had already been defeated.[2]

Thus, while Ludendorff was protesting against Joffe's activities in Berlin, the army in the East was suffering

on July 14, 1918 : " A large number of men and non-commissioned officers who have come back from prison camps in Russia have lost all sense of discipline and brought back so many Bolshevik ideas, owing to their having witnessed the Revolution, that they exercise a bad influence on their comrades " (quoted by General von Kuhl before the Reichstag Commission of Enquiry). [See *The Causes of the German Collapse in 1918*, edited by Ralph Haswell Lutz (Stanford University, Cal., 1934), pp. 143-144.] Such reports from military district commanders were not uncommon at this period.

[1] *Chicago Daily News*, March 13, 1919.

[2] *Memoirs of Prince Max of Baden*, sec. ii. pp. 104-105.

irreparable damage to its morale, and the poison was spreading westwards. Herein lies the answer to the alibi of the " Stab-in-the-back " which Ludendorff built up with such assiduous care in after years. There is no doubt that Joffe did his utmost to destroy the Imperial régime in Germany, from the moment of his ostentatious arrival to the moment of his precipitate departure, but the effect of his propaganda was not sufficiently rapid to contribute to the failure of the German offensives in the West between March and June. These offensives were defeated because the unprecedented and continuous engagements had exhausted the mental and physical energy of the troops and because the reserves and supplies of food and war material were no longer sufficient. The whole German nation, the military and the civilian population alike, was completely exhausted, both physically and psychologically, but the full toll of their exhaustion was not realized, even by themselves, until Ludendorff's defeat was made obvious to all. The nation was so certain that the promises of ultimate victory would be fulfilled, and the army so steeped in the traditions of its history, that it was only when the sudden realization of defeat was borne in upon them that their confidence wavered.

August 8, 1918—" the black day in the history of the German army "—marked the turning point between possible victory and inevitable defeat. For the first time whole divisions failed and in many cases allowed themselves to be captured without resistance. The order to counter-attack could no longer be carried out, and it was from that moment that the defeatist propaganda of the Independents made its greatest inroads on the morale of the army. Up to that time, with the hope of victory before them, the troops had fought with magnificent bravery and had been practically impervious to the widespread sedition of their comrades from the East. Bolshevism took little hold on them while they were winning, but with the shadow of defeat above them their moral resistance weakened and they began to take heed. Retiring troops, meeting a fresh division going into action, greeted them with cries of " Black-legs " and " You're prolonging the war ".[1] Troops in Berlin entraining for the front on September 2 — Sedan Day — sang the " Marseillaise ".[2] Many fought on with sullen courage to the end ; but the virus, once injected, acted swiftly.

It was defeat in the field which destroyed the spirit of the western army and rendered it receptive of revolutionary doctrines. The process was not reversed. The events of October and November were a general strike of a hopelessly conquered army against the madness of its leaders, and the propaganda of the Bolsheviks only weakened German resistance after the tide of battle had turned against them. When, on October 3, 1918, Hindenburg wrote his historic letter to the Chancellor demanding an immediate armistice, he attributed the necessity for so precipitate a step to purely military reasons—the breakdown of the Macedonian Front, the weakening of reserves, the impossibility of making good their very heavy losses —and gave no hint of the " Stab-in-the-back " theory.[3] " The documents dealing with the bolshevizing of the eastern army are plentiful enough to prove how poisoning was done from the East," Dr. Albrecht Philipp said in evidence before the Reichstag Commission of Enquiry ; " but I consider that it is hardly possible to speak of bolshevization of the western army until the moment when the German Revolution broke out ".[4]

It is not to be assumed, however, that the efforts of Joffe and the Independent Socialists were without effect among the civilian population. In conjunction with the Spartacists,

[1] Ludendorff, ii. 683.

[2] Max Beer, *Fifty Years of International Socialism* (London, 1937), p. 178.

[3] Wheeler-Bennett, p. 166.　　　　[4] Lutz, pp. 173-174.

they let slip no opportunity of urging the workers to assert themselves and strike for their freedom. With the advent, on October 1, of Prince Max of Baden as Chancellor, in succession to Count Hertling, and the consequent " Revolution from above ", Joffe, an experienced revolutionary, scented the beginning of the end and redoubled his activities. At a later date, it was his proud boast that he had contributed to the full extent of his power to the triumph of the German Revolution. Every diplomatic privilege was shamelessly abused. The courier service, having the immunity of " the bag ", was remarkably active. The number of people passing between Moscow and Berlin under the protection of *laissez-passer*, and accompanied by a vast amount of luggage, boxes, and bags, was enormous. There was every reason to believe that they contained both arms and revolutionary literature, yet, because of the extraterritorial privileges of the Soviet Embassy, there was no legal means to check the steady flow. In addition, Russian agitators, nominally figuring as attachés on the staff of the Embassy, appeared frequently at Independent Socialist meetings and addressed audiences which were becoming progressively more enthusiastic.

Nor was this all. The Soviet Government in Moscow saw no reason for affording any support whatever to Prince Max of Baden's régime. For, although the new German Government had declared itself, in principle, in favour of a revision of the Brest-Litovsk Peace, it had not actually done anything to change the former eastern policy of Germany. When the news of Prince Max's proposals for the democratization of the German Constitution and of the acceptance of the Fourteen Points was announced by Kamenev to the Central Executive Committee of the Soviet Congress, it was greeted with howls of derision. "He won't stay there long ; Liebknecht will see to that ", was roared from the bursting throats of the enthusiastic delegates.[1]

[1] M. Phillips Price, p. 344.

At Lenin's suggestion the Committee adopted a resolution, on October 4, placing all the "forces and resources" of the Soviets at the disposal of the German proletariat, and very shortly afterwards a tax of ten billion roubles was imposed on the Russian bourgeoisie for the defence of the Russian and international revolutions.[1]

Joffe had already had considerable funds at his disposal for propaganda purposes—a sum of some 12,000,000 marks had been banked with Mendelssohn & Co.[2]—but now he dispensed his money with even greater liberality. He enabled the editors of the famous *Letters of Spartacus* to increase their circulation among workers and soldiers,[3] and gave to Emile Barth, the leader of the shop-stewards and a prominent Independent, not, as was at first alleged, 105,000 marks, " but several hundred thousand marks for the purpose of acquiring arms " in preparation for the coming Bolshevik revolution.[4]

Broadsheets and pamphlets were distributed widely throughout the country. The Independents and Spartacists were convinced that the success of the revolution in Germany was not possible by a compromise with the Majority Socialists, but only by their complete defeat. The revolution must not only sweep away the kings and princes and the military caste, but also those Social Democrats such as Ebert, Scheidemann, and Bauer, who, favouring a middle-class democracy, had allied themselves with the new order of Prince Max. These must go, and for this reason the inflammatory literature with which the country was flooded declared that the new Government

[1] Bunyan, pp. 149-153.

[2] Hoffmann records that, on December 21, 1918, he was informed that the sum lying to Joffe's account at Mendelssohn's, and subsequently sequestrated by the Ebert Government, amounted to 22 million marks. (Hoffmann, i. 252.)

[3] Lutz, p. 108 (evidence of Dr. Ernst Meyer, editor of the *Spartacus Letters*, before the Reichstag Committee of Enquiry).

[4] *Izvestia*, December 6, 1918.

was made up of murderers, who were, however, vastly better than the traitorous Social Democrats.[1]

Even the rural population was affected, and open threats were made by the peasant leaders of East Prussia that they were only awaiting the return of the troops from the front to divide up the estates of the great landlords after the Russian model.[2]

With the release of Karl Liebknecht from prison on October 21, events in Berlin began to move more rapidly. The Government were desperately negotiating with President Wilson for an armistice, and at the same time were endeavouring to persuade the Kaiser to abdicate in the interests of his dynasty and his country. The people, who wanted peace above everything, were apathetic to the dynastic issue, but Liebknecht, seizing the opportunity to link the two together, raised a slogan, which he preached publicly in the streets and halls of the capital, " If we get rid of the Kaiser we shall get a decent peace ".

There was, however, no close co-ordination between the revolutionary movements in Germany. The mutiny of the High Seas Fleet at Kiel on October 29 and 30, which took place on the initiative of the sailors themselves, was not dictated from Berlin. The leaders of the Independents were unaware of what had happened at Kiel until several days later, and on November 2 were agreed that the time was not yet ripe for immediate action.[3]

Joffe, better informed than they, was assured that the naval mutiny indicated the imminence of a general outbreak. He gave a dinner party at the Embassy at which were such prominent German revolutionaries as the Spartacist leaders Karl Liebknecht and Rosa Luxemburg, and

[1] Scheidemann, ii. 533.

[2] Letter from Richard Stovromnek to Prince Max of Baden. (See *Memoirs*, ii. 289, footnote)

[3] Arthur Rosenberg, *The Birth of the German Republic* (Oxford, 1931), p. 262.

Haase, Barth, and Rosenfeld of the Independent Socialist Party. Toasts were drunk—even at that early date the Bolshevik diplomats had established a reputation for the excellent quality of their champagne—and Joffe drank to the day when the German Soviet Government should receive him in the Kaiser's palace. Liebknecht responded warmly to the toast, but regretted that this event was likely to be somewhat distant. " On the contrary ", replied Joffe, " within a week the Red Flag will be flying over the Berliner Schloss." [1]

Joffe's prophesy became true to the very day. On November 9 Liebknecht proclaimed the Soviet Republic from the steps of the Imperial Palace, but Joffe was not there to enjoy his short-lived triumph.

Prince Max's Government, and particularly those of them who belonged to the Social Democratic Party, were seriously embarrassed by the results of the propaganda with which Haase and Liebknecht, with pecuniary assistance from Joffe, were flooding the country. The efforts of the Chancellor to conserve some kind of national stability during the pre-armistice negotiations, in order to preserve the monarchy and to save Germany from too abject a surrender, were hampered at every turn by the rising tide of Leftist opinion, which clamoured for peace and bread and the abdication of the Kaiser. The Majority Socialists, who at the outset had been inclined to ridicule the danger of Bolshevism, were now obsessed with the fear of its proximity, as every day brought a further secession from their ranks to those of Haase. Both they and the Prince were anxious to cut off the Spartacists and Independents from the fountain-head of their supplies.

On October 28 there appeared a particularly obnoxious broadsheet, exceeding even its predecessors in venom, and highly injurious to the vital interests of the country. At

---

[1] The account of this gathering at the Soviet Embassy was given to the author by one of the German participants.

the morning meeting of the Cabinet, Dr. Drews, the
Prussian Minister of the Interior, urged the sharpest possible
control of the Soviet Embassy and its relations, and
Scheidemann proposed that, if necessary, the coal deliveries
to Russia should be stopped as a measure of pressure.[1]
Later in the discussion Scheidemann put forward two
other possibilities : the first was that an official burglary
of the Embassy should be " arranged " and the incriminating documents stolen ; the second, that one of the
Embassy mail-cases should be accidentally " made to go
to pieces " on the station platform. The revolutionary
tracts would then come tumbling out, proving that the
diplomatic privileges of the Embassy were being abused,
and appropriate action could be taken. According to
Scheidemann's own account, " the Cabinet had a good
laugh over these proposals "—though this seems impossible
under the circumstances—but nothing more was said.

When, however, the Cabinet met again on November 5,
Dr. Solf, the Foreign Minister, reported that, strangely
enough, the Soviet courier's packing-case had " come to
pieces " on the Schlesischer Bahnhof the previous evening
and that insurrectionary documents of the most compromising nature—incitements to revolution and assassination—had been disclosed.[2] Joffe was thereupon summoned to the Foreign Office and informed by Solf that,

[1] Prince Max of Baden, ii. 223.

[2] *Ibid. p.* 289 ; Scheidemann, ii. 534-535. Some years later the
Austrian Social Democratic press revealed the fact that the documents
discovered in this particular case " were neither written nor printed,
nor packed, nor despatched from Russia. They were, in fact, inserted
into the diplomatic bag by the German police ; they were written in
Germany by Comrade Levi " (Majority Socialist) (see *Klassenkampf,*
Vienna, December 1, 1927). It would appear, therefore, that, though
Joffe's couriers undoubtedly abused their diplomatic privileges at
every turn—Joffe frequently boasted as much—on this particular
occasion the highly efficient Prussian police either found nothing
sufficiently incriminating or were taking no chances.

on the following morning, he and his entire staff would be deported from Berlin. They were to travel by special train and would be escorted by an armed guard to Pskov, where they would be detained until the remaining members of the German Consular Missions in Moscow and Petrograd had arrived safely within the German lines. In the event of their non-arrival, or of any other untoward happening, Joffe's guards would become his jailers.

Thus, once again, a " sealed train " bore a Bolshevik mission across Germany to Russia, but Joffe had left a sting behind him. On the morning of his departure from Berlin—it is surprising that he was allowed contact with the outside world—he handed over to his German agent, Dr. Oscar Cohn, the sum of a million marks and authority to draw upon the account opened with Mendelssohn's, for the purpose of continuing the work of revolutionary propaganda. A few weeks later, on the eve of the first Spartacist Rising, Dr. Cohn declared : " I have devoted the money to the purpose for which it was given, namely, the spreading of the idea of revolution, and only regret that circumstances rendered it impossible for me to expend the whole amount ".[1]

The news of Joffe's expulsion reached Moscow at the moment when the Sixth All-Soviet Congress was in session.

[1] Wolff Telegraphic Bureau, December 26, 1918. On several subsequent occasions Dr. Cohn endeavoured to minimize these remarks. Both in the National Assembly at Weimar on February 27, 1919, and before the Reichstag Commission of Enquiry on November 15, 1919, he passionately defended himself against the accusation of using Joffe's money for political revolutionary purposes. He had devoted the greater part of it, he said, to the relief of Russian prisoners of war in Germany and of Russian " civilians ". A small sum had been expended on " political aims ", but a certain amount had been given to two party newspapers " for new machinery " and " for literary work ". (See *Verhandlungen der verfassungsgebenden deutschen Nationalversammlung*, vol. 326, February 27, 1919, coll. 337 *seq.*: *Official German Documents relating to the World War*, 1923, p. 756.)

Fortune had smiled on the external affairs of the Bolsheviks. Every day brought news of some fresh collapse among the Central Powers, some new city mounting the Red Flag and organizing Soviets. The Central Executive Committee had seized on the improved international situation to hold new elections in which the Bolsheviks had secured 80 per cent of the seats. The Mensheviks and Right Social Revolutionaries were excluded by decree, and the remnant of the Social Revolutionaries of the Left who had survived the July " purge "—some thirty in all—were anxious for a reconciliation with the Bolsheviks.

It was to this body that Sverdlov, on the evening of November 8 (the anniversary of the Decree of Peace), read the telegram announcing Joffe's expulsion. The news was greeted with cat-calls and cries of derision which became shouts of savage satisfaction when Radek announced that the German Consular and Prisoner of War missions would be immediately expelled, and that hostages had been taken by the Cheka for the safe arrival of Joffe and his staff.[1] Shortly afterwards came the news

[1] Two attempts were made to procure the return of Joffe to Berlin after his departure. Fearing for the fate of the thousands of war prisoners in Russia, the German Commissioner for Exchange requested the Government to allow Joffe to return, without diplomatic privileges and under close supervision, for the purpose of exchange negotiations. He succeeded in gaining the consent of the Foreign Office to send Dr. Cohn to Joffe with this proposal, but Cohn was refused permission by Hoffmann to enter the territory of Ober-Ost.

The second attempt came from Moscow. The Spartacists extended fraternal greetings and a warm welcome to those Bolsheviks who should wish to attend the expected Congress of German Workers and Soldiers, and Joffe, Radek, and Bukharin were commissioned by the Soviet Government to proceed to Berlin. Again Hoffmann refused permission for the agitators to pass through the Ober-Ost district, and Joffe and Bukharin were forced to return to Moscow. Radek, however, disguised in a German uniform and with the forged papers of a released prisoner of war, slipped through the lines and made a dramatic appearance at the Congress on December 30, where he made a forceful appeal to the

that the German fleet had mutinied at Kiel, mounted the Red Flag, and sent fraternal greetings to the Soviet fleet at Kronstadt. Pandemonium reigned in the Congress. Cheering and the singing of the " Internationale " interrupted all further business. " That's the best answer we can give them ", shouted one enthusiastic delegate to his comrade, but the other called back : " No, there's one better. We'll tear up the Treaty of Brest-Litovsk." The cry was taken up by man after man, till the whole Congress was in a fury of denunciation. Gone forever were the days of the oppressors' yoke ; the symbol of their humiliation and sacrifice must be destroyed.

On the afternoon of the following day (November 9) Sverdlov read to the Congress the decree of the Council of Commissars annulling the Brest-Litovsk treaty. A year ago Lenin, on the morrow of the *coup d'état*, had read the Decree of Peace to the Second Congress of Soviets at Smolny, and the delegates had wept with joy at the ending of the war. A peace of conquest and annexation had followed and only Lenin's strength of purpose had forced them along the thorny path of abnegation. Now those who had imposed upon them a dictated peace had been themselves defeated. They were suing for peace even as Russia had

delegates to fight a decisive battle, with the support of the Red armies of Russia, against the forces of capitalism. Radek took a prominent part in the first Spartacist Rising of January 1919, figuring in the notorious doggerel which all Berlin was repeating at that time :

> " Five hundred corpses in a row ;
> Liebknecht, Rosa, Radek and Co.
> Why are they not there also ? "

He was arrested by the Government troops and narrowly escaped execution. During his imprisonment, he held almost daily "audiences" to which came many distinguished members of the bourgeois parties, including Wälther Rathenau. Ultimately he was exchanged for Germans arrested in Moscow, and with his departure ended the last direct effort of the Soviet régime to assist the German Bolsheviks to establish their dictatorship.

sued, and their humiliation was before them. With a glad heart the Congress unanimously endorsed the Decree of Annulment and wrote *finis* to an unhappy chapter.[1]

4

More devastating even than the impact of Brest-Litovsk on German internal affairs was its Nemesis in Germany's relations with the Allied and Associated Powers, both before and after her defeat at their hands. For the signature of the treaties of Brest inspired a unity of purpose and a degree of co-operation between America and the Western Powers which all previous negotiations between them had failed to achieve.

During the first year of American participation in the war there had seemed to be but a lukewarmness in Wilson's pursuit of his policies. His attitude towards the enemy had lacked that *Vernichtungswille* (will to annihilate) which the nations of the Entente had acquired over a longer period of hostilities. The Allies were concerned far more with the defeat of Germany than with her subsequent reformation ; they were fighting Germany as such, despite the protestation of the propaganda departments to the contrary. The hatred of everything German had taken hold of them and was to find its subsequent expression in the Khaki Election of 1918. But Wilson preferred to distinguish between the German people and their rulers. " War upon German imperialism, peace with German liberalism " had been the essence of the presidential speeches since April 1917, and the emphasis had been laid upon the profit which the Liberals would acquire by separating their fortunes from those of Ludendorff and accepting

[1] The resolution, passed by the Council of Commissars and the Congress on November 9, received official force when adopted by the Central Executive Committee on November 13, 1918. For text see Appendix X, p. 447.

the terms which Wilson would persuade the Allies to offer. The fact was even stressed that no designs were entertained against the political structure of Germany. The monarchy might be retained if the power of the old military caste were broken. " We do not intend to inflict any wrong on the German Empire ", ran the President's Message to Congress on December 4, 1917, " nor to interfere in any way in its internal affairs ".[1]

It was largely in this spirit that Wilson had enunciated his Fourteen Points, in the formulation of which the Conference of Brest-Litovsk had played so important a part. On the one hand it had been hoped to encourage the Russians to refrain from making a separate peace, and on the other to endeavour to separate the German people from their rulers by strengthening the belief of the working classes that a just peace could be had upon these terms, and that, should the military leaders refuse to accept them, they were prolonging the war unnecessarily and were responsible for the sufferings of the people.

In entertaining this hope Wilson and his advisers were as ignorant of the psychology of the German working masses as were Lenin and his colleagues, who at the same moment were ardently appealing to the same audience to cast off their rulers and declare a dictatorship of the proletariat. Though the German working man might have been disposed to grasp at the glittering prizes dangled before him by both Wilson and Lenin, he was still held body and soul in the grip of the German High Command ; and not the working man alone, but also the Emperor, the Government, the Foreign Office, and the Reichstag. Whatever may have been the feelings of the German working man towards democracy or Communism, he was totally incapable of giving expression to them, and this lack of receptivity to the blandishments of revolution both

[1] *New York Times*, December 5, 1917.

from America and from Russia was the source of grave disappointment both to Wilson and Lenin.

It was, however, the cynical refusal of the German Government to regard the negotiations with Russia as within the scope of any general settlement that might develop from the Fourteen Points, which first caused Wilson to stiffen his attitude towards Germany as a whole. The Russian question had been intended as something of a criterion of sincerity for Germany. " The treatment accorded to Russia by her sister nations in the months to come will be the acid test of their goodwill ", Wilson had written in Point VIII, and, more than anything else in Hertling's reply, the attitude towards Russia convinced the President that the German desire for peace was insincere.

When, however, this was followed by the barefaced brutality of the peace terms of Brest-Litovsk, their acceptance dictated at the bayonet's point and the whole affair condoned and ratified by the Reichstag almost without protest, Wilson awoke to the fact that for practical purposes there was but one Germany to be conquered, and this was the Germany of the High Command. He realized that it was obviously futile to appeal in conciliatory tones to the working masses of Germany when Ludendorff, already successful in the East, could promise them through victory even greater spoils in the West, and when the *Machtpolitik* of the High Command met with the approval of the Liberal elements in Germany, or at least not with their active opposition. It might be possible to persuade the German masses that in following Ludendorff they were in ultimate error, but the means of persuasion lay in defeat on the field of battle, not in reasoning. The soundest political strategy was to reiterate again and again the impossibility of peace with the kind of government that had imposed the Treaty of Brest-Litovsk.

This change in presidential policy, a change so vital that to it may be attributed the final and speedy victory of the Allied cause, was made public in Wilson's speech at Baltimore on April 6, 1918, in which he frankly admitted his recent change of heart and new resoluteness of purpose:

I do not wish, even at this moment of utter disillusionment, to judge harshly or unrighteously. I judge only what the German arms have accomplished with unpitying thoroughness throughout every fair region they have touched. . . . For myself, I am ready . . . to discuss a fair and just and honest peace at any time that it is sincerely purposed—a peace in which the strong and the weak shall fare alike. But the answer, when I proposed such a peace, came from the German commanders in Russia, and I cannot mistake the meaning of the answer. I accept the challenge.—Germany has once more said that force, and force alone, shall decide whether Justice and Peace shall reign in the affairs of men. . . . There is therefore but one response possible from us : Force, Force to the utmost, Force without stint or limit, the righteous and triumphant Force which shall make Right the law of the world, and cast every selfish dominion down in the dust.[1]

This amounted to a pledge of the last man and gun and dollar in America to the Allied cause. Unanimity between the United States and the nations of the Entente had at last been achieved, and victory was assured, for once the American man-power was made available there could be no doubt of the outcome. The artificer of this compact was Ludendorff—for the High Command by their treatment of Russia had disclosed to the world what defeat at the hands of Germany would entail, and, furthermore, that the supreme power in the country was exercised by them alone. In so doing they had contributed to the Allied cause that final and essential degree of co-operation and oneness of purpose which was necessary for victory.

Nor was this the full measure of Ludendorff's achievement. He had sealed the fate of German arms in the field, but the implacable enmity against imperialism and autocracy which he had aroused in the Presbyterian

[1] *House Papers*, iii. 425-427.

bosom of Wilson would never be assuaged until the monarchy and military caste in Germany had been destroyed. No longer did the President disclaim the intention of the Allies to interfere in the internal affairs of the German Empire. As the summer progressed he showed clearly and definitely that he aimed at " the destruction of every arbitrary power anywhere that can separately, secretly and of its single choice, disturb the peace of the world ".[1] Germany could not have peace until the German people had complied with this demand and had substituted a democratic form of government (preferably republican) for the military imperialism of the Hohenzollerns. Thus even the origins of the Weimar system, later anathema to Ludendorff and his National-Socialist allies, may be numbered among the fruits of Brest-Litovsk.

The fatal results of the policy did not at once become clear to the Supreme Command and the German Government. As the fateful summer of 1918 waned to autumn and the military fortunes of the Central Powers marched steadily towards defeat, it was still considered possible to conserve the spoils of war in the East, even if certain concessions had to be made in the West. On September 12, at a moment when the Austro-Hungarian Empire, then at its last gasp, was proposing a " confidential and non-binding discussion " of peace terms by the belligerents, the German Vice-Chancellor, Herr von Payer, forgetful of Kühlmann's former policy, was breathing defiance at Stuttgart. In any consideration of peace terms, he said, there could be no meddling with the agreements already reached with Russia, the Ukraine, and Rumania. " In the East we have peace, and it remains for us peace,

[1] This statement was made in President Wilson's speech at Mount Vernon on July 18, 1918, and later came to be regarded in the nature of a supplement to the Fourteen Points. It was included as a *conditio sine qua non* of an armistice in the Second and Third Wilson Notes to Germany of October 14 and 23, 1918.

whether it pleases our western neighbours or not."
Germany might consider the restoration of Belgium, but
the position in the East must remain unquestioned and
inviolate.[1]

Back like a lance-thrust came the reply of the Allies
from the lips of President Wilson on September 27 :

We are all agreed that there can be no peace obtained by any
kind of bargain or compromise with the Governments of the Central
Powers, because we have dealt with them already and have seen
them deal with other Governments that were parties to the struggle,
at Brest-Litovsk and at Bukarest. They have convinced us that
they are without honour and do not intend justice. They observe
no covenants, accept no principles but force and their own interests.
We cannot " come to terms " with them. They have made it impossible. The German people must by this time be fully aware that we
cannot accept the word of those who forced this war upon us. We
do not think the same thoughts or speak the same language of
agreement.[2]

Here was deliberate notice served on the German people
of the implacable, uncompromising refusal of the Allied and
Associated Powers to treat with any representatives of the
imperialist military régime in Germany. The Kaiser and the
Generals must go, and the German people must stand upon
their own feet and ask for peace. They had it in their
power to end the conflict immediately. This declaration of
Wilson's was a vastly important factor in destroying the
confidence of the German ruling caste in themselves.

Twenty-four hours later (September 28) Ludendorff
admitted to himself the utter hopelessness of the situation.
For the first time he beheld the face of disaster, a face which
had stalked his dreams since August 8—" that black day "
—but from which he had taken refuge behind the cloak
of his own pride. Now this covering had been ripped away,

[1] Lloyd George, vi. 227.
[2] *Selected Literary and Political Papers and Addresses of Woodrow
Wilson* (New York, 1926-1927), ii. 265.

and the position was revealed in all its stark horror. Germany was defeated. Nothing could alter that, and the sudden realization of this appalling fact sent Ludendorff's highly-strung mind reeling from its moorings of sanity. In panic he appealed to Hindenburg, to the Emperor, to the Chancellor to take some action which should mitigate the catastrophe and stave off the humiliation of a surrender in the field. In a wild frenzy of despair he demanded an instant request for an armistice on the basis of the Fourteen Points and the immediate democratization of the Constitution. No Paul on the road to any Damascus was more suddenly converted than was Ludendorff to the cause of peace and democracy. Never did a dictator take such infinite pains to secure power to his antagonists as did the First Quartermaster-General when he planned the " Revolution from above ". " The parliamentarization of Germany was not fought for by the Reichstag ; it was ordered by Ludendorff." [1]

Despite the efforts of the new Chancellor, Prince Max of Baden, to oppose undue precipitancy in opening negotiations and thereby avoid the appearance of a death-bed repentance on the part of Germany, Ludendorff, dragging an unwilling Hindenburg in his train, insisted that an offer of peace be made at once, and with a heavy heart Prince Max signed the note of October 4.[2]

Again the Germans had misconstrued the situation and under-estimated the *damnosa hereditas* of Brest-Litovsk. It was now too late for them to accept the Fourteen Points as a " basis for negotiations ". In the hey-day of their power they had mocked at the new tables of the law, and now, when they had changed their tune, they found that the Allies had changed theirs also. " The pronouncements of President Wilson were a statement of attitude made before the Brest-Litovsk treaty ", ran an official British Memorandum. ". . . They cannot, therefore, be understood

[1] Rosenberg, p. 242 *et seq.*   [2] Wheeler-Bennett, p. 161 *et seq.*

as a full recitation of the conditions of peace." It was not
sufficient for Germany to express her willingness to
negotiate on the basis of the Fourteen Points, unless the
Allies were in a position to insist upon her accepting their
exegesis of the sacred text.[1]

A hasty process of interpretation at the hands of
Colonel House's Commission followed during the next
six weeks, under which the principles of the Fourteen
Points were brought into line with Wilson's subsequent
pronouncements and with the demands of the Allied
military chiefs for the rendering of Germany incapable of
renewing hostilities. Much of the original golden idealism
was winnowed from them, much was added which later
brought regret, and at the close there emerged a document
steeped in the spirit of Old Testament justice—an eye for
an eye and a tooth for a tooth.

On many issues the new principles were vague, and none
more so than in the case of Russia, the mystery of which
was still unravelled and unsolved ; but one point was clear
before the commentators : " In any case the treaties of
Brest-Litovsk and Bukarest must be cancelled as palpably
fraudulent. Provision must be made for the withdrawal of
all German troops in Russia and the Peace Conference will
have a clean slate on which to write a policy for all the
Russian peoples." [2]

Thus it came about that on the morning of November
8, Erzberger and his colleagues of the Armistice Commission sat in the railway coach of the Allied Commander-
in-Chief at Compiègne, gazing with saddened eyes at the
tanned impassive faces of Foch and Rosslyn Wemyss,
listening with sinking hearts to the cool voice of Weygand
reading the terms of surrender. Their senses were dulled
with disaster as humiliation was piled upon humiliation.
The quiet voice read on relentlessly : " . . . Annulment
of the treaties of Bucharest and Brest-Litovsk and of

[1] Lloyd George, vi. 256.   [2] *House Papers*, iv. 196.

supplementary treaties. . . . Restitution of the Russian and Rumanian gold removed by the Germans or handed over to them. This gold to be delivered in trust to the Allies until the signature of peace. . . ." [1]

In comparison with the mountain of their shame this was but a pebble, but it was the pebble of Brest-Litovsk upon which their feet had stumbled.

---

[1] Articles XV and XIX of the Armistice Agreement of November 11, 1918. Two days later the Treaty of Brest-Litovsk was formally denounced by the Soviets in a resolution of the Central Executive Committee, November 13, 1918. The treaty was formally annulled by the Treaty of Versailles (Article 116). See Appendices X, XI, and XII, pp. 447, 450, 451.

APPENDIX I

THE DECLARATION OF PEACE [1]
(NOVEMBER 8, 1917)

THE Workers' and Peasants' Government, created by the revolution of November 6-7, and drawing its strength from the Soviets of Workers', Soldiers', and Peasants' Deputies, proposes to all warring peoples and their governments to begin at once negotiations leading to a just and democratic peace.

A just and democratic peace for which the great majority of wearied, tormented, and war-exhausted toilers and labouring classes of all belligerent countries are thirsting, a peace which the Russian workers and peasants have so loudly and insistently demanded since the overthrow of the Tsar's monarchy, such a peace the Government considers to be an immediate peace without annexations (*i.e.* without the seizure of foreign territory and the forcible annexation of foreign nationalities) and without indemnities.

The Russian Government proposes to all warring peoples that this kind of peace be concluded at once ; it also expresses its readiness to take immediately, without the least delay, all decisive steps pending the final confirmation of all the terms of such a peace by the plenipotentiary assemblies of all countries and all nations.

By annexation or seizure of foreign territory the Government, in accordance with the legal concepts of democracy in general and of the working class in particular, understands any incorporation of a small and weak nationality by a large and powerful State without a clear, definite, and voluntary expression of agreement and desire by the weak nationality, regardless of the time when such forcible incorporation took place, regardless also of how developed or how backward is the nation forcibly attached or forcibly detained within the frontiers of the [larger] State, and finally, regardless whether or

[1] Reprinted from *The Bolshevik Revolution* by James Bunyan and H. H. Fisher, Stanford University Press, California, by special permission of the authors and publisher ; *Vtoroi Vzerossiiskii Siezd Sovetov R. i. S.D.* p. 59.

not this large nation is located in Europe or in distant lands beyond the seas.

If any nation whatsoever is detained by force within the boundaries of a certain State, and if [that nation], contrary to its expressed desire—whether such desire is made manifest in the press, national assemblies, party relations, or in protests and uprisings against national oppression—is not given the right to determine the form of its State life by free voting and completely free from the presence of the troops of the annexing or stronger State and without the least pressure, then the adjoining of that nation by the stronger State is annexation, *i.e.* seizure by force and violence.

The Government considers that to continue this war simply to decide how to divide the weak nationalities among the powerful and rich nations which had seized them would be the greatest crime against humanity, and it solemnly announces its readiness to sign at once the terms of peace which will end this war on the indicated conditions, equally just for all nationalities without exception.

At the same time the Government declares that it does not regard the conditions of peace mentioned above as an ultimatum ; that is, it is ready to consider any other conditions, insisting, however, that such be proposed by any of the belligerents as soon as possible, and that they be expressed in the clearest terms, without ambiguity or secrecy.

The Government abolishes secret diplomacy, expressing, for its part, the firm determination to carry on all negotiations absolutely openly and in view of all the people. It will proceed at once to publish all secret treaties ratified or concluded by the Government of landlords and capitalists from March to November 7, 1917. All the provisions of these secret treaties, in so far as they have for their object the securing of benefits and privileges to the Russian landlords and capitalists—which was true in a majority of cases—and retaining or increasing the annexation by the Great Russians, the Government declares absolutely and immediately annulled.

While addressing to the governments and peoples of all countries the proposal to begin at once open peace negotiations, the Government, for its part, expressed its readiness to carry on these negotiations by written communications, by telegraph, by parleys of the representatives of different countries, or at a conference of such representatives. To facilitate such negotiations the Government appoints its plenipotentiary representative to neutral countries.

The Government proposes to all governments and peoples of all belligerent countries to conclude an armistice at once ; at the same time it considers it desirable that this armistice should be concluded for a period of not less than three months—that is, a period during which it would be entirely possible to complete the negotiations for peace with the participation of representatives of all peoples and nationalities which were drawn into the war or forced to take part in it, as well as to call the plenipotentiary assemblies of peoples' representatives in every country for the final ratification of the peace terms.

In making these peace proposals to the government and peoples of all warring countries, the Provisional Government of Workers and Peasants of Russia appeals particularly to the class-conscious workers of the three most advanced nations of mankind, who are also the largest States participating in the present war—England, France, and Germany. The workers of these countries have rendered the greatest possible service to the cause of progress and Socialism by the great example of the Chartist movement in England, several revolutions of universal historic significance accomplished by the French proletariat, and, finally, the heroic struggle against the Law of Exceptions in Germany, a struggle which was prolonged, stubborn, and disciplined, which could be held up as an example for the workers of the whole world, and which aimed at the creation of proletarian mass organizations in Germany. All these examples of proletarian heroism and historic achievement serve us as a guaranty that the workers of these three countries will understand the tasks which lie before them by way of liberating humanity from the horrors of war and its consequences, and that by their resolute, unselfishly energetic efforts in various directions these workers will help us to bring to a successful end the cause of peace, and, together with this, the cause of the liberation of the toiling and exploited masses from all forms of slavery and all exploitation.

The Workers' and Peasants' Government created by the revolution of November 6-7, and drawing its strength from the Soviets of Workers', Soldiers', and Peasants' Deputies, must begin peace negotiations at once. Our appeal must be directed to the governments as well as to the peoples. We cannot ignore the governments, because this would delay the conclusion of peace, a thing which a people's government does not dare to do, but at the same time we have no right not to appeal to the peoples. Everywhere governments and peoples are at arm's length ; we must, therefore, help the peoples to take a hand in [settling] the question of peace and war. We shall of course stand by our programme of peace without annexations and without indemnities. We shall not relinquish [that programme], but we must deprive our enemies of the possibility of saying that their conditions are different and that they do not wish, therefore, to enter into negotiations with us. No, we must dislodge them from that advantageous position by not presenting them our conditions in the form of an ultimatum. For this reason we have included a statement to the effect that we are ready to consider any condition of peace ; in fact, every proposal. Consideration, of course, does not necessarily mean acceptance. We shall submit [the proposals] for consideration to the Constituent Assembly, which will then decide, officially, what can and what cannot be granted. We have to fight against the hypocrisy of the governments, which, while talking about peace and justice, actually carry on wars of conquest and plunder. Not one single government will tell you what it really means. But we are opposed to secret diplomacy and can afford to act openly before all people. We do not now close nor have we ever closed our eyes to the difficulties. Wars cannot be ended by a refusal [to fight] ; they cannot be ended by one side alone. We are proposing an armistice for three months—though we are not rejecting a shorter period—[in the hope] that this will give the suffering army at least a breathing-space and will make possible the calling of popular meetings in all civilized countries to discuss the conditions [of peace].

APPENDIX II

THE ARMISTICE AGREEMENT OF BREST-LITOVSK [1]
(December 15, 1917)

I

THE armistice begins on December 17, 1917, at noon (December 4, 1917, at fourteen o'clock, Russian time) and extends until January 14, 1918, noon (January 1, 1918, fourteen o'clock, Russian time). The contracting parties have the right on the twenty-first day of the armistice to give a seven-days' notice of termination ; such not being done, the armistice automatically remains in force until one of the contracting parties gives such seven-days' notice.

II

The armistice applies to all land and air fighting forces of the said Powers on the land front between the Black Sea and the Baltic Sea. In the Russo-Turkish theatres of war in Asia the armistice goes into effect at the same time.

The contracting parties obligate themselves, during the period of the armistice, neither to augment the number of detachments of troops stationed on the said fronts and on the islands of Moon Sound —this applies also to their organization and status—nor to attempt any regroupings in preparation for an offensive.

Further, the contracting parties obligate themselves not to undertake any transfers of troops until January 14, 1918 (January 1, 1918, Russian time), on the front between the Black Sea and the Baltic Sea, unless such transfers had already been begun at the moment of the signing of the armistice.

Finally, the contracting parties obligate themselves not to assemble any troops in the harbours of the Baltic Sea east of 15° longitude east of Greenwich and in the harbours of the Black Sea during the period of the armistice.

[1] *Texts of the Russian " Peace "* (U.S. Department of State, 1918), p. 1.

III

The advance entanglements of each party's position will be considered as demarcation lines on the European Front. These lines may be crossed only under the conditions noted in IV.

In places where entrenched positions do not exist, the demarcation lines for each side will be a straight line drawn through the most advanced occupied positions. The space between the two lines will be considered neutral ground. Likewise, navigable rivers separating the opposing positions will be neutral and closed to navigation, except in case of commercial shipping agreed upon. For sections in which the positions are widely separated it will devolve upon the Armistice Commission (VII) to determine and establish the lines of demarcation.

In the Russo-Turkish theatres of war in Asia, the lines of demarcation, as well as intercourse through them (IV), are to be determined by agreement of the divisional commanders of both sides.

IV

For the development and strengthening of the friendly relations between the peoples of the contracting parties, organized intercourse between the troops is permitted under the following conditions :

1. Intercourse is permitted *parliamentaires* and the members of the Armistice Commission (VII) and their representatives. All such must have passes signed by at least a corps commander or a corps committee.

2. In each section of a Russian division organized intercourse may take place at two or three places.

For this purpose, by agreement of the divisions opposed to each other, centres of intercourse are to be established in the neutral zone between the demarcation lines and are to be distinguished by white flags. Intercourse is permissible only by day from sunrise to sunset.

At the centres of intercourse not more than twenty-five unarmed persons belonging to either side may be present at any one time. The exchange of news and newspapers is allowed. Open letters may be passed for despatch. The sale and exchange of wares of everyday use is permitted at the centres of intercourse.

3. The interment of the dead in the neutral zone is permitted. The special details in each case are to be agreed upon by the divisional commanders on either side or their ranking officers.

4. The question of the return of dismissed soldiers of one country, whose domiciles be beyond the demarcation lines of the other country, can be decided only at the peace negotiations. This applies also to the members of Polish detachments.

5. All persons who—contrary to the agreements 1-4 preceding—cross the demarcation lines of the opposing party will be arrested and not released until the conclusion of peace or the denunciation of the armistice.

The contracting parties obligate themselves to bring to the notice of their troops by strict orders and detailed explanation the necessity for the observance of the conditions of intercourse and the consequences of infraction thereof.

V

With regard to naval warfare the following conditions are agreed upon :

1. The armistice extends to the whole of the Black Sea and to the Baltic Sea east of 15° longitude east of Greenwich, and to all the naval and air forces of the contracting parties within these regions.

Regarding the question of the armistice in the White Sea and in the Russian coastal waters of the northern Arctic Ocean, a special agreement will be entered into by the German and Russian Naval High Command after mutual consultation. Attacks of either party upon mercantile and war vessels in the above-named waters shall cease from now on as far as possible.

In this special agreement shall be included provisions to prevent, as far as possible, the naval forces of the contracting parties from engaging each other on other seas.

2. Attacks by sea and by air upon ports and coasts belonging to one of the contracting parties will be discontinued by both sides on all seas. Similarly, naval forces belonging to one party are forbidden to enter the harbours and approach the coasts occupied by the other party.

3. Flights over the ports and coasts of one of the contracting parties as well as over demarcation lines are forbidden upon all seas to the other party.

4. The demarcation lines run as follows :

    (a) In the Black Sea, from Olinka Lighthouse (St. George's mouth) to Cape Jeros (Trebizond) ;

(b) In the Baltic Sea, from Rogekuel on the West Coast to
Worms to Bogskaer to Svenska to Hoegarne.

The more detailed determination of the line between Worms and
Bogskaer is delegated to the Armistice Commission for the Baltic
Sea (VII, 1) subject to the stipulation that the Russian warships
are granted free passage to the Aaland Islands in all states of the
weather and ice conditions. The Russian naval forces may not pass
the demarcation lines to the south, the naval forces of the four
Allied Powers to the north.

The Russian Government guarantees that the naval forces of
the Entente which at the beginning of the armistice are situated,
or which later may arrive, north of the demarcation lines will conduct
themselves as provided for the Russian naval forces.

5. Commerce and commercial shipping in the sea regions indicated under paragraph 1 are unrestrained. The establishment of all
regulations for commerce as well as the publication of unrestricted
lanes for merchant vessels are delegated to the Armistice Commission
for the Black Sea and the Baltic Sea (VII, 1 and 7).

6. The contracting parties engage, during the duration of the
armistice on the Black Sea and the Baltic Sea, not to undertake
preparations for naval offensive warfare on the high seas.

VI

To prevent disturbances and misunderstandings on the front,
infantry firing-practice nearer than five kilometres, artillery firing-
practice nearer than fifteen kilometres, behind the fronts is prohibited.

Mine warfare on land is to cease completely.

Aerial fighting forces and captive balloons must be kept outside
an air zone of ten kilometres behind the respective demarcation lines.

Work upon positions behind the advanced wire entanglements
is permitted, but not such work as may serve as preparation for
attack.

VII

With inception of the armistice the following " Armistice Commissions " (composed of representatives of each nation fighting on
the section of the front in question) will assemble, before which all

military questions regarding the execution of the provisions of the armistice in the territories in question are to be laid :

1. Riga, for the Baltic Sea ;
2. Dvinsk, for the front from the Baltic Sea to the Disna ;
3. Brest-Litovsk, for the front from the Disna to the Pripet ;
4. Berditschew, for the front from the Pripet to the Dniester ;
5. Koloszvar, and
6. Focsani, for the front from the Dniester to the Black Sea, the boundaries between the two Commissions 5 and 6 to be fixed by mutual agreement ;
7. Odessa, for the Black Sea.

Direct and uncontrolled telegraph lines to the home countries of their members will be placed at the disposal of these Commissions. The lines will be constructed by the respective army commands in their respective countries, as far as midway between the demarcation lines. In the Russo-Turkish theatres of war in Asia similar Commissions will be established in accordance with agreements reached by the Commanders-in-Chief on both sides.

VIII

The treaty concerning cessation of hostilities of December 5 (November 22), 1917, and all agreements concluded up to this time on separate sectors of the front with regard to cessation of hostilities or an armistice, are rendered null and void by this Armistice Treaty.

IX

The contracting parties will enter into peace negotiations immediately after the signature of the present Armistice Treaty.

X

Upon the basis of the principle of the freedom, independence, and territorial inviolability of the neutral Persian State, the Turkish and the Russian Supreme Commands are prepared to withdraw their troops from Persia. They will immediately enter into communication with the Persian Government, in order to regulate the details of the evacuation and the other necessary measures for the guaranteeing of the above-mentioned principle.

XI

Each contracting party is to receive a copy of the agreement in the German and Russian languages, signed by representatives with plenipotentiary powers.

BREST-LITOVSK, the 15th day of December 1917.

(The 2nd day of December 1917, Russian style.)

[Signatures follow]

APPENDIX III

LENIN'S TWENTY-ONE THESES FOR PEACE [1]
(January 20, 1918)

1. THE condition of the Russian Revolution at the present moment is such that practically all the workers and a large majority of the peasants are on the side of the Soviet Government and the Social Revolution. In that respect the success of the Socialist Revolution in Russia seems assured.

2. At the same time the civil war which was caused by the furious resistance of the propertied classes, who realize full well that this is their last and final fight for private property in land and instruments of production, has not reached its highest point. In the end the Soviet Government will win the fight, but it will take much time and a good deal of energy, and a certain period of disorganization and chaos incidental to every war, and especially civil war, is inevitable before the bourgeoisie is finally crushed.

3. Furthermore, the resistance [of the bourgeoisie] in its less active and non-military forms such as sabotage, bribing tramps and other hirelings of the bourgeoisie to join the Socialist ranks with the purpose of undermining their cause, etc. etc., this resistance has proved to be so obstinate and capable of assuming such varying forms that it will take time, several months, perhaps, to put it down. Without a decisive victory over this passive and veiled resistance of the bourgeoisie and its adherents, the success of the Socialist Revolution is impossible.

4. Finally, the task of organizing Russia on a socialistic basis is so huge and difficult that its solution, owing to the abundance of the petit-bourgeois in the midst of the Socialist proletariat and on account of the low cultural level of the latter, will take a considerable time.

5. All these factors taken together show clearly that to make a

[1] Reprinted from *The Bolshevik Revolution* by James Bunyan and H. H. Fisher, Stanford University Press, California, by special permission of the authors and publisher ; *Pravda*, February 24, 1918.

success of Socialism in Russia a certain time, some months at least, is necessary during which the Socialist Government can have a free hand, first to overcome the bourgeoisie of its own country and then to lay the basis for extensive and deep-rooted organizational work.

6. The situation in which the Socialist Revolution in Russia finds itself is to be taken as the point of departure for every definition of the international task confronting the new Soviet Government, because the international situation as it stands during the fourth year of war precludes the possibility of predicting the time of the outbreak of revolutions and the overthrow of the imperialistic governments of Europe (including the German Government). That there will be a Socialist Revolution in Europe there is no doubt. All our hopes in the final triumph of Socialism are based on this certainty, which is in the nature of a scientific prediction. Our propaganda work in general and our fraternization in particular should be strengthened and developed [in order to help bring about the Socialist Revolution]. But it would be a mistake for the Socialist Government in Russia to formulate its policy on the supposition that within the next six months (or thereabouts) there will be a European, to be more specific, a German Socialist Revolution. It is impossible to make such predictions, and every attempt to do so is a blind gamble.

7. The Brest-Litovsk negotiations have made it clear by now (January 20, 1918) that the war party in Germany has the upper hand and has sent us what amounts to an ultimatum . . . either to continue the war or to accept a peace of annexation, that is to say, that we give up all the territory we have seized, while the Germans retain all that they have seized. In addition they impose on us an indemnity in the (concealed) form of paying for the support of the prisoners. This amounts to about three billion roubles and is to be paid over a period of several years.

8. The Russian Socialist Government is confronted with a question which requires an immediate solution, either to accept the annexation peace or to start at once a revolutionary war. No other solution is in fact possible. We cannot put off the decision ; we have already done everything possible and impossible to drag out the negotiations.

9. When we consider the arguments for an immediate revolutionary war we find first of all the argument that a separate peace now is virtually an understanding with German imperialists, an

imperialistic transaction, etc., and that, therefore, such a peace would signify a complete break with the fundamental principles of proletarian internationalism.

This reasoning is fallacious. Workmen who lose a strike and accept conditions not favourable to themselves but favourable for the capitalist do not thereby betray Socialism. They betray Socialism who bargain with the capitalists, accepting favours for part of the workmen in exchange [for conditions] that are favourable to the capitalists. Agreements of this kind are inacceptable.

He betrays Socialism who calls the war against German imperialism a defensive and righteous war and who, at the same time, accepts the help of Anglo-French imperialists and conceals from the people the secret agreements concluded with these imperialists. But he who hides nothing from the people, makes no secret agreements with imperialists, but agrees, because of temporary inability to go on with the war, to sign a peace treaty unfavourable to the weak nation and favourable to one group of imperialists, does not in any way betray Socialism.

10. Another argument for an immediate war is that by concluding peace we become agents of German imperialism because we free German troops on our front in addition to millions of prisoners, etc. This argument is equally fallacious. A revolutionary war at this time would place us in the position of agents of Anglo-French imperialism in so far as we should be aiding the cause of the latter. The English have offered our Supreme Command Krylenko one hundred roubles a month for every one of our soldiers if we continue to fight. Even if we do not accept a penny from them, we should still be helping them by detaining German troops. No matter which way we turn, we cannot wholly escape this or that imperialistic group. That is impossible without the complete destruction of world imperialism. The only true inference to be drawn from this is that from the time a Socialist government is established in any one country, questions must be determined not with reference to preferability of any one imperialistic group but solely from the point of view of what is best for the development and the consolidation of the Socialist Revolution which has already begun. In other words, our tactics must be based not on the consideration of whether it is more expedient to help one or the other of the imperialist groups, but solely on the question of safeguarding the Socialist Revolution in one country until the others are ready to join.

11. It is said that the German Social Democrats who are opposed to the war have become " defeatists " and beg us not to give in to German imperialism. [To this our reply is that] we accepted " defeatism " only with reference to our own imperialistic bourgeoisie, but we always opposed a victory over the imperialism of other countries if that victory had to be obtained through a union, real or formal, with a " friendly " imperialistic Power. The argument is thus a repetition of the preceding one. If the German Left-Wing Socialists should make us a proposal to delay a separate peace for a definite period and guarantee to us that during that time Germany would have a revolution, then we should have a different situation. But they have no such proposition to make. On the contrary, they say this : " Resist as long as you can and then decide in accordance with the best interests of the Russian Socialist Revolution, because at present it is impossible to say anything positive about the German revolution ".

12. It is said that in our party declaration we " promised " that we should wage a revolutionary war and that the conclusion of a separate peace is therefore a failure to keep our word. This is not true. We talked of the necessity for a Socialist government during the period of imperialism " to prepare to wage " a revolutionary war. We advocated this in opposition to the theory of abstract pacifism, against the theory which absolutely rejects the " defence of the fatherland ", and, finally, against the selfish instincts of certain groups of soldiers, but we never assumed the obligation to wage a revolutionary war regardless of whether time and conditions were favourable for such a war.

We should by all means prepare now for a revolutionary war. We live up to our promises now as we have in the past, whenever it is possible to carry them out immediately. We have abrogated the secret treaties, we have offered all nations a just peace, and we have prolonged in various ways the peace negotiations so as to give other nations a chance to join.

The question whether it is possible to undertake at once a revolutionary war must be answered solely from the point of view of actual conditions and the interest of the Socialist Revolution which has already begun.

13. If we summarize the arguments for an immediate revolutionary war, we shall find that the policy advocated in them is capable of giving satisfaction to those who crave the romantic and

the beautiful but who fail completely to take into consideration the objective correlation of class forces, and the real conditions within which the Socialist Revolution is developing.

14. There is no doubt that at the present time (and probably during the next few weeks and months) our army is in no condition to stop a German offensive. In the first place, it is very tired and very hungry, owing to the unprecedented disruption of the army supplies, etc. ; secondly, on account of the shortage of horses our artillery is absolutely doomed ; thirdly, in view of the impossibility of protecting the coast from Reval to Riga, which gives the enemy a good chance to get possession of what remains of Livonia, then Estonia, to attack our troops in the rear, and to occupy Petrograd.

15. There is no doubt whatsoever that, were the question put to a vote, peasants, who constitute the majority in the army, would come out for a peace of annexation rather than for an immediate revolutionary war. The formation of a Socialist army, with the Red Guard as its nucleus, has only just begun. To attempt now, with the present democratization of the army, to force a war against the wishes of a majority of the soldiers would be hazardous. It will take months and months to create an army imbued with Socialist principles.

16. The poorest peasantry in Russia would support a Socialist Revolution led by the working class, but it is not in a position now to wage a revolutionary war. It would be a fatal blunder to overlook the actual strength of the different classes.

17. The question of revolutionary war, therefore, stands as follows : If a revolution should break out in Germany during the next three or four months, then perhaps the tactics of an immediate revolutionary war would not ruin our Socialist Revolution. If [on the other hand] the German revolution does not take place and we go on with the war, Russia would be so badly defeated that she would be forced to sign an even worse separate peace ; such a peace would be signed not by a Socialist government but by some other, by some kind of coalition between the bourgeois *Rada* and the followers of Chernov or some similar government, for after the first shock of defeat the peasant army, which is so badly worn out by the war, would overthrow the Workers' Socialist Government in a few weeks.

18. Under the circumstances it would be very bad policy to risk the fate of the Socialist Revolution on the chance that a revolution

might break out in Germany by a certain date. Such a policy would be adventurous. We have no right to take such chances

19. The German revolution will in no way suffer objectively if we conclude a separate peace. It is probable that the triumph of chauvinism will weaken it [the revolution] for a time, but the position of Germany will remain very critical. The war with England and America will go on for a long time ; the aggressive imperialism of both groups has unmasked itself finally and completely. Under such conditions a Socialist Soviet Republic in Russia will be a model for all other peoples and excellent material for propaganda purposes. On the one side there will be the bourgeois system engaged in a strife between two coalitions of confessed plunderers, and on the other side a Socialist Soviet Republic living in peace.

20. In concluding a separate peace now we rid ourselves, as far as present circumstances permit, of both imperialistic groups fighting each other. We can take advantage of their strife, which makes it difficult for them to reach an agreement at our expense, and use that period when our hands are free to develop and strengthen the Socialist Revolution. We can reorganize Russia on the basis of the dictatorship of the proletariat, nationalize the banks and large industries, bring about a moneyless exchange of products between the city and the small peasant co-operatives in the village. All these are economically feasible provided we have a few months' peace to work out these projects. Such a reorganization would make Socialism unconquerable in Russia and in the whole world, and would at the same time lay the basis for the formation of a powerful workers' and peasants' Red army.

21. A truly revolutionary war at this moment would be a war between a Socialist Republic and the bourgeois countries. Such a war would have to be fully approved by the Socialist army and have as its object the overthrow of the bourgeoisie in other countries. For the time being, however, we cannot make this our object. In reality we should be fighting now for the liberation of Poland, Lithuania, and Courland. There is not a single Marxist who, while adhering to the foundations of Marxism and Socialism, would not say that the interests of Socialism are above the right of nations to self-deter-mination. Our Socialist Republic has done and is doing everything possible to give real self-determination to Finland, the Ukraine, etc. But if the concreté circumstances are such that the safety of the Socialist Republic is being endangered in order to [prevent] the

violation of the right of self-determination of a few nations (Poland, Lithuania, and Courland), there is no question but that the interests of the Socialist Republic must predominate. If that is true, then he who says " we cannot sign a shameful and humiliating peace ; we cannot hand over Poland, etc.", fails to perceive that if we make peace on condition of the liberation of Poland we are only strengthening German imperialism against England, Belgium, Serbia, and the other countries. Peace on condition of the liberation of Poland, Lithuania, and Courland would be a " patriotic " peace from the Russian point of view, but it would be none the less a peace with annexationists and with the German imperialists.

APPENDIX IV

THE TREATY OF PEACE BETWEEN UKRAINE AND THE CENTRAL POWERS [1]

(Signed at Brest-Litovsk, February 9, 1918 [2])

Whereas the Ukrainian People has, in the course of the present world war, declared its independence, and has expressed the desire to establish a state of peace between the Ukrainian People's Republic and the Powers at present at war with Russia, the Governments of Germany, Austria-Hungary, Bulgaria, and Turkey have resolved to conclude a Treaty of Peace with the Government of the Ukrainian People's Republic ; they wish in this way to take the first step towards a lasting world peace, honourable for all parties, which shall not only put an end to the horrors of the war but shall also conduce to the restoration of friendly relations between the peoples in the political, legal, economic, and intellectual spheres.

To this end the plenipotentiaries of the above-mentioned Governments, viz.

For the Imperial German Government : Imperial Actual Privy Councillor Richard von Kühlmann, Secretary of State for Foreign Affairs ;

For the Imperial and Royal Joint Austro-Hungarian Government : His Imperial and Royal Apostolic Majesty's Privy Councillor Ottokar Count Czernin von und zu Chudenitz, Minister of the Imperial and Royal House and Minister for Foreign Affairs ;

For the Royal Bulgarian Government : Dr. Vassil Radoslavoff, President of the Council of Ministers ; the Envoy M. Andrea Tosheff ;

[1] *Texts of the Ukrainian " Peace "* (U.S. Department of State, 1918), p. 9.

[2] Ratifications exchanged between Bulgaria and the Ukraine, July 15, 1918, at Vienna (*Deutscher Reichsanzeiger*, July 17, 1918) ; between Germany and the Ukraine, July 24, 1918, at Vienna (*Neue Freie Presse*, July 25, 1918, morning edition) ; between Turkey and the Ukraine, August 23, 1918 (*Daily Review of the Foreign Press*, August 27, 1918, p. 192).

the Envoy M. Ivan Stoyanovich ; the Military Plenipotentiary Colonel Peter Gantcheff ; and Dr. Theodor Anastassoff ;

For the Imperial Ottoman Government : His Highness the Grand Vizier Talaat Pasha ; Ahmet Nessimi Bey, Minister for Foreign Affairs ; His Highness Ibrahim Hakki Pasha ; and General of Cavalry Ahmet Izzet Pasha ;

For the Government of the Ukrainian People's Republic : M. Alexander Sevruk, M. Mykola Liubinsky, and M. Mykola Levitsky, members of the Ukrainian Central Rada ;—have met at Brest-Litovsk, and having presented their full powers, which were found to be in due and proper form, have agreed upon the following points :

Article I

Germany, Austria-Hungary, Bulgaria, and Turkey on the one hand, and the Ukrainian People's Republic on the other hand, declare that the state of war between them is at an end. The contracting parties are resolved henceforth to live in peace and amity with one another.

Article II

1. As between Austria-Hungary on the one hand, and the Ukrainian People's Republic on the other hand, in so far as these two Powers border upon one another, the frontiers which existed between the Austro-Hungarian Monarchy and Russia, prior to the outbreak of the present war, will be preserved.

2. Further north, the frontier of the Ukrainian People's Republic, starting at Tarnograd, will in general follow the line Bilgoray, Szozebrzeszyn, Krasnostav, Pugashov, Radzin, Miedzyzheche, Sarnaki, Melnik, Vysokie-Litovsk, Kameniec-Litovsk, Prujany, and Vydonovsk Lake. This frontier will be delimited in detail by a mixed commission, according to the ethnographical conditions and after taking the wishes of the inhabitants into consideration.

3. In the event of the Ukrainian People's Republic having boundaries coterminous with those of another of the Powers of the Quadruple Alliance, special agreements are reserved in respect thereto.

Article III

The evacuation of the occupied territories shall begin immediately after the ratification of the present Treaty of Peace.

The manner of carrying out the evacuation and the transfer of the evacuated territories shall be determined by the Plenipotentiaries of the interested parties.

Article IV

Diplomatic and consular relations between the contracting parties shall commence immediately after the ratification of the Treaty of Peace.

In respect to the admission of consuls on the widest scale possible on both sides, special agreements are reserved.

Article V

The contracting parties mutually renounce repayment of their war costs, that is to say, their State expenditure for the prosecution of the war, as well as payment for war damages, that is to say, damages sustained by them and their nationals in the war areas through military measures, including all requisitions made in enemy territory.

Article VI

Prisoners of war of both parties shall be released to their homeland in so far as they do not desire, with the approval of the State in whose territory they shall be, to remain within its territories or to proceed to another country. Questions connected with this will be dealt with in the separate treaties provided for in Article VIII.

Article VII

It has been agreed as follows with regard to economic relations between the contracting parties :

I

The contracting parties mutually undertake to enter into economic relations without delay and to organize the exchange of goods on the basis of the following stipulations :

Until July 31 of the current year a reciprocal exchange of the surplus of their more important agricultural and industrial products, for the purpose of meeting current requirements, is to be effected according to the following provisions :

(a) The quantities and classes of products to be exchanged in accordance with the preceding paragraph shall be settled on both sides by a commission composed of an equal number of representatives of both parties, which shall sit immediately after the Treaty of Peace has been signed.

(b) The prices of products to be exchanged as specified above shall be regulated on the basis of mutual agreement by a commission composed of an equal number of representatives of both parties.

(c) Calculations should be made in gold on the following basis : 1000 German imperial gold marks shall be equivalent to 462 gold roubles of the former Russian Empire (1 rouble $= \frac{1}{15}$ imperial), or 1000 Austrian and Hungarian gold kronen shall be equivalent to 393 karbovantsi 76 grosh gold of the Ukrainian People's Republic, or to 393 roubles 78 copecks in gold of the former Russian Empire (1 rouble $= \frac{1}{15}$ imperial).

(d) The exchange of goods to be determined by the commission mentioned under (a) shall take place through the existing Government central offices or through central offices controlled by the Government.

The exchange of such products as are not determined by the above-mentioned commissions shall be effected on a basis of free trading, arranged for in accordance with the conditions of the provisional commercial treaty, which is provided for in the following Section II.

II

In so far as it is not otherwise provided for under Section I hereof, economic relations between the contracting parties shall be carried on provisionally in accordance with the stipulations specified below until the conclusion of the final Commercial Treaty, but in any event until a period of at least six months shall have elapsed after the conclusion of peace between Germany, Austria-Hungary, Bulgaria, and Turkey on the one hand, and the European States at present at war with them, the United States of America and Japan on the other hand :

A

For economic relations between the German Empire and the Ukrainian People's Republic, the conditions laid down in the following provisions of the Germano-Russian Commercial and Maritime Treaty of 1894–1904,[1] that is to say :

Articles 1-6 and 7 (including Tariffs " a " and " b "), 8-10, 12, 13-19 ; further, among the stipulations of the final Protocol (Part I), paragraphs 1 and 3 of addendum to Article 1 ; paragraphs 1, 2, 4, 5, 6, 8, 9 of addenda to Articles 1 and 12 addendum to Article 3 ; paragraphs 1 and 2 of addendum to Article 5 ; addenda to Articles 5, 6, 7, 9, and 10 ; addenda to Articles 6, 7, and 11 ; to Articles 6-9 ; to Articles 6 and 7 paragraphs 1, 2, 3, 5, of addendum to Article 12 ; further in the final Protocol (Part IV), §§ 3, 6, 7, 12, 12b, 13, 14, 15, 16, 17, 18 (with the reservations required by the corresponding alterations in official organizations), 19, 20, 21, and 23.

An agreement has been arrived at upon the following points :

1. The General Russian Customs Tariff of January 13-26, 1903,[2] shall continue in force.

2. Article 5 shall read as follows :

" The contracting parties bind themselves not to hinder reciprocal trade by any kind of import, export, or transit prohibitions, and to allow free transit.

" Exceptions may only be made in the case of products which are actually, or which may become, a State monopoly in the territory of one of the contracting parties ; as well as in the case of certain products for which exceptional prohibitory measures might be issued, in view of health conditions, veterinary police, and public safety, or on other important political and economic grounds, especially in connection with the transition period following the war."

3. Neither party shall lay claim to the preferential treatment which the other party has granted, or shall grant to any other State, arising out of a present or future Customs Union (as, for instance, the one in force between the German Empire and the Grand Duchy of Luxembourg), or arising in connection with petty frontier inter-course extending to a boundary zone not exceeding 15 kilometres in width.

4. Article 10 shall read as follows :

[1] 86 British and Foreign State Papers, pp. 442, 449, 482 ; 97 British and Foreign State Papers, p. 1040.

[2] New General Customs Tariffs for the European Frontiers of Russia, British Parliamentary Papers (1903), Cd. 1525.

" There shall be reciprocal freedom from all transit dues for goods of all kinds conveyed through the territory of either of the parties, whether conveyed direct or unloaded, stored and re-loaded during transit."

5. Article 12 (a) shall be revised as follows :

" (a) With regard to the reciprocal protection of copyright in works of literature, art, and photography, the provisions of the Treaty concluded between the German Empire and Russia on February 28, 1913,[1] shall prevail in the relations between Germany and the Ukrainian People's Republic.

" (b) With regard to the reciprocal protection of trade-marks, the provisions of the Declaration of July 11-23, 1873,[2] shall be authoritative in the future."

6. The provision of the final Protocol to Article 19 shall read as follows :

" The contracting parties shall grant each other the greatest possible support in the matter of railway tariffs, more especially by the establishment of through rates. To this end both con-tracting parties are ready to enter into negotiations with one another at the earliest possible moment."

7. § 5 of Part IV of the final Protocol shall read as follows :

" It has been mutually agreed that the customs houses of both countries shall remain open on every day throughout the year, with the exception of Sundays and legal holidays."

B

For economic relations between Austria-Hungary and the Ukrainian People's Republic, the agreements shall be valid which are set forth in the following provisions of the Austro-Hungarian–Russian Commercial and Maritime Treaty of the 15 February, 1906,[3] being Articles 1, 2, and 5 (including Tariffs " a " and " b ") ; Articles 6, 7, 9-13 ; Article 14, paragraphs 2 and 3 ; Articles 15-24 further, in the provisions of the final Protocol, paragraphs 1, 2, 4, 5, and 6 of addenda to Articles 1 and 12 ; addenda to Article 2 ; to Articles 2,

[1] 107 British and Foreign State Papers, p. 871.

[2] 63 British and Foreign State Papers, p. 58.

[3] 99 British and Foreign State Papers, p. 599.

3, and 5 ; to Articles 2 and 5 ; to Articles 2, 4, 5, 7, and 8 ; to Articles 2, 5, 6, and 7 ; to Article 17, and likewise to paragraphs 1 and 3, Article 22.

An agreement has been arrived at upon the following points :

1. The General Russian Customs Tariff of January 13-26, 1903,[1] shall remain in force.

2. Article 4 shall read as follows :

" The contracting parties bind themselves not to hinder reciprocal trade between their territories by any kind of import, export, or transit prohibition. The only permissible exceptions shall be :

" (a) In the case of tobacco, salt, gunpowder, or any other kind of explosives, and likewise in the case of other articles which may at any time constitute a State monopoly in the territories of either of the contracting parties ;

" (b) With respect to war supplies in exceptional circumstances ;

" (c) For reasons of public safety, public health, and veterinary police ;

" (d) In the case of certain products for which, on other important political and economic grounds, exceptional prohibitory measures might be issued, especially in connection with the transition period following the war."

3. Neither party shall lay claim to the preferential treatment which the other party has granted or shall grant to any other State arising out of a present or future Customs Union (as, for instance, the one in force between Austria-Hungary and the Principality of Liechtenstein), or arising in connection with petty frontier intercourse, extending to a boundary zone not exceeding 15 kilometres in width.

4. Article 8 shall read as follows :

" There shall be reciprocal freedom for all transit dues for goods of all kinds conveyed through the territory of either of the contracting parties, whether conveyed direct or unloaded, stored and re-loaded during transit."

---

[1] New General Customs Tariffs for the European Frontiers of Russia, British Parliamentary Papers (1903), Cd. 1525.

5. The provision of the final Protocol to Article 21 shall read as follows :

" The contracting parties shall grant each other the greatest possible support in the matter of railway tariffs, and more especially by the establishment of through rates. To this end both contracting parties are ready to enter into negotiations with one another at the earliest possible moment."

C

In regard to the economic relations between Bulgaria and the Ukrainian People's Republic, these shall, until such time as a definitive Commercial Treaty shall have been concluded, be regulated on the basis of most-favoured-nation treatment. Neither party shall lay claim to the preferential treatment which the other party has granted or shall grant to any other State arising out of a present or future Customs Union, or arising in connection with petty frontier intercourse, extending to a boundary zone not exceeding 15 kilometres in width.

D

In regard to the economic relations between the Ottoman Empire and the Ukrainian People's Republic, these shall, until such time as a definitive Commercial Treaty shall have been concluded, be regulated on the basis of most-favoured-nation treatment. Neither party shall lay claim to the preferential treatment which the other party has granted or shall grant to any other State arising out of a present or future Customs Union, or arising in connection with petty frontier intercourse.

III

The period of validity of the provisional stipulations (set forth under Section II hereof) for economic relations between Germany, Austria-Hungary, Bulgaria, and the Ottoman Empire on the one hand, and the Ukrainian People's Republic on the other hand, may be prolonged by mutual agreement.

In the event of the periods specified in the first paragraph of Section II not occurring before June 30, 1919, each of the two contracting parties shall be entitled as from June 30, 1919, to denounce within six months the provisions contained in the above-mentioned section.

IV

(a) The Ukrainian People's Republic shall make no claim to the preferential treatment which Germany grants to Austria-Hungary or to any other country bound to her by a Customs Union and directly bordering on Germany, or bordering indirectly thereon through another country bound to her or to Austria-Hungary by a Customs Union, or to the preferential treatment which Germany grants to her own colonies, foreign possessions, and protectorates, or to countries bound to her by a Customs Union.

Germany shall make no claim to the preferential treatment which the Ukrainian People's Republic grants to any other country bound to her by a Customs Union and bordering directly on the Ukraine, or bordering indirectly thereon through any other country bound to her by a Customs Union, or to colonies, foreign possessions, and protectorates of one of the countries bound to her by a Customs Union.

(b) In economic intercourse between territory covered by the Customs Convention of both States of the Austro-Hungarian Monarchy on the one hand, and the Ukrainian People's Republic on the other hand, the Ukrainian People's Republic shall make no claim to the preferential treatment which Austria-Hungary grants to Germany or to any other country bound to her by a Customs Union and directly bordering on Austria-Hungary, or bordering indirectly thereon through another country which is bound to her or to Germany by a Customs Union. Colonies, foreign possessions, and protectorates shall in this respect be placed on the same footing as the mother country. Austria-Hungary shall make no claim to the preferential treatment which the Ukrainian People's Republic grants to any other country bound to her by a Customs Union and directly bordering on the Ukraine, or bordering indirectly thereon through another country bound to her by a Customs Union, or to colonies, foreign possessions, and protectorates of one of the countries bound to her by a Customs Union.

V

(a) In so far as goods originating in Germany or the Ukraine are stored in neutral States, with the proviso that they shall not be exported, either directly or indirectly, to the territories of the other contracting party, such restrictions regarding their disposal shall be abolished so far as the contracting parties are concerned. The two contracting parties therefore undertake immediately to notify the Governments of the neutral States of the above-mentioned abolition of this restriction.

(b) In so far as goods originating in Austria-Hungary or the Ukraine are stored in neutral States, with the proviso that they shall not be exported, either directly or indirectly, to the territories of the other contracting party, such restrictions regarding their disposal shall be abolished so far as the contracting parties are concerned. The two contracting parties therefore undertake immediately to notify the Governments of the neutral States of the above-mentioned abolition of this restriction.

Article VIII

The establishing of public and private legal relations, and the exchange of prisoners of war and interned civilians, the amnesty question, as well as the question of the treatment of merchant shipping in the enemy's hands, shall be settled by means of separate Treaties with the Ukrainian People's Republic, which shall form an essential part of the present Treaty of Peace, and, as far as practicable, come into force simultaneously therewith.

Article IX

The agreements come to in this Treaty of Peace shall form an indivisible whole.

Article X

For the interpretation of this Treaty, the German and Ukrainian text shall be authoritative for relations between Germany and the Ukraine ; the German, Hungarian, and Ukrainian text for relations between Austria-Hungary and the Ukraine ; the Bulgarian and Ukrainian text for relations between Bulgaria and the Ukraine ; and the Turkish and Ukrainian text for relations between Turkey and the Ukraine.

Final Provision

The present Treaty of Peace shall be ratified. The retifications shall be exchanged in Vienna at the earliest possible moment.

The Treaty of Peace shall come into force on its ratification, in so far as no stipulation to the contrary is contained therein.

In witness whereof the plenipotentiaries have signed the present Treaty and have affixed their seals to it.

Executed in quintuplicate at Brest-Litovsk this 9th day of February 1918.

[Signatures follow]

APPENDIX V

THE PEACE OF BREST-LITOVSK—THE TREATY OF PEACE BETWEEN RUSSIA AND GERMANY, AUSTRIA-HUNGARY, BULGARIA, AND TURKEY [1]

(SIGNED AT BREST-LITOVSK, MARCH 3, 1918 [2])

GERMANY, Austria-Hungary, Bulgaria, and Turkey for the one part, and Russia for the other part, being in accord to terminate the state of war, and to enter into peace negotiations as speedily as possible, have appointed as plenipotentiaries :

On the part of the Imperial German Government :

The Secretary of State for Foreign Affairs, the Actual Imperial Privy Councillor, Herr Richard von Kühlmann ;

The Imperial Envoy and Minister Plenipotentiary, Dr. von Rosenberg ;

Royal Prussian Major-General Hoffmann, Chief of the General Staff of the Commander-in-Chief of the East ;

Naval Captain Horn.

On the part of the Imperial and Royal Joint Austro-Hungarian Government :

The Minister of the Imperial and Royal House and for Foreign Affairs, the Privy Councillor of His Imperial and Royal Apostolic Majesty, Ottokar Count Czernin von und zu Chudenitz ;

The Envoy Extraordinary and Plenipotentiary of His Imperial

---

[1] *Texts of the Russian " Peace "* (U.S. Department of State, 1918), p. 13.

[2] Ratifications exchanged between Russia and Germany, March 29, at Berlin (*Neue Freie Presse*, July 6, morning edition) ; between Austria-Hungary and Russia, July 4, at Berlin (*Neue Freie Presse*, July 6, morning edition) ; between Turkey and Russia, July 12, at Berlin (*Neue Freie Presse*, July 13, evening edition) ; between Bulgaria and Russia, July 9, at Berlin (*Daily Review of the Foreign Press* (British), July 13, 1918. p. 602).

and Royal Apostolic Majesty, the Privy Councillor, Kajetan [*sic*] Merey von Kapos-Mere ;

General of Infantry, His Imperial and Royal Apostolic Majesty's Privy Councillor, Maximilian Csiscerics von Bacsany.

On the part of the Royal Bulgarian Government :

The Royal Envoy Extraordinary and Minister Plenipotentiary in Vienna, Andrea Tosheff ;

Colonel Peter Gantcheff of the General Staff, Royal Bulgarian Military Envoy Plenipotentiary to His Majesty the German Emperor and Aide-de-Camp of His Majesty the King of the Bulgarians ;

The Royal Bulgarian First Legation Secretary, Dr. Theodor Anastassoff.

On the part of the Imperial Ottoman Government :

His Highness Ibrahim Hakki Pasha, former Grand-Vizier, Member of the Ottoman Senate, Envoy Plenipotentiary of His Majesty the Sultan to Berlin ;

His Excellency, Zekki Pasha, General of Cavalry, Adjutant general of His Majesty the Sultan, and Military Envoy Plenipotentiary to His Majesty the German Emperor.

On the part of the Russian Federal Soviet Republic :

Grigory Iakovlevitch Sokolnikov, Member of the Central Executive Committee of Councillors to the Deputies of the Workingmen, Soldiers, and Peasants ;

Lew Mikhailovitch Karakhan, Member of the Central Executive Committee of Councillors to the Deputies of the Workingmen, Soldiers, and Peasants ;

Georgy Vassilievitch Chicherin, Assistant to the People's Commissioner for Foreign Affairs ;

Grigory Ivanovitch Petrovsky, People's Commissioner for Internal Affairs.

The plenipotentiaries met in Brest-Litovsk to enter into peace negotiations, and after presentation of their credentials, and finding them in good and proper form, have agreed upon the following stipulations :

Article I

Germany, Austria-Hungary, Bulgaria, and Turkey, for the one part, and Russia for the other part, declare that the state of war between them has ceased. They are resolved to live henceforth in peace and amity with one another.

Article II

The contracting parties will refrain from any agitation or propaganda against the Government or the public and military institutions of the other party. In so far as this obligation devolves upon Russia, it holds good also for the territories occupied by the Powers of the Quadruple Alliance.

Article III

The territories lying to the west of the line agreed upon by the contracting parties which formerly belonged to Russia, will no longer be subject to Russian sovereignty ; the line agreed upon is traced on the map submitted as an essential part of this treaty of peace (Annex I). The exact fixation of the line will be established by a Russo-German Commission.

No obligations whatever toward Russia shall devolve upon the territories referred to, arising from the fact that they formerly belonged to Russia.

Russia refrains from all interference in the internal relations of these territories. Germany and Austria-Hungary purpose to determine the future status of these territories in agreement with their population.

Article IV

As soon as a general peace is concluded and Russian demobilization is carried out completely, Germany will evacuate the territory lying to the east of the line designated in paragraph 1 of Article III, in so far as Article VI does not determine otherwise.

Russia will do all within her power to ensure the immediate evacuation of the provinces of Eastern Anatolia and their lawful return to Turkey.

The districts of Ardahan, Kars, and Batum will likewise and without delay be cleared of Russian troops. Russia will not interfere in the reorganization of the national and international relations

of these districts, but leave it to the population of these districts
to carry out this reorganization in agreement with the neighbouring States, especially with Turkey.

Article V

Russia will, without delay, carry out the full demobilization of
her army inclusive of those units recently organized by the present
Government.

Furthermore, Russia will either bring her warships into Russian
ports and there detain them until the day of the conclusion of a
general peace, or disarm them forthwith. Warships of the States
which continue in a state of war with the Powers of the Quadruple
Alliance, in so far as they are within Russian sovereignty, will be
treated as Russian warships.

The barred zone in the Arctic Ocean continues as such until the
conclusion of a general peace. In the Baltic sea, as far as Russian
power extends within the Black Sea, removal of the mines will be
proceeded with at once. Merchant navigation within these maritime
regions is free and will be resumed at once. Mixed commissions will
be organized to formulate the more detailed regulations, especially
to inform merchant ships with regard to restricted lanes. The navigation lanes are always to be kept free from floating mines.

Article VI

Russia obligates herself to conclude peace at once with the
Ukrainian People's Republic and to recognize the treaty of peace
between that State and the Powers of the Quadruple Alliance. The
Ukrainian territory will, without delay, be cleared of Russian troops
and the Russian Red Guard. Russia is to put an end to all agitation
or propaganda against the Government or the public institutions of
the Ukrainian People's Republic.

Estonia and Livonia will likewise, without delay, be cleared of
Russian troops and the Russian Red Guard. The eastern boundary
of Estonia runs, in general, along the river Narva. The eastern
boundary of Livonia crosses, in general, lakes Peipus and Pskov,
to the south-western corner of the latter, then across Lake Luban
in the direction of Livenhof on the Dvina. Estonia and Livonia will
be occupied by a German police force until security is ensured by
proper national institutions and until public order has been established. Russia will liberate at once all arrested or deported inhabi-

tants of Estonia and Livonia, and ensures the safe return of all
deported Estonians and Livonians.

Finland and the Aaland Islands will immediately be cleared of
Russian troops and the Russian Red Guard, and the Finnish ports
of the Russian fleet and of the Russian naval forces. So long as the
ice prevents the transfer of warships into Russian ports, only limited
forces will remain on board the warships. Russia is to put an end to
all agitation or propaganda against the Government or the public
institutions of Finland.

The fortresses built on the Aaland Islands are to be removed as
soon as possible. As regards the permanent non-fortification of these
islands as well as their further treatment in respect to military and
technical navigation matters, a special agreement is to be concluded
between Germany, Finland, Russia, and Sweden ; there exists an
understanding to the effect that, upon Germany's desire, still other
countries bordering upon the Baltic Sea would be consulted in
this matter.

Article VII

In view of the fact that Persia and Afghanistan are free and
independent States, the contracting parties obligate themselves to
respect the political and economic independence and the territorial
integrity of these States.

Article VIII

The prisoners of war of both parties will be released to return
to their homeland. The settlement of the questions connected therewith will be effected through the special treaties provided for in
Article XII.

Article IX

The contracting parties mutually renounce compensation for their
war expenses, i.e. of the public expenditures for the conduct of the
war, as well as compensation for war losses, i.e. such losses as were
caused them and their nationals within the war zones by military
measures, inclusive of all requisitions effected in enemy country.

Article X

Diplomatic and consular relations between the contracting
parties will be resumed immediately upon the ratification of the

treaty of peace. As regards the reciprocal admission of consuls, separate agreements are reserved.

Article XI

As regards the economic relations between the Powers of the Quadruple Alliance and Russia the regulations contained in Appendices II-V are determinative, namely Appendix II for the Russo-German, Appendix III for the Russo-Austro-Hungarian, Appendix IV for the Russo-Bulgarian, and Appendix V for the Russo-Turkish relations.

Article XII

The re-establishment of public and private legal relations, the exchange of war prisoners and interned civilians, the question of amnesty as well as the question anent the treatment of merchant ships which have come into the power of the opponent, will be regulated in separate treaties with Russia which form an essential part of the general treaty of peace, and, as far as possible, go into force simultaneously with the latter.

Article XIII

In the interpretation of this treaty, the German and Russian texts are authoritative for the relations between Germany and Russia ; the German, the Hungarian, and Russian texts for the relations between Austria-Hungary and Russia ; the Bulgarian and Russian texts for the relations between Bulgaria and Russia ; and the Turkish and Russian texts for the relations between Turkey and Russia.

Article XIV

The present treaty of peace will be ratified. The documents of ratification shall, as soon as possible, be exchanged in Berlin. The Russian Government obligates itself, upon the desire of one of the Powers of the Quadruple Alliance, to execute the exchange of the documents of ratification within a period of two weeks. Unless otherwise provided for in its articles, in its annexes, or in the additional treaties, the treaty of peace enters into force at the moment of its ratification.

In testimony whereof the plenipotentiaries have signed this treaty with their own hand.

Executed in quintuplicate at Brest-Litovsk, March 3, 1918.

APPENDIX VI

SPEECH BY LENIN ON THE RATIFICATION OF THE PEACE TREATY, MARCH 14, 1918 [1]

COMRADES, to-day we have to decide a question which signifies a turning-point in the development of the Russian, and indeed not alone of the Russian, but of the international Revolution; in order to find the correct solution of the question regarding the terribly onerous peace concluded by the representatives of the Soviet Government at Brest-Litovsk and which the Soviet Government proposes to confirm or ratify, it is above all essential for us to comprehend the historical meaning of the turning-point at which we now stand, to understand what has been the main characteristic of the development of the Revolution so far, and what is the fundamental cause of the heavy defeat and of that period of bitter trials through which we are now passing.

It seems to me that the chief source of the disagreements on this question within the Soviet parties is the fact that some are giving way too much to the feeling of legitimate and just indignation at the defeat of the Soviet Republic by imperialism. They are sometimes too prone to give way to despair, and, instead of taking into account the historical conditions for the development of the Revolution as they emerged before the conclusion of the peace and as they appear after the peace—instead of doing this they try to formulate the tactics of the Revolution relying on their own immediate emotions. But the experience of all the histories of revolutions teaches us that when we have to deal with any mass movement or class struggle, particularly such as that of the present day, which is developing, not alone in one, albeit a huge country, but embraces the whole of international relations—in such a case one must base one's tactics before all and above all on the objective position. One must examine the question analytically as to the course of the Revolution so far, and why it has changed so threateningly, so sharply, so disadvantageously for us.

If we look at the development of our Revolution from this point

[1] Published in *Pravda*, March 16 and 17.

of view we shall see clearly that, up to the present time, it has passed
through a period of comparative and, to a considerable extent, apparent self-reliance and temporary independence of international
relations. The path taken by our Revolution from the end of February
1917 to February 11 of the current year, when the German attack
commenced, was, in general and on the whole, one of facile and rapid
successes. If we glance at the development of this Revolution on the
international scale, from the point of view of the development of the
Russian Revolution alone, then we shall see that during this year
we have lived through three periods. The first period when the
working class of Russia, together with all who were most advanced,
conscious, active among the peasantry, supported not only by the
petty bourgeoisie, but also by the big bourgeoisie, wiped out the
monarchy within a few days. This delirious success is to be explained,
on the one hand, by the fact that the Russian people had piled up an
enormous reserve of ability for revolutionary struggle from the
experience of 1905 ; on the other hand, by the fact that Russia, being
an extremely backward country, had suffered most disastrously from
the war, and had particularly early reached a state of complete
inability to continue the war under the old régime.

After the short impetuous success when a new organization was
formed—the organization of Soviets of Workers', Soldiers', and
Peasants' Deputies—there followed for our Revolution long months
of a transition period—a period when the power of the bourgeoisie,
undermined at one blow by the Soviets, was sustained and
strengthened by the petty bourgeois conciliation parties—the Mensheviks and the Socialist Revolutionaries who supported this power.
This was an authority which supported the imperialist war and
imperialist secret treaties, it was an authority which fed the working
class with promises, did practically nothing, and left the devastation
of the country untouched. During this period—a long one for us, for
the Russian Revolution—the Soviets built up their forces. This was a
period, lengthy for the Russian Revolution, but short from the
point of view of the international revolution, because, in the majority
of the central countries, the period during which they shed their
petty bourgeois illusions, the period during which they passed
through the process of conciliation of different parties, fractions, and
shades of views, occupied not months but long, long decades—this
period in the Russian Revolution from May 3 (April 20) and the
renewal in June of the imperialist war by Kerensky, who carried in

his pocket the secret imperialist treaty, this period played a decisive rôle. During this period we lived through the July defeat, we lived through the Kornilov days, and only after the experience gained in the mass struggle, only when the wide masses of the workers and peasants—not as a result of propaganda, but because of what they had themselves gone through—realized the complete futility of the petty bourgeois conciliation policy; only then, after a long political development, after long preparation and transformation in the temper and views of the party groups, was the soil for the October coup ready, and then we entered into the third period of the Russian Revolution in its first phase—detached or temporarily separated from the international revolution.

This third period, the October period, was a period of organization, extremely difficult, but at the same time it was a period of the most important and most rapid triumphs. Since October—our Revolution having put power into the hands of the revolutionary proletariat; having established the dictatorship of the latter and secured for this dictatorship the support of the overwhelming majority of the proletariat and of the poorest peasants—since October our Revolution went forward at a victorious, triumphal pace. Throughout the length and breadth of Russia civil war broke out in the form of the resistance of the exploiters, the landed estate owners and bourgeoisie, supported by a part of the imperialist bourgeoisie.

The civil war began, and in this civil war the forces of the enemies of the Soviet power, the forces of the enemies of the toiling and exploited masses, proved to be negligible; the civil war was a complete triumph for the Soviet Government, because the enemies of the latter, the exploiters, the landed estate owners, the bourgeoisie, had neither political nor economic points of support, and their attack was smashed. The struggle with them resolved itself not so much into a military campaign as into an agitation; layer after layer, one section of the masses after another, right up to the toiling Cossacks, left those exploiters who had endeavoured to lead them away from the Soviet power.

This period of the victorious, triumphal march of the dictatorship of the proletariat and the Soviet Government, when it attracted to its side, unconditionally, decisively, and once for all, the great numbers of the toiling and exploited masses of Russia, signalized the last and highest point of development of the Russian Revolution, which during all this time had gone forward as though quite independent of international imperialism. This was the reason why the country, which was the most backward but the most prepared for revolution by its experience of 1905, so rapidly, so readily, so plannedly moved forward to power, one class after another ; passing through various political structures, at last reaching that political structure which was the last word, not only of the Russian Revolution but also of the Western European working-class revolutions ; for the Soviet power consolidated itself in Russia and won the unchangeable sympathy of the toilers and exploited because it destroyed the old oppressive machinery of State power, because it created a fundamentally new and higher type of State, such as the Paris Commune had been in embryo. It overthrew the old State machine and put in its place the directly armed forces of the masses. It substituted the bourgeois parliamentary democracy by the democracy of the labouring masses, at the same time excluding the exploiters and systematically suppressing the resistance of the latter.

This is what the Russian Revolution had done during this period, and this is the reason why a small part of the vanguard of the Russian Revolution had the impression that this triumphal march, this rapid progress of the Russian Revolution could count on further victories. And this was their mistake, because the period during which the Russian Revolution developed, when it handed over State power in Russia from one class to the other, ridding itself of class conciliation within the confines of Russia alone— this period could exist historically only because the greatest, most gigantic robbers of world imperialism were temporarily halted in their attacks against the Soviet power. A revolution which within a few days had overthrown the monarchy, which within a few months had exhausted all the attempts at conciliation with the bourgeoisie, and within a few weeks of civil war had overcome the resistance of the bourgeoisie—such a revolution, a revolution of the Socialist Republic, could only accommodate itself in the midst of the Imperialist Powers, in surroundings where world robbers held sway, and exist side by side with the beasts of international imperialism, only in so far as the bourgeoisie, locked in a death struggle amongst themselves, was paralyzed in its attack on Russia.

And now came the period which stands so vividly before us, and which we feel so deeply—the period of the most distressing defeat, of the most bitter trials for the Russian Revolution, a period when, instead of rapid, direct and open attack on the enemies of the Revolution, we had to experience the most grievous defeats and to retreat before forces immeasurably greater than our forces; before the forces of international imperialism and finance capital, before the forces of military might, which the whole bourgeoisie with its modern technique and its organization has mustered against us for the purpose of despoiling, oppressing and throttling the small nationalities. We had to ponder the question of the balance of forces, we were faced with a most difficult problem. We had to encounter not an enemy, such as Romanov or Kerensky, who could not be taken seriously. We had to meet the forces of the international bourgeoisie in all its military imperialist might; we were face to face with the world robbers. Naturally, in view of the retardation of help from the international Socialist proletariat we were forced unaided to accept battle with these forces and to suffer heavy defeat.

This epoch is the epoch of heavy defeats, the epoch of retreat, the epoch when we have to save, if only a small part of the position, retreating before imperialism, waiting for the time when the international position in general will have changed, when to our aid will come those forces of the European proletariat which do exist, which are maturing, which could not so readily as ourselves overcome their own enemies, for it would be the greatest delusion and the gravest mistake to forget that it was easy for the Russian Revolution to start, but more difficult for it to take the next steps. This was inevitably so, because we had to start with the most rotten, the most backward political structure. The European revolution, on the other hand, has to start with the bourgeoisie, it has a far more powerful enemy, and the conditions for its struggle are immeasurably more difficult. It will be immeasurably more difficult for the European revolution to start; we see how terribly difficult it is for the working class to make the first breach in that structure which is oppressing it. It will, however, be much easier for it to enter the second and third stages of its revolution, and it cannot be otherwise in view of the correlation of forces between the revolutionary and reactionary classes which now exist on the international arena. This is the fundamental turning-point which is constantly ignored by people who regard the present position, the very difficult present position of the Revolution not from an historical point of view, but from the point of view of their own emotions and indignation. The experience of history shows us that always, in all revolutions—with the exception of periods when the revolution lives through an acute break and a transition from rapid victory to a period of serious defeats—there arrives a period of pseudo-revolutionary phrases which always did an enormous amount of harm to the development of the revolution. And so, Comrades, we shall only then be able to appraise correctly our tactics if we take into account that conjecture of events which has thrown us from rapid, facile and full victories into a period of bitter defeats. This question (an immeasurably difficult, immeasurably thorny question) which represents the result of the turning-point in the development of the Revolution at the present time (from easy victories within the country to extraordinarily heavy defeats from outside) as well as the turning-point in the whole international revolution, from the epoch of the propaganda-agitational activities of the Russian Revolution, whilst imperialism was still passing through a waiting period, to the starting of the offensive by imperialism against the Soviet Government—all this presents a very serious and very acute question to the whole Western European movement. If we do not forget this historic point we shall have to examine what relation the basic circle of interest of Russia bears to the question of the present most onerous so-called impudent peace.

In my polemics against those who denied the necessity for us to accept this peace I have been told many a time that the point of view which advocates the signing of peace only represents the special interests of the exhausted peasant masses, the declassed soldiers and so on. And always I have been amazed when examining these expressions of opinions how the comrades seem to have forgotten the class scale of the national development. They seem to have delved deep for their explanations—as though the party of the proletariat having taken power had not beforehand considered that only the union of the proletariat and the poorest peasant masses, that is the majority of the Russian peasantry, that only such a union could give power in Russia to a revolutionary government of the Soviets—to a majority, to a real majority of the nation—that without this it would be absurd to make any attempt at forming a government, particularly at difficult turning-points in history. As though we could now do without this generally recognized truth, and confine ourselves to innuendos regarding the exhausted conditions of the peasants and the declassed soldiers. With respect to the exhausted condition of the peasantry and the declassed soldiers we must declare that the country will not permit resistance ; that the poorest peasantry can resist only within the definite limits of its ability to fight.

When we took power in October it was clear that the course of events was necessarily approaching the point when the conversion of the Soviets to Bolshevism signified a similar change over the whole country, that the rise of Bolshevism to power was inevitable. When we, recognizing this, took steps to assume power in October we said quite clearly and definitely both to ourselves and to the whole nation, that power was being transferred into the hands of the proletariat and the poorest peasantry, that the proletariat knows that the peasantry will support them, and what it is that they would support you yourselves know—the active struggle for peace, the readiness to continue the further fight against big finance capital. In this we are not mistaken, and no one who still retains any foothold at all within the confines of the class forces and class relationships can detach himself from this indubitable truth that we cannot ask a small peasant country, which has given so much both to the European and the international revolution, we cannot ask it to maintain the struggle in those terribly difficult conditions, when although our comrades among the Western European proletariat are undoubtedly coming towards us—this is proved by such facts as strikes, etc.— this help, although we shall get it eventually, has certainly been delayed. This is why I say that such references to the exhaustion of the peasant masses, etc., are being used by those who are devoid of arguments, who are completely helpless and who are quite unable to comprehend all the class relationships as a whole, in their totality— the revolution of the proletariat and the peasantry in its mass ; only when at every acute turning-point in history we appraise the relationship of classes as a whole, of all classes, and do not select separate examples and separate peculiar cases, only then can we feel that we stand solidly on an analysis of probable facts. I quite understand that the Russian bourgeoisie is now urging us on towards a revolutionary struggle, at a time when we are quite unable to engage in it. This is demanded by the class interests of the bourgeoisie.

When they merely cry : "An impudent peace", without saying a word as to who drove the army to this position, I quite understand that it is the bourgeoisie with the Dielo-Narodists, Mensheviks, Tseretellites, Chernovites, and their underlings. I quite understand that it is the bourgeoisie who cry for a revolutionary war. This is demanded by its class interests. It is demanded by their desire to cause the Soviet Government to make a false step. It is quite comprehensible on the part of people who, on the one hand, fill pages with their counter-revolutionary dribble . . . (voices : " They have all been closed "). Unfortunately not all have yet been closed, but we shall close them. I should like to see the proletariat which would permit the counter-revolutionaries, the supporters of the bourgeoisie, and those who would form coalitions with the latter to continue to utilize their monopoly of wealth for fooling the people with their bourgeois opium. There has never been such a proletariat.

I quite understand that the pages of such publications are full of howls, groans, and shrieks against the impudent peace. I quite understand that the people who stand for this revolutionary war, from the Cadets to the Right Socialist Revolutionaries, meet at the same time the Germans when they make an attack and solemnly declare : Here are the Germans ; and then let their officers, in full uniform, swagger about in the areas occupied by the German imperialists. Yes, I am not at all surprised to hear pleas for a revolutionary war made by such bourgeois, such conciliators. They desire that the Soviet Government should fall into a trap. They have shown what they are, these bourgeois and these conciliators. We have seen them and will yet see living examples of them : we know that in the Ukraine there are Ukrainian Kerenskys, Ukrainian Chernovs, and Ukrainian Tseretellis—here they are the Messieurs Vinnichenkos. Here are these gentlemen, the Ukrainian Kerenskys, Chernovs, Tseretellis, who concealed from the people the peace which they concluded with the German imperialists and who now with the help of German bayonets are trying to overthrow the Soviet power in the Ukraine. This is what these bourgeois and these conciliators and those who think with them have done. These are the acts of those Ukrainian bourgeois and conciliators, whose example now stands before our very eyes, who have concealed and still conceal from the people their secret treaties and who now come forward with their German bayonets against the Soviet power. This is exactly what the Russian bourgeois wants. This is where, consciously or unconsciously, the underlings of the bourgeoisie are trying to drive the Soviet power. They know well enough that the Soviet Government is quite unable at the present moment to engage in war with powerful imperialists. This is why it is only by realizing these international circumstances, these general class circumstances, that we can comprehend the vastness of the mistakes made by those who, like the party of the Left Socialist Revolutionaries, have permitted themselves to be carried away by a theory which is to be found in the histories of all revolutions at difficult moments, and which is made up half of despair, half of phrases, when, instead of soberly looking at realities and appraising the problems of the Revolution in relation to the internal and external enemies from the point of view of the class forces, they call upon us to resolve a most serious and difficult question under pressure of emotions, only from the point of view of one's personal feelings. They imagine that having abused this peace, having proved that it is so impudent, so shameful, so burdensome—undoubtedly they think that they are demonstrating the whole extent of these defeats which, as a matter of fact, we have never concealed, for we have ourselves promulgated it. I myself have had occasion in the press and in declarations and speeches to characterize this peace many a time as a Tilsit peace, which the conqueror Napoleon forced upon the Prussian and German people after a series of heavy defeats. Yes, this peace constitutes a heavy defeat and humiliates the Soviet Government, but if because of this and limiting yourself to this fact you appeal to emotions, arouse indignation, and in this way try to solve the greatest historical question, you fall into the same absurd and pitiful position in which the whole party of Socialist Revolutionaries at one time found itself when in 1907, in a situation somewhat similar in regard to certain features, they in the same way appealed to the feelings of the revolutionary ; when after the severest defeat of our Revolution in 1906-7 Stolypin dictated to us the laws regarding the third Duma—the most disgraceful and mortifying conditions of work in one of the most abominable representative institutions—when our party, after a certain amount of wavering (the vacillations on this question were greater than now), decided the question on the principle that we had no right to succumb to emotions ; that, however great our indignation against and disgust with the most disgraceful third Duma, we were nevertheless bound to recognize that we had to deal not with an accident, but with a historical necessity of the developing class struggle ; for the time being the latter had no more strength to fight, but it would be able to gather such strength even under these disgraceful dictated conditions. We proved to be right. Those who endeavoured to entice us with revolutionary phrase-mongering, with appeals to justice, in so far as it expressed a feeling thrice justified, those received a lesson which will not be forgotten by any reflecting, sensible revolutionary.

The course of revolutions is not so smooth as to assure us rapid and easy prógress. There has not been a single great revolution, even within the framework of merely national revolutions, which has not lived through a period of heavy defeats. And one's attitude towards a serious question of mass movements of a developing revolution cannot be such that, whilst declaring the peace to be predatory, humiliating, a revolutionary is unable to reconcile himself to accepting it. It is insufficient to bandy about fine propaganda phrases, to smother us with reproaches regarding this peace—this is the veritable abc of the revolution. It is the well-known experience of all revolutions. We must remember our experience in 1905—and if we are rich in anything, and if, thanks to anything, the Russian working class and the poorest peasantry could take upon themselves the most difficult, most honourable rôle of beginning the international Socialist revolution, it is just because the Russian people succeeded, thanks to a particular conjuncture of historical circumstances, in carrying out two great revolutions at the beginning of the twentieth century—we must study the experience of these revolutions, we must understand that only by taking into account the change in the correlations of the class ties, of one state with the other, can one lay down definitely that we are not in a position to accept battle at the present moment. We must take this into account and say to ourselves : Whatever the respite, however precarious, however short, however burdensome and humiliating the peace, it is better than war, for it will give the national masses an opportunity to take breath; because it will give us an opportunity to rectify the misdeeds of the bourgeoisie which is now sounding the alarm everywhere, particularly there, where it is under the protection of the Germans in the occupied province.

The bourgeoisie cries that the Bolsheviks have destroyed the army, that there is no longer an army, and that the Bolsheviks are to blame for it ; but let us look at the past, Comrades, let us look before all at the development of our Revolution. Do you not know that the desertions from, and the dispersal of, our army began long before the Revolution—already in 1916, and that everyone who has seen the army must recognize this ? And what has our bourgeoisie done to prevent it ? Is it not clear that the only chance of saving ourselves from the imperialists was then in its hands, that there was such a chance in March–April, when the Soviet organizations could have taken power by a simple movement of their hands against the bourgeoisie ? And if the Soviets had indeed taken power then, if the bourgeois intelligentsia and the petty bourgeoisie together with the Socialist Revolutionaries and Mensheviks, instead of helping Kerensky to deceive the people, to conceal the secret treaties, and to lead the army into an attack, if they had then come to the help of the army, supplied the army with arms, with food, forcing the bourgeoisie to aid the Fatherland with the help of the whole intelligentsia—not the Fatherland of the hucksters, not the Fatherland of the secret treaties which are instrumental in destroying the people—if the Soviets, having forced the bourgeoisie to help the Fatherland of the toilers, of the workers, had helped the ragged, barefooted, starving army—only in that case might we perhaps have had a period of ten months sufficient to give the army the opportunity of a respite, we could then have given it wholehearted support, so that without retreating one step from the front, a general democratic peace could have been proposed. The secret treaties would have been torn up, but the army would have remained at the front, it would not have made one step away from it. This was the opportunity for peace which the workers and peasants gave and approved, these the tactics of the defence of the Fatherland, not the Fatherland of the Romanovs, of the Kerenskys, of the Chernovs, not the Fatherland of the secret treaties, the Fatherland of the mercenary bourgeoisie, but the Fatherland of the labouring masses. Those who failed to do all this are the people who have caused the transition from war to revolution and from the Russian Revolution to international socialism to stumble against so many dire difficulties. This is why the proposal of a revolutionary war is so much empty phrase-mongering, when we know that we have no army, when we know that we could not restrain desertions from the army, and people who know the circumstances could not but realize that our demobilization order was not something devised by us but was the result of self-evident necessity, the simplest impossibility of retaining the army. We could not retain the army. And quite right was the officer, not a Bolshevik, who declared even before the October coup that the army cannot and will not fight. This is what the months of bargaining with the bourgeoisie and all the talk about the necessity of continuing the war has led to. However noble the feeling which dictated such speeches by many or a few revolutionaries, in actual fact they have proved empty revolutionary phrases. International imperialism only obtained further opportunities for encroachments, so that it might continue to rob as much and more than it had already succeeded in robbing after our tactical or diplomatic mistake—after the signature of the Brest Treaty. When we said to those who opposed signing the peace treaty : if the breathing-space should be a fairly long one, you will then realize that the need to heal the army, the interests of the toiling masses, stand above everything, and that peace must be concluded for the sake of this—they asserted that there could be no respite.

But our Revolution differentiated itself from all previous revolutions in that it gave rise to a tremendous longing for construction and creative work within the masses. In the most out-of-the-way villages the toiling masses, humiliated, crushed, oppressed by Tsars, landlords, and the bourgeoisie, are raising themselves, and this period of the Revolution is only now coming to a head, when the Revolution in the villages now in full swing is constructing life anew. And for the sake of this respite, however slight and short it might be, we must, if we place the interests of the labouring masses above those of the bourgeois warriors who rattle their sabres and call us to the battle, sign this treaty. This is what the Revolution teaches us : the Revolution teaches us that when we make diplomatic mistakes, when we imagine that the German workers will come to our help on the morrow, in the hope that Liebknecht will win immediately (and we know that in one way or another Liebknecht will win, this is inevitable in the development of the working-class movement), this signifies that, carried away on a wave of enthusiasm the revolutionary slogans of a difficult Socialist movement have been transformed into mere phrase-mongering. Not a single representative of the labouring people, not a single honest worker, will refuse to make the greatest sacrifices to help the Socialist movement in Germany, because during all this time at the front he has learned to differentiate between the German imperialist and the soldiers, exhausted by German discipline, who for the most part sympathize with us. This is why I say that the Russian Revolution has in practice rectified our mistakes. It has corrected it by giving us this respite.

In all probability the breathing-space will be very short, but we are able even in the shortest respite to render the exhausted, starving army conscious of the fact that it has at last received the possibility of catching its breath. It is clear to us that the present period of imperialist wars has ended, and new horrors and the beginning of new battles are threatening, but in many historical epochs there have been periods of such wars and they have usually become all the more acute just before their conclusion. And it is essential that this should be understood, not only at meetings in Petrograd and Moscow, but also by the tens of millions in the villages ; it is necessary that the better informed sections of the villagers, those who have lived through all the horrors of the war, when returning from the front should help the others to understand this, and that the masses of peasants and workers should be convinced of the need for a revolutionary front and should say that we have acted correctly.

We are told that we have betrayed the Ukraine and Finland—oh, what a disgrace ! But the position of affairs was such that we were cut off from Finland, with which we had earlier concluded a tacit peace before the Revolution, and now we have concluded a formal peace with her. It is said that we are giving away the Ukraine which Chernov, Kerensky and Tseretelli are going to devastate. We are told that we are traitors, that we have betrayed the Ukraine ! but I reply : Comrades, I know the history of revolutions too well to be in any way disconcerted by the hostile views and cries of people who give themselves up to their emotions and are incapable of reasoning. Let me give you a simple example : Imagine that two friends are walking along at night and suddenly ten people attack them. If these rascals cut off one of them, what can the other man do ? He cannot go to the help of his comrade. If he starts running away, is he a traitor ? But imagine that we are dealing not with individuals, not with cases in which personal feelings play the leading rôle, but that five armies each with a hundred thousand soldiers surround an army of two hundred thousand people, and that another army has to go to its assistance. But if the latter army knows that it will certainly fall into a trap, then it must retreat ; it cannot do anything but retreat, even though in order to cover its retreat it is necessary to sign a vile, predatory peace—you can inveigh against it as much as you like, but still this peace must be signed. One cannot consider the question from the point of view of the feelings of a duellist who draws the sword from his scabbard, and says : I must die because I am being forced to conclude a humiliating peace. But we all know that, whatever the solution, we have no army, and no fine gestures will save us from the necessity of retreating in order to gain time, so that the army may have a respite ; and everyone will agree with this who looks facts in the face and is not deceiving himself with revolutionary phrases.

If we know this, it is our revolutionary duty to sign even an onerous, a super-onerous and forced treaty, for thereby we shall attain a better position both for ourselves and for our allies. Have we lost anything by signing the peace treaty on March 3 ? Everyone who desires to look on things as they are from the point of view of mass relationship and not from that of the little aristocrat-duellist, will understand that not having an army, or having only the sick remains of any army, to accept battle and to call this a revolutionary war, is only self-illusion and the greatest possible deception of the people. It is our duty to tell the people the truth: Yes, the peace is terribly burdensome. The Ukraine and Finland are perishing, but we have to accept this peace. And the whole conscious labouring masses of Russia will accept it because they know the unadorned truth, because they know what war is; they know that to put everything on the cards in the hope that a German revolution will start immediately is nothing but self-deception. Having signed such a peace we have attained this—that our Finnish friends have received from us a breathing-space ; help, and not ruin.

I know examples in the history of peoples when even a more brutally compulsory peace had to be signed: when that peace handed over other peoples to the tender mercies of the conqueror. Let us compare our peace with the Tilsit peace. The Tilsit peace was forced by the victorious conqueror on Prussia and Germany. This peace was so onerous, that not only did the conqueror seize all the capitals of all the German States ; not only were the Prussians thrown back to Tilsit—which can be compared with the state of affairs which would arise if we were thrown back to Omsk or Tomsk—but the worst horror of all was that Napoleon forced the defeated nations to give him auxiliary troops for his wars, when nevertheless the position of affairs was such that the German peoples had to suffer the onslaught of the conqueror. When the epoch of the revolutionary wars of France was succeeded by the epoch of the imperialist wars of conquest, then became clear that which people, carried away by revolutionary phrases, people who represent the signature of peace as a national decline, refuse to understand. From the point of view of the little aristocrat-duellist, such a psychology is quite comprehensible, but not from that of the worker and peasant. The latter has gone through the severe school of war and has learnt to calculate. There have been even more difficult trials and even more backward peoples have lived through them. More onerous peace terms have been accepted and were concluded by the Germans at a time when they had no army, or their army was sick as our army is now sick. They concluded a most burdensome peace with Napoleon, but this peace did not signify the decline of Germany—on the contrary, it was actually a turning-point in the national defence and rise of the country. And we too now stand on the eve of such a turning-point, and are going through analagous conditions. We must look truth in the face and spurn mere phrases and declamations. We must declare that if it is necessary then peace must be concluded. A war of liberation, a class war, a people's war, will take the place of a Napoleonic war. The system of Napoleonic wars will pass, peace will take the place of war, war will follow peace, and from each new most burdensome peace there has always resulted a more extensive preparation for war. The most onerous of peace treaties—the Tilsit Peace—is now regarded by history as a turning-point of that time, as the start of the turning-point in the history of the German nation. Germany, though forced to retreat to Tilsit, to Russia, was actually gaining time, waiting until the international situation, which at one time had permitted the triumph of Napoleon—a robber similar to the present-day Hohenzollern Hindenburg—should change in her favour, and until the consciousness of the German people, exhausted by the decades of the Napoleonic wars and defeats, should heal and the people be resurrected to new life. This is what history teaches us. This is why it is criminal to indulge in despair and phrase-mongering. This is why everyone will say : Yes, the old imperialist wars are coming to an end. The historic turning-point has arrived.

Beginning with October, our Revolution had been a complete triumph, but now long and difficult times have begun. We do not know how long they will be, but we do know that we have before us a long and difficult road of defeats and retreats ; because such is the relationship of forces ; because by our retreat we give the people an opportunity of resting. We shall make it possible for every worker and peasant to understand this truth, that new wars of the imperialist robbers against oppressed people are about to start : then the worker and peasant will realize that we have to stand for the defence of the Fatherland, for after our October triumph we are ready to defend it. Since November 7 [October 25] we have said quite openly that we now stand for the defence of the Fatherland, because we now have such a Fatherland from which we have driven the Kerenskys and

Chernovs; because we have destroyed the secret treaties; because we have suppressed the bourgeoisie. We are still passing through bad times, but we shall learn how to make them better.

Comrades, there is a still more important difference between the condition of the Russian people who have suffered a severe defeat at the hands of the German conquerors and the German people. There is the greatest of differences which must be mentioned, although I have already dealt with it in brief in the preceding part of my speech. Comrades, when the German people a hundred and more years ago found themselves in a period of the most grievous wars of conquest, in a period when they had to retreat and to sign one humiliating peace after another, before the German nation awoke— at that time the German nation was only weak and backward— only such. Against the German people were ranged not only the military forces and might of the conqueror Napoleon—but against them also stood a country which was above Germany in respect of her revolutionary and political experience; above her in every way. A country which had raised herself above all other countries; which in this respect had said the last word. France stood immeasurably higher than the nation which was being starved and frozen in subjection to the imperialists and landowners. The Germans were then a nation which was, I repeat it, only weak and backward; but they were able to learn from their bitter lessons and to raise themselves.

We are better situated. We are not simply a weak and backward nation. We are that nation which could—not thanks to any special merit or historical predetermination, but thanks to a peculiar chain of historical circumstances—take upon itself the honour of raising the banner of the international Socialist revolution.

I know very well, Comrades, as I have said more than once, that this banner is in weak hands and the workers of the most backward country will be unable to retain it if the workers of all the advanced countries do not come to their aid. Those Socialist transformations which we have succeeded in carrying out are in many ways incomplete, weak, and insufficient. But our experience will be a guide to the Western European advanced workers, who will say to themselves: " The Russians have started things not quite in the right way ". It is, however, important that, in relation to the German people, our people are not simply weak, not simply a backward nation, but a nation which has raised the banner of the Revolution.

Although the bourgeoisie of any country, taken at random, fills the columns of its press with calumnies on the Bolsheviks—the press of imperialist France, England, Germany, etc., are at one in vilifying the Bolsheviks—in not a single country would it be possible to hold a meeting of workers at which the names and slogans of our Socialist Government would call forth exclamations of indignation [a voice : " Lies "]. No, this is not a lie, but the truth, and everyone who has been in Germany, in Austria, in Switzerland, or America, during recent months will tell you that it is not a lie but the truth ; that the names and slogans of the representatives of the Soviet Government in Russia meet with the greatest enthusiasm in working-class circles ; that in spite of all the lies of the bourgeoisie in Germany, France, etc., the working masses have understood that, however weak we may be, their own aims are being realized here, in Russia. Yes, our people must bear the heavy burden which it has taken upon itself, but a people which has been capable of creating the Soviet power cannot perish. And I repeat, not a single conscious Socialist, not a single worker, reflecting on the history of revolution can dispute the fact that, in spite of all the shortcomings of the Soviet Government—which I know only too well and know how to appraise—the Soviet Power is the highest type of State, the direct successor to the Paris Commune. Our Revolution has risen a step higher than all other European revolutions, and consequently we are not in such a difficult position as the German people were a hundred years ago. At that time the only hope of the oppressed was an alteration in the relative strengths of the robbers—the robber Napoleon, the robber Alexander I, the English monarchical robbers —the one chance of the oppressed was to take advantage of the conflicts between the robbers and utilize them for their own purposes. Nevertheless, the German people was not crushed as a result of the Tilsit peace. But, I repeat, we are at the present moment better situated, since we have in all the Western European countries a most powerful ally—the international Socialist proletariat who are with us, whatever our enemies may say. True, this ally may find it difficult to raise his voice, just as it was by no means easy for us to do so before the end of February 1917. This ally lives underground, under conditions of the military penal prison into which all the imperialist countries have been transformed, but he knows us and understands what we are doing. He finds it difficult to come to our help, consequently the Soviet troops will have to have considerable time and much patience ; they will be constrained to go through difficult trials whilst waiting for that time—and we shall seize every opportunity to gain time, for time is on our side. Our cause is gaining in strength, whilst the forces of the imperialists are becoming weaker, and whatever trials and defeats we may suffer from our " Tilsit " peace, we are starting the tactics of retreat, and I repeat once again : there is no doubt whatever that both the conscious proletariat and the conscious peasants are on our side, and we shall prove ourselves capable not only of heroic attack, but also of heroic retreat. We shall know how to wait till the international Socialist proletariat comes to our aid and we shall then start a second Socialist revolution on a world scale.

APPENDIX VII

SUPPLEMENTARY TREATY TO THE TREATY OF PEACE BETWEEN RUSSIA AND THE CENTRAL POWERS [1]

(SIGNED AT BERLIN, AUGUST 27, 1918 [2])

GUIDED by the wish to solve certain political questions which have arisen in connection with the Peace Treaty of March 3-7, 1918, between Germany, Austria-Hungary, Bulgaria, and Turkey, for the one part, and Russia, for the other part, in the spirit of friendly understanding and mutual conciliation, and, in so doing, to promote the restoration of good and confidential relations between the two Empires, for which a way was paved by the conclusion of peace, the German Imperial Government and the Government of the Russian Socialist Federal Soviet Republic have agreed to conclude a supplementary treaty to the Peace Treaty with this object, and have appointed as their plenipotentiaries :

For the Imperial German Government :

The Secretary of State for Foreign Affairs, the Imperial Privy Councillor, Rear-Admiral Paul von Hintze, retired ; and
The Director in the Foreign Office, the Imperial Privy Councillor, Dr. Johannes Kriege.

For the Government of the Russian Socialist Federal Soviet Republic :

Its diplomatic representative accredited to the German Imperial Government, M. Adolf Joffe.

After exchanging their credentials, and finding them in correct and proper form, the plenipotentiaries agreed to the following provisions :

[1] *Texts of the Russian " Peace "* (U.S. Department of State, 1918), p. 179.
[2] Ratifications exchanged at Berlin, September 6, 1918 (*Frankfurter Zeitung*, 2nd morning edition, September 7, 1918).

Part I

Demarcations and Frontier Commissions

Article 1

In so far as this has not yet been done, Russo-German Commissions will immediately be formed to fix demarcation lines for all fronts where German and Russian troops face one another. Exact details as to this shall be agreed on by the commanders of the troops on each side.

These demarcation lines shall be so drawn that there are neutral zones between the respective fronts, which zones must not be trodden by any members of the respective armies, with the exception of *parlementaires*. In so far as there is not regular traffic between the respective fronts, such traffic will be established by the demarcation commissions.

Article 2

The Russo-German Commission for fixing the frontier line, provided for in Article 3, paragraph 1, of the Peace Treaty, shall also fix the eastern frontiers of Estonia and Livonia, agreed on in Article 6, paragraph 2, of that Treaty, more exactly.

After the fixing of the eastern frontier of Estonia and Livonia, provided for in paragraph 1, Germany will evacuate the territory occupied by her east of this frontier without delay.

Article 3

Germany will evacuate the territory occupied by her east of the Beresina, even before the conclusion of general peace, in proportion as Russia makes the cash payments stipulated in Article 2 of the Russo-German Financial Agreement of this date ; further provisions as to this, particularly the fixing of the individual sectors to be evacuated, are left to the Commission referred to in Article 2, paragraph 1, of this Supplementary Treaty.

The contracting parties reserve the right to make further agreements with regard to the effecting of the evacuation of the occupied territory west of the Beresina before the conclusion of general peace, in accordance with the fulfilment by Russia of the remaining financial obligations undertaken by her.

Part II

Separatist Movements in the Russian Empire

Article 4

In so far as is not otherwise prescribed in the Peace Treaty or in this Supplementary Treaty, Germany will in no wise interfere in the relations between the Russian Empire and parts of its territory, and will thus in particular neither cause nor support the formation of independent States in those territories.

Part III

North Russian Territory

Article 5

Russia will at once employ all the means at her disposal to expel the Entente forces from North Russian territory in observance of her neutrality.

Germany guarantees that during these operations there shall be no Finnish attack of any kind on Russian territory, particularly on St. Petersburg.

Article 6

When the Entente forces shall have evacuated North Russian territory, the local Russian coast shipping within the three-mile limit from the north coast, and the fishing boats within a stretch of thirty miles along this coast shall be relieved of the barred zone menace. The German naval command shall have an opportunity, in a way to be further agreed upon, of convincing itself that this concession shall not be taken advantage of to forward contraband goods.

Part IV

Estonia, Livonia, Courland, and Lithuania

Article 7

Russia, taking account of the condition at present existing in Estonia and Livonia, renounces sovereignty over these regions, as well as all interference in their internal affairs. Their future fate shall be decided in agreement with their inhabitants.

No obligations of any kind towards Russia shall accrue to Estonia and Livonia through their former union with Russia.

Article 8

To facilitate Russian trade through Estonia, Livonia, Courland, and Lithuania the following is agreed :

§ 1. In Estonia, Livonia, Courland, and Lithuania the through transport of goods to and from Russia on routes liable to the payment of duty shall be absolutely free, and the goods to be transported shall not be subject to any transit duties or general transport dues.

§ 2. On the railways connecting Russia with Reval, Riga, and Windau, the freight tariffs on the goods to be forwarded in through trade with Russia are to be kept as low as possible. They may only be raised above the rates in force on August 1, 1914, by taking the average of the amount by which a general rise in the freight tariffs of the lines in question may be necessary to cover the cost of working and upkeep, including the payment of interest, and timely redemption of the capital invested. Neither must they be higher than the freight tariffs for goods of the same kind of inland origin or destination, which are forwarded over the same lines and in the same direction.

§ 3. Shipping on the Dvina between Russia and the open sea, as well as between all places on the Livonian-Courland Dvina, and on the Russian Dvina, is, subject to prevailing police regulations, to be free for the transport of goods and passengers, without any discrimination in regard to the ships and the subjects of the one or the other party. It is not to be subject to any tax based solely on the fact of the navigation. It is not to be subject to any stations, slips, depôt, turnover, or harbourage dues.

Exclusive shipping privileges must not be granted either to companies or corporations, or to private persons of any kind.

Taxes for the use of works and institutions which are created, or may be created in future, to facilitate traffic, or to improve and maintain the navigation of the river, may only be raised uniformly in accordance with published tariffs and to the extent necessary to cover the cost of restoration and upkeep, inclusive of payment of interest and redemption of the capital invested. The cost of restoring and keeping up the works and institutions which are not for the facilitation of traffic and the improvement and maintenance of the navigation of the river, but are intended to further other objects and interests, may be raised only to a proportionate extent by shipping dues.

The provisions of paragraphs 1 to 3 preceding apply also to rafts.

§ 4. At Reval, Riga, and Windau, Russia shall have suitably situated free port zones assigned to her in which the storing and unpacking of goods, coming from or intended for Russia, can take place without hindrance, and the work of despatching goods from or to the Russian Customs zone can be done by Russian officials.

§ 5. The individual questions connected with the provisions of §§ 1 to 4, particularly the restrictions to which these provisions may be subjected in war-time out of consideration for war necessity or for urgent sanitary reasons, shall be regulated by a special agreement.

Article 9

The water of Lake Peipus is not to be artificially diverted on either side to such a degree as to lower the water level. No methods of fishing calculated to diminish the stock of fish will be permitted ; a further agreement as to this is reserved.

The water power of the Narva is to be made available as soon as possible for the supply of electricity for the St. Petersburg municipality according to a special agreement to be made regarding this.

Article 10

With regard to Estonia, Livonia, Courland, and Lithuania, agreements, among others, are to be concluded with Russia, as to the following points :

1. With regard to the nationality of the former Russian inhabitants of these territories, as to which they must in any case be allowed the right of option and departure.

2. With regard to the return of the property in Russia belonging to subjects of these territories, particularly that belonging to publicly recognized societies, establishments, and institutions, as well as the property in these territories which belongs to Russian subjects.

3. With regard to an arrangement concerning the property of the communal districts cut up by the new frontiers.

4. With regard to an arrangement concerning the archives, the documents of the legal and administrative authorities, the legal and administrative trusts, and the register of births, marriages, deaths, etc.

5. With regard to the regulation of the new frontiers.

6. With regard to the effect of the territorial alterations on the State treaties.

PART V

RUSSIAN BLACK SEA TERRITORY WITH EXCEPTION OF CAUCASUS

Article 11

With reservation of the provisions of Article 12, Germany will evacuate the Russian Black Sea territory occupied by her outside the Caucasus after the ratification of the treaty of peace to be concluded between Russia and the Ukraine.

Article 12

The parts of the occupied territory which do not belong to the districts referred to in the third Ukrainian Universal of November 7, 1917,[1] shall be evacuated by the German forces at latest on the conclusion of the general peace, in so far as the peace between Russia and the Ukraine shall not have come into being before then.

The evacuation of the railway line Rostov–Voronesh, as well as of the occupied territory east of it, and a suitable frontier district west of it, including the town of Rostov, will follow as soon as this is demanded on the Russian side. Until the evacuation, Germany will permit the forwarding of grain and other goods for the Russian Government, under the supervision of Russian officials, on those portions of the railway situated in the occupied territory ; the same applies for the portions of the railway line Taganrog–Rostov and Taganrog–Kursk, lying in the occupied territory, for the duration of the occupation.

So long as the Donets Basin is occupied by German troops in accordance with Article 11 and Article 12, paragraph 1, Russia shall receive monthly from the quantities of coal extracted there a three-times greater number of tons than it lets Germany have of crude oil or crude oil products from the Baku district in accordance with Article 14, paragraph 2, and a four-times greater number of tons for the consignments of benzine contained therein. In so far as the coal supply in the Donets Basin is not sufficient for this, or must be used for other purposes, it will be supplemented by German coal.

[1] Old Style (November 20, New Style). See *Texts of the Ukrainian " Peace "*, p. 1.

Part VI

The Caucasus

Article 13

Russia agrees to Germany's recognizing Georgia as an independent State.

Article 14

Germany will give no assistance to any third Power in any military operations in the Caucasus outside Georgia or the districts mentioned in Article 4, paragraph 3, of the Peace Treaty. She will also take measures to prevent the military forces of any third Power in the Caucasus overstepping the following lines : The Kuban, from its mouth to Petropavlovskoje ; from there onwards, the boundaries of the district Shemakha to Agrioba ; thence a straight line to the point where the boundaries of the district of Baku, Shemakha, and Kuban meet ; thence along the northern boundary of the district of Baku to the sea.

Russia will do her utmost to further the production of crude oil and crude oil products in the Baku district, and will supply to Germany a quarter of the amount produced, or at least a number of tons, to be agreed upon later, per month. In so far as the quantities produced in the Baku district are not sufficient to supply this number of tons, or must be used for other purposes, they will be supplemented by quantities produced elsewhere. The price will be reckoned by the price of the coal Russia is to be allowed to have in accordance with Article 12, paragraph 3, and moreover, by the amount of goods to be supplied by Russia to Germany in accordance with Article 3, § 2, of the Russo-German Financial Agreement of this date.

Part VII

Treatment of Russian Warships and Russian Stores seized by German Military Forces after the Conclusion of Peace

Article 15

Germany recognizes Russia's ownership of the Russian warships seized by German forces after the ratification of the Peace Treaty, subject to Russia coming to terms with Finland and the Ukraine as to the national capital of the former Russian Empire.

The warships seized will remain under German care until the conclusion of the general peace.

Article 16

Germany admits Russia's claim to be compensated for the Russian stores which have been seized outside the Ukraine and Finland by German forces after the conclusion of peace. This compensation will be reckoned when Germany's and Russia's financial obligations arising from the Supplementary Treaty to the Peace Treaty are discussed.

PART VIII

FINAL PROVISIONS

Article 17

This Supplementary Treaty shall be ratified, and the ratification documents shall be exchanged not later than September 6, 1918, in Berlin.

The Treaty comes into force on the day the ratification documents are exchanged.

In witness whereof the plenipotentiaries have signed and sealed this Supplementary Treaty.

Executed in duplicate in Berlin on this 27th day of August 1918.

(L.S.) VON HINTZE

(L.S.) KRIEGE

(L.S.) A. JOFFE

APPENDIX VIII

NOTE HANDED BY THE GERMAN SECRETARY OF STATE
FOR FOREIGN AFFAIRS, REAR-ADMIRAL VON
HINTZE, TO THE SOVIET AMBASSADOR, M. ADOLF
JOFFE.[1]

(BERLIN, AUGUST 27, 1918)

DEAR SIR,

Following our conversation regarding the agreement signed
to-day in complement to the Peace Treaty, I have the honour to
confirm herewith confidentially in the name of the Imperial German
Government some details of the provisions of this complementary
agreement.

1. With regard to Article 2, paragraph 1. The border line to be
determined by the German-Russian Commission shall follow the
bed of the river Narva at the distance of one kilometre from its
eastern bank, due consideration being given to the communal
frontiers, and shall include the city of Narva with the territory
required by its economic interests ; at the same time the eastern
protruding end of Courland, south from the Düna on the general
line Dunaburg–Driswiaty, shall be rounded off, consideration being
given to the communal border lines. Along the line beginning at the
south-western part of the lake of Pskov (or Pleskau) and leading to
the lake of Luban and further to Liwenhof, the frontier shall be
established in accordance with the following viewpoints and with
due consideration being given to the administrative borders : the
economic conditions of the city of Pskov and the situation of the
Russian monastery Petchory make it desirable, on the one hand,
to establish the frontier as far to the west as possible ; on the other
hand, there should be established to the south-west of the Pskov
Lake a border line which would facilitate the defence of Livonia.

2. With regard to Article 4. Germany undertakes also, in connection with the execution of these provisions, to see that the formation
of independent State units within the Russian State should not
obtain military support from the Ukraine.

[1] Translated from *Europäische Gespräche*, March 1926.

3. With regard to Article 5. The presence in the Northern Russian regions of armed forces of the Allies represents a permanent and serious menace to the German troops stationed in Finland. Should, therefore, the Russian action provided for in Article 5, paragraph 1, not reach the expected results, Germany would find herself obliged to undertake this action, if necessary with the help of Finnish troops ; the Russian territory lying between the Finnish Gulf and Lake Ladoga, as well as the regions to the south and south-east of this lake, would not thereby be touched by German or Finnish troops unless at the special request of the Russian Government. The German Government expects that the Russian Government will not consider such action as an unfriendly act and will not oppose it in any way whatever. Under such conditions Germany guarantees that the Russian regions occupied in the course of this action shall be again evacuated by German and Finnish troops upon the departure of the Entente forces and after the conclusion of a general peace, in so far as these regions are not to be incorporated into the Finnish territory in accordance with the Russo-Finnish Treaty of Peace ; Germany will also re-establish, as soon as possible after the expulsion of the Entente armed forces, the Russian civil administration in these regions.

4. With regard to Article 7. In the course of the negotiations concerning Estonia and Livonia, the Russians expressed the desire that Germany should undertake the guarantee for the permanent dismantling of the Reval fortifications. The German Government believes that it is not able to undertake such a binding obligation in this sense, for such agreements, as experience has shown, become the source of international conflicts. It does not hesitate, however, to declare that it is the intention of the German Government to dismantle the fortifications of Reval after the conclusion of the general peace, and not to allow the future maintenance of Reval as a fortress.

5. With regard to Article 12, paragraph 2. The German Government expects that the Russian Government will take all possible measures in order to crush immediately the insurrection of General Alexeiev and of the Czechoslovaks ; Germany, on her part, will adopt all measures at her disposal against General Alexeiev. In view of this, Russia shall insist on the evacuation of the railway section mentioned in Article 12, paragraph 2, sentence 1, only when the military situation will allow such evacuation and upon the decision specially agreed upon at the time.

6. With regard to Article 12, paragraph 3. Germany will exercise her influence in the negotiations for the peace treaty to be concluded by Russia with the Ukraine, to the end that Russia shall obtain the adequate part of the Don Basin as required by her economic interests; on the other hand, Russia shall not insist on the evacuation of that part of the Don Basin which will thus come into her possession before the conclusion of the general peace, independently from the provisions of Article 12, paragraph 2. Germany will further exercise her influence with the Ukraine so that one-third of the Ukrainian production of iron shall be put at the disposal of Russia in accordance with a special agreement to be concluded on the subject.

7. With regard to Article 13. Germany will exercise her influence to enable Russia to export from Georgia one quarter of the manganese ore extracted there in accordance with the provisions of a special agreement to be concluded on the subject.

8. With regard to Article 14, paragraph 1. The agreement by Germany not to support any third Power in possible military operations in the Caucasus outside Georgia or the regions mentioned in the Treaty of Peace, Article IV, paragraph 3, will also extend to such cases when, in the course of such operations, it should come unfortunately to an armed conflict between the Russian troops and the troops of a third Power. Such conflicts will not involve any intervention on the part of Germany, as long as the Russian troops do not cross the frontier of Turkey, including the above-mentioned regions, or the borders of Georgia.

9. With regard to Article 14, paragraph 2. The German Government expects to hear by September 30, 1918, the proposals of the Russian Government regarding the amounts of monthly minimum supplies of petroleum and oil products to be supplied by Russia.

10. With regard to Article 15. Germany reserves to herself the use for peaceful aims, in particular for the trawling of mines and coastal harbour and police service, of the men-of-war of the Black Sea fleet, including the warships returned from Novorossisk to Sebastopol, as long as they remain under German control in conformity with paragraph 2 of the present article ; in case of war necessity they might also be used for military aims. The German Government will pay the Russian Government full indemnity for the damages and losses which may be suffered by these ships during this service.

11. Germany will speak in favour of the Red Guards imprisoned by the Finnish Government, and will try to obtain for them, as long

as they are not under indictment for any ordinary crime, their liberation from Finnish citizenship, if they request it, and their free passage to Russia. Russia, on her side, will undertake to grant these persons Russian citizenship and will promise not to use them in the armed forces operating against Finland, or in the regions bordering on Finland, nor to insist on their settling in these regions.

Would you kindly communicate to me the consent of the Russian Government to the settlement of the questions as provided herewith in points 1 to 11, and an undertaking to keep the contents of this present note confidential.

I have the honour . . . [etc.]

VON HINTZE

[The reply of the Soviet Government, agreeing to the terms of the German Note and undertaking to keep the correspondence secret, was handed by M. Joffe to Rear-Admiral von Hintze on the same day (August 27, 1918).]

APPENDIX IX

FINANCIAL AGREEMENT SUPPLEMENTING THE RUSSO-GERMAN SUPPLEMENTARY TREATY TO THE TREATY OF PEACE BETWEEN RUSSIA AND THE CENTRAL POWERS [1]

(SIGNED AT BERLIN, AUGUST 27, 1918)

On the basis of Article 35, paragraph 2, of the Russo-German Supplementary Treaty to the Peace Treaty between Germany, Austria-Hungary, Bulgaria, and Turkey, for the one part, and Russia, for the other part, the plenipotentiaries for the German Empire, namely :

> The Secretary of State for Foreign Affairs, the Imperial Privy Councillor, Rear-Admiral Paul von Hintze, retired ; and
> The Director in the Foreign Office, the Imperial Privy Councillor, Dr. Johannes Kriege ;

as well as the plenipotentiary of the Russian Socialist Federal Soviet Republic, namely :

> The diplomatic representative of the Soviet Republic accredited to the German Imperial Government, M. Adolf Joffe ;

have agreed to regulate the financial obligations of Germany and Russia arising from the Russo-German Supplementary Treaty, the reciprocal return of bank deposits and bank balances due, as well as the adjustment of certain differences in the mutual economic system, and for these purposes to conclude a supplementary agreement to the Russo-German Supplementary Treaty, taking into consideration the Russian decisions with regard to annulling the Russian State loans and State guarantees, and as to the nationalization of certain financial property in Russia.

After exchanging their credentials, and finding these in correct and proper form, the plenipotentiaries agreed to the following provisions :

[1] *Texts of the Russian " Peace "* (U.S. Department of State, 1918), p. 191.

Part I

GERMANY'S AND RUSSIA'S FINANCIAL OBLIGATIONS ARISING FROM THE RUSSO-GERMAN SUPPLEMENTARY TREATY TO THE PEACE TREATY

Article 1

The following provisions of the Russo-German Supplementary Treaty to the Peace Treaty between Germany, Austria-Hungary, Bulgaria, and Turkey, for the one part, and Russia, for the other part, shall be null and void : Article 2 ; Article 8, in so far as it relates to the Russian National Debt, including State guarantees ; Article 9, § 1, paragraph 2, in so far as it does not deal with remission of obligations incurred ; Article 9, § 3, clause 2 ; Article 12, paragraph 2, clause 2, sub-clause 1 ; Articles 13 to 15 ; Article 16, paragraph 1 ; Article 16, paragraph 2, in so far as it relates to Russian expropriations before July 1, 1918 ; and Article 17, § 3, and § 4, paragraph 2.

Article 2

Russia shall pay Germany a sum of 6,000,000,000 marks as compensation for the loss to Germans caused by Russian measures, having regard to the corresponding Russian counter-claims, and taking into account the value of the stores seized by German military forces after the conclusion of peace.

Article 3

§ 1. The payment of the 6,000,000,000 marks mentioned in Article 2 shall be effected in the following manner :

A sum of 1,500,000,000 marks shall be paid by the transfer of—
    245,564 kilogrammes of fine gold, and
    545,440,000 roubles in bank notes, consisting of—
        363,628,000 roubles in notes of 50, 100, or 500 roubles, and
        181,812,000 roubles in notes of 250 or 1000 roubles.

The transfer shall be effected by 5 instalments, namely :

1. An amount payable September 10, 1918, of—
    42,860 kilogrammes of fine gold, and
    90,900,000 roubles in bank-notes consisting of—
        60,600,000 roubles in notes of 50, 100, or 500 roubles, and
        30,300,000 roubles in notes of 250 or 1000 roubles.

2. Four amounts payable September 30, October 31, November 30, and December 31, 1918, each of 50,676 kilogrammes of fine gold, and 113,635,000 roubles in bank-notes consisting of—

75,757,000 roubles in notes of 50, 100, or 500 roubles, and 37,878,000 roubles in notes of 250 or 100 roubles.

The instalments shall be handed over to the representatives of the German Government at Orscha or Pskov. The representatives will, on receipt, furnish a provisional discharge, which, after the examination and checking of the gold and the notes, shall be replaced by a final discharge.

§ 2. A sum of 1,000,000,000 marks shall be cancelled by delivery of Russian commodities in accordance with the special agreement to be made in regard thereto. The commodities are to be delivered to the value of 50,000,000 marks each time by November 15 and December 31, 1918, to the value of 150,000,000 marks each time by March 31, June 30, September 30, and December 31, 1919, and to the value of 300,000,000 marks by March 31, 1920. In so far as the deliveries cannot be effected within these periods, the amount lacking on each occasion shall be made up forthwith either in German imperial bank-notes at their face value or in fine gold and rouble notes in the proportion of three to two at the rate of exchange then obtaining.

§ 3. An amount of 2,500,000,000 marks shall up to December 31, 1918, be met by handing over securities of a loan at 6 per cent from January 1, 1919, with a sinking fund of $\frac{1}{2}$ per cent, which will be taken up in Germany by the Russian Government to the nominal value of the sum mentioned, and the terms of which shall form an essential part of this agreement.

As security for the loan referred to in paragraph 1 preceding, specific national revenues shall be pledged, in particular the rental dues for certain economic concessions to be granted to Germans. The securities are to be settled in detail by a special agreement in such a form that the estimated income from them exceeds the yearly sum required for interest and sinking fund by at least 20 per cent.

§ 4. With regard to the balance of 1,000,000,000 marks, in so far as its payment is not in agreement with Germany, taken over by the Ukraine and Finland in their financial agreement with Russia, a special agreement shall be concluded.

Article 4

Property of Germans situated in Russia which before July 1, 1918, was appropriated to the use of the State or of a Commune, or otherwise withdrawn from the owner's power of disposal, shall be handed back to him on request, subject to the return of the compensation received by him out of the sum mentioned in Article 2, and with due regard to possible improvements or damage, if the property has not remained still in the possession of the State, or of the Commune, or if an appropriation or other withdrawal of similar property has not been effected in regard to inhabitants of the country or subjects of a third Power. The request for a return must be made within a year from the period when it can be claimed.

Article 5

The following provisions of the Supplementary Treaty of the Peace Treaty remain unaffected : Those of Article 8, in so far as they do not relate to the Russian Public Debt ; those of Article 16, paragraph 2, in so far as they relate to Russian expropriations after July 1, 1918 ; those of Article 19, paragraph 1, clause 2 ; those of Article 22, clause 1 ; and those of Articles 28 to 32. In regard to the payment and assurance of the financial obligations arising out of these provisions, in so far as the settlement has not been already effected in Part III of this Convention, a further agreement shall be concluded.

Article 6

The contracting parties will mutually furnish all possible information for the establishment of the civil damages suffered by their nationals within the sphere of the other party, and will respond to requests for the production of proofs relating to such damages.

Part II

Surrender of Bank Deposits and Credits

Article 7

Each contracting party shall take care that the assets within its territory, lodged with banking and financial institutions (bank deposits) by subjects of the other party, including the moneys and certificates deposited on their behalf with a central deposit office, a public trustee, or other State-empowered collecting office, shall be made over on demand to the authorized persons with the right to despatch them to the territory of their native country free of State taxes and duties.

Each party shall, without further formality, treat the bank deposits of subjects of the other party in the sense of paragraph 1, if they are deposited in the name of such subjects. If not so deposited, it must be shown that the deposits are those of subjects of the other party. Possible differences of opinion in regard hereto shall be decided by a commission consisting of a representative of both Governments and a neutral chairman.

Commissions of the kind specified in paragraph 2 shall be set up in Berlin, Moscow, and St. Petersburg immediately after this agreement comes into force. The chairman shall, subject to the consent of the Royal Swedish Government, be appointed by the Swedish consuls in these places.

Article 8

Each contracting party shall take care that the money claims (bank credits) payable by banking and financial institutions within its territory to subjects of the other party shall, immediately after the coming into force of this agreement, be paid out on demand to the authorized persons without reference to the period of grace provided by Article 7, § 3, paragraph 1, clause 1. Those entitled may also despatch the sums obtained to their own country free of State taxes and duties.

The provisions of Article 7, paragraphs 2 and 3, apply in corresponding manner to the bank's credits referred to in paragraph 1 of this Article.

Article 9

In order to accelerate to the utmost the delivery provided by Articles 7 and 8, of bank deposits and credits on both sides, each contracting party shall forthwith appoint a State Commissioner, with whom their respective subjects may lodge their claims up to January 31, 1919. The two Commissioners shall give each other notice of these claims for the first time by September 25, 1918, at the latest; for the second time by November 15, 1918, at the latest; and for the third time by February 15, 1919, at the latest; and shall take care that the bank deposits and credits to be made over shall be given up on October 25, 1918, December 31, 1918, and

March 31, 1919, and, in so far as the claims under Article 7, paragraph 2, and Article 8, paragraph 2, have to be examined by a mixed commission, they shall be given up immediately after the decision of the commission, on the side of Germany in Berlin, and on the side of Russia in Moscow.

Each contracting party shall take care that the delivery, in so far as the rights of banks of third parties to the bank deposits or credits are not in conflict, shall be effected against an authenticated release of the person in whose name the deposit or credit stood, or who is recognized as authorized by a decision of the commission referred to in Article 7, paragraph 2. Should another person claim the deposit or credit on the ground of an hereditary title or a legal succession to the whole assets of a juridical person, the release can be furnished by this other person if he is a subject of the same contracting party as the original claimant, and if his title is supported by a declaration from the State Commissioner of that party. In all other cases definite evidence of the title must be given to the banking or financial institution with which the deposit or credit rests.

The rightful claimants, who desire to make good their claims without the intervention of the State Commissioner, may apply direct to the banking and financial institutions in the case of German subjects only after October 25, 1918, and in the case of Russian subjects only after December 31, 1918.

Article 10

The provision of Articles 7 and 8 find corresponding application to the bank deposits and credits in Russia of subjects of Courland, Livonia, Estonia, and Lithuania, in particular to the moneys, certificates, and other valuables abstracted in these districts during the war, as also to the bank deposits and credits in these districts of Russian subjects, including the Russian State Bank as successor in title to the nationalized Russian private banks.

Part III

Adjustment of Certain Differences in the Economic System of Both Sides

Article 11

Property of Germans shall in future be expropriated in Russia, or otherwise withdrawn from the owner's power of disposal, only under the proviso that the expropriation or other withdrawal is carried out in favour of the State or a Commune under legislation applying to all inhabitants and subjects of a third country and to all articles of a similar kind, and the further proviso that the owner is immediately compensated in cash.

The amount of the compensation to be paid, in accordance with paragraph 1, shall be fixed by two experts, of whom one shall be appointed by the Russian Government, and the other by the rightful claimant. Should no agreement be reached between them, they shall call in a third expert as chairman, whom the competent Swedish Consul shall be asked to appoint in default of agreement to the contrary.

Article 12

Property, which in accordance with Article 11 has been expropriated or otherwise withdrawn from the owner's power of disposal, shall be handed back to him on request against return of the compensation paid to him and with regard being had to possible improvement or damage, if the property no longer remains the public possession of the State or of the Commune, or if the expropriation or other withdrawal of similar property is annulled as regards inhabitants of the country or subjects of a third Power ; the request for transfer must be made within a year of the time when it can be claimed.

Article 13

The provisions of Article 11, paragraph 2, and Article 12 find corresponding application, in so far as property of Germans in Russia has been expropriated or otherwise withdrawn from the owner's power of disposal after July 1, 1918, and before the coming into force of this agreement.

The request for transfer can be made, in the cases mentioned in paragraph 1, even when an expropriation or other withdrawal of similar property has not been carried out in regard to inhabitants of the country, or subjects of a third Power. Such a request must be made within a year after the coming into force of this agreement.

Article 14

German creditors, in respect of their claims arising before July 1, 1918, may, immediately after these have fallen due, require them to be satisfied from their creditors' balances with Russian banks, if their claim is recognized as valid by both the debtor and the bank. The debtor's acknowledgment may be replaced by a judicial decision having the force of law ; if the bank contests the validity of the claim, the commissions in Moscow and St. Petersburg referred to in Article 7, paragraph 3, shall decide in regard thereto.

Article 15

The Russo-German Deceased Estates Convention of November 12/October 31, 1874,[1] shall remain in force, with the proviso that, in regard to all cases of inheritance since the new law of inheritance in Russia, the provisions for movable property shall apply to immovable property also, and the proviso that a duty on the inheritance may be levied only by the country of the deceased, and the further proviso that, inasmuch as the law of inheritance in Russia is annulled or essentially limited, the Convention cannot be annulled.

The contracting parties further reserve the right to supersede certain provisions of the Deceased Estates Convention which have not been observed in practice by new ones more in harmony with existing conditions.

Part IV

Final Provisions

Article 16

The Convention shall be ratified and the ratification documents exchanged in Berlin by September 6, 1918.

The Convention comes into force at the date of the exchange of the ratification documents.

In witness whereof the plenipotentiaries have signed and sealed this agreement.

Executed in duplicate in Berlin this 27th day of August 1918.

> (L.S.) Von Hintze
> (L.S.) Kriege
> (L.S.) A. Joffe

---

[1] *65 British and Foreign State Papers*, p. 250.

APPENDIX X

DECREE OF THE ALL-RUSSIAN CENTRAL EXECUTIVE COMMITTEE OF THE SOVIETS ON THE CANCELLATION OF THE BREST-LITOVSK TREATY [1]

(SIGNED NOVEMBER 13, 1918)

947]

To all peoples of Russia, to the population of all occupied regions and territories :

The All-Russian Central Executive Committee of the Soviets hereby declares solemnly that the conditions of peace with Germany signed at Brest on March 3, 1918, are null and void. The Brest-Litovsk treaty (and equally the annexed agreement signed at Berlin on August 27, and ratified by the All-Russian Central Executive Committee on September 6, 1918), in their entirety and in all their articles, are herewith declared as annulled. All obligations assumed under the Brest-Litovsk treaty and dealing with the payment of contributions or the cession of territory or regions, are declared void.

The last act of the Government of Wilhelm, who compelled our acceptance of this peace imposed upon us with the object of weakening and aggravating the position of the Russian Socialist Federative Soviet Republic, and with a view to unlimited exploitation of the peoples bordering on the Republic, was the expulsion of the Soviet Embassy from Berlin because of its activities directed towards the destruction of the bourgeois-imperial régime of Germany. The first act of the revolting workmen and soldiers of Germany, who have overthrown the imperial régime, was to call back the Soviet Embassy.

The Brest-Litovsk peace of violation and brigandage has thus fallen beneath the joined blows of the German and Russian proletarian revolutionaries.

[1] Translated from *Sobranie Uzakonenii i Rasporiazhenii Rabochego i Krest'ianskogo Pravitel'stva* (The Collection of Laws and Ordinances of the Workers' and Peasants' Government), December 25, 1918, N.95. First Section.

The masses of the working people of Russia, Livonia, Estonia, Poland, Courland, Lithuania, the Ukraine, Finland, the Crimea, and the Caucasus, delivered by the German revolution from the yoke of the rapacious agreement dictated by German militarists, are now called upon to decide their fate for themselves. The imperialist peace must be replaced by Socialist peace concluded between the masses of working peoples of Russia, Germany, Austria-Hungary, liberated from the yoke of the imperialists. The Russian Socialist Federative Soviet Republic offers to the brother nations of Germany and of former Austria-Hungary, represented by their soviets of workmen's and soldiers' deputies, an immediate beginning of the regulation of the questions connected with the cancellation of the Brest-Litovsk treaty. The real peace among nations can only be based on those principles which correspond to the brotherly relations existing among the working peoples of all countries and nations, as proclaimed by the November Revolution and upheld by the Russian delegation at Brest. All the occupied regions of Russia must be evacuated. The right to self-determination must be fully recognized as inherent in the working peoples of all nations. All losses must be charged to the account of the real authors of the war, the bourgeois classes.

The revolutionary soldiers of Germany and Austria, who are at present establishing in the occupied regions soviets of soldiers' deputies in conjunction with the local workmen's and peasants' soviets, must be collaborators and allies of the labouring people in the fulfilment of their tasks.

In brotherly alliance with the peasants and workers of Russia they will heal the wounds inflicted upon the population of the occupied regions by the German and Austrian generals who supported the interests of counter-revolution.

Built on such an international basis, the relations between Russia, Germany, and Austria must not only be peaceful relations. They will represent the alliance of the working classes of all nations in their struggle for the creation and the strengthening of the Socialist structure on the ruins of militarism and economic slavery. This alliance is offered by the working masses of Russia, represented by the Soviet Government, to the peoples of Germany and Austria-Hungary. They hope that the peoples of all other countries which have not yet shaken off the yoke of imperialism will adhere to this powerful union of the liberated peoples of Russia, Poland,

Finland, the Ukraine, Lithuania, the Baltic countries, the Crimea, the Caucasus, Germany, and Austria-Hungary. Until that moment, however, this alliance of peoples will stand against every attempt to impose upon them the capitalistic yoke of foreign bourgeoisie. The peoples of Russia, liberated by the German revolution from the yoke of German imperialism, will the more oppose submission to the yoke of Anglo-American and Japanese imperialism.

The Government of the Soviet Republic has offered to conclude peace with all Powers with which it is in a state of war. Until the moment, however, when the working masses of these Powers will compel their Governments to accept the conditions of peace with the workers, peasants, and soldiers of Russia, the Government of the Republic, supported at present by the revolutionary forces of entire Central and Eastern Europe, will oppose all attempts to bring Russia back under the yoke of slavery of foreign or national capital. Welcoming the population of all regions liberated now from the yoke of German imperialism, the Russian Socialist Federative Soviet Republic invites the working masses of these regions to conclude a brotherly alliance with the workers and peasants of Russia, and promises them complete and lasting support in their struggle for the establishment in their territories of the Socialist power of workers and peasants.

The dictated peace of Brest-Litovsk is annulled. Welcome to real peace and the world alliance of the workers of all countries and nations.

(*Signed*)   President of the All-Russian Cen-
tral Executive Committee of the
Soviets   IA. SVERDLOV
Secretary of the All-Russian Cen-
tral Executive Committee of the
Soviets   V. AVENESOV

November 13, 1918.

APPENDIX XI

EXTRACT FROM CONDITIONS OF AN ARMISTICE WITH GERMANY
(Signed November 11, 1918)

(B) Clauses relating to the Eastern Frontiers of Germany

12. All German troops at present in any territory which before the war belonged to Austria-Hungary, Rumania, or Turkey, must at once withdraw within the frontiers of Germany as these existed on August 1, 1914. All German troops at present in territories which before the war formed part of Russia shall likewise withdraw within the German frontiers as above defined, as soon as the Allies shall consider this desirable, having regard to the interior conditions of those territories.

13. Evacuation by German troops to begin at once, and all German instructors, prisoners, and civilian or military agents now within Russian territory (as defined on August 1, 1914), to be recalled.

14. German troops to cease at once all requisitions, seizures, or coercive measures for obtaining supplies intended for Germany in Rumania and Russia (according to frontiers existing on August 1, 1914).

15. Annulment of the Treaties of Bucharest and Brest-Litovsk and of supplementary treaties.

16. The Allies shall have free access to the territories evacuated by the Germans on their eastern frontier, either via Danzig or by the Vistula, in order to revictual the populations of those territories or to maintain order.

(D) General Clauses.

19. *Financial Clauses.* With the reservation that any future claims and demands of the Allies and United States shall remain unaffected, the following financial conditions are required. . . .

Restitution of the Russian and Rumanian gold removed by the Germans or handed over to them. This gold to be delivered in trust to the Allies until the signature of peace.

APPENDIX XII

TREATY OF VERSAILLES [EXTRACTS]

PART III, SECTION XIV, RUSSIA AND RUSSIAN STATES. *Article 116.*

Germany acknowledges and agrees to respect as permanent and inalienable the independence of all the territories which were part of the former Russian Empire on August 1, 1914.

In accordance with the provisions of Article 259 of Part IX (Financial Clauses) and Article 292 of Part X (Economic Clauses), Germany accepts definitely the abrogation of the Brest-Litovsk treaties and of all other treaties, conventions, and agreements entered into by her with the Maximalist Government in Russia.

The Allied and Associated Powers formally reserve the rights of Russia to obtain from Germany restitution and reparation based on the principles of the present Treaty.

Article 117.

Germany undertakes to recognize the full force of all treaties or agreements which may be entered into by the Allied and Associated Powers with States now existing or coming into existence in future in the whole or part of the former Empire of Russia as it existed on August 1, 1914, and to recognize the frontiers of any such States as determined therein.

PART IX, FINANCIAL CLAUSES. *Article 259.*

(6) Without prejudice to Article 292 of Part X (Economic Clauses) of the present Treaty, Germany confirms the renunciation provided for in Article XV of the Armistice of November 11, 1918, of any benefit disclosed by the Treaties of Bucharest and of Brest-Litovsk and by the treaties supplementary thereto.

(7) The sums of money and all securities, instruments, and goods of whatsoever nature, to be delivered, paid, and transferred under the provisions of this Article, shall be disposed of by the Principal Allied and Associated Powers in a manner hereafter to be determined by those Powers.

PART X, SECTION II, TREATIES. *Article 292.*

Germany recognizes that all treaties, conventions, or arrangements which she concluded with Russia, or with any State or Government of which the territory previously formed a part of Russia, or with Rumania, before August 1, 1914, or after that date until coming into force of the present Treaty, are and remain abrogated.

Article 293.

Should an Allied or Associated Power, Russia, or a State or Government of which the territory formerly constituted a part of Russia, have been forced since August 1, 1914, by reason of military occupation or by any other means or for any other cause, to grant or to allow to be granted by the act of any public authority, concessions, privileges, and favours of any kind to Germany or to a German national, such concessions, privileges, and favours are *ipso facto* annulled by the present Treaty.

No claims or indemnities which may result from this annulment shall be charged against the Allied or Associated Powers or the Powers, States, Governments, or public authorities which are released from their engagements by the present Article.

PART XIV, SECTION II, EASTERN EUROPE. *Article 433.*

As a guarantee for the execution of the provisions of the present Treaty, by which Germany accepts definitely the abrogation of the Brest-Litovsk Treaty, and of all treaties, conventions, and agreements entered into by her with the Maximalist Government in Russia, and in order to ensure the restoration of peace and good government in the Baltic Provinces and Lithuania, all German troops at present in the said territories shall return to within the frontiers of Germany as soon as the Governments of the Principal Allied and Associated Powers shall think the moment suitable, having regard to the internal situation of these territories. These troops shall abstain from all requisitions and seizures and from any other coercive measures, with a view to obtaining supplies intended for Germany, and shall in no way interfere with such measures for national defence as may be adopted by the Provisional Governments of Estonia, Latvia, and Lithuania.

No other German troops shall, pending the evacuation or after the evacuation is complete, be admitted to the said territories.

[Similar provisions were included in the treaties of peace signed by the Principal Allied and Associated Powers with Austria, Hungary, Bulgaria, and Turkey. (See Treaty of St. Germain, Articles 72, 227, 228 ; Treaty of Neuilly, Articles 58, 171, 172 ; and Treaty of Sèvres, Articles 135, 259, 277, 278.)]

BIBLIOGRAPHY

I. OFFICIAL DOCUMENTS

Foreign Relations of the United States, 1918 : Russia. (Washington, D.C., 1919.)

Krasni Arkhiv. (Moscow, 1929.)

Mirnye peregovary v Brest-Litovske. (Moscow, 1920.)

Parliamentary Debates, House of Commons. (London, 1917–1918.)

Piatyi Vserossiiskii Siezd Sovetov Rabochikh, Krestianskikh, Soldat-skikh ; Kazachikh Deputatov. Stenograficheskii otchet. (Moskova 4-10 iiwlia 1918. g.)

Proceedings of the Brest–Litovsk Conference. (Department of State, Washington, D.C., 1918.)

Protokoly siezdov i konferentsii vsesoiuznoi Kommunisticheskoi Partii (V.) Sedmoi siezd. Mart 1918, goda. (Moscow-Leningrad, 1928.)

Texts of the Russian " Peace ". (Department of State, Washington, D.C., 1918.)

Texts of the Ukrainian " Peace ". (Department of State, Washington, D.C., 1918.)

Texts of the Rumanian " Peace ". (Department of State, Washington, D.C., 1918.)

Texts of the Finland " Peace ". (Department of State, Washington, D.C., 1918.)

United States Congressional Record. 65th Congress, 3rd Session. (Washington, D.C., 1919.)

United States Senate Documents. 65th Congress, 3rd Session. (Washington, D.C., 1918.)

Ursachen (Die) des deutschen Zusammenbruches im Jahre 1918. (Berlin, 1925–1928.)

Verhandlungen des Reichstages. (Berlin, 1917–1918.)

Verhandlungen der verfassungsgebenden deutschen Nationalversammlung. (Berlin, 1920.)

II. UNOFFICIAL COLLECTIONS OF DOCUMENTS

BUNYAN, JAMES. Intervention, Civil War and Communism in Russia, 1918. (Baltimore, 1936.)

BUNYAN, JAMES, and FISHER, H. H. The Bolshevik Revolution, 1917–1918. Documents and Materials. (Stanford University, Cal., 1934.)

CUMMING, C. K., and PETTIT, WALTER W. Russian-American Relations. (New York, 1920.)

GOLDER, FRANK ALFRED. Documents of Russian History, 1914–1917. (New York, 1927.)

Interrogatoires des Ministres, Conseillers, Généraux, Hauts Fonctionnaires de la Cour Impériale Russe par la Commission Extraordinaire du Gouvernement Provisoire de 1917. (Paris, 1927.)

LUDENDORFF, LIEUTENANT-GENERAL ERICH. The General Staff and its Problems. (London, 1920.)

LUTZ, RALPH HASWELL. The Causes of the German Collapse in 1918. (Stanford University, Cal., 1934.)

The Fall of the German Empire. (Stanford University, Cal., 1932.)

MAGNES, JUDAH P. Russia and Germany at Brest-Litovsk. (New York, 1919.)

" Novy dockumenti Lenina ", *Krasnaia Lietopis*. (Leningrad, 1929.)

Official German Documents relating to the World War. (Carnegie Endowment for International Peace. New York, 1923.)

III. GENERAL WORKS

ANTONELLI, ÉTIENNE. Bolshevist Russia. (London, 1920.)

ASTROV, NICHOLAS J., and GRONSKY, PAUL P. The War and the Russian Government. (New Haven, 1929.)

BADEN, PRINCE MAX OF. Memoirs. (London, 1928.)

BECHMANN, K. H. Der Dolchstossprozess in München. (Munich, 1925.)

BEER, MAX. Fifty Years of International Socialism. (London, 1937.)

BROWN, WILLIAM ADAMS (Jnr.). The Groping Giant. (New Haven, 1920.)

BRUSSILOV, GENERAL A. A. A Soldier's Notebook. (London, 1930.)

BUCHANAN, SIR GEORGE. My Mission to Russia. (London, 1923.)

BÜLOW, PRINCE VON. Memoirs. (London, 1932.)

CHAMBERLIN, W. H. The Russian Revolution. (London, 1935.)

CHERNOV, VICTOR. The Great Russian Revolution. (New Haven, 1936.)

CHICHERIN, GEORGE VASSILI. Two Years of Soviet Foreign Policy. (New York, 1920.)

CHURCHILL, RT. HON. WINSTON S. The Aftermath. (London, 1929.)

The World Crisis. (London, 1927.)

COATES, W. P., and ZELDA. Armed Intervention in Russia, 1918–1922. (London, 1935.)

CZERNIN, COUNT OTTOKAR. In the World War. (London, 1919.)

DANILOV, GENERAL YOURI. La Russie dans la guerre mondiale. (Paris, 1927.)

DENIKIN, GENERAL. Ocherki russkoi smuty. (Berlin, 1924–1926.)

DENNIS, ALFRED L. P. The Foreign Policies of Soviet Russia. (New York, 1924.)

DOROSHENKO, D. Istoriia Ukraini 1917–1923. (Uzhgorod, 1930–1932.)

DUGDALE, BLANCHE E. C. Arthur James Balfour. (London, 1936.)

ERZBERGER, MATHIAS. Erlebnisse im Weltkrieg. (Berlin, 1920.)

FAINSOD, MERLE. International Socialism and the World War. (Cambridge, Mass., 1935.)

FISCHER, LOUIS. The Soviets in World Affairs. (London, 1930.)

FLORINSKY, MICHAEL T. The End of the Russian Empire. (New Haven, 1931.)

FOKKE, COLONEL IVAN. " Kulisanii brestkoi tragikomedie " (in *Arkhiv Russkoi Revolutsii*. Edited by Hessen : Berlin, 1926–1934.)

FRANCIS, HON. DAVID R. Russia from the American Embassy. (New York, 1922.)

GERMAN CROWN PRINCE. Memoirs. (London, 1922.)

GRATZ, GUSTAV, and SCHÜLLER, RICHARD. The Economic Policy of Austria-Hungary during the War. (New Haven, 1928.)

HARD, WILLIAM. Raymond Robins' Own Story. (New York, 1920.)

HAUSSMANN, CONRAD. Journal d'un député au Reichstag pendant la guerre et la révolution. (Paris, 1928.)

HELFFERICH, KARL. Der Weltkrieg. (Berlin, 1919.)

HERTLING, KARL GRAF VON (RITTMEISTER). Ein Jahr in der Reichkanzlei. (Freiburg, 1919.)

HINDENBURG, FIELD-MARSHAL VON. Out of My Life. (London, 1920.)

HITLER, ADOLF. Mein Kampf. (München, 1938.)

HOFFMANN, MAJOR-GENERAL MAX. War Diaries and Other Papers. (London, 1929.)

JOFFE, A. A. " The Fight for Peace " (in *Illustrated History of the Russian Revolution*. London, 1928.)

JONES, E. ELWYN. Hitler's Drive to the East. (London, 1937.)

Journal intime de Nicholas II, 1914–1919. (Paris, 1934.)

KERENSKY, ALEXANDER. The Crucifixion of Liberty. (London, 1934.) Révolution Russe. (Paris, 1928.)

KRASSIN, LUBOV. Leonin Krassin. (London, 1929,)

KRÖGER, THEODOR. Brest-Litovsk. Beginn und Folgen des bolschewistischen Weltbetrugs. (Berlin, 1937.)

KRUPSKAYA, N. K. Memories of Lenin. (London, 1930.)

LENIN, N. Collected Works. (London and New York, 1930.)
" Left-wing " Communism ; an Infantile Disorder. (New York, 1934.)
Letters of Lenin, edited by Elizabeth Hill and Doris Mudie. (London, 1937.)

LENIN, N., and TROTSKY, LEON. The Proletarian Revolution in Russia. (New York, 1918.)

Letters of the Tsar to the Tsaritsa. (London, 1929.)

Letters of the Tsaritsa to the Tsar. (London, 1923.)

LEVINE, ISAAC DON. The Man Lenin. (New York, 1924.)

LLOYD GEORGE, RT. HON. DAVID. War Memoirs. (London, 1933–1936.)

LOCKHART, BRUCE. Memoirs of a British Agent. (London, 1932.)

LUDENDORFF, LIEUTENANT-GENERAL ERICH. My War Memories, 1914–1918. (London, 1919.)

458   BIBLIOGRAPHY

LUTZ, RALPH HASWELL. The German Revolution, 1918–1919. (Stanford University, Cal., 1922.)

MARCU, VALERIU. Lenin. (London, 1928.)

MASARYK, T. G. The Making of a State. (London, 1927.)

MAVOR, J. The Russian Revolution. (London, 1928.)

MIRSKY, PRINCE D. S. Lenin. (London, 1931.)

NABOKOFF, CONSTANTIN. The Ordeal of a Diplomat. (London, 1921.)

NOULENS, JOSEPH. Mon ambassade en Russie soviétique 1917–1919. (Paris, 1933.)

NOWAK, KARL FRIEDRICH. The Collapse of Central Europe. (London, 1924.)

PALÉOLOGUE, MAURICE. An Ambassador's Memoirs. (London and New York, 1923–1925.)

PIONTKOVSKY, S. A. Khrestomatiia po istorii oktobrskoi revoliutsii.

"PRAGMATICUS." "Germany's Present Eastern Policy and the Lessons of Brest-Litovsk." (*Slavonic and Eastern European Review*, XV, No. 44.)

PRICE, M. PHILLIPS Germany in Transition. (London, 1923.)
    Reminiscences of the Russian Revolution. (London, 1921.)

REED, JOHN. "How Soviet Russia Conquered Imperial Germany." (*Liberator*, New York, January 1919.)
    Ten Days that Shook the World. (New York, 1919.)

ROSENBERG, ARTHUR. The Birth of the German Republic, 1871–1918. (London, 1931.)

ROSS, EDWARD ALSWORTH. The Russian Soviet Republic. (London, 1923.)

SADOUL, CAPTAIN JACQUES. Notes sur la révolution bolchévique. (Paris, 1920.)

SCHACHER, DR. GERHARD. Germany Pushes South-East. (London, 1937.)

SCHEIDEMANN, PHILLIP. The Making of a New Germany. (New York, 1929.)

SCHUMAN, FREDERICK L. American Policy towards Russia since 1917. (New York, 1928.)

SCOTT, JAMES BROWN. President Wilson's Foreign Policy. (New York, 1918.)

SEMMENIKOV, U. P. Monarkhia Pered Krusheniem. 1914–1917. (Moscow, 1929.)

    Romanovy Germanskie Vliyania. 1914–1917. (Moscow, 1929.)

SEYMOUR, CHARLES. The Intimate Papers of Colonel House. (New York, 1928.)

    Woodrow Wilson and the World War. (New York, 1926.)

SISSON, EDGAR. One Hundred Red Days. (New Haven, 1931.)

STALIN, I. D. L. Leninism. (London, New York, 1928.)

STRAKHOVSKY, LEONID I. The Origins of American Intervention in North Russia, 1918. (Princeton, 1937.)

STRÖBEL, HEINRICH. The German Revolution and After. (London, 1923.)

STUPOTSHENKO, LEO. " The Fight for Peace " (in *Illustrated History of the Russian Revolution*. London, 1928.)

TROTSKY, LEON. Collected Works. (Leningrad-Moscow, 1926.)

The History of the Russian Revolution. (London, 1932–1933.)

The History of the Russian Revolution to Brest-Litovsk. (London, 1919.)

Lenin. (London, 1925.)

My Life. (London, 1930.)

The Stalin School of Falsification. (New York, 1937.)

Terrorismus und Kommunismus. (Hamburg, 1920.)

VANDERVELDE, EMILE. Three Aspects of the Russian Revolution. (New York, 1918.)

VOLKWART, JOHN. Brest-Litovsk. Verhandlungen und Friedensverträge im Osten, 1917. (Stuttgart, 1937.)

WHEELER-BENNETT, J. W. Hindenburg, The Wooden Titan. (London, 1936.)

WHITE, WILLIAM C. Lenin. (New York, 1936.)

WILLIAMS, MRS. ARIADNA TYRKOVA. From Liberty to Brest-Litovsk. (London, 1919.)

WILSON, WOODROW. Selected Literary and Political Papers and Addresses. (New York, 1926–1927.)

INDEX